Scripture:Canon::Text:Context
Essays Honoring Lewis Lancaster

Lewis R. Lancaster

Scripture:Canon::Text:Context
Essays Honoring Lewis Lancaster

Edited by
Richard K. Payne

Institute of Buddhist Studies and
BDK America, Inc.
2014

Contemporary Issues in Buddhist Studies

Series Editor, Richard K. Payne

Photo of Lewis Lancaster © Bart Nagel

First Printing, 2014
ISBN: 978-1-886439-57-3
Library of Congress Catalog Card Number: 2014955577

Published by
BDK America, Inc.
2620 Warring Street
Berkeley, California 94704

Printed in the United States of America

Contents

Foreword

Richard K. Payne
Institute of Buddhist Studies, Berkeley

Lewis Rosser Lancaster established the Group in Buddhist Studies at the University of California, Berkeley, in 1972. Among other supportive members of the Cal faculty, his primary colleague in this venture was Padmanabh Jaini, and the two areas of expertise they brought to the program design—East Asian and South Asian, respectively—demonstrates the interdisciplinary nature of the the Group, itself a reflection of the scope of the field of Buddhist studies.

Lancaster completed his doctoral work at the University of Wisconsin, Madison, with a dissertation entitled "An Analysis of the *Aṣṭasāhasrikāprajñāparamitāsūtra* from the Chinese Translations." By comparing the seven different Chinese translations of this important text with the Pāla dynasty Sanskrit text, he was able to examine the strata by which the text had been expanded. This kind of textual study has been the primary focus of his scholarly accomplishments, and has led to a variety of undertakings, including creating, with Sung-bae Park, *The Korean Buddhist Canon: A Descriptive Catalogue*, published in 1979 (www. acmuller.net/descriptive_catalogue/).

The study of Buddhism in Korea was an overlooked area, and it is worth noting that part of Lancaster's contributions to the field of Buddhist studies includes bringing greater attention to this subject. In addition to the role of Korea in the study of the Buddhist canon, Korean monks and monasteries were also important to the overall history of Buddhism in East Asia. It is in part due to Lancaster's efforts that any history of East Asian Buddhism that does not include Korea cannot be considered adequate.

Placing the the Korean canon catalogue online also reflects Lancaster's longstanding awareness of the power of technology to improve scholarship. I can personally recall his insistence on the utility of email, at a time when that medium was just beginning to move from the arcane world of governmental agencies into academia.

More recently, Lancaster has been instrumental in the development of a data analysis system that allows for the systematic examination of patterns of Chinese characters in the canon, locating phrases such as "original awakening" (本覚) in terms of their frequency in different texts and across spans of textual history. This project is discussed in an article coauthored with Howie Lan and Ping Auyeung, "Pattern Recognition and Analysis in the Chinese Buddhist Canon: A Study of 'Original Enlightenment,'" *Pacific World: Journal of the Institute of Buddhist Studies,* 3rd. series, no. 11 (2009): 141–181.

Such work has led to an important shift in understanding the nature of "texts" in Buddhist studies. In a recent publication, "Critical Editing of Buddhist Texts" (www.academia.edu/7284930/ Critical_Editing_of_Buddhist_Texts, n.p.), Lancaster talks about his own changing conceptions of what a text is. For more than a century and a half the field of Buddhist studies has been influenced by the model of "text" inherited from Biblical studies, which seeks to identify the first version, the *Urtext,* as being closest to the spoken words and actual life of Jesus. As Lancaster notes, however, "The results [of my efforts] always frustrated me and I could never seem to move smoothly toward an *Ur* version." While the electronic search methods he had helped pioneer for the Buddhist canon seemed to offer the means to discover the *Urtext,* it became increasingly clear that a text is an "event," that it "has a history, a context in which it has developed in relationship to time, place, and people." Instead of texts being like tree branches that grow from a single source, the *Urtext,* Lancaster instead suggests that texts are like networks, river systems, or the warp and weft of cloth—or, we might add, like Indra's net:

> The network analysis is showing us that there were multiple streams of content (clusters of words) that flowed together, much like rivers that merge and create a single waterway and can then later diverge and split into delta-like structures.

The title of this collection, *Scripture:Canon::Text:Context,* employs set theory notation, and may be understood as "scripture is to canon as text is to context." The four elements of this comparison were all important to the education that Lancaster provided his students. The collection as a whole stands as a tribute to each contributor's appreciation for his wisdom, kindness, and guidance through the travails of our doctoral studies. It is our way of saying "Thank you."

I would also like to thank all of the contributors for their support of and patience with the development of this project. Special thanks to

Marianne Dresser for copyediting and production work, and to Arlene Kato for another beautiful cover design. My thanks also to Sanjyot Mehendale of the UC Berkeley Group in Buddhist Studies for her assistance with gathering historical information and with documentary archaeology. As always, my deep appreciation to Bukkyō Dendō Kyōkai America and Rev. Brian Nagata for their continuing support of this series. A deep *gasshō* of thanks to the Fraternal Benefit Association of the Buddhist Churches of America. From very humble beginnings more than a century ago, the BCA has benefited from visionary leaders, both ministerial and lay, who have established the largest single Buddhist organization in the United States today.

Scripture:Canon::Text:Context
Essays Honoring Lewis Lancaster

The Mountain Spirit: Dōgen, Gary Snyder, and Critical Buddhism[1]

Carl Bielefeldt
Stanford University

In this essay I will discuss three books, beginning with the *Shōbōgenzō,* the collection of essays by the famed thirteenth-century Japanese Zen master Dōgen. I am involved in a project to translate and annotate the complete scriptural canon of the Sōtōshū.[2] Given the technical task set by the project, my way of reading the *Shōbōgenzō* has been narrowly philological. I have rarely looked up from the text, and the piles of sources and reference works I need to make my way through it, to ask what it might mean as a philosophical or religious teaching. The *Shōbōgenzō,* one of the most famous works of philosophical and religious teaching in the history of Zen, and more broadly in the history of Japanese Buddhism, has been for me largely a set of textual and linguistic puzzles.

Two other books, however, have nudged me from my philological slumbers and prodded me to reflect a bit on the sort of book I am translating. The *Shōbōgenzō,* as the primary scriptural basis of the Sōtōshū, has been the focus of a long tradition of scholarly and religious study. Beginning in the early Edo period with the first modern editions, study of this work gathered momentum in the late nineteenth and early twentieth centuries with the development of modern Sōtō scholarship and the dissemination of the book to the general public, and developed in the postwar period into what is now a major intellectual industry. In recent years this industry has been rocked by the movement known as "critical Buddhism" (*hihan bukkyō*), which has, among other items on its wide-ranging agenda, raised a set of questions about the nature of the *Shōbōgenzō* itself in its various redactions, and its interpretation by Sōtō tradition.

Unlike other products of postwar Japanese industry, most study of the *Shōbōgenzō* has been produced for and consumed by the domestic market. In an important sense, this seems particularly true of the products of critical Buddhism, both the writings of the movement itself and the responses prompted by those writings. The "movement" (if we can in fact call it that) is almost entirely the work of two former professors of Komazawa University, whose agenda, while wide ranging, is primarily focused on reform of Sōtōshū doctrine and social practice. Thus, while recent debates over the *Shōbōgenzō* have cast up several significant new issues for the study of the text, much of this work, even at the most basic textual level, derives its force from and speaks most powerfully to the politics of the contemporary Japanese Buddhist—especially Sōtō Buddhist—scene. In my own work with the Sōtōshū Administrative Headquarters I have been exposed to various opinions about such politics but, given the philological nature of my work, I have viewed them more as interesting church gossip than as serious intellectual or religious challenges.

Not long after its publication I was asked to review *Pruning the Bodhi Tree: The Storm Over Critical Buddhism* edited by Jamie Hubbard and Paul Swanson,[3] which collects several articles by Hakamaya Noriaki and Matsumoto Shirō, the prime advocates of critical Buddhism, along with various responses to their work by Japanese and American scholars. Here and there in earlier reading I had encountered most of the arguments in the book, and had put them down to the passing passions of sectarian squabble. Seeing the arguments collected in one volume, however, drove home to me just how odd and confusing are these debates over critical Buddhism, and as I read through them I found myself becoming both more interested and more troubled than I had expected—interested not so much by the content as by the fact of the volume itself, and troubled by both the content and the fact. That learned American scholars from several different fields of Buddhist studies had felt moved to contribute to and produce such a volume made me realize that there may be more to the so-called "storm" over critical Buddhism than mere church gossip. And the fact that an American academic publishing house brought out the volume suggested to me that there was a presumed international audience for a topic I had believed was largely a matter of religious politics specific to Japan.

Except for Steven Heine's excellent piece summarizing the debates over the twelve-fascicle *Shōbōgenzō,* little of the material in the collection speaks directly to Dōgen's text.[4] Yet in much of it, including some that is itself critical of critical Buddhism, we find an approach to reading Buddhist texts that does not bode well for a work like the *Shōbōgenzō* or for the Sōtōshū's hope that the book's translation will foster an appreciation for Sōtō religion. This approach to reading could be called "philosophical reductionism," and I discuss my forebodings about this approach in this article.

First, however, I want to introduce the third book, Gary Snyder's *Mountains and Rivers Without End,* which stands on the opposite side of the *Shōbōgenzō* from critical Buddhism, and thus offers a quite different perspective on the religious possibilities of Dōgen's text.[5] Snyder is a poet, not a Buddhologist, and his book is a work of art, not of Buddhist studies. Unless they also happened to be interested in American literature, probably few Buddhist scholars would know of Snyder's work, and even those who might be interested in American literature would hardly think to look there for a guide to reading the *Shōbōgenzō.* I myself never thought to do so. Why, then, do I introduce this book here?

The publication of *Mountains and Rivers Without End* in 1996 marked the completion of a project that had occupied fully forty years of the author's life. When Snyder was invited to read this poem at our university in 1997, he mentioned to me, perhaps only partly in jest, that my translation of one fascicle of the *Shōbōgenzō* in the early 1970s had delayed his work on the project by a decade—a decade spent brooding over the meaning of the fascicle and its implications for the vision of his own poem. While not a Buddhologist, Snyder is a lifelong student of Buddhism, both of its texts and its practices. Whether or not he can be labeled a "Buddhist" poet, the fact that Snyder would contemplate at length a Zen text and seek to incorporate its vision into his own work will come as no surprise to anyone familiar with his life and work.

Mountains and Rivers Without End is a difficult text, bringing together in a complex structure many shorter pieces written over the long period of its creation. At first glance, the poem might be seen simply as a celebration of the natural world of mountains and rivers, especially the wilderness of the American west through which Snyder has wandered for years. In fact, like Snyder himself, the poem wanders not only among the high peaks of the Sierras and the desolate canyons of the Great Basin but along old U.S. Highway 99 and down into the basement of the Goodwill store on Howard Street in San Francisco (as well as many other places around the globe). Meandering through town and country, the poem is an extended meditation on the intimate intertwining of the worlds of nature and culture—a song about the land to be sure, but also about how we inhabit the land and build it up, not only with our roads and settlements but also with our dreams and memories, our art and song.

The title of the work refers both to the mountains and rivers of the natural world and to an anonymous Song-dynasty landscape painting in the Cleveland Museum of Art that represents the natural world and recreates it as cultural artifact. Snyder's epic work may be seen as coming to a climax in a poem (based on the Noh drama *Yamamba*) entitled "The Mountain Spirit," in which the spirit of the mountain, having challenged the poet from the city to speak of real "minerals and stone," accepts his poem with the whisper,

> "All art and song
> is sacred to the real,
> As such."[6]

As I understand it, Snyder's poem suggests two related points, or perhaps one point viewed from two angles. First, the natural world is cultural. It is not a given, not simply the raw stuff of objective reality: the stuff is always already cooked, the world already mapped as human landscape. We cannot, as it were, get out of town into the unexplored wilderness; someone has always been there before us, leaving a beer can at the campsite. Or to put it in traditional Buddhist terms, we might say that *pratyakṣa,* direct perception, is always shot through with *anumāna,* conceptual grasp, and even the *dharmakāya* preaches the dharma. Second, the cultural world is natural. The beer can belongs to the land; it is just as wild as the rock on which it rests. The wilderness is everywhere—in our rooms, in our computers, in our words on the computer. At some epistemological level, all of our experience is raw, all our *anumāna* is shot through with *pratyakṣa;* scripture is itself a separate transmission, not dependent on words or letters.

Snyder signals this intimate intertwining of the natural and cultural in his epigraph for the poem, which quotes Dōgen's mysterious comments on the famous Zen metaphor of the painted rice cake that cannot satisfy hunger:

> "If you say the painting is not real, then the material phenomenal world is not real, the Dharma is not real.
>
> "Unsurpassed enlightenment is a painting. The entire phenomenal universe and the empty sky are nothing but a painting.
>
> "Since this is so, there is no remedy for satisfying hunger other than a painted rice cake. . . ."

These comments come from the *Gabyō* ("Painted Rice Cake") fascicle of the *Shōbōgenzō.* But the fascicle that so preoccupied Snyder during his writing of *Mountains and Rivers Without End* is the *Sansuikyō* ("Mountains and Waters Sūtra"). The poet's interest in this essay is hardly surprising when we remember that the *Sansuikyō* is itself explicitly concerned with the theme of the intertwining of the buddhadharma and the natural world, expressed in its very title. As Dōgen explains in the opening line of the *Sansuikyō,* "The mountains and waters of the present are the expression of the old buddhas." The text is not to be understood simply as a sūtra (scripture) on mountains and rivers: the landscape is itself a sūtra, teaching us the meaning of the dharma. The natural world around us is somehow, it seems, a subjectivity that expresses and even itself pursues the spiritual life.

While reading Snyder's *Mountains and Rivers Without End,* I went back to Dōgen's *Sansuikyō* to try to see what the poet saw in the text's vision of the natural world that so preoccupied him. I cannot say that I have fully understood either Snyder or Dōgen, but here I want to suggest three layers of reading the Zen master's text that might make it a rich source for the poet. We can call the first of these the "metaphysical" layer.

A haunting refrain runs through *Mountains and Rivers Without End:*

Walking on walking,
under foot earth turns.

Streams and mountains never stay the same.[7]

Here the natural world becomes a kind of walking itself that is "underneath" the walking human foot. The mind leaps immediately to the words of Furong Daokai quoted at the beginning of the *Sansuikyō:* "The blue mountains are constantly walking." Dōgen goes on to comment at length on this saying, playing with the famous Buddhist doctrine of impermanence, in which the seemingly solid mountain is reduced to a stream of momentary mountain dharmas. He then extends this kind of metaphysical analysis to the human sphere, to the life of the individual and the history of the buddhadharma, both of which are constantly "walking" with the mountain.

In the final poem of *Mountains and Rivers Without End,* "Finding the Space in the Heart," Snyder has a brief passage that will be recognized immediately to by anyone familiar with the *Heart Sūtra:*

Sound swallowed away,
no waters, no mountains, no
bush no grass and
because no grass
no shade but your shadow.

No flatness because no not-flatness.
No loss, no gain. So —
nothing in the way![8]

No mountains and rivers remain in the space cleared by the *Heart Sūtra.* Like Dōgen in the *Sansuikyō,* the poet clearly senses the emptiness implied in his constant walking. As the Zen master puts it in his usual literary style, walking has been going on "since the very time 'before any subtle sign,' since the other side of the King of Emptiness (*kūō nahan*)." Or again, in his opening lines, "because they are circumstances 'prior to the *kalpa* of emptiness (*kūkō*),'" mountains and rivers are "this life in the present"; they are liberated because they are "the self 'before the germination of any subtle sign.'" Or more simply, later on, mountains are "constant" because they are constantly "walking."

For the poet, the Zen master's logic of impermanence and emptiness opens up images of nature at once restless and still, a dynamic world always recreating itself in time through the constant thrust and erosion of peaks and gorges, and yet a world at peace in the present, stretching itself on space as the vast, vacant expanse of the landscape. There is opportunity here for language to play with the sharp consonants and smooth vowels of such a world. But, as we know, the same logic of impermanence and emptiness has dangers for language. It can empty words of their referents and render them merely "conventional." It can cut off the poet's art and song from the Mountain Spirit's "real as such." It can end in the Zen master's silence, or perhaps in a shrug and a muttered "thus."

Here the poet finds a friend in Dōgen. As we know from his comments in the *Gabyō* fascicle, the walking world is a world of art as well as of nature. As we know from the title of the *Sansuikyō,* it is a talking world, speaking the language of scripture. Indeed, in the latter text (and elsewhere in the *Shōbōgenzō*) Dōgen goes out of his way to chastise those Zen types who hold that language does not get at nature and that a saying such as Yunmen Wenyan's "The East Mountain moves over the water" does not really describe the mountain. These types, says Dōgen, are not only not Buddhists, they are not even human; they are dumber even than animals. In fact, he concludes in a turn on the "liar's paradox" that if they claim language is false, they falsify their own claim. Rather, we should realize that Yunmen's saying is the very "'bones and marrow' of the buddhas and ancestors." The mountains do indeed "walk over the water, [t]he tips of [their] feet setting [the waters] dancing." For those with eyes to see them, the mountains actually "mount the clouds and stride through the heavens."

With what eyes should we see mountains "striding through the heavens"? To the artist, such language may appear as an elegant image of towering ranges on the horizon; to the philosopher, it can be a coded signal that the temporal stream of mountain dharmas has a transcendental status, in the emptiness beyond our earthly categories of understanding. But to those with an eye for Buddhist cosmology, it can also be a reminder that mountains walk not only back and forth in time but also up and down through the hierarchies of the dharma realm. This is true not only of mountains. Indeed, such movement "up and down" is particularly clear in the *Sansuikyō*'s treatment of water. As Dōgen says, water does not just flow down from the mountains, it flows across the sky; it reaches everywhere throughout the dharma realm, from the highest heavens to the deepest hells. Water extends into every buddha land, and "incalculable buddha lands" appear in "a single drop of water."

In language like this, we are moving toward the second layer of the *Shōbōgenzō* text, what I shall call, with some trepidation, the "mystical" reading. By "mystical" I mean a view of the natural world that sees it not simply as empty dharmas but as the expression, or embodiment, of a sacred order; that sees the mountains and rivers of this apparent world as participating in, or communicating with, higher realms hidden from view, in the heavens and beyond. Here, the dharmas come together in a cosmic whole; here, emptiness comes alive as Vairocana, whose body, speech, and thought generate and enliven all things. As conscious processes of the living cosmic body, the walking and talking of mountains and rivers become more than metaphors, and "grasses and trees become buddhas." The mountains do not merely walk, Dōgen says in the *Sansuikyō,* they have their own "way of life" (*kakkei*). Their way of life is their "investigation" (*sangaku*) of their own walking, their study of themselves. In studying themselves, "mountains become the buddhas and ancestors," "wise men and sages."

Through this vision of mountains and rivers as conscious being engaged in spiritual activity, Dōgen brings the Song Chan nostalgia for the natural landscape into conversation with the mystical hierarchies of his Heian Japanese esoteric Buddhism. In the process, he brings his religion out of the cloistered world of philosophy into the imagination of the gods. He creates a space for the Mountain Spirit, a realm of archaic meanings from which she appears to the poet to demand a song, a realm that makes the song not merely pretty or true but "sacred to the real as such." The poet sings her a Zen song.

Mountains will be Buddhas then

when — bristlecone needles are green!
Scarlet penstemon
flowers are red![9]

The color green is familiar in China, Korea, or Japan, where buddhas see that bamboo is green, but the bristlecone pine grows only in the New World. The heavens of hidden meanings stretch all around the globe, as gods come and go at will; but the range of this Mountain Spirit is the White Mountains of the Great Basin. She seeks a song about her own range, her own buddhahood; the poet, camped in her range, responds. This is the way the dharma travels, by converting the gods in their own abodes and addressing people where they actually live. The sophisticated systems of the *śāstra*s circle back to the ancient patterns of the people; the *maṇḍala*s migrate and settle down in sites long sacred in local lore: pools and falls, caves and crags, groves of pine and cryptomeria.

The idea of local lore brings me to the final layer of the *Sansuikyō,* what I shall call the "mythic." By this I mean an approach that reads the landscape through the historical narratives of a community that sees the countryside as the storied sites of song and legend, the places where memories take place. The world of *Mountains and Rivers Without End* is such a storied place, crisscrossed by the myths of many peoples. In one central poem, we find the ancient Native American cultural hero Kokop'ele, the humpbacked flute player, traveling with (or perhaps as) the Chinese Buddhist pilgrim Xuanzang across a landscape that is at once the Great Basin of the American west and the Tarim Basin of Central Asia. "Logicians of emptiness" at Nālandā join in the Native American ghost dance that liberates the land and returns it to its inhabitants. Later, the poet sings to the Mountain Spirit:

Ghosts of lost landscapes
herds and flocks,
towns and clans,
great teachers from all lands
tucked in Wovoka's empty hat,
stored in Baby Krishna's mouth,
kneeling for tea
in Vimalakīrti's one small room.[10]

In practice, of course, what I am calling the mythic and the mystic often intersect, as gods descend into human form and heroes pass into the pantheon. But Dōgen, as a Zen missionary seeking to convert his countrymen from their esoteric ways, was likely loath to overpopulate his landscape with the familiar divinities of the Mahāyāna mystical pantheon. Rather, like the Chinese Chan literary tradition he sought to introduce to Japan, he favored the mythic powers of the patriarchs and historical legends of the masters. The very title *Shōbōgenzō*, of course, refers to the tradition of these patriarchs and masters, whose legends and sayings provide the inspiration for most of the essays in the book. The mountains and rivers of the *Sansuikyō* are the haunts of the ancients, from the historical buddha Śākyamuni himself, through the sages of early Daoist lore, to the Chan master Chuanzi Dezheng, who lived as a boatman on the Huating River and one day disappeared into its waters. Indeed, such is the intimacy between sage and mountain in the text that at one point their relationship is described in effect as a mating: the mountains are said to love their masters, and therefore the sages enter the mountains, charming the trees, rocks, birds, and beasts, and giving the mountains delight.

These, then, are my three layers of the *Sansuikyō*. If I may be granted for the moment something like these three possibilities for the text, the question remains as to how they are related. I have been using the metaphor of layers, but in my own mind the disparate readings are more like seams of meaning running through the text, twisting and crossing each other along the way. Dōgen's mountains are not built up from a bedrock of metaphysics, overlaid with the sedimentary deposits of mysticism and mythology. I do not have, and would tend to resist, a cosmogony of the text that posits a primordial philosophy preceding the appearance of the gods and the time of the heroes. For me, the legends of the masters who practiced in the mountains are as important for understanding the meaning of these mountains as any abstract analysis of their being.

This way of reading perhaps puts me at odds with the Sōtō tradition that would ground the text in the doctrine of the universal buddha-nature, as well as with recent critics of the tradition who would dig out the original Indian emptiness buried beneath the rubble of East Asian cultural accretion. Being thus at odds, I want to return to the first book mentioned in this essay, *Pruning the Bodhi Tree,* and offer a few closing words about the vexed subject of critical Buddhism.

The subject of critical Buddhism is both vexed and vexing in part because it covers such a wide range of issues and is argued from so many angles. The editors of *Pruning the Bodhi Tree* have made a noble effort to organize the material into three loosely coherent categories, dealing with broad themes of methodology, substantive debates over Buddhist texts and doctrines, and social issues. The arguments, however, are such that they often bounce back and forth between and beyond such categories, and the effect on the reader is rather like trying simultaneously to watch several different games—of philosophy, philology, history, ethics, religion, politics, and more. Rather than blunder into all these games, I here raise only a question about the one troubling feature of critical Buddhism I introduced previously: its tendency toward what I call philosophical reductionism.

An argument appearing in the writings of both Prof. Hakamaya and Prof. Matsumoto goes something like this: "We are Buddhists. As Buddhists, we must take a stand on the essential teaching of the religion and reject all that violates such teaching as not true Buddhism." Both authors stand on the Buddhist teachings of *pratītyasamutpāda* ("dependent origination") and *śūnyatā* ("emptiness") and from that stance they reject all forms of "topical Buddhism" or "original enlightenment" (*hongaku shisō*), or "essentialism" (*dhātuvāda*) as expressions of the "indigenous (religious) thought" of Asian cultures, whether Hinduism, Daoism, Shintō, and the like, that has found its way into the Buddhist tradition. On these grounds, it would appear that not only Snyder's poem (which is clearly dedicated to mixing the dharma with various traditions of indigenous thought) but also Dōgen's essay (at least large parts, as I read them) must be rejected. If so, they will be in good company, in a large pile along with most texts of the tradition.

I see no point in arguing here about whether and why Buddhists should take *pratītyasamutpāda* and *śūnyatā* as the essential teachings of the religion, let alone whether and why these particular teachings are likely to be more conducive than other alternatives to the social reform sought by adherents of critical Buddhism. Much more can be, and has been, said on these issues than appears in *Pruning the Bodhi Tree.* My own question here is more simpleminded: Why, as Buddhists, must we start by taking a stand in an essential teaching and rejecting most texts of the tradition? There is certainly plenty of historical precedent for this way of being a Buddhist, especially perhaps in the so-called "selective" (*senchaku*) styles of Japanese Buddhism often associated with some reformers (including Dōgen) in the Kamakura period. But since most people, even in the Kamakura period, have not been Buddhists of this sort, clearly we cannot establish the argument on precedent.

One of the nasty consequences of the argument for taking a stand on orthodox doctrine is the view that those who do not are not Buddhists. "Objective historians," who rest on mere precedent and accept as Buddhism whatever Buddhists have actually said and done, are dismissed as outsiders, nonbelievers uncommitted to the dharma. But what about the rest of us, Buddhists who may not know what the essential teachings are, let alone what to do about them, and who search the tradition in faith for guidance? What about those of us, perhaps like Gary Snyder, who may be struggling to make the dharma come alive in our own historical situation and who look to the tradition for the ways that past Buddhists such as Dōgen have done this in their own situations?

Perhaps it is no surprise that there is much in critical Buddhism that reminds us of Dōgen, in his emphasis on the need to read Buddhist texts with the "eye of the way" (*dō gen*), and in his slashing attacks, such as those we have seen in the *Sansuikyō,* on anyone who lacks this eye. But for Dōgen the eye of the way was not a natural gift, either of reason or intuition; it was a gift of the tradition itself. Dōgen could be sure that he himself had the eye in large measure because of his faith in the historical lineage of the buddhas and patriarchs. It was first of all the historical fact of his membership in this lineage that gave him the confidence to judge the tradition, and it was through participation in this lineage—in its historical forms as he had received them—that he sought to bring the dharma alive in his community. In this sense, for Dōgen, history came first and philosophy second.

Faith in a particular version of sacred history was a common starting point for many Buddhists in Dōgen's day. It is far less common today, and surely it is not the starting point for the proponents of critical Buddhism. Although they must necessarily argue at times for their vision of orthodoxy from the historical precedents of particular texts, their selection and interpretation of those texts rests less on faith in the dharma as an historical tradition than on belief in the dharma as a philosophical system.

Where does this belief come from? Surely some of it comes from the fact that the professors are specialists in doctrinal texts—rather than, say, texts of ritual, history, or literature—that themselves seek to define the dharma as an intellectual system. But I suspect that this belief (and likely the professors' choice of specialization) is more deeply rooted in the modern need to define Buddhism as a coherent system of beliefs, so that it can take its rightful place among the religions (thus defined) of the world. This need has been felt in Japan since the Meiji period, when

Japanese Buddhists first came into contact with the new "science of religion" and a nascent Western Buddhology already at work on such a definition.

I am not myself drawn to what might be called the "Protestantization" of the dharma, which weeds out the rich overgrowth of art and literature, myth and ritual, and in the process cuts off most possibilities for being Buddhist. My larger point here, however, is not to condemn this work so much as to remind the professors that their call to take a stand on orthodox doctrine and reject the rest, whatever value it may have in challenging and reforming the Sōtōshū, belongs to a particular historical context and is but one more example of how Buddhists must always struggle to bring the dharma alive in their own situations. I wish to remind them of this and to suggest that if they look around for other Buddhists in other situations, both in past and present, they may find more friends than they think, even among those who take refuge in their original enlightenment or sing at night to the Mountain Spirit.

Notes

1 This essay is based on a talk originally given at the International Conference on Korean Sŏn Buddhism, Paekyang-sa, 1998. I offer it to Lew Lancaster here after so many years in fond recollection of his work with me on the *Shōbōgenzō sansuikyō,* when I first became his student at UC Berkeley in the early 1970s.

2 *Sōtō Zen Texts,* edited with Griffith Foulk, in progress. Sponsored by the Sōtōshū Administrative Headquarters (Sōtōshū Shūmuchō), Tokyo, Japan.

3 Jamie Hubbard and Paul Swanson, eds., *Pruning the Bodhi Tree: The Storm Over Critical Buddhism* (Honolulu: University of Hawai'i Press, 1997).

4 Steven Heine, "Critical Buddhism and Dōgen's *Shōbōgenzō:* The Debate over the 75-Fascicle and 12-Fascicle Texts," in Hubbard and Swanson, eds., *Pruning the Bodhi Tree: The Storm Over Critical Buddhism* (Honolulu: University of Hawai'i Press, 1997), pp. 251–285.

5 Gary Snyder, *Mountains and Rivers Without End* (Washington, DC: Counterpoint Press, 1996); page references below are to the recent deluxe edition reprint, which includes a CD with audio recordings of Snyder reading the work (Berkeley: Counterpoint Press, 2013).

6 Snyder, *Mountains and Rivers Without End,* p. 133.

7 Snyder, *Mountains and Rivers Without End,* p. 8.

8 Snyder, *Mountains and Rivers Without End,* pp. 137–138.

9 Snyder, *Mountains and Rivers Without End,* p. 132.

10 Snyder, *Mountains and Rivers Without End,* p. 133.

References

Bielefeldt, Carl, and Griffith Foulk, eds. *Sōtō Zen Texts,* in progress. Soto Zen Text Project, Sōtōshū Shūmuchō International Division. http://scbs.stanford.edu/sztp3/index.html.

Heine, Steven. "Critical Buddhism and Dōgen's *Shōbōgenzō:* The Debate over the 75-Fascicle and 12-Fascicle Texts," in Jamie Hubbard and Paul Swanson, eds., *Pruning the Bodhi Tree: The Storm Over Critical Buddhism,* pp. 251–285. Honolulu: University of Hawai'i Press, 1997.

Hubbard, Jamie, and Paul Swanson, eds. *Pruning the Bodhi Tree: The Storm Over Critical Buddhism.* Honolulu: University of Hawai'i Press, 1997.

Snyder, Gary. *Mountains and Rivers Without End.* Washington, DC: Counterpoint Press, 1996. Berkeley: Counterpoint Press, 2013, reprint.

Sectarian Rationalization: *Shūgaku* in Tokugawa Japan Ninchō, Gizan, and Monnō of the Jōdo-shū

Mark L. Blum
University of California, Berkeley

The study of Buddhist experience in Japan has been focused on the ancient, medieval, and modern periods of the Japanese Buddhist experience, that is, from its inception up through the Muromachi period (1336–1467) and then again from the Meiji period (1868–1912) forward. The religious and philosophical developments in the leapfrogged Edo or Tokugawa period (1605–1868), by contrast, have generally drawn the attention of scholars interested in the developments of Confucian, Neo-Confucian, and National Learning (*kokugaku*) movements. While there have been studies of individual religious figures in the Buddhist tradition, such as Hakuin, Suzuki Shōzan, Bankei, Takuan, or Jiun,[1] in fact there were momentous changes occurring in this period. We lack an appraisal of the dominant intellectual and political trends taking place within Buddhist institutions, among Buddhist intellectuals, and in the interaction between both and society as a whole during the Tokugawa period.

Because of the close involvement by the *bakufu* in monastic affairs both administratively and financially, Tokugawa institutions and individuals were heavily influenced by the benefits afforded those who pursued religion in ways that closely hewed to government policies. The usual understanding is that this resulted in the pursuit of stronger institutional structures at the cost of spiritual innovation. Some of these institutional changes were purely internal as, by and large, each sect maintained an administrative structure quite different from the one organized for it by the *bakufu*. Other innovations directly resulted from *bakufu* decrees, such as the *danka* system of family affiliation in which the vast majority of lay Japanese developed inherited sectarian ties to particular monasteries or temples that provided care and housing for the family dead.

This paper is an attempt to contribute to a broader understanding of Tokugawa religion by drawing attention to an important aspect of the Buddhist tradition that has been all but ignored: namely, the rich intellectual activity known today as *shūgaku* 宗學, in which the authoritative doctrines, practices, and texts, both written and oral, of each school underwent intense scrutiny, codification, and canonization such that the existing religious structures of each school were deepened and rationalized with an added philosophical rigor not seen previously. This activity was so dynamic and its effects so far reaching that what was undertaken during the Edo period amounts to no less than an attempt at a complete reinvention of the Buddhist tradition along sectarian lines.

Also known as *shūjō* 宗乘, *shūgaku,* or "sectarian studies," resulted in a long process of reexamining everything held sacred by each tradition, a process that continues to the present day.[2] Often the internal values exhibited in this process seem conservative, even anachronistic at times, but this is no accident considering the intellectual climate outside the monasteries where similar attempts were made to reestablish ancient orthodoxies in the contemporaneous Neo-Confucian and National Learning movements. The fact that similar intellectual values can be seen motivating the discourse in Buddhist circles at the same time that Neo-Confucian studies in Japan were enjoying new vigor is clearly not a coincidence, and I hope to show how Buddhists were part of that discourse in that they shared much of the same methodology and many of the same intellectual concerns as their "secular" counterparts, though they may have explained their motivations differently.

The term *shūgaku* is commonly used today in Japanese universities affiliated with Buddhist organizations to refer to a form of critical yet apologetic Buddhist scholarship, which is distinguished from *bukkyōgaku,* or Buddhist studies, a term that generally denotes the study of all other forms of Buddhism. Many people point to the printing of the *Shutsujō kōgo* by Tominaga Nakamoto in 1745 as the beginning of *bukkyōgaku* in Japan. Although the precise history, development, and implications of the *shūgaku* tradition have yet to be clarified, we can say with confidence that the work of a scholar such as Ekū (1644–1721) points to an active *shūgaku* discourse by at least the beginning of the Genroku period (1688–1704).[3]

In this essay I will discuss in some detail the achievements of three influential scholar-monks of the Jōdo-shū as an example of the areas of intellectual concern and scholarship pioneered during this formative period, when the *shūgaku* we know today was created among Buddhist scholars in the greater Kyoto area. Kyoto was the focus of most of this work simply because most centers of ecclesiastic power were gathered there, where many of the best libraries were, where a great many publishers were based that readily supported and undoubtedly profited from the work of these scholars, and where a keen intellectual culture that supported this kind of critical scholarship in all fields flourished.

The closest parallel with *shūgaku* in the West would be theology—both are academic disciplines aimed at clarifying a sectarian religious message as well as the historical processes that led to the internal philosophical structures of that message, and that employ a methodology that can be highly critical but which nevertheless presumes a religious truth underlying their traditions. Just as with the history of theology, the history of *shūgaku* has been subject to enormous political pressures, both external and internal, to the sectarian organizations that spawned it, supported it, and gave it its particular identity in support of each sect. *Shūgaku* represents none other than the path to religious truth and liberation as defined by a particular Buddhist sect, but in the process of defining their soteriological mission in this way the Buddhist organizations of the Tokugawa period grew increasingly dependent on *shūgaku* for their own legitimacy.

While some of the finest Buddhist scholars have come from the *shūgaku* tradition, the sometimes tenuous relationship between a church and its theology can be seen in the fact that while *shūgaku* journals and courses devoted to the religious traditions of each sect are an important part of the academic culture of Buddhist universities in Japan today, very little interest has been shown in the study of *shūgaku* itself. When we consider that during the century from approximately 1675 to 1775 the very concept of creating critical editions of sectarian canons was born, that huge compendiums of bibliographies of model Buddhist monks (often referred to as saints) were undertaken on an unprecedented scale, and that the distribution of scriptures and canons became an issue for the first time in Japan, it is clear that an enormous project to legitimize its own truth sources was underway within the Buddhist community. *Shūgaku* thus began as the great enterprise of rationalizing sectarian Japanese Buddhism.

With this in mind, in this essay I present the example of three individual case studies from the *shūgaku* tradition of the Jōdo-shū—Ninchō, Gizan, and Monnō—noting, particularly in the last example, the kinds of issues in which a dialogue ensued not only among *shūgaku* scholars but with the *kogaku* and *kokugaku* community as well. I hope to further the discussion of the nature of the discourse during this early period of *shūgaku* formation by raising questions regarding what hermeneutic values were operative when these canons of scripture and bibliography were compiled and editorial decisions made.

In order to have a more complete picture of the intellectual discourse during the Edo period we must look at the concerns of the Buddhists alongside the various forms of Confucian and Nativist learning. As discussed below, when appropriate, it was not beyond the scope of normative behavior for scholars in any of these traditions to cross lines and make use of knowledge from someone of what may appear today to be an ideologically oppositional camp, and at times even to support their work. At other times it was appropriate to attack the opinions expressed in what was seen as polemical writing coming from one of these opposing traditions.

What I hope to show in this paper is simply that the philosophical and often ideological debates identified with Neo-Confucians such as Kaibara Ekken, Ancient Learning scholars associated with Ogyū Sorai, and Nativist thinkers in the line of Motoori Norinaga did not occur in isolation from the work of the Buddhist *shūgaku* tradition, in which we find a similarly intense reexamination of tradition. In short, Buddhism was part of this discourse and monk-scholars often pursued similar lines of research, particularly in the area of phonology, to those done by *kogaku, shūgaku,* or *kokugaku* scholars.

Concerning the study of Edo-period Buddhism itself, although the works of such charismatic religious figures as Hakuin, Suzuki Shōzan, or Ryōkan are well read (all of which are available in translation), the equally influential legacies of such pivotal *shūgaku* intellectuals as Gizan, Ekū, Muchaku Dōchū, or Menzan[4] are certainly not, with the exception of Menzan. I contend that the impact of these scholar-monks who served as the doxographers, the curriculum creators, the canon compilers, the editors of liturgical texts, etc., should also be recognized as of critical importance to these religious traditions, for they created both the form and often the content in which these religious traditions presented themselves to the world. In other words, these are the people who articulated the formulas with which Jōdo Shinshū discusses itself as something distinct, as a form of Pure Land Buddhism somehow different from the Pure Land Buddhism of Jōdo-shū; how Sōtō Zen distinguishes itself from the Zen Buddhism of Rinzai or Ōbaku; how one identifies Shingi Shingon-shū as a form of Vajrayāna other that that found in Tendai, the other branches of Shingon-shū, Shugendō, etc.

I do not attempt to map out this entire process or even the major events within the critical discourse that led to the formation of sectarian Buddhism as we know it today; that story differs somewhat for each sect, school, or branch, and such a discussion is well beyond the confines of this essay. Instead, I consider the example of arguably the most influential intellectual leaders in one particular school, the dominant Chinzei branch of the Jōdo-shū, under the admittedly unsubstantiated assumption that the types of discussions that preoccupied and ultimately reshaped the religious consciousness of the Jōdo-shū were relevant to sectarian Buddhism in the Tokugawa period as a whole.

I have selected the Jōdo-shū for a number of reasons. One is that many of its scholars from this period have had a demonstrable impact outside the school itself, indicative of the intersectarian and interscholastic discourse I am affirming. An important aspect of this new *shūgaku* culture was philology, expressed by the term *kōshōgaku,* discussed below. And one expression of this climate among all Buddhist schools was, as mentioned above, the felt need to produce their own canons. In the case of the Jōdo-shū, this developed into a considerable effort devoted toward the creation of a common Buddhist canon as well.

As all canons embody what its editors deem to be philosophically and at least potentially ideologically normative, the movement to create canons represents a particular stage of self-consciousness in the organizational development of a tradition. In this way, the enterprise of sectarian canon formation in the Edo period embodies contested notions of institutional identity and individual spiritual liberation. The final editions of these canons were usually printed immediately and made available throughout the country, a process that opened up the religious truth inherent in scripture on a geographical scale unprecedented in Japanese history. They also express a resultant administrative agenda within each school aimed at codifying their notion of the sacred in ritual, praxis, and ultimately a normative version of the textual bases behind the doctrinal presumptions of their faith.

Within the culture of Tokugawa *shūgaku,* this process reflects a crucial stage in the formation of sectarian identities through the formalization of the authoritative in doctrine and institutionalization of lineage. The history of the canon in each Buddhist country has always been a politically sensitive issue, as evidenced by the disparity in canonical sūtras among Buddhist schools manifest in Abhidharma debates in India and the close connection with the imperial court in the copying and printing of the various canons in all Buddhist nations.

The process of canon formation thus reflects one of the most far-reaching elements of the *shūgaku* tradition: its explicit sectarianism. Sectarian consciousness is so strong in Japan today that many people assume Japanese institutionalized Buddhism has always displayed an expressly exclusive personality. In fact, this is far from the case, as the use of the term *shū* 宗 (commonly translated as "sect" or "school") has always been somewhat ambiguous. In its earliest usage to denote the so-called six sects or schools of Buddhism in the Nara period, *shū* decidedly did not mean independent sectarian organization. The six Nara schools were nothing more than philosophical disciplines within Tōdaiji, Kōfukuji, and the other major monastic centers. Only with the arrival of Ganjin (688–763) did the government build Tōshōdaiji as a center of Ritsu studies of the Vinaya for him; Kusha, Jōjitsu, and Sanron never enjoyed any organizational base.

The Heian (794–1185), Kamakura (1185–1333), and Muromachi (1336–1573) periods are filled with examples of monks crossing "sectarian" lines when moving from one teacher to another. Contemporary accounts of Yōsai's Kenninji testify to pluralisitc practices of Tendai, Shingon, and even nenbutsu being pursued alongside its focus on Zen,[5] and one of the most authoritative historical records of the Pure Land movement in the Kamakura period, the *Jōdo hōmon genrushō,* was written by Gyōnen, the leading Kegon intellectual of his day. Even a figure with such strong sectarian concerns as Rennyo studied in a monastery of the Seizan branch of the Jōdo-shū, something unthinkable today for a Jōdo Shinshū priest, let alone for the heir who would succeed the head of Honganji. The political impact of government administrative supervision under the Tokugawa *bakufu* undoubtedly contributed to sectarianism through religious policies that encouraged the expansion of academic training centers for monks and demanded statements of doctrinal identities from within each sect but forbade debates between them.[6]

The case of Pure Land Buddhism illustrates this trend of sectarian-specific efforts made to achieve doctrinal and ritual distinctiveness. Since all branches of the Jōdo-shū and Jōdo Shinshū derive from Hōnen and hence hold authoritative the same sūtras and treatises he designated as such, intellectual energy devoted to enunciating sectarian identity was channeled into two major areas: publicly codifying traditional lines of interpretation through the editing and publishing of exegetical texts selected from the works of both pre-Edo and Edo-period scholars, and standardizing liturgical and ritual forms of practice. Sectarian interpretations of the same Chinese texts were expressed by conscious differences in the application of *kundoku* readings of the same passages among the different Pure Land schools. Lineages developed of how Chinese scriptures were to be read that fell along sectarian lines and these continue to the present day. This is most easily seen in differences in pronunciation of the same canonical material, even the names of texts. For example, Hōnen's authoritative treatise is called the *Senchakushū* in Jōdo-shū and the *Senjakushū* in Jōdo Shinshū; Tanluan's commentarial treatise is called the *Jōdoron-chū* in Jōdo-shū and the *Ōjōron-chū* in Jōdo Shinshū; the Chinese word *laiying* 來迎, denoting the salvific event of being greeted by the Buddha and his bodhisattvas at the moment of death, is pronounced *raikō* in Jōdo-shū and *raigō* in Jōdo Shinshū. But the relative freedom in *kundoku* readings also led to doctrinal differences, most famously in the sectarian authority bestowed upon the idiosyncratic ways in which Dōgen and Shinran read sutras.

The Honganji branch of Jōdo-Shinshū was originally split into the Nishi and Higashi factions by Tokugawa Ieyasu, who exploited a family feud among the descendants of Rennyo regarding whether or not to lay down their arms in their fight against Hideyoshi.[7] By the eighteenth century, however, they had somehow managed to redefine themselves in terms of doctrinal positions on a number of key issues.[8] Today these two branches have grown into distinct churches whose philosophical differences are the cornerstones of their sectarian identities, at least to scholars.

Each major Buddhist school expanded their educational facilities at this time, spurred on internally by institutional pressure to fashion a canonical set of doctrinal sources to be used for standardization of religious activities and externally by a system of rewards from the *bakufu* that not only encouraged greater administrative centralization and academic achievement but also placed strict controls over the amount of praxis required for monastic ranks.[9]

Evolving out of study and practice centers that for most Buddhist organizations began in the Kamakura period, called either *dangisho* 談義所, *danrin* 檀林・談林, or simply *dansho* 談所, formalized schools institutionalized in the Tokugawa period not only increased in number[10] but in turn spawned academies usually called *gakuryō* 學寮 or *gakurin* 学林. These were seminaries for prospective priests where teachers and students lived together and pursued intensive study and practice; some have continued to the present day, while others evolved into the sectarian Buddhist universities of the twentieth century, such as Komazawa, Risshō, Taishō, or Ōtani. The *gakuryō* thus became centers for the pursuit of *shūgaku* for all Buddhist sects. The most famous are those built by

Shingon-shū at Chishaku'in in Kyoto and Hasedera in Nara, by Sōtō-shū at Kichijōji in Edo, by Jōdō-shū at Zōjōji, by Shinshū at Nishi and Higashi Honganji in Kyoto, and by Tendai-shū at Kan'eiji in Edo.

The task of developing a canon came out of the combined efforts of the scholars in the *gakuryō* and those working directly for the *honzan*. It required a certain text-critical rigor in which extant manuscripts considered most reliable were compared, character by character. This led to concern over correct pronunciation of Buddhist technical terms in Chinese as well as how traditional pronunciation should be noted for sounds that no longer existed in the Japanese language. Concerns over phonology were common among many of the sectarian scholars of this period. Because corrupted Confucian texts were problematic for the tradition and phonetic changes in Japanese created similar problems for the close reading of all ancient literature, these concerns were shared by all philologically sensitive scholars at this time.

Newly edited texts were made available through the medium of printing, which had become a burgeoning industry by the 1650s; prior to this, most classical texts existed only in manuscript form and had thus received only limited distribution. The Edo xylograph editions of these texts appear to have completely supplanted the manuscripts upon which they were based: while we can often find printed editions from the Tokugawa period, which in turn form the basis of modern editions printed with movable type, the original manuscripts have generally disappeared. Presumably they were not preserved after the printing blocks were carved.

Although the Tokugawa period was supposedly one of isolation, we now know that in addition to the impact of the steady flow of European technology and ideas, there was also significant interaction with China. Both the Ancient Learning (*kogaku*) and National Learning (*kokugaku*) movements grew out of the new trends in early Qing-period Confucian studies in the seventeenth century that eventually received strong support from the Qing court. There is much to suggest that the philological direction of classical study seen among Buddhists, Confucians, and the Kokugakusha was directly influenced by the direction Confucian studies had taken in China. Here I am referring to the importance of the rise of the Qing dynasty Confucian tradition of so-called "empirical scholarship," *kaozheng* (考證; in Japan usually called *kōshōgaku* 考證学). As Benjamin Elman has shown,[11] the rise of this form of scholarship had tremendous political implications for Chinese society as a whole, but it is also true that this new methodology transformed Japanese scholarship and society as well.

Although it remains unclear as to when and in what form these ideas were brought to Japan, it is probably no accident that the rise of this form of scholarship during the reign of the Kangxi Emperor (康熙帝 1661–1722) parallels the appearance of such *shūgaku* scholars as Ekū, Ninchō, Mujaku Dōchū, and Menzan, etc., not to mention Keichū, Kaibara Ekken (1630–1714), Ogyū Sorai (1666–1728), and his disciples, including Yamanoi Konron (1690–1728) and Daizai Shundai (1680–1747). This is precisely the time of the fall of the Ming court in 1644, which created an exodus of intellectuals and artisans from China, among whom were the Ōbaku monks, most significant for the Japanese Buddhist world, and whose impact was not limited to Zen, as we shall see below.

We know, for example, that Monnō sought out immigrant native speakers of Chinese to answer his phonological questions in the mid-eighteenth century. Although *kōshōgaku* is generally assumed not to have firmly established itself in China until the second half of the eighteenth century, many of its assumptions appear quite prominently among Neo-Confucian and Buddhist intellectuals in Japan from the late seventeenth and early eighteenth centuries. While the philological values of *kōshōgaku* appear particularly strong among Buddhist *shūgaku* scholars at this time, the same methodology can be seen in Yamanoi's thirty-two–volume exegetical commentary on the Confucian classics, *Shichikei mōshi kōbun* (七經孟子考文), a work that appears in the *Shi-ku zhuan-shu* compendium completed in 1782.[12]

Ninchō, Gizan, and Monnō, the three prominent scholar-monks profiled below, are from the critical century of 1675–1775, when *shūgaku* grew into a discipline with a new philological and sectarian mission. As the example of these three scholars will show, during this time the term *shūgaku* took on an entirely new scope of meaning beyond mere doctrinal formulations, incorporating such goals as canon formation, the production of standardized source texts, dissemination of religious literature, devotion to monastic rigor and the value of continuous practice, phonology study, and the proper reading of both classical Chinese and Japanese texts.

Ninchō (忍澂, 1645–1711)

Ninchō was born in Edo in 1645. He lost his parents at a young age and entered the priesthood at age eleven with the dharma name Denjō (傳貞). Four years later he changed teachers and was thereafter known by the name Ninchō. In 1669 he moved to Kyoto, taking up residence in a temple called Shōhōji (正法寺) in the Hachiman section of Yamashiro, where he studied Shintō, supposedly to understand the anti-Buddhist polemics coming out of Shintō at that time. In 1676, Ninchō is said to have made a renewed commitment to upholding the precepts, and announced that he would lead a campaign to reform the Jōdo-shū in this direction. It is not clear to what this specifically refers; unlike the Jōdo Shinshū, the Jōdo-shū had always insisted on its clerics living a traditional monastic existence as in the other sectarian forms of Buddhism. But the frequent lampooning of Buddhist monks during the Tokugawa period attests to the continual decline of monastic discipline in all forms of Buddhism.

In 1680, Ninchō moved to an area called Shishigatani[13] in the Higashiyama section of Kyoto to build a new monastery, which he called Hōnen'in Manmuji (法然院萬無寺)—named for his teacher Manmu and to commemorate an area where Hōnen (1133–1212) was known to be active. Due to the *bakufu* policy banning new temple construction, work began only after he received permission from the shōgun himself, Ietsuna. Ninchō publicly designated the new site as a *hanju-dōjō* (般舟道場), a "center for the practice of nenbutsu-*samādhi* (*pratyutpanna-samādhi*)," and composed a seventeen-article list of rules for the monastery.

Ninchō put considerable effort into teaching proper deportment to all monks as part of their monastic training, made ambitions plans for his succession, and in the process built quite a substantial monastic complex. He succeeded in "converting" a number of aristocrats, including members of the Tokugawa family, and in all these endeavors we know that he was supported politically not only by the Jōdo-shū administration but by the *bakufu* as well.[14] In fact, the *bakufu* was so pleased with Ninchō's work that twenty-two years after granting him permission for the creation of Hōnen'in, the monastery was designated an official administrative temple (*kanji*, 官寺), for which it received an allotment of tax revenue in exchange for performing administrative tasks for the *bakufu*.

How did Ninchō achieve success both in building an entirely new temple and managing to have it receive financial assistance from the government? Unlike some professional religious, he did not have a powerful family to support him in the halls of power. I draw attention to this fact because it illustrates another aspect of the religious culture of this period. The *bakufu* government's religious dealings with Buddhism were complicated by its attempts to impost a new administrative system on preexisting sectarian administrative structures. The most salient area of conflict was between the central government's desire for a sectarian network based on geographic relationships that were convenient to the *bakufu*—for example, all sects were required to establish a *honzan,* or central administrative monastery, in Edo—a scheme inherently in opposition to the previously evolved sectarian institutional structure based on teacher-disciple lineages.

The *bakufu* was therefore eager to reward temples that would comply with its own administrative agenda, which in principle aimed to streamline the crazy-quilt networks of branch lineages scattered throughout Japan. In general, a new monastery was the last thing the government wanted to see. On the other hand, if a religious group centered around a charismatic teacher promoted religious values seen to be good for society and could demonstrate success in those values, that group would be rewarded. In this way, the central government influenced, or at least tried to influence, the direction of all religious activity at this time. Ninchō's story looks very much like a textbook example of the embodiment of religious values that were in accordance with government policy, and were therefore seen to promote social stability. He embodied, or at least propounded, the following agenda:

1. Dedication to a religious life along idealistic, almost anachronistic lines regarding traditional religious values. Ninchō represents a bulwark against the modernization process that was taking place in Japanese society, in which economic growth and political stability created an increasingly secularized culture. This is Ninchō standing against hedonism.

2. Commitment to strict observation of the monastic precepts as embodied in the Vinaya tradition and commitment to seeing that this renewed devotion to traditional monasticism succeeds not only in his own monastery but is held up as a model by his entire sectarian organization. Ninchō as sectarian reformer valorizing monasticism.

3. Earnest pursuit of religious praxis, here expressed as the attainment of trance states of *samādhi* in which visions of Amida Buddha appear. Pure Land Buddhism has always had a dual identity regarding praxis, i.e., the so-called "easy" practice of unfocused nenbutsu that anyone can do regardless of their state of mind, and the traditional monastic pursuit of *buddha-anusmṛti samādhi* through nenbutsu taken from the fourfold *samādhi* tradition in Tendai.[15] By the seventeenth century the unfocused practice of nenbutsu had already become a centuries-old tradition in Japan, and the emphasis on its simplicity obviated the need for a disciplined lifestyle, thus significantly reducing the moral imperative inherent in the notion of a sangha. The political implications of simple,

unfocused nenbutsu as the core of Jōdo-shū (and Jōdo Shinshū) thus implied moral laxity in a time of moral license. This is Ninchō sounding the call to disciplined practice.

4. Devotion to scholarship, specifically the kind of scholarship that esteemed the legacy of Buddhist scholars of past centuries. On this point, the *bakufu* took a similar policy line to that of the Qing dynasty court: it wanted to support academic work that was basically revisionist in nature because such study kept the intellectuals focused on the past, dissuading them from forging ahead with new and potentially socially disruptive ideas. Ninchō as canonical scholar.

As the first three points require little explanation, we will examine the salient achievements in Ninchō's career as a scholar to begin to unpack what kind of scholasticism brought renown as *shūgaku.* He devoted himself to three major projects: printing texts and devotional material traditional to the Jōdo-shū,[16] printing and distributing moral and ethical Chinese texts,[17] and seeking out and eventually printing reliable reference books for the study of the Chinese Buddhist canon.

At the onset of the revolution that led to the Qing, a wave of immigrants from the continent came to Japan, most of whom apparently settled initially in the Kinki region. This influx of refugees from China appears to have been one of the catalysts for the growth in interest among educated Japanese in both ancient and contemporary Chinese language and culture, which began to manifest during Genroku and probably peaked during the mid-eighteenth century. As part of this exodus, what was known in Japan as the Ōbaku branch of Rinzai Zen was invited to Japan, and Ingen and his disciples arrived in 1654, some ten years after the official fall of the Ming court.

In 1668 the Ōbaku monk Tetsugen set about raising money to print the entire Buddhist canon, a project that took him ten years to complete. Although the so-called Tenkai canon had been carved and printed only twenty years earlier (completed in 1648), barely twenty impressions had been made before printing was halted.[18] Thus, despite being the first Buddhist canon printed in Japan, the Tenkai canon was virtually invisible: each institution lucky enough to obtain a copy revered it as an object of worship and it was thus never available for study. Tetsugen's vision was to create a canon that anyone could purchase. The impact of this on Japanese Buddhism was enormous, for it meant that for the first time all scholars interested in studying the content of Buddhist scriptures had access to the entire body of canonical writings as held by the Chinese tradition.

Ninchō's pursuit of canon studies focused on two themes: phonology and text-critical editing. He was not directly involved with Tetsugen's project (he was only twenty-three at the time Tetsugen began his effort) but had been approached afterward by the Ōbaku monk Dokutan, the fourth abbot of Mampukuji, with a request to print an image called the *safuku nenbutsu-zu* (作福念佛圖). This picture had been used for centuries as a proselytizing tool in China but it had not yet been introduced in Japan.[19] Ninchō immediately agreed to help, had the blocks carved, and began making impressions, with the total quantity finally reaching over 200,000 prints. Thereafter Ninchō enjoyed close relations with Mampukuji, and we know that the temple's members helped him with the design of the Hōnen'in.

Ninchō's biography states that he installed a Buddhist canon in the storehouse when he moved into the newly completed Hōnen'in in 1681. It does not state what type of canon this was or where it had come from, but we can assume that it was a copy of the Ōbaku Ming canon. Over the next twenty or so years, Ninchō's study of this canon brought to light a number of difficult passages, and he came to seriously doubt some of its readings. Around 1705 to 1706 he decided to launch a project to compare different versions of texts in the canon, with the goal of creating a reliable edition for everyone to work from. He concluded it would be prudent to compare the Korean canon with the Ming because the Korean represented the oldest compete canon in Japan and was known to have been transmitted from the Southern Song. In fact there are two Korean canons; the blocks for the first had been destroyed during the Mongol invasion, and although Zōjōji had a complete edition of the second Korean canon in Edo, Ninchō knew an impression of the first Korean edition was held by the Rinzai temple Kenninji in Kyoto. Without having seen the Kenninji canon, he nonetheless decided it was the more reliable of the two because of its antiquity.[20]

The notion of a Buddhist canon was considered to total 6,000 fascicles at the time. Ninchō asked Zōjōji for assistance, and no fewer than ten young scholars were sent down to help him for as long as it took to finish the project. Under *bakufu* tutelage as the *bodaiji* of the Tokugawa family, Zōjōji had by this time become the predominant monastery of the Jōdo-shū. Its decision to underwrite such an unprecedented large-scale research project, in which every line of the entire 6,000-fascicle Ming canon would be checked, reflects not only its economic prowess but also the kind of support *shūgaku* could command at this time.

Ninchō threw himself into study of the canon just three years after Hōnen'in was designated as an administrative temple by the *bakufu*. After receiving this honor, he personally traveled to Edo to show his appreciation and was invited to lecture on Buddhism to the shōgun Tsunayoshi and his pious mother. The goodwill between Ninchō and the shogunate proved extremely useful for his project. When he personally asked the abbot of Kenninji to borrow the Korean canon, he was initially refused, as there had been a rule in place within Kenninji for centuries that the old canon must never pass beyond the temple gate. Ninchō appealed to Edo and through the intercession of the *bakufu*, a former *kwanpaku* and *sesshō* sent his minister of public works down to Kyoto to hand-deliver an official message that the authorities felt Ninchō should have his way. The elders at Kenninji had to comply but they managed to save face by insisting that he and his staff could only examine the texts within the temple walls. So every morning for the next four years, the group walked down the eastern side of the city of Kyoto from Hōnen'in to Kenninji, carrying relevant texts from the Ōbaku canon and their own paper, ink, and brushes, and worked there until dark.

Ninchō must have complained about the difficult conditions of his work because another directive from the *bakufu* finally led to Kenninji relenting and allowing Ninchō to borrow a maximum of fifty texts per day to take back to Hōnen'in for examination. But he had to promise the abbot of Kenninji that his staff would bathe before each examination and maintain strict observance of the precepts during this period. Every time the Jōdo-shū monks came to the book repository at Kenninji to return or borrow something, the temple bell would be rung and the Kenninji monks would line up on either side of the path leading up to the depository to observe the Hōnen'in monks coming and going.

In the end, Ninchō did not endeavor to edit an entirely new canon but rather decided to take the notes he and his staff had made and compile them into a massive reference work in fifty-eight fascicles called the *Daizō taikōroku* (大藏対校録), which was eventually printed in 1783, seventy years after Ninchō's death. This work is the only one of its kind in Japan, and became the inspiration not only for the *Shukusatsu daizōkyō* canon, published in 1882 and the basis for the texts used in the *Manji zōkyō* canon, completed in 1905, but is also famous for being the first Japanese canon reference with *kundoku* readings printed alongside the Chinese characters.[21] With the variety of different editions of the Chinese canon available to scholars today, Ninchō's *Daizō taikōroku* has lost all relevance to Buddhist scholarship. But in eighteenth-century Japan, when scholarly interest in the canon was extremely high, this work provided the only access anyone outside of Kenninji had to the first Korean canon. By exhaustively noting all variant readings to the Ming canon, one could actually reconstruct the Korean canon from Ninchō's record.

Below is an example of how the *Taikōroku* worked, taken from a section on Taishō no. 159, *Dasheng bensheng xindi guanjing* 大乘本生心地觀經.

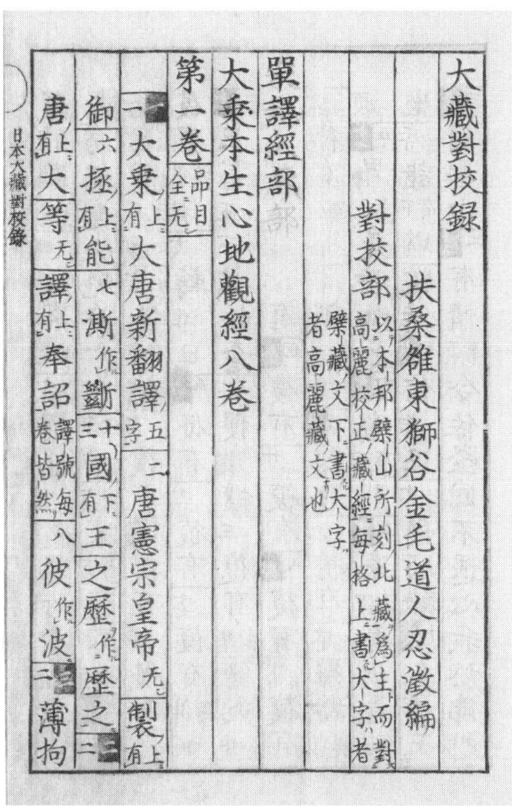

大藏對校録

扶桑雒東獅谷金毛道人忍徵編

對校部 以本邦檗山所刻北藏為主而對高麗校正藏經每格上書大字者檗藏文下書小字者高麗藏文也

單譯經部

大乘本生心地觀經八卷

第一卷 品目全无

一 大乘 有上 大唐新翻譯 字五 二 唐憲宗皇帝 无 製 有上

御 六 拯 有上 能 七 漸 作 斷 十三 國 有下 王之歷 作 歷之 二

唐 有上 大 等 无 譯 有上 奉詔 譯號每卷皆然 八 彼 作 波 二 薄拘

日本大藏對校錄

This is a page from an extant manuscript of Ninchō's 100-fascicle *Daizō taikōroku* regarding variants in fascicle eight of the *Dasheng bensheng xindiguan jing* 大乘本生心地觀經 (T. 159, K. 1385). It was when Ninchō was having trouble reading this text in the recently printed Ōbaku canon (based mostly on the Ming period Jiaxing canon) that he felt the need to compare it with the same text in the Korean canon. Individual characters are presented as deviations from the Korean, and the layout is prepared as a model for a printed edition.

One important and influential aspect of Tokugawa-period scholarship was the focus on the proper reading of Chinese. Ninchō not only pursued his own study and teaching of Chinese but also devoted considerable time and resources to the printing of reference materials for general distribution.[22] In this regard, one of the most important achievements of his canon study is that he edited and endeavored to have blocks carved for the printing of the 100-fascicle dictionary of difficult terms found in the Buddhist canon. This work, called the *Yiqie yinyi* or the *Issaikyō ongi* (一切經音義) in Japanese, had taken the Tang-period monk Huilin (慧林, 737–820) thirteen years to compile. Ninchō succeeded only in getting the first ten fascicles of Huilin's work printed by the time of his death, but his disciples continued the project and the Ninchō edition is today the standard text used in both Japan and China.[23]

Ongi are dictionaries for problematic words, both translations and transliterations from Sanskrit/Prakrit sources, found throughout the Chinese Buddhist canon. They are of great value to Confucian scholars as well, both because they serve as detailed dictionaries on Chinese language as understood in the Tang and because they frequently quote contemporary non-Buddhist sources. They are thus known as repositories of numerous nonextant treatises in the Confucian tradition.[24]

Gizan (義山, 1648–1717)

Born in Kyoto just three years after Ninchō, Gizan was also a prodigious scholar with a methodology that was remarkably advanced philologically for his time. Gizan's focus was on the Jōdo-shū itself.

At the age of fourteen Gizan took the tonsure in a local temple but the next year he was sent to study at Zōjōji in Tokyo. He then went to study with a teacher named Monshō, with whom he moved to a temple in Musashino in 1675. Gizan remained there until his return to Kyoto in 1683, and we know he was lecturing not only on Pure Land Buddhism at that time, but also on Abhidharma, Yogācāra, and even Buddhist logic. After his return to Kyoto, Gizan resided at a temple close to Chion'in, the administrative head of the Jōdo-shū for western Japan, called Nyūshin'in (入信院), where he enjoyed increasingly close ties with the administration of his church.

At this point, after his return to Kyoto, Gizan turned his attention to *shūgaku* and began to consider the textual tradition of his own school. It is not clear if he was commissioned to pursue this by the powers-that-be in Chion'in, or if it came out of his own intellectual need for clarity, but Gizan thereupon embarked upon a text-critical study of all of the major works in the Sino-Japanese Pure Land Buddhist tradition. He went about the laborious task of collecting all the editions he could find of each continental treatise and commentary in the Pure Land tradition and then compared them word by word until he produced a critical edition that could serve as an authoritative source text. He then brought the same methodology to the works of Hōnen as well as to those of his disciples in the Chinzei branch, which formed the basis of his own lineage.

All the critical editions edited by Gizan were printed and thus made available to the public. The impact of Gizan's achievements in textual editing were certainly on a par with, if not even more significant than, those of Ninchō. We can say this because in the work of Gizan we see for the first time the formation of a canon for the Jōdo-shū. Based as a rule on texts edited by Gizan, in the early part of the twentieth century the collection known today as the *Jōdo-shū zensho*, or *Complete Works of the Jōdo-shū,* was published and it has remained the de facto canon of this school until 1995 when volumes of a newly edited canon called *Jōdo-shū seiten* began appearing, but even those texts are usually based on, if not duplications of, Gizan's editions. If Hōnen is the founder of the Pure Land school of Buddhism in Japan, then Gizan is the founder of its canon. The way in which we know Hōnen and his legacy has been undeniably shaped by Gizan.

This fact is particularly apparent in the canonical Hōnen biographies. Of all Gizan's textual editing, the one achievement that has brought him the most fame within the Jōdo-shū is his editing and commentary on the long, forty-eight–fascicle biography of Hōnen completed at the end of the thirteenth century, sometimes called the "Imperial Biography" (*Chokuden*). According to Gizan's biographies, he was urged to undertake this task by his teacher Monshō, but this story may have arisen from a desire to share responsibility for the massive impact his editing and commentary of the text entailed.

We can infer that he carefully read the texts he was able to collect and, according to Gizan's biography, with one of his disciples he worked on a detailed commentary on nearly every line in the entire work. When the disciple suddenly died in the middle of the project, Gizan continued alone until the entire commentary, totaling sixty fascicles, was completed in 1704. Because the biography itself is the largest and most detailed work concerning the life not only of Hōnen but all of his major disciples and religious acquaintances, Gizan's edited text and commentary are today divided into five sections: events and doctrines, geography, monasteries, people, and written works.

In the nearly 300 years since its completion, Gizan's edition of the biography and accompanying commentary have become thoroughly canonical, in the sense that no one has ever attempted to rival his work with a competing interpretation on this scale. But it is also canonical in another sense: the *Complete Works* of the Jōdo-shū in fact does not contain the original forty-eight–fascicle biography of Hōnen from the thirteenth century but only Gizan's commentary on it, in which each line from the original biographical text is quoted. The result is that one can only read this authoritative biography of Hōnen within the context of Gizan's interpretation of it.

Among the three scholars discussed here, Gizan thus represents *shūgaku* in its purest form, as his legacy has been limited to the textual tradition of his sect. I have included him as an example both of Buddhist *kōshōgaku* and of how one dedicated scholar impacted the scriptural tradition of his church so thoroughly at this time when efforts toward the formation of sectarian canons began. While certainly not all the texts of the Jōdo-shū canon were edited by Gizan, his edited texts dominate and his xylograph editions are those most likely to be found in libraries in Japan today.

Monnō (文雄, 1700–1763)

Even within the Jōdo-shū, Monnō is a relatively obscure figure compared to Ninchō and Gizan, and the details of his life are thus much more sketchy. He was born in a farming village in Tanba, in the mountains north of Kyoto, and entered the local monastery at fourteen. Soon after he went to Kyoto to study at a temple called Ryōgeji (了華寺). Around the age of sixteen he moved to Denzūin in Edo to pursue his studies, where it is recorded that he worked on both Buddhist and non-Buddhist materials. He was probably in Edo for no more than five or six years.[25]

In particular, Monnō wanted to study phonology and with this aim he became a student of the Confucian scholar Dazai Shundai (太宰春台, 1680–1747), a scholar of contemporary Chinese among other intellectual pursuits. Shundai was a student of Ogyū Sorai (1666–1728) and it was from Shundai (and possibly Sorai himself) that Monnō learned the principles of philology and phonology, studying together with Watanabe Mōan (渡辺蒙庵, b. 1687), the Chinese teacher of Kamo Mabuchi (賀茂眞淵, 1679–1769).[26] Monnō returned to Kyoto to serve as the abbot of Ryōgeji, where he stayed until the early 1750s, when he retired to a monastery called Keirinji. He died while traveling in 1763, returning to Kyoto from a visit to the Awa and Sanuki regions.

In a mode similar to Ninchō, Monnō vigorously pursued the study of Buddhist thought and phonology simultaneously. Today Monnō's name is far more commonly associated with historical linguistics in Japan and his religious efforts have been all but overlooked.

There is no record of people with whom Monnō might have been close or even knew outside of mention of his teachers and students in his biography. Although the time gap makes any direct link with Ninchō or Gizan impossible (Ninchō died when Monnō was only eleven, Gizan when he was seventeen), Monnō lived in Kyoto when many of Ninchō's and Gizan's students were still active. His focus on Chinese studies was clearly influenced by Shundai, Mōan, and quite possibly Mabuchi as well. Monnō's example is therefore one of a Buddhist scholar from this period who actually studied under masters in Sorai's line and was therefore at least trained in the Ancient Learning school's methodological approach to Chinese studies.

Monnō's most famous phonological work is the *Makō inkyō* (磨光韻鏡), a study and newly edited presentation of a famous Chinese phonological study from the late Tang/Five Dynasties era called the *Yunjing* 韻鏡, or *Inkyō* in Japanese pronunciation. The *Yunjing* had been lost after the Southern Song dynasty but was well known in Japan from the time of its transmission in the Kamakura period. Japanese studies of this text date back at least to the work of Shinpan (信範, 1223–1296),[27] and Monnō was another in a long line of monks to tackle this text.[28] In the Edo period for the first time we see works written on the *Yunjing* from non-clerics, such as the Confucian scholars Ōta Shiki and Mōri Teisai.[29]

Monnō's study was a considerable breakthrough in the understanding of this important text, because he was the first person to seriously attempt to learn how Chinese was actually spoken on the continent as a living language. The result was that his understanding of the *Yunjing* was completely new for Japan and served to stimulate renewed interest in this work among seventeenth-century scholars of Chinese from all philosophical camps.[30] It is now accepted that Norinaga's *Jion kanazukai* is largely based on Monnō's *Makō inkyō*.[31]

Further evidence of the broad nature of the discourse concerning such philological subjects is the fact that all editions of the *Makō inkyō,* dating from the very first carved in 1744, contain both a preface written by Shundai, Monnō's teacher of Chinese philology and phonetics in the Sorai line, and a colophon written by an unidentified Buddhist monk called Hōe (法慧). The best edition of this work is the *Makō inkyō yoron* (餘論) prepared by the Jōdo Shinshū monk Rihō (利法) and carved in 1807; this includes a complete commentary on not only the *Makō inkyō* but on the preface by Shundai and the colophon by Hōe as well.[32] The participation of Shundai, an heir to the Sorai line, as well as of Rihō, a monk-scholar from the Jōdo Shinshū school—direct sectarian rivals to Monnō's own school for the Pure Land believer—would be unthinkable for one of Monnō's *shūgaku* compositions, as these works represented overt sectarian interests. This tells us that phonology was politically "open" as an academic discipline with concerns shared by people from all fields of classical studies, but also that such work was not seen to fetter Monnō's status as a *shūgaku* scholar.

Shundai was a close disciple of Sorai and an influential Confucian teacher in his own right. His views on humanity, however, differed from those of Sorai and his contemporary Kamo no Mabuchi. Shundai had little faith the realization of an idealized society created by morally perfected individuals. This may explain his friendship with Monnō, which seems to have continued after Monnō return to Kyoto. In fact, one of Shundai's pastimes was visiting with learned monks from the same Jōdo-shū monastery where Monnō lived in Edo, discussing classical Chinese and writing Chinese poetry:

> In the past, when the Shōnin (上人) was living in the dormitory at Denzū'in . . . we once gathered several tens of monks together and amused ourselves by composing Chinese poetry together. The Shōnin gathered all the poems and created a collection called the *Nensai kanka;* it was truly an achievement.[33]

The "Shōnin" here is Monnō Shōnin, and the title *Nensai kanka* 念西間課 is a clear reference to Amida's Pure Land in the West, but what is most interesting is that Monnō left it up to his teacher to choose the name for the collection, so the Buddhist allusion came from Shundai, a Confucian.[34]

Needless to say, Monnō and Shundai shared a passion for the Chinese language, particularly the enormously complex study its phonology. In a similar vein to Sorai's attempt to return to the "original" Confucian texts resulting from a loss of confidence in Song interpretations, Shundai and Monnō were well aware of the problems in the reconstructions of Chinese phonology that existed not only in the Japanese commentaries but in the Chinese phonological texts themselves. What Shundai shows us in his Introduction is that both men understood that the problems stemmed in large part from trying to apply Sanskrit phonetic principles to Chinese. Considered together, Monnō's study with Shundai's Introduction detail for us the state of knowledge at that time in Japan on this complex problem. From Shundai's preface to Monnō's study:

Since the Qin 秦 and Han 漢 [periods] (249 B.C.E.–25 C.E.), the people in China have moved around incessantly, and foreign peoples from the four directions have come in, adding to the mixture of all who live in China. Then, up through the time of the two Jin 晉 [periods] (266–420 C.E.), Han people and non-Han people encroached upon each other throughout the country. The natural sound of China['s language] was then mixed up with unknown foreign words. This led to there being old and new pronunciations that are not identical,[35] and is the reason for the study of [Chinese] phonology.

Sunyan of the Jin (晉孫炎, d. 260?) first created the *fanyin* (反音) [system].[36] Shenyue of the Liang (梁沈約, 441–513) first divided characters into four tones and established the scheme listing 206 phonemes. Sometime afterward—no one knows how many generations later—the monk Shengong composed the sound chart in the *Qieyin* 切韻,[37] which is included in the end of the *Yupian* 玉篇.[38] This configuration is the probably the beginning of the study of phonology. It is unclear who created the *Yunjing* 韻鏡,[39] but it appeared after [the] Song linguists.[40] In this work a chart is created with the four tones on the vertical and the seven [consonant] sounds on the horizontal.

Xianru 先儒[41] thought [that] this [scheme] was transmitted [initially] by monks from India and later scholars (i.e., Zhang Linzhi) took this to have captured the genuine nature [of Chinese]. The appellation "four tones" probably first came from Shenyue and the explanation of the seven consonants[42] emerged from [transliterations,] as in the word *futu* 浮屠 [for *buddha*].[43] The distribution of these seven consonants and four tones over the warp and weft charts the phonemes of natural human speech. But [words like] *futu* represent the study of Siddham, which is precisely for the [linguistic] rules of Sanskrit. The *Yunjing* [therefore] is applying the rules for speakers of Siddham to [the] sounds of Chinese characters. This [principle] assuredly does not represent the original [sounds] of China. Thus these rules must be carefully [examined] as to their accurate representation of [Chinese] phonemes. We must discern what is native and what is foreign.

In a similar way, these phonological studies have come after what happened earlier, so there is both gain and loss. In terms of clarity, these are not like the *Yunjing,* so the phonological work done by these later [Chinese scholars] is more accurate. Among people [working in this field] here in our own contemporary Japan, there are a fair number who have been fond of the *Yunjing,* and since the monk Yūsaku (宥朔, n.d.)[44] opened this box no one knows how many have tried to make sense of it. But none of them have studied the [current] *ka-on* (華音, i.e., Ming) pronunciation. . . .

My dear Master Monnō is not like this. Monnō is someone from Heian (Kyoto) who, when he was young, came to Kantō to learn from me about characters (*moji*). Whenever he asked me about something, I answered him, and he came to appreciate *ka-on.* He also appreciated the *Yunjing* and after

> returning to the West[45] sunk his mind into a study of it for more than ten years, saying it was very valuable for him. He did not respect his elders who had mastered the *Yunjing* because none of them had completely [understood] it and did not know the usefulness of the *Yunjing*. Ultimately he took his discoveries about the text and collected them into this work. This year his students asked him to publish it and he sent what he had written to me, asking me to write a preface. For me, because of the effort the honorable Master has made in his phonological studies, he has been able to provide us with this broad study. Anyone who carefully examines the import of his composition with the kind of effort he put into it will understand his contribution.
>
> First year of Enkyō (延享) (1744)

Shundai's respect for Monnō thus stems from recognition that there is a serious gap in the methodology of the *Yunjing*, based on Sanskrit phonological rules, and the actual phonetics of spoken Chinese, and he praises Monnō's efforts at learning the contemporary linguistic situation in China. Although the politics of eighteenth-century Japan prohibited travel to China, this reference to Monnō's study of Chinese phonetics is supported by his biographies, which tell us he traveled to Nagasaki to speak with translators of Chinese and query them about their language usage, and even made a trip to Tsushima to be able to converse with Koreans living there to get answers to his questions about the authentic pronunciation of Korean.

The long involvement of the Buddhist community in the history of phonological studies was not only true for Japan but for China as well. The very concepts of grammar and phonetics appear in East Asia for the first time with the advent of Buddhist monks traveling from India and Central Asia. The enormous project of translating Buddhist texts into the phonetically and orthographically complex Chinese language from heavily inflected Sanskrit and Prakrit sources presented formidable linguistic challenges that did not abate for centuries.

The problem was exacerbated from the Indian side by the fact that many crucial philosophical terms and names were transliterated rather than translated into Chinese, as well as the prevalence of sacred sounds contained in mantras and *dhāraṇīs* in which the practitioner is empowered by the phonemes themselves, coupled with an unknown range of grammatical and phonemic forms of the same word or passage used by the transmitters who came from various locales. On the Chinese side, there was enormous regional variation in the pronunciation of Chinese mixed with changes in the concept of what constitutes a national language from dynasty to dynasty.

In Japan, phonological studies begin with the works on Sanskrit written or edited by the early Heian-period monks who traveled to study in China, such as Kūkai (774–835), Ennin (794–864), Shuei (809–884), and Annen (841–902). It is well known that the Japanese syllabary is organized on Sanskrit phonetic principles, reflecting this intellectual tradition in Japan, even if Kūkai was not the architect of the *iroha kana* poem. Because the Buddhist canon remained in Chinese until the modern period, and the canonical sūtras in particular were all thought to have come from Sanskrit or at least Indic originals, Japanese Buddhist scholarship from its inception has exhibited strong concern for phonological accuracy regarding both Chinese and the Sanskrit that Chinese at times expresses. Ninchō's many years of work on the Ming canon and the *Issaikyō ongi* thus reflect two aspects of the same spiritual orientation.

Despite the long history of Confucian studies in Japan, the impact of Sorai and his students in trying to erect a Confucian ethical system for ideological purposes brought out a new level of concern in Confucian circles for philological issues in the late seventeenth century. Here is where *kōshōgaku, oningaku* (phonology), and *shūgaku* intersect. Of course the Buddhist roots in phonological study also bear fruit in the mid-Tokugawa period, not only in the study of the phonology of Chinese but of Japanese as well.

It is well known that the influence of the Shingon monk Keichū (契沖, 1640–1701) on the *kokugaku* movement was extremely important, particularly for Motoori Norinaga (1730–1801). Keichū's creation of a phoneme chart for ancient Japanese is based on a passage in the *Nirvāṇa Sūtra*, also thought to have been the original basis of the *iroha* formulary.[46] Since certain ancient phonetic distinctions were lost from speech by the end of the Heian period, Fujiwara Teika (1162–1241) noted a system for his own usage in his *Gekanshū* that compromised contemporary speech with historical usage, and this was later standardized by the monk Gyōa (ordained 1363).[47] While spoken Japanese had undergone even more changes in the 400 years since Teika, Keichū, through his detailed study of the *Man'yōshū* and other early texts, asserted the importance of returning to the orthodox original *kana* usage, what is now called *rekishiteki kanazukai*. In his work *Waji shōran shō* (和字正濫鈔), published in 1695, Keichū proposed a new standard of *kana* that "corrected" Teika's rules of usage. This work persuaded Norinaga to adapt Keichū's scheme as normative, and through Norinaga's influence it was adopted and taught in Japanese schools until 1946.

Monnō also worked on Japanese phonology and was an advocate of the *rekishiteki kanazukai* approach, as can be seen in his treatise on Japanese phonology, the *Waji taikan-shō* (和字大觀鈔), first printed in 1754. As both Keichū and Monnō both studied the Sanskrit phonetics in the Siddham script (Jp. *shittan*), it is not clear from whom Norinaga learned of this idea, but in his *Jion kana yōkaku* he asserts that the vowel *A* is the most basic of all vowels and that all sounds of the Japanese language evolve from it.[48] This notion is an exact replica of the mythology surrounding the first letter *A* in the Sanskrit phonetic system, as used in mantras beginning with *A,* such as *aum,* so there is little doubt of a Buddhist origin of this idea.

Shinmura Izuru 新村出 (1876–1967), the original editor of the *Kōjien,* has written an interesting article assessing the achievements of Monnō's scholarship.[49] He mentions three areas in which Monnō lectured and published: Pure Land Buddhist studies, astronomy, and phonology. Shinmura quotes evaluations of Monnō's historical contributions to both Chinese and Japanese phonology as made by other Chinese scholars and *kokugaku* scholars who worked after him in eighteenth- and nineteenth-century Japan, such as Ōta Zensai (太田全斎, 1759–1829), Hirata Atsutane (平田篤胤, 1776–1843), and Kurokawa Harumura (黒川春村, 1799–1866).[50]

All these later scholars pointed out mistakes in Monnō's studies of Chinese and Japanese phonology but at the same time praised him as a man of extraordinary talent. Shinmura finds Monnō to have been much more of a pioneer than any of these later scholars, and he is particularly interested in speculating upon Monnō's influence on Norinaga. Although there is no textual evidence of any direct communication between the two men, Norinaga was in Kyoto as a young scholar when Monnō was most active in publishing his phonological works. Shinmura points out that Monnō's treatises on the correct reading of *kanji,* such as the *Makō inkyō* published first in 1744 (later revised) and the *San'on seika* (三音正譌) published in 1752, significantly presage some of Norinaga's conclusions of similar content, such as his *Kanji san'on-kō* (漢字三音考), dated 1768, and the *Jion kana yōkaku* (字音假名用格), dated 1776.

Writing in 1907, Shinmura argued his point skillfully but it remained only speculative. With the publication of the *Motoori Norinaga zenshū* between 1968 and 1973, we now have ample evidence of Norinaga's awareness of Monnō's presence as a scholar. Among Norinaga's *zuihitsu* in volume 13 there are whole sections copied from Monnō's *Waji taikan-shō,* which he names and identifies as Monnō's work,[51] and volume 14 contains a small essay in which Monnō's name is even mentioned in Norinaga's title.[52] In 1754 Monnō wrote a monograph called *Kyūsen hakkai gechō-ron* (九山八海解嘲論), in which he defended traditional Buddhist cosmology against its critics. In what amounts to a review article entitled "Monnō's argument in his *Kyūsen hakkai gechō-ron*,"[53] Norinaga critiques Monnō's reasoning in light of the fact that since Westerners have sailed to Japan from the east, this asserts the greater plausibility of Western notions of cosmology.

Does Monnō betray some ideological motivation in his study of Japanese? If so, he does not mention such. Was he aware of the ideas of earlier Shintō revivalists like Masuho Zankō (増穂残口, 1655–1742) regarding the religious significance of the language in the earliest historical Japanese texts such as the *Kojiki* and the *Man'yōshū*? Monnō's lack of personal commentary regarding his linguistic predecessors precludes a definitive answer to such questions, but he shows too many similarities in method to Keichū to suggest that he did not read them, and his associations with Shundai and Watanabe Mōan certainly lead us to assume that he was aware of the more ideological studies of the *Man'yōshū* by his contemporary, the *kokugakusha* scholar Kamo Mabuchi.

What was Monnō's motivation? Shinmura quotes this passage from one of his works:

> Phonology is of primary significance in reading sacred texts. When the Indians came to China and transmitted their language, each person had their own way of speaking such that [the entire transmission] was not unified and there were also dialectic differences from among the five regions of India. When the Han people accepted the translation from Yuezhi (月支)[54] people the language was not always the same. There are differences between the language of an official and the man in the street, between the Zhang (漳),[55] Fu (福),[56] and Wu (呉).[57] Without clarifying these dialects any reading of the corresponding Chinese transcription cannot ultimately yield the correct Sanskrit pronunciation. Eminent monks in these times as a rule do not know the pronunciation of characters. They simply cling to the oral tradition they have received and say with pride, "this is the correct pronunciation." They go on and on reading, on and on making mistakes, getting further and further from the [original] Sanskrit sound. Even the Sanskrit scholars take a pronunciation from one region and group together a variety of transliterated sounds under that one pronunciation. This is akin to walking for fifty steps but trying to laugh for a hundred. If you read Chinese transcriptions without knowing that [one] pronunciation can take a variety of forms, the crucial element in the Sanskrit pronunciation cannot possibly be obtained.[58]

This suggests that Monnō's interest in phonology was not motivated by the nativist arguments found in lapsed Buddhists such as Zankō or Fujiwara Seika. In fact, Buddhism had always represented the universal and transcendent, as opposed to the particular, in Japanese intellectual discourse, offering an analysis of the human condition that in general deconstructed the significance of the Japanese cultural environment.[59] The heroes of *setsuwa* literature are just as likely to be Indian, Chinese, or Central Asian as Japanese. What Monnō's statement shows is that despite his serious work in philological and phonological studies, an area of research that he shared in the main with people from various ideological movements, some of whom did emphasize the uniqueness of Japan, the Buddhist canon remained, for him, the locus of spiritual truth.

The above quote also shows, however, a similar attitude to Norinaga's regard for the sacred nature of ancient language, only for Monnō that sacredness is not immanent in Japanese prior to continental influence but in the language of Buddhist scripture, first in Sanskrit and then in Chinese as the coded form of that transmission for East Asia. We know that Monnō studied Sanskrit phonology to the point of recognizing regional differences in Sanskrit pronunciation embedded in Chinese transliterations, but there is no evidence that he actually endeavored to read canonical material in Sanskrit as did Jiun (1718–1804), for example. Instead, Monnō fixed his sight on the proper decoding of the Chinese transmission as well as the Japanese transcription of how canonical Chinese should be read. Without knowing the proper pronunciation of Buddhist Chinese, the full impact of the religious truth embodied in the Buddhist canon would be lost.

While Buddhism's dominance in determining the values of intellectual discourse in Japan had declined significantly by the second half of the seventeenth century, and continued to lose ground to other models of the human condition throughout the eighteenth and nineteenth centuries, it is important to remember that Buddhism never lost its role representing the authoritative statement of the universal in Japanese intellectual thought.

Shinmura comments here that Monnō's appreciation of regional varieties in the pronunciation of Sanskrit and Chinese went far beyond any other scholar in Japan. It should also be noted that Monnō invented a method for demarking accent and stress in his writings and even had the foresight to separate words. Today these aspects of his works are of tremendous value to historical linguists; he is thought to provide one of the best records of the Kyoto manner of speech in the mid-eighteenth century.

Another work of Monnō attests to his spiritual grounding in the Jōdo-shū. Barely one year after his completion of the *Makō inkyō,* Monnō published something of a comprehensive introduction to Buddhist doctrine from the point of view of the Jōdo-shū, entitled *Jōdo shinmon shoshin gakusoku* (淨土眞門初心學則). Written as a textbook for his students, it serves as an excellent example of the state of *shūgaku* at the time and provides a glimpse into the curricula in the sectarian academies of the Jōdo sect in use at that time.

In the Norinaga archives in Matsuzaka there are manuscript copies of two works by Monnō: the *Makō inkyō* (both the original and the revised edition) and the *Hi-shutsujō kogo.* My final example of the interscholastic discourse[60] of this period concerns the latter. The 1745 printing of the *Shutsujō kōgo* (出定後語) by Tominaga Nakamoto (富永仲基, 1715–1746) was a watershed event in the intellectual culture of the Tokugawa period. This work has been hailed as the first "objective" study of the Buddhist literary tradition, and supposedly formed the basis of modern Buddhist studies in Japan because of its methodology that judged all sūtras after the original Āgamas to have not originated in Śākyamuni's discourses.

At the time it was made public, however, the book was seen by many in the Buddhist world as an attack on the Japanese Buddhist tradition. As the son of one of the founders of the Kaitokudō school in Edo, Nakamoto engaged in what we would call critical scholarship not only on Buddhism but on Shintō and Confucianism as well. Whatever were Nakamoto's personal motivations, this work fueled the already incipient anti-Buddhist sentiment among National Learning scholars. Among the Buddhist responses, Monnō's treatise, the *Hi-shutsujō kōgo,* is one of the best known.[61] There is no room here to present the details of the arguments in Monnō's essay, but his sentiments are well expressed by this comment from his introduction:

> Ah, [from what I heard], I thought, this Nakamoto must be a superb fellow. Recently I was able to obtain a copy of this work and when I started to read it at first I was awed by it. But then in the middle I thought, this must be denounced. When I got to the end I only felt pity. . . . Nakamoto is someone with white clothes and a yellow mouth (i.e., a laymen with no experience).[62]

Monnō's was not the only apologia written in defense of the Buddhist tradition; other contemporary refutations of Nakamoto's treatise include the *Kakuretsu jamō-hen* (摑裂邪網編)[63] by the Shinshū scholar Chō'on (潮音, 1783–1836) and the *Ben shutsujō kōgo* (辨出定後語) by Hōkō (放光). The xenophobic National Learning scholar Hirata Atsutane also responded with a polemic in his *Shutsujō shōgo* (出定笑語) of 1811, in which he not only attempts to repel the Buddhist defenders but also expresses a much more pointed attack against Buddhism than Nakamoto's. Despite the fact that Monnō's work has nothing to do with phonology, a copy is kept at the Norinaga archives, and it is assumed to have been copied by Norinaga himself (or by his son) in 1788. We can therefore deduce that Atsutane was responding at least to Monnō's treatise.

Although a detailed study of all these texts would be necessary to confirm just who was reading whose treatise, there is no question that a lively debate ensued over Nakamoto's methodology and conclusions. Despite Atsutane's vigorous attack on Buddhism as the self-appointed leader of the National Learning movement in his day, such as in his *Kamōsho,* which clearly assails Shundai for his sympathetic view of Buddhism, the *shūgaku* tradition of Buddhist scholarship continued to feel empathy with the goals of Norinaga's study. This is evidenced by the linguistic work of the Shinshū scholar Gimon (義門, 1786–1843) who, like Monnō, saw religious meaning in his linguistic study and spent time discussing such matters with Norinaga's students, or with linguists like Ōta Zensai (太田全斎, 1759–1829), whose own work owed a debt to Monnō. I will have to leave discussion of this area for a later opportunity.

Conclusion

In this essay I have tried to show how the work of these Buddhist scholars impacted their own traditions as well as humanistic scholarship in general during the mid-Tokugawa period. The methodology of Monnō, and particularly that of Gizan, is generally labeled by Japanese scholars today as an "evidential methodology."[64] Insofar as the Confucian scholars in China and Japan called their work "Han study" (Jp. *kangaku*), they first saw themselves as returning to the kind of text-critical scholarship that was represented by Han-period Confucian study, as opposed to the Neo-Confucian trends of Zhu Xi and Wang Yangming. It is telling that Japanese scholars interested in this reformation generally see it only in terms of the two dimensions of Chinese Confucian learning and Japanese Confucian learning.

For example, in a well-cited article on the import of *kōshōgaku* scholarship to Japan in the Tokugawa period, Yoshida Atsushi cites only the names of Confucian scholars in Japan.[65] This article is revealing for two reasons. First is the fact that supposedly the advent of *kōshōgaku* studies in Japan, as measured by the fact that scholars began using this term to refer to their own work, is pegged on the figure of Ōta Kinjō (1765–1825), significantly later than any the three figures I have discussed here. The second reason is that as a precursor to Kinjō, the earliest figure Yoshida mentions is none other than Dazai Shundai, who was a great supporter of Monnō's work, as was discussed above. In the same way, Buddhist scholars writing on *shūgaku* generally ignore the trends in Confucian, Ancient Learning, or National Learning scholarship.[66]

Yet not only is it clear that the same trends were occurring in traditional Buddhist, traditional Confucian, and the new National Learning forms of intellectual readings of sacred scripture, we also know that Buddhist reformist scholars like Monnō were learning from reformist Confucian teachers in Sorai's line, as well as the fact that National Learning scholars such as Norinaga, Atsutane, and Zensai were closely reading (and correcting) the pioneering phonological work of such Buddhist monks as Keichū and Monnō. Phonology was a topic of study that crossed all philosophical boundaries, with contributions made not only by Ninchō, Monnō, Keichū, Shundai, and Norinaga but also Neo-Confucians such as Kaibara Ekken and Arai Hakuseki.[67] This is precisely why I label this an interscholastic discourse, indicating shared values in methodology and content. Starting from this point of view, we must ask what kinds of critical methodologies were being adopted by whom, and when and where, without restricting ourselves to one field of learning.

I have provided examples of some of the most influential figures within one school of *shūgaku* during this critical period from 1675 to 1775. As only three figures are presented in this essay, and all of them from the same school, I cannot make any claims about their concerns being representative. It is nonetheless striking that unlike the Shintō-Confucian rapprochement that occurred at this time, these Buddhist intellectuals displayed no interest in resurrecting the paradigm of Shintō-Buddhist conflations such as *honji-suijaku* or *shinbutsu shūgō*. In contrast, even the most stubborn of all Buddhist groups that resisted the accommodation of Shintō beliefs, Jōdo Shinshū, had since Rennyo's time torn down the walls of separation and accepted the legitimacy of the Shintō faith without trying to sublimate it necessarily into a Buddhist form.

As seen above in Ninchō's case, insofar as its tradition of social ethics is concerned, Confucianism remained a positive part of the discourse for many Buddhist intellectuals. As long as it did not seek to denigrate the Buddhist tradition to legitimize its own political ambition, Buddhist intellectuals continued to cede Confucian thought the same social role it had played in Japan since ancient times, when the two systems enjoyed a more harmonious relationship and Confucian morals were taught by Buddhist monks. Indeed the lack of antipathy toward Confucian learning—as opposed to Confucian ideology—among Buddhist thinkers is reflected in the Confucian content included in the curricula of their *danrin* academies. In this regard, Jiun's attempt to create a Buddhist social ethic based on the ten rules of good conduct to compete with Confucian schema was doomed to fail.

Monnō's study of proper Chinese pronunciation came from a tradition in *shūgaku* of reading the Confucian classics alongside Buddhist scriptures, a tradition attested to in ancient Buddhist hermeneutic schema such as *naiten/geten* (内典/外典), *naikyō/gekyō* (内經/外經), and *naidō/gedō* (内道/外道) that express tacit recognition of the fact that Confucian and Daoist scriptures and teachings were also available as other ways of learning. Since the phonological problems inherent in Buddhist Chinese had plagued the Buddhist community for so many centuries, the tradition of careful philological and linguistic study of Chinese naturally led to the appearance of influential phonologists such as Keichū and Monnō from within the Buddhist tradition. This development is only to be expected: as all scholastic groups dedicated to the understanding of Chinese shared the same concerns, their interaction should come as no surprise.

Notes

1 A notable exception is Jeanine Sawada's study of the mixing of Zen and Confucian values in the Shingaku movement of the eighteenth century, *Confucian Values and Popular Zen: Sekimon Shingaku in Eighteenth-Century Japan* (Honolulu: University of Hawai'i Press, 1993).

2 There was no standardized term for the "inside" study of a sect or tradition common to all schools of Buddhism until the Meiji period, when a number of terms were established based on earlier usage that distinguished different forms of study. Among them, the distinction with the most long-lasting effect was between *shūgaku* and *bukkyōgaku,* where the former refers the intellectual study of the system of beliefs and practices at the core of one's own school, and *bukkyōgaku* as the historical study of Buddhism as a whole. The term *shūgaku* is not found in Genshin and Hōnen uses it only once, but it appears frequently in Kamakura- and Muromachi-period exegesis; a term like Tendai *shūgaku* 天台宗学 can be found in Nichiren, for example, though what he meant by it may not be entirely the same as its modern usage. In Edo-period scholarship, the Zen and Jōdo schools typically employed *shūjō* for what is now called *shūgaku,* and though still seen in some sectarian publications into the twentieth century, *shūjō* has largely fallen out of use today.

3 There were numerous treatises written in earlier periods, particularly during the Kamakura, which consciously set out to delineate the doctrinal positions

of one's own school of Buddhist thought. These are often referred to by sectarian scholars in Japan today as instances of *shūgaku*, and they do express one important aspect of Edo-period *shūgaku:* the explication of doctrine. But I am using the word in a somewhat different sense, i.e., as a moniker for a specific intellectual and sectarian political movement beginning in the late seventeenth century that sought to articulate each school's sectarian identity through a variety of reformations, including those of doctrine, administration, relations with the government, relations with the lay communities, hagiographic biography, canon formation, liturgical standardization, etc.

4 Ekū (慧空, 1644–1721) was an influential teacher and text-critical scholar in the Ōtani branch (Higashi Honganji) of Jōdo Shinshū. Mujaku Dōchū (無着道忠, 1653–1744) was a profound scholar of the Rinzai school from the same period. Like Monnō, he was also interested in phonology. See Urs App, "Chan/Zen's Greatest Encyclopedist Mujaku Dōchū," *Cahiers d'Extrême-Asie* 3 (1987), 155–174. Mujaku's opposition to Obaku Zen while asserting his own syncretic view of Zen is discussed briefly by Michel Mohr, "Zen Buddhism during the Tokugawa Period: The Challenge to Go Beyond Sectarian Consciousness," *Japanese Journal of Religious Studies* 21/4 (1994): 350–351, 355. Menzan (面山瑞方, 1683–1769) played a very similar role for the Sōtōshū and has been the subject of recent study by David Riggs, "The Life of Menzan Zuihō, Founder of Dōgen Zen," *Japan Review* 16 (2004): 67–100. See also the supporting analysis by Peter Haskel in his translation of a biography written by Menzan of an otherwise obscure monk, *Letting Go: The Story of Zen Master Tōsui* (Honolulu: University of Hawai'i Press, 2001). Gizan will be discussed below. All of these monk-scholars served as models for later forms of sectarian scholarship for their careful reading of texts and preparation of critical editions.

5 See *Shasekishū* 10末, entry 3; translated in Robert E. Morrell, *Sand and Pebbles (Shasekishū): The Tales of Mujū Ichien, A Voice for Pluralism in Kamakura Buddhism* (New York: State University of New York Press, 1985), p. 263.

6 Cf. Akamatsu Toshihide and Kasahara Kazuo, eds., *Shinshū-shi gaisetsu* (Kyoto: Heirakuji Shoten, 1963), p. 391.

7 In fact there has been a great deal of scholarship over the possible causes of the split between the two branches of Honganji. For a summary of the philological evidence and the relationship between Higashi Honganji and Ieyasu, see Akamatsu and Kasahara, *Shinshū-shi gaisetsu*, pp. 323–330.

8 There are many points of difference, but one key difference can be seen in the way each branch of Honganji views a seminal text called the *Anjin ketsujōshō.* Rennyo revered this text and quotes from it repeatedly in his writings, but it contains a controversial doctrine of unity between human beings and the salvific buddha, known as *kihō ittai,* wherein the time of Amida's ascension into buddhahood is affirmed as the time in which the birth in the Pure Land of all sentient beings was confirmed. The Higashi branch, under the influence of the *shūgaku* scholar Ekū, declared this text to be heretical, meaning outside of proper Jōdo Shinshū dogma, and to this day it is not considered authoritative in the Higashi Honganji. But the Nishi Honganji never agreed to the exclusion and the text remains one of the cornerstones of Nishi doctrine.

9 In the Sōtōshū, for example, according to a directive called the *Sōtōshū hōdo* 曹洞宗法度 issued in 1612, twenty years of practice were required for the rank of *gōko-tō* 江湖頭 and thirty years for the higher rank of *hattō* 法幢. Cf. G. Kagamishima, "Nihon Zenshū-shi—Sōtō-shū—," in Nishitani Keiji and Suzuki Daisetsu, eds., *Kōza zen* 4 (Tokyo: Chikuma Shobō, 1967), pp. 114–125.

10 For example, the Nichiren school supported a total of nineteen between its Itchi and Shōretsu branches, in Kantō alone the Tendai had ten and Jōdo eighteen.

11 Benjamin Elman, *From Philosophy to Philology* (Cambridge: Harvard University Press, 1984).

12 I am referring to the *Siku quanshu zongmu tiyao* 四庫全書総目提要, a two hundred-volume annotated catalog completed under the editorial leadership of Ji Yun in 1782 by order of the Kanlung emperor. This shows that there was communication among scholars from Japan and the continent. Yamanoi's work was presented to the *bakufu* and later printed, but it does not appear to have been printed in the twentieth century. Cf. *Ajia rekishijiten* (Tokyo: Heibonsha, 1960), vol. 4, no. 153.

13 Shishigadani is usually written 鹿ケ谷 but also appears as 獅谷 and 獅ケ谷.

14 Ieyasu had already set a precedent of taking refuge in this form of Buddhism, and throughout the Edo period the Jōdo-shū continued to enjoy close relations with the Tokugawa family.

15 This is based on such texts as the *Hanju zammai kyō* 般舟三昧經 (Skt. *Pratyutpanna-buddha-saṃmukhāvasthita samādhi-sūtra*); see Paul Harrison, *The Samadhi of Direct Encounter with the Buddhas of the Present* (Tokyo: The International Institute for Buddhist Studies, 1990); Zhiyi's *Maha shikan* (摩訶止觀), *Taishō shinshū daizōkyō,* vol. 46, no. 1.

16 For example, as Shandao's authoritative commentary on *The Sūtra of Contemplation on the Buddha of Immeasurable Life,* known in Japanese as *Kangyōshō* 觀經疏 (T.1753.7:245), the important commentary on Hōnen's *Senchakushū* called the *Senchaku dengu ketsugishō* (*Jōdo-shū zensho,* vol. 7, no. 186) by the third patriarch of Jōdo-shū, Ryōchū (良忠, 1199–1287), etc.

17 According to Etō Chōei's *Ninchō Shōnin* (Tokyo: Zōjōji, 1935), the *Zizhi lu* 自知録 (Jp. *Jichi-roku*) by Zhu Hong (袾宏, 1535–1615) was his first project, printed in 1701. Then he had the *Taishang ganying bian* 太上感應編 (Jp. *Taijō kannō-hen*), printed, a Daoist collection of morality tales attributed to Ge Hong (葛洪, 283–343), author of the *Baopuzi* 抱朴子 that became popular in the Song dynasty. It first came to Japan in 1494, according to the *Sanetake kōki* 實隆公記 (cf. *Nihon kokugo daijiten* 12.570b). Ninchō also printed the *Kanchō hōkun* 勸懲寶訓, an anonymous morality tract. The term *kanchō* 勸懲 is an abbreviation of *kanzen chōaku* 勸善懲悪 (Ch. *quanshan cheng'e*), "to promote good and punish evil," an ancient Chinese phrase dating back to the *Zuo Zhuan* adopted in the Edo period to describe a genre of Edo fiction and theatrical performances in which good characters struggle against bad, with the good always coming out on top and the bad are destroyed. See Morohashi Tetsuji, ed., *Dai kanwa jiten* 大漢和辭典 (*Great Chinese-Japanese Dictionary*) (Tokyo: Taishūkan shoten, 1955–1960); vol. 2, p. 421c.

18 The *Kaneiji-ban* 寛永寺版 (also called *Tenkai-ban* 天海版) was completed in 1648, over fifty years before Ninchō began his work; there is no mention made in Ninchō's biography of this work. The Kaneiji canon was made with movable wooden type, an experiment that was dubbed a failure, and everyone went back to carving blocks. It was based upon the Southern Song *Sixi Baozi-fusi* 思渓 寶資福寺 (Sixi) edition, which also formed the basis of the Yuan canon.

19 In the middle is the Amida trinity standing on a cloud with *nianfo*/nenbutsu (*namo amituo fo* 南無阿彌陀佛; *namu amida butsu*) written across the top horizontally in big characters. Beneath the triad is the phrase "nenbutsu disciples" (*nianfo dizi* 念佛弟子; *nenbutsu deshi*), under which is a space to write in a believer's name. Sometimes there are strings visible from the Buddha's hand to the name. On either side are drawn the merits of nenbutsu practice and a series of circles all around from top to bottom in different colors: white, yellow, red, blue, and black; one advances from one to another with each 1,000 utterances of the nenbutsu, eventually leading up to a goal of 1 million recitations. There are now two extant editions from 1704, one is from Ōbaku Shishirin (獅子林) and the other from Shishigatani (= Hōnen'in). Both of these have the same colophon by the Ōbaku monk Dokutan, also known as Shōkei Dokutan (性瑩獨湛, 1628–1706), and the Ōbaku text also has a postscript written by Ninchō. The Shishigatani one is a little longer and has a "Chinese grass" motif on top and bottom, which is missing in the other edition.

Dokutan was the fourth abbot of Mampukuji, following Yinyuan bringing the lineage from China. In addition to receiving the seal of transmission in his lineage, he is noted for setting out a place for Pure Land practice and reciting both the *Amidakyō* and the nenbutsu as part of his daily liturgy. In his teaching, Dokutan is said to have only taught the merits of nenbutsu practice and so gained the nickname "Nenbutsu Dokutan." Ninchō and Dokutan seem to have become extremely close friends spiritually, and Dokutan came to the construction site of the Hōnen'in to make suggestions. Dokutan is said to have lamented the absence of this picture from Japanese Buddhism and gave one to Ninchō from which to carve a block and circulate.

20 The first Korean Buddhist canon was destroyed in the Mongol invasion of Korea and very little of it is extant today. The second Korean canon is thought to have been more carefully edited under the supervision of the masterful scholar Sugi. In general this second Korean canon is closest to the Khitan Liao edition and forms the basis of the Japanese Taishō canon. Its blocks have been preserved. See the article by Robert E. Buswell, Jr., "Sugi's *Collation Notes* to the Koryŏ Buddhist Canon and Their Significance for Buddhist Textual Criticism," pp. 57–118 in this volume.

21 The *Manji zokuzōkyō* followed the *kundoku* of Ninchō's *Taikōroku* work.

22 Such as the *Inshitsu-roku* 陰隲録 (author unknown).

23 There were numerous *yinyi/ongi* compiled in China during the Tang period and two works called *Yiqiejing yinyi/Issaikyō ongi*, with Huilin's work reaching to four times the early work of Xuanying (玄應, 627–649). Ninchō's edition of Huilin's work can be found at T.2128.54:311. It was also recently printed in five volumes along with the addendum added by the Liao dynasty prelate

Xilin (希麟) and an index, *Zhengxu yiqiejing yinyi* 續正一切經音義 (Shanghai: Shanghai Guji Chubanshe, 1986).

24 As a measure of how important the quotations that can be found in Huilin's work are, in 1936 the Commercial Press in Taipei put out a five-volume index to all the works quoted in his *Yiqiejing yinyi*, the *Huilin Yiqiejing yinyi yinyongshu suoyin* 慧琳一切經音義引用書索引.

25 The *Makō inkyō yoron*, discussed below, states that Monnō probably came to Edo at the age of fifteen or sixteen and returned to Kyoto at around twenty, making his dates there 1715–1720. Shinmura Izuru confers in "Monnō Shōnin no kōgyō," published in two parts: *Shūkyōkai* 宗教界 2/12 (1906) and 3/4 (1907); reprinted as an appendix in Itō Yūkō, *Jōdoshūshi no kenkyū*, pp. 409–433 (Kyoto: Itō Yūkō-shi Ikō Kankōkai, 1937; Tokyo: Kokusho Kankōkai, 1984, reprint) and in *Shinmura Izuru senshū* (Tokyo: Kōchō Shorin, 1944), vol. 3, pp. 137–163. There are two major biographical sources on Monnō's life: the *Musō Shōnin ryakuden* 無相上人略傳 by his disciple Monryū, and the *Zoku nihon kōsōden* 續日本高僧傳. Denzūin (傳通院) was the dharma name given to Tokugawa Ieyasu's mother. She had asked that upon her death she be interred in a temple founded by Shōgei in 1415 in Edo called Muryōjukyōji. She died in 1602 in Fushimi, and her remains were then carried up to Edo to fulfill her request, at which point the temple was renamed after her.

26 It should be noted here that while all these figures shared a passion for the study of Chinese literature, the Confucian classics, and the ancient Japanese texts from the Nara period, they were often at odds about how to interpret them. In particular, Shundai is considered an inheritor of Sorai's so-called Ancient Learning (*kogaku*) school, while Mabuchi along with Norinaga worked to advance the rival National Learning (*kokugaku*) school that affirmed the value of native Japanese values prior to the import of Confucianism.

27 Also known as Myōryōbō (明了房); Shinpan was a monk in the Shingon school.

28 The *Kokugogaku kenkyū jiten* gives the following list from the Kamakura to Sengoku periods: Shinpan 信範, Gensei 元盛, Dōe 道恵, In'yū 印融, Kakusan 覺算, Raisei 頼勢. Satō Kiyoji 佐藤喜代治, ed., *Kokugogaku kenkyū jiten* 国語学研究事典 (Tokyo: Meiji Shoin, 1977), p. 859.

29 Satō, *Kokugogaku kenkyū jiten*, p. 859, lists the *Inkyō shochū-shō* 韻鏡庶中鈔 written in 1660 by Ōta Shiki 大田子規 (嘉方), and the *Inkyō shūchū shō* 韻鏡袖中鈔 written by Mōri Teisai 毛利貞齋 in 1695, etc.

30 Satō, *Kokugogaku kenkyū jiten*, p. 680.

31 See Haruo Aoki's article "*kana*" in Edwin O. Reischauer and Gen Itasaka, eds., *Kodansha Encyclopedia of Japan* (Tokyo: Kodansha, 1983), vol. 4, p. 134.

32 A photo reproduction of the 1804 xylograph is available in Hayashi Shiten, ed., *Makō inkyō yoron* (Tokyo: Benseisha, 1981), based on the edition held by the National Diet Library.

33 From the *Fuku Monnō Shōnin sho* 複文雄上人書, quoted in Tajiri Yūichirō 田尻祐一郎, *Dazai Shundai, Hattori Nankaku* 太宰春台, 服部南郭 (Tokyo: Meitoku Shuppan, 1995), p. 140.

[34] *Fuku-Monnō Shōnin sho,* quoted in Tajiri, *Dazai Shundai, Hattori Nankaku*, p. 140. The colophon explains that the title means "Lessons while Thinking of [the Pure Land in] the West."

[35] Rihō comments that this is a reference to the Wu pronunciation (呉音, *go-on*) that was used as the standard in the southern courts. He remarks that it is not certain what the northern pronunciation was at this time; Hayashi, *Makō inkyō yoron,* p. 38.

[36] More commonly referred to as either *fanqie* 反切 or *fanniu* 反紐, this is a method whereby the pronunciation of the entry character is indicated by the listing of two characters, from which the initial sound of the first is combined with the final sound of the second to produce a facsimile of the entry character's sound.

[37] This work is considered to date from the Sui period (589–618) but Shengong (神珙) is referred to as a Tang figure, though his dates are unknown. Morohashi, *Dai kanwa jiten*, vol. 8, p. 448, describes Shengong as a Central Asian monk from the Tang period.

[38] The *Yupian* was originally compiled during the Liang dynasty (502–557) by Gu Yewang (顧野王) but it underwent significant revision during the Tang by Sunqiang (孫強) and again in the Song by Chen Pengnien (陳彭年) and others. Shengong's chart first appears in the Song edition.

[39] The *Yunjing* is another important milestone in the history of the study of Chinese phonology. It contains for the first time the chart of 206 phonemes divided up over four tones.

[40] The word here is *songji* 宋季, and refers to the important linguists of the Southern Song, here specifically Zhang Linzhi (張麟之), who wrote the preface to the *Yunjing* dated 1161, and Zheng Qiao (鄭樵, 1104–1160).

[41] Xianru is the sobriquet of Zheng Qiao. Shundai here is referring to Zheng Qiao's *Tongzhi qiyinlüe* 通志七音略.

[42] Labial, palatal, velar, dental, laryngeal, half-palatal, and half-dental: *shinsetsu-ga-shi-kō-hanshin-hanshi* 唇舌牙歯喉半舌半歯.

[43] One of many unsuccessful transliterations of the word *buddha* in early Chinese translations of Buddhist texts. Another common form, also pronounced *futu,* is 浮圖.

[44] According to the *Makō inkyō yoron,* Yūsaku was not a monk at all but a doctor who lived in the Tōrinji 常林寺 monastery in eastern Kyōto. He also called himself Tōan Hōkyō 等菴法橋. We have no other information about him.

[45] According to the *Makō inkyō yoron* (47), in 1726.

[46] I am grateful to Ann Wehmeyer for learning of this connection between Keichū and the *Nirvāṇa Sūtra.*

[47] Teika's work is best known by the name *Gek'anshū* 下官集 but its actual title was *Hekian* 僻案. Gyōa's work is called either *Kana mojizukai* 假名文字遣, *Gyōa kanazukai* 行阿假名遣, or *Teika kanazukai* 定家假名遣.

[48] Satō, *Kokugogaku kenkyū jiten*, p. 682.

49 See n. 25.

50 Ota Zensai's work *Kangō onzu* 漢呉音図 is clearly based on Monnō's precedent, but with major corrections. Ota himself acknowledged his debt to Monnō, and in the following comment expresses both his admiration for Monnō's pioneering efforts as well as his justification for writing his own treatise:

> In former times there was a phonologist monk in Kyoto named Monnō who wrote the *Makō inkyō* and many other compositions. It is truly painful to recommend this study but it should also be said that scholars of later generations have been particularly blessed [by his efforts].

51 Ōno Susumu and Ōkubo Tasashi, eds., *Motoori Norinaga zenshū* (Tokyo: Chikuma Shobō, 1972), vol. 13, pp. 75–77.

52 See *Kokusho sōmokuroku, hoteiban* (Tokyo: Iwanami Shoten, 1989–1991), vol. 2, p. 470. Monnō's treatise is a highly academic statement of the traditional Buddhist myth, which quotes numerous canonical sources and contains a number of carefully drawn pictures of the configuration of continents and mountains such as Sumeru, Cakravāla, etc.

53 Motoori Norinaga, "Shamon Monnō ga kyūsen hakkai gechō-ron no ben (文雄が九山八海解嘲論の弁)," in Ōno and Ōkubo, eds., *Motoori Norinaga zenshū*, vol. 14, p. 163 ff. Monnō's monograph is an academic outline of traditional Buddhist myths of sacred geography, quoting canonical sources and using a number of carefully drawn pictures of the configuration of continents and mountains such as Sumeru and Cakravāla. There is no modern edition but impressions from the original 1754 blocks exist in a number of libraries in Japan, such as those at the National Diet, Kyoto University, etc. See *Kokusho sōmokuroku, hoteiban*, vol. 2, p. 470. Ōno and Ōkubo, the editors of the *Motoori Norinaga zenshū*, assert in their *kaidai* on Norinaga's essay (vol. 14, p. 20) that he was well aware of Monnō's work from his early years studying in Kyoto.

54 The Yuezhi were a nomadic people of Central Asia, one branch of which settled in Bactria in the second century B.C.E. and set up the Kuṣāṇa kingdom in the following century. Their origins are unknown other than being Indo-European; they have been called Iranian, Tocharian, Tibetan, and even Turkish. Most of the important early translators of Buddhist sūtras into Chinese were Yuezhi, such as Lokakṣema, Dharmarakṣa, and Zhiqian. Monnō appears to understand something here that is still perplexing scholars today, the fact that the language of the sūtras used by the Yuezhi was not pure Sanskrit but a Prakrit dialect, perhaps many Prakrit dialects, as Monnō is saying here. This contributed to the lack of uniformity in transliterations of Buddhist technical terms as well as translation mistakes.

55 Probably indicates Central China, as this is the name of a river running from Shanxi through Hunan to Hubei. Note that Zhang 漳 was also used for the Fujian area.

56 Probably represents Fujian province in the south.

57 Although the name of a number of different kingdoms in Chinese history, as a place name Wu 呉 generally represents the the Jiangsu area.

58 Itō, *Jōdoshū shi no kenkyū,* p. 416. Unfortunately Shinmura does not identify this source of these comments.

59 Even though the Nichiren tradition appears to be the counter-example of this statement, Nichiren's valorization of Japan as a sort of "chosen" land for the future incarnation of Śākyamuni is still rationalized on the basis of a universalist argument—that Japan is the ideal environment for Buddhism to spread throughout the world. Thus ultimately the goal remains the universal application of Buddhist principles of liberation to a sphere that is not limited to a specific nation.

60 The reason I do not use the more usual term, intersectarian, is that it implies that we should consider the Ancient Learning and National Learning schools as "sects." Despite the fact that they display a great deal of what can be called religious discourse and religious values, these were more philosophical movements than organized religious organizations; hence, using the term "sect" to describe them is inappropriate.

61 The exact year of this work is not known. The text was printed in Washio Junkei 鷲尾純敬, ed., *Nihon shisō tōjō shiryō* 日本思想闘諍史料 (Tokyo: Tōhō Shoten, 1930), vol. 3, but no date is given for the manuscript used. I was able to photograph the manuscript held in the Motoori Norinaga archives, but it was dated 1788, i.e., twenty-five years after Monnō's death.

62 Washio, *Nihon shisō tōjō shiryō,* p. 239.

63 Also known as the *Dan shutsujō kōgo* 彈出定後語. This text is also located in Washio, *Nihon shisō tōjō shiryō,* vol. 3.

64 *Jisshōteki hōhō* 實證的方法. This is precisely the kind of language used by Elman to describe the "empirical scholarship," or *kaozheng-xue* (*kōshō-gaku*), movement in China. Other descriptive terms used are "text-critical philology," *kōkan-gaku* 校勘學, and "bibliography" in the broadest sense, or *shoshi-gaku* 書誌學.

65 Yoshida Atsushi 吉田篤志, "Edo kōki no kōshōgaku—Matsuzaki Kendō no baai," *Ōkurayama ronshū* 23 (March 1988): 203–224.

66 There has been very little written on *shūgaku* in any form by Japanese scholars, much less outside Japan. What has been done generally tends to frame the problem from the point of view of sectarian identity and what the contributions of individual scholars has been toward that development. In general there is thus no consideration of the parallel developments in methodology and theme in non-Buddhist areas of learning. For example, see Kaneko Daiei, *Shinshū no kyōgi to sono rekishi* (Kyoto: Chōjiya, 1942), pp. 224–235; Kagamishima Genryū, "Nihon zenshū-shi—Sōtō-shū," *Kōza zen,* vol. 4: *Zen no rekishi* (Tokyo: Chikuma Shōbō, 1967), pp. 114–125; and Furuta Shōkin "Nihon zenshū-shi—Rinzai-shū," *Kōza zen,* vol. 4: *Zen no rekishi,* pp. 80–88.

67 Dazai Shundai's best-known work on Chinese language study is his *Wadoku yōryō* 倭讀要領. See Arai Hakuseki's *Dōbun tsūkō* 同文通考, written in 1705, and the *Tōon-fu* 東音譜, dated 1719, the latter specifically a study of Chinese phonology. Kaibara Ekken is known for his *Wajikai* 和字解 on *kana* usage and the *Nihon shakymyō* 日本釋名 on Japanese etymology, both dated 1699. His nephew Kaibara Yoshiko also contributed the *Wajiga* 和字雅 in 1688.

References

Akamatsu, Toshihide 赤松俊秀, and Kasahara Kazuo 笠原一男, eds. *Shinshū-shi gaisetsu*. Kyoto, Heirakuji Shoten, 1963.

App, Urs. "Chan/Zen's Greatest Encyclopedist Mujaku Dōchū," *Cahiers d'Extrême-Asie* 3 (1987): 155–174.

Aoki, Haruo. "Kana," in Edwin O. Reischauer and Gen Itasaka, eds. *Kodansha Encyclopedia of Japan*, vol. 4, pp. 131–135. Tokyo: Kodansha, 1983.

Elman, Benjamin. *From Philosophy to Philology*. Cambridge, MA: Harvard University Press, 1984.

Etō, Chōei 江藤澂英. *Ninchō Shōnin*. Tokyo: Zōjōji, 1935.

Furuta, Shōkin 古田紹欽. "Nihon Zenshū-shi—Rinzai-shū," in *Kōza zen*, vol. 4: *Zen no rekishi*, pp. 5–88. Tokyo: Chikuma Shōbō, 1967.

Harrison, Paul. *The Samadhi of Direct Encounter with the Buddhas of the Present*. Studia Philologica Buddhica Monograph Series V. Tokyo: The International Institute for Buddhist Studies, 1990.

Haskel, Peter. *Letting Go: The Story of Zen Master Tōsui*. Hawaii: University of Hawai'i Press, 2001.

Hayashi, Shiten 林史典, ed. *Makō inkyō yoron* 摩光韻鏡餘論. Tokyo: Benseisha, 1981.

Huilin 慧琳 (737–820). *Huilin Yiqiejing yinyi yinyongshu suoyin* 慧琳一切經音義引用書索引, 5 vols. Changsha: Shangwu yinshuguan (Commercial Press), 1938.

Itō, Yūkō 伊藤祐晃. *Jōdoshūshi no kenkyū* 浄土宗史の研究. Kyoto: Itō Yūkō-shi Ikō Kankōkai, 1937. Tokyo: Kokusho Kankōkai, 1984, reprint.

Kagamishima, Genryū 鏡島元隆. "Nihon Zenshū-shi—Sōtō-shū—," in Keiji Nishitani and Daisetsu Suzuki, eds., *Kōza zen* 4: *Zen no rekishi*, pp. 89–125. Tokyo: Chikuma Shobō, 1967.

Kaizuka, Shigeki 貝塚茂樹, ed. *Ajia rekishijiten*, 10 vols. Tokyo: Heibonsha, 1960.

Kaneko, Daiei 金子大榮. *Shinshū no kyōgi to sono rekishi*. Kyoto: Chōjiya, 1942.

Kokusho sōmokuroku, hoteiban 国書総目録 補訂版. Tokyo: Iwanami Shoten, 1989–1991.

Mohr, Michel. "Zen Buddhism during the Tokugawa Period: The Challenge to Go Beyond Sectarian Consciousness," *Japanese Journal of Religious Studies* 21/4 (1994): 341–372.

Morohashi, Tetsuji 諸橋轍次, ed. *Dai kanwa jiten*, 13 vols. Tokyo: Taishūkan shoten, 1955–1960.

Morrell, Robert E. *Sand and Pebbles (Shasekishū): The Tales of Mujū Ichien, A Voice for Pluralism in Kamakura Buddhism*. New York: State University of New York Press, 1985.

Motoori Norinaga 本居宣長. "Shamon Monnō ga kyūsen hakkai gechō-ron no ben (文雄が九山八海解嘲侖の弁)," in Ōno Susumu and Ōkubo Tadashi, eds., *Motoori Norinaga zenshū*, vol. 14, pp. 161–717. Tokyo: Chikuma Shobō, 1972.

Ōno Susumu 大野晋 and Ōkubo Tadashi 大久保正, eds. *Motoori Norinaga zenshū*, 14 vols. Tokyo: Chikuma Shobō, 1972.

Riggs, David. "The Life of Menzan Zuihō, Founder of Dōgen Zen," *Japan Review* 16 (2004): 67–100.

Ryōchū 良忠 (1199–1287). *Senchaku dengu ketsugishō* 選擇傳弘決疑鈔, 5 vols. *Jōdo-shū zensho* 7.186–347.

Satō, Kiyoji 佐藤喜代治, ed. *Kokugogaku kenkyū jiten* 国語学研究事典. Tokyo: Meiji Shoin, 1977.

Sawada, Jeanine. *Confucian Values and Popular Zen: Sekimon Shingaku in Eighteenth-Century Japan.* Honolulu: University of Hawai'i Press, 1993.

Shinmura, Izuru 新村出. "Monnō Shōnin no kōgyō 文雄上人の功業," published in 2 parts in *Shūkyōkai* 宗教界 2/12 (1906) and 3/4 (1907). Reprinted as an appendix in Itō Yūkō 伊藤祐晃, *Jōdoshūshi no kenkyū* (Kyoto: Itō Yūkō-shi Ikō Kankōkai, 1937; Tokyo: Kokusho Kankōkai, 1984, reprint), pp. 409–433; and in *Shinmura Izuru senshū* (Tokyo: Kōchō Shorin, 1944), vol. 3, pp. 137–163.

—. *Shinmura Izuru senshū* 新村出選集, 4 vols. Tokyo: Yūtokusha, 1943–1947.

—. *Shinmura Izuru zenshū* 新村出全集, 15 vols. Tokyo: Chikuma Shobō edition, 1968–1973.

Tajiri, Yūichirō 田尻祐一郎. *Dazai Shundai, Hattori Nankaku* 太宰春台, 服部南郭. Tokyo: Meitoku Shuppan, 1995.

Washio Junkei 鷲尾純敬, ed. *Nihon shisō tōjō shiryō* 日本思想闘諍史料, 10 vols. Tokyo: Tōhō Shoten, 1930–1931.

Yoshida, Atsushi 吉田篤志. "Edo kōki no kōshōgaku—Matsuzaki Kendō no baai," *Ōkurayama ronshū* 23 (March 1988): 203–224.

Sugi's *Collation Notes* to the Koryŏ Buddhist Canon and Their Significance for Buddhist Textual Criticism

Robert E. Buswell, Jr.
University of California, Los Angeles

The publication of the thirteenth-century Korean Buddhist canon (Koryŏ taejanggyŏng 高麗大藏經) was arguably the greatest cultural achievement of the Koryŏ 高麗 dynasty (918–1392). Emulating their predecessors in the Chinese Northern Song 北宋 dynasty, who published the first xylographic canon in 983, Koryŏ began the first such carving (which I will henceforth call Koryŏ I) in 1011; it was completed sometime around 1087, only to be destroyed in 1234 during an invasion by the Mongols.[1] The woodblocks of its replacement (which I will call Koryŏ II) were carved between 1236 and 1251,[2] and the 81,258 blocks (the canon's popular name is the "Eighty Thousand Canon," or P'alman taejanggyŏng 八萬大藏經) have been stored in paired wooden archives at the monastery of Haeinsa 海印寺 in South Kyŏngsang province 慶尙南道 since 1398. These massive compilations of scripture, disciplinary manuals, commentary, doxography, and history collect Buddhist materials translated from Indian and Central Asian languages into Chinese (the lingua franca of educated discourse throughout East Asia, including Korea), as well as a limited selection of indigenous East Asian writings in literary Chinese. Creating these enormous canons would have required a national commitment of money and manpower on a par with U.S. efforts to launch the lunar missions in the 1960s.

No scholar in the West has done more to bring the Korean Buddhist canon to the attention of the broader academy than Lewis Lancaster, the scholar, mentor, and friend to whom this *festschrift* volume is dedicated. The University of California, Berkeley, was one of only twelve institutions worldwide to receive a complete copy of the Korean canon when the full set of xylographs was last printed in the 1960s. However, since no catalogue of the bound volumes was available, the set was difficult to use. Soon after Professor Lancaster arrived in Berkeley in 1967, he began the massive task of cataloguing the complete set of xylographs, aided by Sung-bae Park (now at Stony Brook University, New York) who arrived as a graduate student in Buddhist Studies in 1974. Their joint efforts led to the 1979 publication of *The Korean Buddhist Canon: A Descriptive Catalogue,* the first Western-language catalogue detailing this canon.[3]

Professor Lancaster has returned periodically to this canon over the course of his career, helping to identify fragments of the first Koryŏ canon and consulting with the Korean team that produced the digital edition of the second Koryŏ canon in the 1990s, the first complete Buddhist canon to be made available in digital form. Indeed, many of the broader areas of research that continue to fascinate Professor Lancaster, such as the digitization of Buddhist texts and virtual realities in the Humanities, his ever-expanding Electronic Cultural Atlas Initiative, and his "blue-dot" method for high-dimensional visualization of large-scale canonical metadata, all build upon his early interest in the second Koryŏ canon. This chapter on the editing of this canon is my own small tribute to this influential aspect of Professor Lancaster's long career.[4]

I. The Importance of Sugi's *Collation Notes*

The Carving of the Second Koryŏ Canon

With the destruction of the woodblocks of the first Koryŏ canon, the kingdom began the task of recarving this "great treasure of the country" in 1236. The editorial office was reestablished, with the main headquarters for the undertaking at Kanghwa Island 江華島, an easily defendable yet readily accessible island off the west-central coast of Korea. There was also a branch at Namhae 南海 in the far south of the Korean peninsula. Special care was taken with this second canon to produce an edition that would be worthy of the sacred contents of the scriptures, thereby ensuring the intercession of the buddhas and bodhisattvas in the protection of the kingdom.

The editors consulted a number of new versions of the canon that had been published since the first Koryŏ project in the eleventh century. Foremost among these was the Liao 遼 canon of the Khitans, which Koryŏ had received in 1064. Although no complete prints of the Khitan canon are extant today, at the time it was reputed to have been the most carefully edited of all East Asian Buddhist canons. Several revisions of the canon also appeared in China in 1104, 1137, and 1172, but these were all private printings, produced with little attention to philological accuracy.

The Koreans gathered a veritable army of scholars, first to collate the various editions of the scriptures and establish the correct reading, then to proofread meticulously the finished blocks to ferret out any misprints. Birchwood from several offshore islands was harvested and cured in seawater for three years to protect the wood against warping and cracking. The logs were hewn and the resulting blocks were again soaked in saltwater and then dried and planed. The texts of the scriptures were written on paper by some of the finest calligraphers in Korea and transferred to the blocks; the style of the calligraphy was carefully checked to insure its consistency across the thousands of blocks. Finally, skilled woodworkers carved the calligraphy onto each block, producing the finished xylograph.

The blocks themselves measure approximately 69.5 cm. by 23.9 cm. (27.4 by 9.4 inches) and usually include 23 lines of 14 Sinographs apiece, with text on both sides of the block. After sixteen years of labor by thousands of scholars and craftsmen, the entire set, consisting of some 1,514 texts in 6,815 fascicles, carved on 81,258 individual blocks, was completed in 1251. All of the texts that had been published in previous editions of the canon were included, making the Koryŏ II canon the most comprehensive collection of East Asian Buddhist literature assembled up to that time,[5] and it was the finest edition of the canon ever produced in East Asia. When compared with the earlier Northern Song 北宋 edition and all subsequent editions produced in China or Japan, the careful scholarship and vigilant quality control that went into the project are still recognized as exceptional, even by modern standards.

Sugi and his *Collation Notes*

Beginning in 1904 with Sekino Sada 關野貞, who published the first accounts of this canon outside Korea,[6] scholars in both Japan and the West have lauded the Koryŏ II canon for its advanced editorial standards.[7] Yet despite the widespread recognition of this canon's editorial quality, a work that documents in remarkable detail the process followed by the editorial team in compiling the canon has received little attention from the scholarly community. This work is the *Koryŏguk sinjo taejang kyojŏng pyŏllok* 高麗國新雕大藏校正別錄 (*Supplementary Record of Collation Notes to the New Carving of the Great Canon of the Koryŏ Kingdom*), compiled in thirty fascicles (*kwon* 卷) by Sugi 守其 (d.u.), the editor-in-chief of the Koryŏ II canon, and his associates.[8] Sugi's notes are even more valuable because they are the only extant record of how East Asian Buddhist scholars in the premodern era went about the task of collating and editing multiple recensions of thousands of scriptures into a definitive canon.

Despite Sugi's importance to the textual history of East Asian Buddhism, he remains a nearly forgotten figure. There are no references to him in the *Koryŏsa* 高麗史 (*History of Koryŏ*) or any other Korean historical source. About all we know of Sugi is that he seems to have hailed from Kaet'aesa 開泰寺, one of the major Hwaŏm 華嚴 monasteries during the Koryŏ dynasty and the merit cloister of the founder of Koryŏ, King T'aejo 太祖 (r. 918–943). There were two principal lineages of Hwaŏm during the Koryŏ: one derived from the Silla monk Ŭisang 義湘 (625–702) and the early Koryŏ monk Kyunyŏ 均如 (923–973); a second traced its lineage from the Silla monk Wŏnhyo 元曉 (617–686) to Ŭich'ŏn 義天 (1055–1101). Sugi was associated with the Ŭisang-Kyunyŏ lineage, which had close political connections to the Ch'oe 崔 military regime; Ŭich'ŏn's line had closer connections with a group of high-status clans known as the Munbŏl 門閥.[9]

Virtually the only other allusion to Sugi the man appears in an encomium written by his contemporary, the renowned Koryŏ literatus Ch'oe Cha 崔滋 (1188–1260), recorded in Ch'oe's *Pohan chip* 補閑集 (*Supplementing Idleness Collection*) compiled in 1254.[10] Ch'oe Cha writes:

> The *sŭngt'ong* 僧統 (*saṃgha* overseer) Sugi of Kaebongsa 開奉寺: his scholarship was broad and his understanding seminal. He honored an imperial order to edit the canon, adjudicating the correct and incorrect [readings] as if he had himself translated the texts before.

Sugi is also mentioned in a late work, the *Yŏnsan sam taejang yŏn'gi* 緣山三大藏經緣起 (*Background on the Three Great Canons of Yŏnsan*), written in 1748 by Such'ŏn 隨天 (d.u.) of Chŭngsangsa 增上寺, which refers to Sugi's role in editing the Koryŏ II canon.[11] Apart from these few cryptic references, Sugi is a mystery to us, as he will probably forever remain.

In editing the Koryŏ II canon, Sugi and his team drew principally upon three other canons: first, the canon of the Northern Song dynasty, carved during the Kaibao 開寶 reign era between 971 and 983 (commonly referred to in the scholarship as the Kaibao canon); Sugi refers to this canon variously as the Old Song edition (*Ku-Song pon* 舊宋本), the Song canon (*Songjang* 宋藏), the Song-canon edition (*Songjang pon* 宋藏本), or simply the Song edition (*Song pon* 宋本); second, the Khitan edition of the Liao dynasty, printed circa 1031–1055, which he generally referred to as the Khitan edition (*Tan pon* 丹本), or other variants similar to those used for the Kaibao; and third, the Koryŏ I canon of 1011, which he usually referred to as the State edition (*Kuk pon* 國本).[12]

Virtually all of the consideration given to Sugi's work in Buddhist scholarship to date has concerned its value for documenting the textual genealogies of the various East Asian canons. In fact, it was through using Sugi's work that Japanese scholars in the first part of the twentieth century were able to verify conclusively the existence of an independent Khitan edition of the canon, the authenticity of which had previously been contested.[13] Sugi's detailed records provided definitive proof that, in style and format, the Koryŏ II canon imitated the Song Kaibao canon and the Koryŏ I canon (which was itself based on the Kaibao), though its readings followed more closely those found in the Liao canon of Koryŏ's Khitan neighbors.

The Koryŏ II canon's reputation for scholarly accuracy was so well established that Japanese scholars adopted it as the *textus receptus* for the modern Taishō printed edition of the Buddhist canon, the *Taishō shinshū daizōkyō* 大正新修大藏經,[14] compiled in Japan between 1922 and 1934. Unfortunately, although the Taishō editorial team had access to the *Collation Notes* and could have easily drawn on Sugi's discussions of the variant readings he had confronted in making their own editorial decisions, they chose not to do so. Instead, they simply appended a number of Sugi's annotations to independent texts included in the Koryŏ II canon and reprinted these verbatim in the Taishō (though with more than the occasional misprint).[15] Despite both this fact and the considerable historical interest of Sugi's *Collation Notes,* the Taishō editors did not attempt to sort through and mark the specific points of controversy addressed in his annotations. The Taishō is therefore not a true critical edition of the canon; instead the first fifty-five volumes constitute substantially a reprint of Koryŏ II, with a listing of alternate readings from other canons.

In the Appendix to this chapter, I list all of the texts treated by Sugi, and summarize Sugi's annotation to each text, including the specific page, column, and line references (as keyed to the Taishō canon) to the passages in question. His annotation will prove to be an extremely valuable source for detailing medieval Chinese xylographic lineages, and in several cases will demonstrate that the texts appearing in Taishō are not merely Koryŏ II recensions but instead derive originally from the Khitan and occasionally the Kaibao and/or Koryŏ I canons.

Sugi's *Collation Notes* thus also serves as a valuable resource for establishing the textual lineage of individual scriptures, which can be of considerable value to Buddhist scholars in establishing the precise canonical affiliations of texts appearing in the Taishō. This information will also help to verify the authenticity of fragments of these nonextant canons—fragments (some quite substantial) that continue to be discovered and published in East Asia—and to reconstruct other portions. Indeed, this can already be shown in some specific instances: for example, the readings of some published sections of the Fangshan 方山 lithic canon carved during the Liao dynasty converge nicely with the Koryŏ II readings and, by extension, the Khitan state canon.[16]

Sugi does not, of course, cover all potential points of controversy in the different canonical recensions. Minor variations in readings of a few Sinographs were not covered in his notes, a fact that can be gleaned from such comments as "Although the wording of the State and Song editions is different from the Khitan edition, their meaning is indistinguishable" (國宋兩本與彼丹本文雖有異,義則無殊; K.1402.38:614c). Sugi generally covered only major issues of structure, translator attribution, textual lineage, and the like. In a typical entry for a specific text, he lists the case character in the Koryŏ II canon where the work appears; the title of the text and the fascicle or roll (Kor. *kwŏn;* Ch. *quan* 卷) in which the disputed point appears (if relevant); followed by the passage itself, generally indicated by *kwŏn*, scroll (*p'ok* 幅), and line (*haeng* 行) numbers.[17] He then evaluates the discrepancies in the three editions, and indicates which reading he prefers. Often, information appearing in such bibliographical catalogues as the *Kaiyuan Shijiao lu* 開元釋教錄 (*Kaiyuan-era Catalogue of Śākyamuni's Teachings,* hereafter KYL; T. 2154) is cited in support of his analysis. Finally, Sugi commonly ends with the stock phrase:

> Furthermore, for the sake of those who may read the Old Song canon (viz., the Kaibao), I record [either in its entirety or in brief] the correct passage to the left (i.e., below). (又爲看舊藏經者, 略錄正文于左; K.1402.38:512b et passim)

This "correct passage" (*chŏngmun* 正文) is the reading as it appears in the actual blocks of the Koryŏ II edition of the text. Of course, it would have been more valuable in establishing textual genealogies if Sugi had given the readings that he rejected. However, if we follow precisely the information he provides about scroll and line numbers, the readings Sugi found in these variant editions can be reconstructed. This information offers important data that documents the text-critical methodology followed by editors of Buddhist texts in East Asia and details the decision-making processes they followed in preparing their editions.

One minor point on which Sugi's *Notes* can also contribute is in establishing the relative order of texts within a particular case (*ham* 函) of the Koryŏ II canon—no small task for some of the cases that include large numbers of shorter scriptures. There traditionally was no sequential numbering of the texts included in the canon, as was done in the modern Taishō edition, only an ordering of case characters;[18] the order of texts within a specific case was arbitrary and up to the editors to decide. In their catalogues to Koryŏ II, Prof. Lancaster and Prof. Yi Sŏn'gŭn 李瑄根 have done an admirable job of attempting to provide a coherent listing of the included texts, and their collaboration in establishing a definitive numbering system for the canon has considerably aided the efforts of all scholars who use the Korean canon.[19]

Sugi's *Collation Notes,* however, provides additional clues about the correct ordering of a few scriptures, and seems to call for some fine-tuning of the present listing. Since the *Notes* go through the canon case by case, one would assume that the order in which he treated the texts within a single case represents his intended ordering of the scriptures. According to Sugi's listings, we should thus transpose K. 117 and K. 112, K. 640 and K. 639, and K. 871 and K. 864. Given the some 1,500 works that appear in Koryŏ II, however, three such corrections hardly call into question the overall accuracy of Sugi's adopted numbering scheme.

The *Collation Notes* was apparently compiled during the ongoing process of editing each text for inclusion in Koryŏ II canon. The date appearing on the final edited text is 1251 (*Kojong* 高宗 38), which corresponds to the completion date of the canon as a whole. The blocks of the case in which the *Collation Notes* is included, however, are said to have been carved in 1247, some four years earlier.[20] This discrepancy is probably due to putting a projected date for completion of the entire project in the *Collation Notes.* Sugi has placed his work in the *chun* 俊, *ye* 乂, and *mil* 密 cases, replacing an earlier scriptural catalogue, the *Yiqie jing yuanpin cilu* 一切經源品次錄 (*Sequential Listing of the Original Chapters of All the Scriptures*), in thirty fascicles, compiled by the *śramaṇa* Congfan/Chongbŏm 從梵 (d.u.).[21] As that catalogue was not of much value in using the present canon, Sugi replaced it with his own *Collation Notes* (K. 1402).

Motivations for Compiling the Koryŏ Buddhist Canons

A complex set of motivations prompted the compilation of the two Koryŏ canons. Scholars have suggested three major motivations behind Koryŏ I: its value as a means for the project's sponsor, King Hyŏnjong 顯宗 (1009–1031) to show his filial piety and to transfer merit to his deceased parents; as a focus for state protection; and as a way to demonstrate Koryŏ's "cultural self-sufficiency" (to borrow a phrase from Michael Rogers), especially when the dynasty's achievement in producing a complete canon was contrasted with the depradations of the pillaging invaders.[22] By the time of the second carving (after Mongol invaders had ravaged Korea once more and destroyed the xylographs of the first canon), the need for protection of the state came to be of overriding importance. The invocation offered by the noted statesman and Buddhist adherent Yi Kyu-bo 李奎報 (1168–1241) at the time of the initiation of the second project strongly indicates that the canon was intended to serve as an apotropaic "talisman,"[23] empowered by Korea's Buddhist faith with the ability to ward off future invaders.

Sugi's *Collation Notes* also provides oblique indications of the role of the Koryŏ II canon in supporting Korean aspirations to cultural self-sufficiency. The invasion of Koryŏ by the Khitans, their rivals in northern Asia, at least accelerated, if not actually prompted, the carving of the Koryŏ I canon in 1011 C.E. After the destruction of Koryŏ I in 1232, the Khitan canon achieved near-universal renown throughout East Asia as the preeminent canon, both in its selection of texts and its editorial quality.[24] By compiling a canon that would be impeccable critically and representative of the highest aspirations of the Korean intellectual elite, Sugi and the Koryŏ leadership may have hoped that their product would surpass even that pinnacle of East Asian canons and thus help to restore Koryŏ national pride.

There is no disputing that state protection, cultural prestige, and Buddhist faith were important concerns in the production of the canon and provided ready justification for the enormous expense obviously incurred by its production. We must recognize, however, that these factors alone may not have been enough to compel the exacting standards for which the Koryŏ canon is renowned.[25] Rather, the Koryŏ II canon was a product of deep faith, refracted in the lens of exacting scholarship. Indeed, if faith had been the sole reason for the canon's compilation, it is highly unlikely that specific scriptures would have been proscribed from the canon on purely textual grounds, as was sometimes done by the Koryŏ II editors.[26]

In Sugi's case, in fact, scholarship seems to have provided the grounding for faith: in order to gain the full efficacy forthcoming from the inherent power of the word of the Buddha (*buddhavacana*), it was necessary to ensure that textual errors, spurious materials, or other misrepresentations of content, authorship, or provenance did not sully the canon's exactitude as a precise record of those sacred words. These concerns explain why the critical sense displayed by Sugi and his colleagues was so prized by the royal court that sponsored the project.

Regardless of the specific reasons that may have prompted the carving of the canon, it should come as no surpise that the Koryŏ court would undertake the compilation of its own Buddhist canon—and not once, but twice. Koryŏ Buddhists were heirs to a flourishing Buddhist exegetical and scholarly tradition that rivaled anything then current in China. The Koryŏ II canon is arguably the preeminent example of this scholarly dimension of the Korean Buddhist tradition.

Unresolved Issues in Sugi's *Collation Notes*

Although it is clear that Sugi drew principally upon the Kaobao, Koryŏ I, and Khitan Liao canons in editing his canon, he mentions other editions in a few places in his annotation. Identifying these canons has created more than a few problems. In his collation note to the *Banzhou sanmei jing* 般舟三昧經 (*Bhadrapālasūtra;* K. 67), Sugi makes a cryptic reference to "eastern" and "northern" canons that he uses to correct the Kaibao:

> Now while this [verse section] was originally nonextant in the Song edition, there was a prose passage consisting of over ten pages of text. Scrutinizing its phraseology, I found that, while the wording was slightly different from that of the "Wuzuo pin" 無著品 and "Sibi pin" 四輩品 of the second *kwŏn,* its major purport is indistinguishable. Therefore, there was no precedent for the dittography of this prose passage. I fear that the Song edition was mistaken in adopting the text of an alternate translation and including it here. Consequently, *relying on the two editions of East and North* (emphasis added), I have deleted those passages, which are identical to the later dittographed sections.
>
> 今此宋本本無, 而有長行十餘紙文. 詳其文相, 與中養無著品, 四輩品文, 雖少異, 大旨無殊, 則長行之文例無重疊,恐宋本錯. 將異譯之文連書耳. 故依東, 北二本, 去彼同後重疊之文. (K.1402.38:515c)

It remains uncertain exactly what Sugi means by this reference. Ikeuchi Hiroshi 池内宏 assumes that Sugi is referring to the Koryŏ I and Khitan editions, respectively,[27] as the region of Liao was north and the Koryŏ was east of Song territory. This supposition seems plausible from the context, for Sugi commonly used the Khitan and Koryŏ I canons to correct the Kaibao readings.

A much more controversial point appears in Sugi's collation note to *quan* 13 of *Genben shuo yiqie youbu pinaiye posengshi* 根本說一切有部毗奈耶破僧事 (*Mūlasārvastivādavinaya-saṃghabhedakavastu;* K. 1390), where Sugi uses a "later State edition" (*Kukhu pon* 國後本) to correct both an "earlier State edition" (*Kukchŏn pon* 國前本) and the Kaibao edition. Some scholars, including Murakami Ryūkichi 村上龍佶, Ono Genmyō 小野玄妙,[28] and Paul Demiéville, cite this and other circumstantial evidence to prove that there were actually three Koryŏ state canons. Demiéville advocates, for example, that in addition to the thirteenth-century Koryŏ II there was a royal canon carved in the first half of the eleventh century, and a second published sometime after 1063 that reflected the readings of the newly introduced Khitan canon.[29] This proposal goes against the weight of historical evidence, however; there is no reference in the Koryŏsa to three separate canon-carving projects.

Ikeuchi also points out that in the collation note to K. 1390 Sugi states that the readings of the "earlier State edition" and the Song Kaibao edition were identical, as was also the case for the "later State edition" and the Khitan recension. Thus, the "earlier State edition" may have been the Koryŏ I canon, or perhaps a single-edition scripture based on the Kaibao or Koryŏ I editions, while the "later State edition" was a separate single-edition text that incorporated readings from the Khitan. Accordingly, this "later edition" could not have predated the introduction of the Khitan canon to Koryŏ.[30]

It is now accepted by scholars that there was only one royal carving during the eleventh century.[31] This is not, of course, to deny that separate editions of scriptures or perhaps even substantially complete canons for private monastic use were carved at various times and places during the dynasty. Indeed, such new carvings could very well have been made in conjunction with the publication of Ŭich'ŏn's *Koryŏ sokchang* 高麗續藏 (*Koryŏ Supplementary Canon*), begun around 1091,[32] which is well known to have incorporated many Khitan texts and readings. This in no way implies, however, that a new official Koryŏ carving of the entire canon was made at that time.

As valuable as Sugi's *Collation Notes* proves to be, it does not allow us to resolve all of the outstanding issues concerning the Koryŏ II canon. One such problematic point is the unusual format of the version of the *Dafangguang fo huayan jing* 大方廣佛華嚴經 ([*Buddha*]*Avataṃsakasūtra;* K. 80) that appears in the canon. The standard textual arrangement adopted in Koryŏ II, following the earlier Kaibao and Koryŏ I editions, is 14 Sinographs per line, 23 lines per block. The Koryŏ II edition of the *Avataṃsakasūtra,* however, uses a peculiar format of 17 Sinographs per line.[33] Sugi's *Notes* provides no information as to this discrepancy. It could be that Sugi simply followed the style of the Khitan canon, which used the seventeen-Sinograph format, though why he would have adopted this variant formatting here and not elsewhere remains a mystery.

A clue to this discrepancy may be found in Sugi's discussion of another text, the *Daji jing* 大集經 (*Mahāsannipāta-sūtra;* K. 56), in which Sugi notes a discrepancy in the structure and divisions of this large anthology between the identical Kaibao/Koryŏ I recension and the later Khitan edition. After establishing the relationship between the two different recensions, he concludes that neither of their textual divisions can be shown to be unequivocably correct. As he cannot decide which of the two to follow in his edition, he finally decides simply to follow the edition of the text as it had been transmitted in Korea:

> This sixty-*kwŏn* recension is the one that has been chosen and disseminated by the Punhwangjong 芬皇宗 of the present dynasty; its dissemination has continued for some time now. Since it has gone on for so long, it is just too difficult to change. (以此六十卷本, 是本朝芬皇宗選行, 經行來已久, 久則難變耳.) (K.1402.38:514c)

Sugi apparently did not follow in this instance any of the three official canons in deciding on the correct structure of the text and instead adopted the version that was accepted within the Korean Punhwangjong (viz., Hwaŏm school). Just as he followed the Punhwangjong's recension of the *Daji jing* in making his edition of that text for the new canon, Sugi may well have been similarly influenced when editing the *Avataṃsaka-sūtra:* the high esteem for this sūtra in the Korean tradition may have prompted Sugi to retain the distinctive and anomalous style of a particularly venerated recension of the text.

Perhaps our best bet for resolving the issue of the *Avataṃsaka-sūtra*'s format lies in simple utility and convenience. As was shown above in reference to the collation note for K. 1390, separate editions of individual texts were available in Korea. It is known that not all of the xylographs used in the Koryŏ II canon were newly carved during the compilation project; some blocks seem to have been incorporated from other collections, especially for texts appearing in the later cases of the canon. The case-character numberings of Koryŏ II end at the *tong* 洞 case with the *Yiqie jing yinyi* 一切經音義 (K. 1498), but there are an additional fifteen exegetical works, primarily Sŏn and Hwaŏm materials (K. 1499–1514) appended at the end; these texts show a remarkable diversity in format, ranging from 17 to 24 Sinographs per line.[34] Indeed, the most reasonable explanation for this anomalous format of the *Avataṃsaka-sūtra* seems to be that where there was no controversy in readings between different editions used in the collation (as witnessed by the lack of any collation note to the *Avataṃsaka-sūtra* in Sugi's work), Sugi and his team simply appropriated some previously carved blocks in order to accelerate the project.

A final piece of evidence for this anomalous format is found in Ŭich'ŏn's *Supplementary Canon*. In the few xylographs remaining from that collection there is a copy of the *Huayan jing helun* 華嚴經合論, a text that combined this translation of the *Avataṃsaka-sūtra* with Li Tongxuan's 李通玄 (635–730) commentary to the scripture, the *Xin Huayan jing lun* 新華嚴經論 (T. 1739). While most texts in the *Supplementary Canon* generally were carved in a format of 20 to 22 Sinographs per line,[35] the *Huayan jing helun* was carved in a format of 17 Sinographs per line, apparently reflecting the Khitan recension. The fact that this *Helun* was found in the archives at Songgwangsa 松廣寺 is particularly important, since during the thirteenth century the monastery is known to have held a copy of the Khitan canon. This is verified by the text of *Tanbon taejang kyŏngch'an so* 丹本大藏慶讚疏 (*Encomium to the Khitan Edition of the Canon*), written by the sixth State Preceptor of Songgwangsa, Ch'ungji 沖止 (1226–1292; posthumous name Wŏn'gam *kuksa* 圓鑑國師).[36] The 17 Sinographs-per-line format is virtually certain to have derived from the Khitan edition. During this period the prevailing custom may have been to carve Śikṣānanda's (652–710) translation of the *Avataṃsaka-sūtra* in this format, a custom that might account for its unusual format in the Koryŏ II edition.

II. "Tripiṭaka" vs. "*Dazangjing/ Taejanggyŏng*"

Before I turn to specific issues treated in Sugi's *Collation Notes*, let me offer a brief aside on what it was that Sugi was collating. The *Koryŏ taejanggyŏng*, the object of Sugi's notes, has long been referred to in the scholarly literature as the *Tripiṭaka Koreana*, using a hybrid Sanskrit-Latin term. But calling this canon a *tripiṭaka* (*samjang* 三藏), literally, "three baskets" or "three repositories" in the Chinese translation, is very much a misnomer. East Asian canons such as the *Koryŏ taejanggyŏng* were actually titled "scriptures of the great repositories" (*dazangjing/taejanggyŏng* 大藏經), a term that supplanted the Sanskrit term *tripiṭaka* (*sanzang/samjang* 三藏) in East Asia. *Sanzang/samjang* was more commonly employed in East Asia to translate the term *trepiṭaka*, meaning a monk who was a scholarly translator of Buddhist materials, such as Xuanzang 玄奘 (600/602–664 C.E.); this rendering is used, for example, in the title *sanzang fashi/samjang pŏpsa* 三藏法師, "*trepiṭaka* Dharma master." The term *sanzang/samjang* was typically not used to refer to indigenous East Asian collections of scriptures.

The switch from *sanzang/samjang* to *dazangjing/taejanggyŏng* is due to the fact that East Asian Buddhists included in their canons not only materials from the tripiṭakas of several independent schools of Indian Buddhism, but also different recensions of various Mahāyāna scriptures and commentaries, sometimes in multiple translations. As the East Asian tradition evolved its own scholarly traditions, indigenous writings by native East Asian authors, composed in literary Chinese, also came to be included in the canon. These materials included scriptural commentaries, doctrinal treatises, biographical and hagiographical collections, edited transcriptions of oral lectures, Chinese-Sanskrit dictionaries, catalogues of scriptural rosters (*jinglu/kyŏngnok* 經錄), and so on. Because the scope of the Buddhist canon in China was therefore substantially broader than the traditional tripartite structure of an Indian tripiṭaka, the Chinese coined alternative terms to refer to their collection of Buddhist materials, such as "all the books" (*yiqie jing/ilch'e kyŏng* 一切經), until eventually settling on the term *dazangjing* ("scriptures of the great repositories").

The term *dazangjing* may have derived from a Northern Song dynasty term for an officially commissioned "great library" (*dazang/taejang* 大藏) that was intended to serve as a repository for "books" (*jing/kyŏng* 經) sanctioned by the court. Recent research by Professor Fang Guangchang 方廣锠 of Shanghai Normal University instead suggests that the term may already have been in use in China prior to the Huichang 會昌 Persecution of 842–845.[37] Buddhist monasteries were the first places other than imperial palaces where such officially sanctioned libraries were established. These collections of the official canonical books of Chinese Buddhism were arranged not by the sūtra, vinaya, and abhidharma categories of India, but instead in shelf lists that followed the categorizations used in court libraries. Thus, although these Buddhist "great repositories" include materials that align with a traditional tripiṭaka—that is, they include sections of sūtra (including both scriptures and major commentaries to scriptures), vinaya, and abhidharma—they are much more inclusive.

The Koryŏ II canon is arranged with pride of place given to texts (both sūtra and *śāstra*) from the Mahāyāna tradition:

1. Major Mahāyāna scriptures (K. 1–548), beginning with the *Prajñāpāramitā,* followed by the *Mahāratnakūṭa* collection, and continuing through all the major Mahāyāna sūtras and sūtra collections, from the *Avataṃsaka* to the *Parinirvāṇa, Saṃdhinirmocana,* and *Laṅkāvatāra.*

2. Mahāyāna *śāstra*s and scriptural commentaries, beginning with the *Dazhidu lun* 大智度論 (**Mahāprajñāpāramitā-śāstra*) (K. 549–646).

3. Āgama collections and "Hīnayāna" sūtras (K. 647–888).
4. Vinaya materials (K. 889–937).
5. Abhidharma texts (K. 938–977).
6. *Avadāna* and *Jātaka* tales and miscellaneous materials (K. 978–1034).
7. Biographies of individual monks, starting with Aśvaghoṣa, Nāgārjuna, etc. (K. 1035–1049).
8. Rosters of numerical lists, scriptural catalogues (K. 1050–1064).
9. Travelogues and anthologies of biographies of eminent monks (K. 1065–1086).
10. Miscellaneous sūtras, *dhāraṇī* scriptures, and *dhāraṇī* anthologies (K. 1087–1242).
11. Other miscellaneous sūtras (K. 1243–1496).
12. References, Chan anthologies, indigenous Korean works (all in literary Chinese) (K. 1497–1514).

As this roster makes clear, the *Koryŏ taejanggyŏng* and other East Asian Buddhist canons place Mahāyāna *śāstras* and scriptural commentaries before sūtra literature associated with the "Hīnayāna," thereby obscuring the distinction between sūtras and *śāstras*. These collections also vastly expand the scope of the canon to include a whole range of literary genres not found in an Indian tripiṭaka, including catalogues, biographies, and travelogues.

Given this breadth of coverage, I believe we have been doing a disservice to the *Koryŏ taejanggyŏng* and other East Asian canons by referring to them as "tripiṭakas"; we should simply call them either a "Buddhist canon" or transcribe the Sinographs *dazangjing/taejanggyŏng*. It is misleading to use the pedantic term *Tripiṭaka Koreana* and I believe it should be abandoned.

III. Specific Issues Addressed in Sugi's Collation Notes

Returning now to Sugi's *Collation Notes,* of the 1,514 texts included in the Koryŏ II canon,[38] Sugi collated seventy-six passages from sixty-five different texts.[39] I will explore here the types of textual problems that warranted the attention of the Koryŏ II compilers, the specific methodology adopted by Sugi in editing the texts included in his canon, the standards of textual authenticity employed in adjudicating suspect texts, evidence corroborating the structure and content of earlier canons, and a few extraneous issues of special interest. The Appendix provides the specific data gathered for each of the texts where such editorial issues were addressed. Here I present only a representative survey of the types of concerns Sugi covers in his work, and a few typical examples of how his collation notes address these concerns.

Dittographies

Of all the types of textual problems noted by Sugi, certainly the most common were transpositions of passages (*chŏnhu toch'ak* 前後倒錯) and dittographies (*chungsa* 重寫; *chungch'ŏm* 重疊), i.e., unintended repetitions of identical passages, a common occurrence in Buddhist texts, which frequently used mnemonic repetition for rhetorical effect. Such errors occurred most commonly in the Kaibao edition and were generally corrected following the Khitan readings. In his discussion of the Kaibao edition of the *Jueding pini jing* 決定毗尼經 (*Upālipariprcchā;* K. 35), for example, Sugi notes three problematic passages in which

> the text is corrupt, the meaning cannot be construed, and it is difficult to find a way of interpreting them (*mundan ŭigyŏl nan ch'wi haech'ŏ* 文斷義絶難取解處). . . . Now, collating against the other editions, [I find that] the Song edition is mistaken. (今檢他本, 則宋本錯; K.1402.38:512a)

After listing the three passages according to their scroll (*p'ok* 幅) and line numbers, he then goes on to show that 487 Sinographs belonging in the first passage and 517 Sinographs from the last passage have been transposed, a mistake that has been retained in the later Song and Yuan 元 editions, as the Taishō collation notes to the passage indicate (see Appendix).

> We can show in this wise that the text of these three passages is corrupt. . . . The prior and subsequent [passages] have been transposed in error. (致令如是三節文斷. 前後倒錯; K.1402.38:512b)

Sugi then collates the text against the Koryŏ I carving and the Khitan canon and chooses to follow their readings instead. This particular passage is revealing because it indicates that both the earlier Koryŏ I edition as well as the Khitan canon did not blindly follow the readings appearing in earlier recensions. They too edited their own distinct versions of the canon, probably in ways very similar to those followed by Sugi and his associates, in light of textual evidence in other recensions, either manuscript or xylograph, that are no longer available to us. (Such Kaibao dittographies are found also in K. 67 and K. 943.)

Even the Khitan edition was not immune from such problems, however. There are a few instances noted by Sugi in which the Khitan editors have incorrectly allowed dittographed sections to stand, as in the case of the *Xuzhen tianzi jing* 須眞天子經 (*Suvikrāntadevapūtraparipṛcchā;* K. 372). By rejecting the Khitan readings for this text, Sugi demonstrates that he did not slavishly follow the readings of the Liao canon, and thereby avoided the trap of using the "best" manuscript into which many textual critics (including the Japanese Taishō editors) have fallen.

In some cases, Sugi has been compelled to use evidence appearing in the preface to a scripture to resolve apparent dittographed passages. For example, in his collation note to *quan/kwŏn* 8 of the *Apitan ba jiandu lun* 阿毘曇八犍度論 (*Jñānaprasthāna;* K. 943), Sugi observes that there is a thirty-five–line passage missing in the Khitan edition that is found in both the Kaibao and Koryŏ I editions. The sense is not easily construed in the latter two editions, however, and Sugi discovers that the passage is a near-verbatim repetition of a passage appearing later in the same *quan/kwŏn* of this text. Sugi examines Dao'an's 道安 (312–385) preface to this text and discovers that its initial translation by Zhu Fonian 竺佛念 (ca. late fourth to early fifth centuries) was said to have been full of misconstructions that were corrected over a forty-six–day period. Sugi therefore assumes that the first translation by Zhu Fonian included both an earlier translation and a later revision, apparently implying that this repetition might have been drawn from one of these two different recensions (although he never spells this out explicitly). Suspecting that the Koryŏ I and Kaibao editions wrongly dittographed that section, Sugi follows the Khitan reading and removes it.

Textual Divisions

Sugi also treats matters such as textual division in great detail. For example, Xiangong's 先公 (d.u.) translation of the *Yuedeng sanmei jing* 月燈三昧經 (*Samādhirāja-sūtra;* K. 182) in the Koryŏ II canon is the Khitan edition of the text, which differs in both letter and meaning from the Koryŏ I/Kaibao edition (K. 183). Both, however, are said to derive from *quan/kwŏn* 7 of the *Da Yuedeng jing* 大月燈經 (K. 181). Sugi accepts that the Khitan recension (K. 182) is the authentic translation by Xiangong because its structure and size match the information on the text given in the headnote to the sūtra, as cited in KYL. Sugi notes, however, that there is a discrepancy with the KYL statement that this text derives from *quan* 7 of the longer text; his collation determines instead that it is excerpted from the first half of the sixth *quan*. Sugi assumes that ". . . the division of the *quan* was different or else the six was mistakenly copied as seven [in KYL]" (分卷有異,或書寫錯六爲七耳; K.1402.38:522c).

Variant Titles

The issue of differing titles for the same work is yet another area that Sugi is compelled to take up time and again. In the case of K. 912, for example, both the Kaibao and Koryŏ I editions give the title as *Shaminili jie wen* 沙彌尼離戒文 (**Śramaṇerī-vinaya*). The Khitan has instead *Shamini zajie wen* 沙彌尼雜戒文. Collating against the actual text of the scripture, Sugi senses that all three editions are wrong, and that the *li* 離 of this translation is simply a different transliteration of the Sanskrit phoneme *ri*, which is represented by *ni* in other translations; the correct title should therefore read *Shamili jie wen* 沙彌離戒文. However, as none of the three editions gives this title, Sugi does not dare make the revision, and simply records his notes to help later scholars resolve the discrepancy.

Preference for the Khitan Readings

In the great majority of Sugi's collation notes, he acknowledges that he follows the readings of the Khitan canon. This preference for the Khitan canon is reflected in the inclusion of texts in Koryŏ II that were missing entirely in the Kaibao and Koryŏ I canons, such as Yijing's 義淨 (635–713) translation of the *Mile xiasheng chengfo jing* 彌勒下生成佛經 (*Maitreya-vyākaraṇa;* K. 199) and the *Shi Moheyan lun* 釋摩訶衍論 (K. 1397),[40] as well as shorter texts within larger collections, such as the *Zhong ahan jing* 中阿含經 (*Madhyamāgama;* K. 648), the *Za ahan jing* 雜阿含經 (*Saṃyuktāgama;* K. 650), and the *Bieyi za ahan jing* 別譯雜阿含經 (*Saṃyuktāgama;* K. 651). These scriptures are all examples where the Khitan editors seemed to have had access to a different textual lineage than what was known to other regions of China, and therefore preserved in their canon what would otherwise have been a lost textual recension.

At the same time, there are also several places in the Kaibao and Koryŏ I editions where missing passages of several hundred Sinographs are added from the Khitan edition, as, for example, in *quan* 5 of the *Shisong lü* 十誦律 (*Sarvāstivāda-vinaya;* K. 890). But it was not only with missing texts or dittographies that the Khitan edition often served as the *textus receptus* for Sugi; even translator attributions were sometimes viewed as correct in Khitan and incorrect in the other two editions. For example, the Kaibao and Koryŏ I editions record that the *Qishi jing* 起世經 (K. 660) was translated by Jñānagupta (523–600) together with Dharmagupta (d. 619), while the Khitan names only Jñānagupta. On the other hand, in the Koryŏ I and Kaibao editions the *Qishi yinben jing* 起世因本經 (K. 661) is recorded as translated by Jñānagupta, while the Khitan edition attributes it instead to Dharmagupta. Sugi follows the KYL citation for these texts to show that the Khitan information should be accepted.

In cases where the Koryŏ I canon included a text that was not found in the Kaibao, as for example, the *Putichang suoshuo yizi dinglunwang jing* 菩提場所說一字頂輪王經 (*Bodhimaṇḍanirdeśaikākṣaroṣṇiṣacakravartirāja-sūtra;* K. 1290), national pride did not preclude Sugi from using the Khitan reading to correct his own country's earlier canon. Conversely, however, there are two cases in which he follows the reading of the Koryŏ I edition against the Kaibao and/or Khitan editions. In quan 1 of the *Daloutan jing* 大樓炭經 (K. 662), Sugi adds fifteen lines of text that are missing in the Kaibao and Khitan editions. In the *Shibabu lun* 十八部論 (*Samaya-bhedoparacanacakra;* K. 976), Sugi finds a mistake in the title copied in the Kaibao edition and corrects it according to the Koryŏ I edition.

There are several instances in which Sugi follows the evidence of two canons in order to correct mistakes in a third. This is seen most frequently when the Khitan and Koryŏ I editions are used to correct the Kaibao. For example, in the *Puyao jing* 普曜經 (*Lalitavistara;* K. 112) the Kaibao edition confuses the *quan* numbering and inadvertently drops chapter 4; Sugi corrects these errors according to the Koryŏ I and Khitan editions. More extensive discussion on the use of the Koryŏ I and Khitan canons is found in Sugi's collation note to the *Moni jing* 魔逆經 (*Mañjuśrī-vikurvāṇaparivarta;* K. 463), where he demonstrates that the Kaibao edition is identical to the *Wenshushili huiguo jing* 文殊師利悔過經 (K. 538). Similar decisions in favor of the Koryŏ I/Khitan editions are seen also for the texts of K. 549 and K. 552, as well as omissions or dittographies in K. 35, K. 598, K. 600, K. 612, K. 650, K. 664, K. 936, K. 946, K. 952, K. 1069, and K. 1076.

There are also mistakes in Koryŏ I that Sugi corrects according to the Kaibao and Khitan editions; e.g., in the *Apitan biposha lun* 阿毘曇毘婆沙論 (*Abhidharmavibhāṣā;* K. 951). This instance may indicate that the Koryŏ I editors inadvertently introduced this mistake during their editing or that they were following a different manuscript tradition in Korea.

Finally, there are a few places where Sugi finds major differences in both the Kaibao and Khitan editions, but is unable to decide which of the two recensions is correct. In the case of the Kaibao edition of the *Dong-fang zuishengdengwang tuoluoni jing* 東方最勝燈王陀羅尼經 (*Agrapradīpa-dhāraṇīvidhārāja;* K. 349) and its Khitan counterpart (K. 350), the latter edition is more than twice the length of the former and Sugi was uncertain which was the legitimate scripture. Based also on the "archaic language and structure" (*ko ŏjil* 古語質) of the Kaibao recension, Sugi suspects that it was probably not translated by Jñānagupta. Nevertheless, since he cannot determine which of the two versions is authentic he enters both into the canon, leaving it to later scholars to determine the correct one.

Despite his overall respect for the readings established by the Liao editors, Sugi did not hesitate to follow alternate readings if errors in the Khitan edition could be confirmed. In *quan* 15 of the *Zhong ahan jing* (*Madhyamāgama;* K. 648), for example, the Khitan has misread the title and mistakes *shi* 世 ("time," in cursive form) for *sanshi* 三十 ("thirty"). In this case Sugi accepts *sanshi* as correct, following Kaibao and Koryŏ I. In the *Hujing jing* 護淨經 (K. 864) an important section of 255 Sinographs missing in the Khitan edition is added from the Kaibao/Koryŏ I editions. In the first *quan* of the *Pusa benyuan jing* 菩薩本緣經 (K. 988) the Khitan recension wrongly dittographs a section of 26 lines in 412 Sinographs from the second *quan* of this text; Sugi removes it following the Kaibao/Koryŏ I reading. In *quan* 5 of the *Za baozang jing* 雜寶藏經 (K. 1001) the Khitan includes a section of six episodes (*yuan* 緣) that was mistakenly recopied from its earlier appearance in *quan* 4; Sugi deletes it, following the other two editions.

However, considering that Sugi was able to find only four such instances of mistaken readings throughout the entire Khitan canon, it is clear that the Khitan editors followed extremely strict standards in producing their canon. It is also telling that in only one place did Sugi follow the Kaibao reading alone, in his collation note for the *Xuzhen tianzi jing* 須眞天子經 (*Suvikrāntadevapūtraparipṛcchā;* K. 372). In all other instances, Sugi refused to follow the Kaibao reading unless it was corroborated in one of the other two official state canons. The large number of errors Sugi uncovered in the Kaibao canon seems to have compromised its reputation in his eyes, thus diminishing its influence in his editing of the second Koryŏ II canon.

In a few instances, readings found in texts other than those appearing in the Kaibao, Koryŏ I, or Khitan canons were used to resolve problematic passages. This is the case with transposed passages in *quan* 59 of the Kaibao/Koryŏ I edition of the *Daji jing* (*Mahāsannipāta-sūtra;* K. 56). Unfortunately, this fascicle is missing in the Khitan edition, and Sugi is forced to collate it against a separate edition of the text appearing in the *Mingdu wushi jiaoji jing* 明度五十校計經 (K. 411).

Case-Character Designations

Sugi is also diligent about correcting case-character (*ham* 函) designations for several of the works included in the various canons. A text entitled *Shousui jing* 受歲經 (K. 688) is found in the Khitan canon but not in the Kaibao, while the *Shou xinsui jing* 受新歲經 (K. 871) is found in the Kaibao but not in the Khitan. Dharmarakṣa (230?–316) is presumed to have translated both texts, but despite their similar titles the content is completely different. Using KYL, Sugi verifies that the *Shousui jing* is the sūtra, also translated by Dharmarakṣa, that is parallel to a sūtra in the *Zhong ahan jing,* which is included in the *yong* 容 case. The Khitan edition is correctly placed here, and he deletes the Kaibao edition.

Issues of Textual Authenticity

Like the bibliographical cataloguers who preceded him, Sugi was also compelled to treat issues of textual authenticity in the course of editing his canon. His approach to such topics demonstrates the close affinities between the canonical editors and the bibliographical cataloguers. One of the major concerns of both was to ascertain the legitimacy of different translations of a presumed Indian original. Several scriptures included in the East Asian canons underwent multiple translations during the long course of the transmission of Buddhist texts to China, and the authenticity of some of these variant translations had occasionally been called into question. It is not surprising, then, that Sugi often compared translator ascriptions noted in the Buddhist catalogues with the information appearing in the texts he was editing.

Sugi's major sources for deciding such questions were earlier critiques by the cataloguers of such works as the *Kaiyuan Shijiao lu* (T. 2154; KYL) by Zhisheng 智昇 (658–740), the *Chu sanzang jiji* 出三藏記集 (T. 2145) by Sengyou 僧祐 (445–518), and the *Zhongjing mulu* 衆經目錄 (T. 2146) by Fajing 法經 (d.u.). Given the reverence with which earlier translators such as An Shigao 安世高 (fl. c. 148–180 C.E.) or Kumārajīva (344–413) were regarded, anonymous translations and reworked versions of earlier translations were sometimes falsely attributed to these eminent personages, a tendency that was particularly pronounced in the *Lidai sanbao ji* 歷代三寶記 (T. 2034), a catalogue by Fei Changfang 費長房 (d.u.).[41] These attributions were eventually adopted by Zhisheng, the compiler of the definitive KYL, and thereby entered the mainstream of the East Asian Buddhist tradition.

In collating these catalogue accounts, Sugi was sometimes able to discover that texts attributed to different translators were actually identical, and he eliminated a number of these "multiple" translations from the Koryŏ II canon. In his discussion of Dharmarakṣa's translation of the *Xumoti pusa jing* 須摩提菩薩經 (*Sumatidārikāparipṛcchā;* K. 39), for example,

Sugi attempts to deal with the problems of variant translations and multiple ascriptions. He adopts in this note many of the criteria of textual authenticity followed in the catalogues, with a critical sense rivaling that of his predecessors. This passage, translated here in its entirety, offers one of the best examples of Sugi's approach to textual criticism found in his *Collation Notes:*

> The *Kaiyuan lu* says, "There were four earlier and later translations made of this text; three are extant and one is nonextant."[42] Dharma master Bodhiruci made two translations, an earlier and a later one, of which the former is the one that is not extant. Now, collating all the canons, I have found that both the State and Song canons include the translations by Dharmarakṣa and the second of Bodhiruci's two renderings, but not Kumārajīva's translation. Although the Khitan canon does not include Bodhiruci's latter translation, it does include the translations made by Dharmarakṣa and Kumārajīva. If the two canons (i.e., Kaibao/Koryŏ I and Khitan) are combined together, it seems that all three extant versions are included.
>
> Now, examining what the Khitan canon has called the "Kumārajīva translation" (T. 335), [I find that] from beginning to end it is indistinguishable from the Dharmarakṣa translation (K. 39; T. 334) that is included in both of the other canons. Furthermore, there is no precedent for such a sūtra translated by Kumārajīva, so why was this said to be Kumārajīva's translation? If two men from different countries each translated it sumultaneously, then we would have to admit that there were two translations that were inadvertently identical; but this precedent is unknown for any sūtra. Moreover, it could not be the case that, some one hundred years after Dharmarakṣa, Kumārajīva came from the west and commenced his translation activities by copying down verbatim Dharmarakṣa's translation and calling it a "retranslation." If it were claimed that, while remaining unaware of Dharmarakṣa's translation, Venerable Kumārajīva retranslated it, then there are indeed surprising similarities. At that time, the holy teachings were not yet widely disseminated and his adherents studied diligently. With more than eight hundred people who were members of his congregation—who were the valiant and sagacious ones of the eastern territory [of China]—how is it possible that none would have noticed [these similarities]? Furthermore, any retranslation wants to be different from its predecessors; if it were completely identical, then what is the point of retranslating [it]? There is no such precedent in any retranslated sūtra.

開元錄云:「此經前後四譯三存一闕.」流志法師有先後二譯. 其先譯者卽一闕也. 今撿諸藏, 國宋二藏有法護譯, 流志後譯, 而無什譯. 丹藏雖無流志後譯, 而有法護, 羅什二譯, 則若二藏互備, 乍似三存具矣. 今詳丹藏所謂什譯者, 與諸藏法護譯始終無異.又非羅什譯經之例, 而謂之什譯何也? 若同時, 異國二人各譯, 則容有二譯偶同而諸經無此

> 例者, 況護之後一百餘年, 羅什西來始事翻譯.應直書法護之譯而云重譯. 若云什 // 公未見法護而重譯之, 乃偶同耳, 則彼時聖教未廣, 人又勤學其會下參譯八百餘人竝是東土英賢何必人人皆不見耶? 又凡重譯者欲異於前, 若全同者何煩重譯耶? 諸重譯經亦無此例. (K.1402.38:513b–c)

As Sugi's analysis makes clear, the KYL was in error in accepting the authenticity of Kumārajīva's assumed translation of this scripture. Sugi indicts the Khitan canon for following the judgment of KYL and including both of these versions in its canon. He therefore decides to delete the "Kumārajīva" translation (T.335.12:79c–81c) from the canon.[43] Even a cursory comparison of the translation attributed to Kumārajīva with the one by Dharmarakṣa (K. 39; T. 334) reveals the truth of Sugi's statements: apart from a few minor textual variants, the two texts are virtually identical.

Title and translator attributions appearing in KYL are also discussed with reference to the Kaibao and Koryŏ I editions of the *Yuedeng sanmei jing* (*Samādhirāja-sūtra;* K. 183), which both canons attribute to the Liao-Song translator Xiangong. Sugi doubts this attribution, however, as those recensions omitted the alternate title of Xiangong's translation, and both are twice the length of the text mentioned in the KYL's notice. Sugi suspects that the Kaibao/Koryŏ I edition was actually the earlier translation by An Shigao, which had been presumed lost by KYL. He notes:

> As there was no translator's name [in the colophon to the scripture], they (the Koryŏ I editors) checked the catalogues and found a reference to a *Yuedeng sanmei jing* translated by Xiangong. They then mistakenly ascribed his name to this text. (無譯主之名者, 見目錄中有月燈經名, 是先公譯者, 乃錯題其名; K.1402.38:527a–b)

Not all such problems with translator ascriptions could be resolved by Sugi, however, and occasionally he "defers to later sages" (*i yu huhyŏn* 以遺後賢, among many variants), whom he hoped would be able to resolve the discrepancies. For example, KYL states that there were six translations made of the *Mile xiasheng jing* 彌勒下生經 (K. 197), of which three were no longer extant. This particular recension was found only in the Kaibao edition, not in the Khitan. There is a listing for such a scripture as translated by Dharmarakṣa in the KYL section on nonextant translations, and Sugi first thought this must be the text in question. However, he discovered that elsewhere in KYL, in the discussion on Kumārajīva's translation of this same text, there was a direct reference to the parallel text by Dharmarakṣa. Sugi realized that the nonextant text was different. The fact that this scripture differs from the nonextant text listed was also corroborated by evidence from its structure. Citing the *Jingang bore houxu*

金剛般若後序 by Gushan Zhiyuan 孤山智圓 (981–1027),[44] Sugi notes that, traditionally, one page of a scripture had 25 lines, and one line had 17 Sinographs. The notice to the nonextant translation of this text states that it was 17 pages long, for a total of 7,222 Sinographs.[45] This sūtra had only 3,176 Sinographs, however, so it was less than half the length of that text. Because Sugi cannot resolve the discrepancy, he "defers to later sages" to determine the authenticity of the attribution to Dharmarakṣa.

In another problematic case, four translations of the *Shenri jing* 申日經 (*Candraprabhakumārasūtra;* K. 234) are noted in the catalogues, of which one was nonextant; these texts were included only in the Kaibao canon, not in the Khitan. According to KYL, the listings for translations made by Dharmarakṣa include a reference to a *Yueguang tongzi jing* 月光童子經 (*Candraprabhakumāra-sūtra;* K. 219) with the alternate name *Shenri jing*—that is, a single text with two different titles. Complicating matters even further, Sugi notes that the canon (presumably the Kaibao canon, though he does not specify) had already included a *Yueguang tongzi jing* by Dharmarakṣa, "so how can there be another *Shenri jing* that was also translated by Dharmarakṣa?" (此何更有申日經亦是法護之譯耶; K.1402.38:530a).

To resolve the problem, Sugi mentions that KYL included a listing for a *Shenri jing* among the translations attributed to Zhi Qian 支謙 (fl. ca. 220–252), and Zhisheng's 智昇 annotation to that text stated that it was a different translation of the *Yueguang tongzi jing*. Sugi thus determines that earlier canons had included a translation of the *Shenri jing* (also known as the *Yueguang tongzi jing*) by Zhi Qian, which was not included in any of the present canons. He therefore suspects that the *Shenri jing* (K. 234) is actually the translation by Zhi Qian, but that it had been mistakenly attributed to Dharmarakṣa. He suspects that all four of the translations made of this text are actually extant, rather than one being nonextant, but he cannot say this definitively and again leaves the matter to "later sages."

The Kaibao and Koryŏ I canons (in the *cai/chae* 才 case) included a *Liuzi shenzhou jing* 六字神呪經 (*Ṣaḍakṣaravidyāmantra;* K. 316), translation attributed to Bodhiruci, a text not found in the Khitan canon. According to KYL, this text was actually a different translation of two other texts: the *Wenshushili pusa zhoufa* 文殊師利菩薩咒法, included in *quan* 6 of the *Tuoluoni ji jing* 陀羅尼集經 (*Dhāraṇīsamuccaya;* K. 308), and the *Liuzi tuoluoni* 六字陀羅尼 included in the *Zhou wushou* 咒五首 (K. 312). Sugi corroborates this information through his own collation of the texts. Nevertheless, since he finds no evidence supporting the attribution of the translation to Bodhiruci, Sugi assumes that the Song canon must have found the same text, the *Liuzi zhouwang jing* 六字咒王經 (*Ṣadakṣaravidyāmantra;* K. 341), which was included later in the *zhi/chi* 知 case "by an anonymous translator, now appended to the *Liang lu* 梁錄" (失譯人名今附梁錄者耳)—and, presuming that K. 316 was an alternate translation of K. 341, had mistakenly added Bodhiruci's name to it. Thus, following the Khitan editors, Sugi does not include this text in his canon.

> Therefore, I have now deleted it from this [*chae*] case; if later sages wish to know what text it is that has been deleted, they should know that it is the *Liuzi shenzhou wang jing* 六字神呪王經 included in the *chi* case. (故今刪去此函中者. 後賢欲知今所去經是何等者, 請見知函六字神呪王經則是耳; K.1402.38:530b)[46]

The *Fenbie gongde lun* 分別功德論 (K. 973) is a commentary to *pin* 品 1–4 of the *Zengyi ahan jing* 增壹阿含經 (*Ekottarāgama;* K. 649); the translation of the latter scriptural anthology is attributed to Gautama Saṃghadeva (d.u.). The KYL ascribes the translation of this commentary to Dharmarakṣa, but other catalogues all attribute it instead to an anonymous translator. Sugi accepts the latter judgment, but, noting the parallels between the passages cited in the commentary and the actual text itself, he suggests that the translators of these two texts were probably the same. The *Chu sanzang jiji* states that Kāśyapa and Ānanda composed the commentary, a claim summarily rejected by Sugi. Since the first *quan* of the commentary quotes "foreign monks" (*waiguo shi* 外國師) and the Sarvāstivāda school, he maintains that it could not have been composed by these two ancient Indian patriarchs.

Sugi at times also rejected the judgment of the cataloguers, Zhisheng in particular. The *Shou xinsui jing* (*Pravāraṇa;* K. 871) is the Kaibao/Koryŏ I counterpart of the parallel Khitan edition, the *Shousui jing* (K. 688). This text seems to be a variant translation of the *Xinsui jing* 新歲經 (*Pravāraṇa;* K. 872); despite some minor differences in the vocabulary, the content is identical. Sugi therefore presumes that KYL is wrong to catalogue the *Xinsui jing* (K. 872) as a single-edition translation (*danyi* 單譯).

In some cases, only internal evidence such as phraseology allowed any determination of the translator's identity to be made. The Kaibao and Koryŏ I editions included in their *shu/suk* 孰 case a *Foshuo muhuan jing* 佛說木槵經 (cf. *Muhuanzi jing* 木槵子經; K. 862), translated by Amoghavajra (705–774). Sugi collated this text against a similar text that appeared earlier in the *jing/kyŏng* 竟 case, the *Muhuanzi jing* (K. 862) by an anonymous translator, which was included in the *Dongjin lu* 東晉錄 (317–420 C.E.), and discovered that they were absolutely identical. "Examining the phraseology (*munch'e*

文體), [I discovered] that this was a translation of the Han-Jin 漢晉 [period] (ca. first to fifth centuries C.E.)" (詳其文體卽是漢晉之譯). He therefore rejected this sūtra and refers the reader to K. 862 (listed earlier).

There are also instances where neither the catalogue information nor internal evidence allowed any resolution of translator attribution. For example, the cataloguers generally ascribed the translation of the *Shibabu lun* 十八部論 (*Samayabhedoparacanacakra;* K. 976) to Paramārtha 眞諦 (499–569). Sugi notes that the opening section of the text cites the "Fenbu pin" 分部品 of the *Wenshushili wen jing* 文殊師利問經 (*Mañjuśrīparipṛcchā;* K. 412), and at the conclusion of the quotation he includes the note: "Compiled by Dharma Master Kumārajīva" (see T.2032.49:17b29). Sugi remarks:

> Even assuming that this treatise was translated by Kumārajīva, during the Qin period there was not as yet [a translation of] the *Wenshushili wen jing* so it could not have been quoted and placed at the beginning [of the treatise]. (方是論若是羅什所翻, 秦時未有文殊問經, 不合引之置於初也; K.1402.38:701c)

Having showing that even if the text were the product of an anonymous compiler the same problem would remain, Sugi then explores whether the *Wenshushili wen jing* might have been a retranslation by Paramārtha, which was then included in the treatise. Sugi notes, however, "Examining the phraseology (*mulli* 文理) [of the treatise], much of it derives from the Qin-period translations of Kumārajīva" (詳其文理多是秦時羅什譯出; K.1402.38:701c). This means that all of the accounts of the translation of this treatise are suspicious, and as he cannot definitively resolve the issues Sugi leaves the problem to "later ones of vast learning" (*hu pangmun* 後博聞) to resolve.

Abbreviated Scriptures

Like the bibliographical cataloguers, Sugi also had no tolerance for the canonical pretensions of so-called "abbreviated scriptures" (*chaojing/ch'ogyŏng* 鈔經). These were texts intended for mass consumption that summarized the major points of generally a single, but sometimes multiple, texts. While such abridged texts originally had no pretensions to being separate sūtras, they were readily amenable to expansion through the assimilation of indigenous elements, and eventually many of them came to be passed off as independent translations in their own right. As one example, the *hoe* 迴 and *han* 漢 cases of Koryŏ I included a *Foming jing* 佛名經 (*Names of the Buddhas Sūtra*) in 18 *kwŏn*. After collating the text, however, Sugi discovered that it was identical to another text bearing the same title that appeared later (K. 1404). Sugi assumes that the eighteen-*kwŏn* text was a spurious abbreviation of the thirty-*kwŏn* text (K. 1404), which had subsequently been mistaken for a separate scripture: "Later people saw that the number of *kwŏn* of this [particular text] was different and assumed it was a different scripture; therefore they reincluded it [in the canon]" (後人見其卷數有異, 認爲異經, 故重編入; K.1402.38:723c). Sugi therefore deletes the eighteen-*kwŏn* recension from the Koryŏ II edition.

In another example, KYL claims that the *Pinpisuoluo wang yifo gongyang jing* 頻毘娑羅王詣佛供養經 (K. 716) is a variant translation of a sūtra appearing in the *Zengyi ahan jing* (viz., K. 649 [34.5]). While all three editions of the canon include a text bearing the identical title and translator ascription, the versions in Kaibao and Koryŏ I differ markedly from that in the Khitan edition. The Kaibao and Koryŏ I editions are, however, identical to the text in the *Zengyi ahan jing* and are simply excerpted from that larger collection; they are not variant translations. Sugi finally decides that the Kaibao/Koryŏ I edition is simply a *chaojing* and, being spurious, he deletes it and instead enters the Khitan edition into the canon.

In a last example, Sugi shows that there are six major errors in the Kaibao/Koryŏ I edition of the *Sifen biqiuni jiemo fa* 四分比丘尼竭磨法 (*Dharmaguptabhikṣuṇīkarman;* K. 919), which indicate that the text was the "reckless abbreviation" (*nanch'o* 亂鈔) of an unknown person from a later period. Sugi rejects it and enters the Khitan edition into the canon.

Non-Buddhist Works

The East Asian Buddhist canons also included some works that were not Buddhist at all: treatises of rival Indian philosophical schools, for example, the *Jin qishi lun* 金七十論 (*Sāṃkhyakārikā;* K. 1032), a central treatise of the Sāṃkhya school, one of the six *darśana*s of classical Indian philosophy. Sugi notes that in the listings of Paramārtha's translations appearing in Fei Changfang's *Lidai sanbao ji* and Daoxuan's 道宣 (596–667) *Datang neidian lu* 大唐內典錄 (T. 2149) there is a reference to both this text in two *quan* and a *Sengqie lun* 僧佉論 (an alternate rendering of *Sāṃkhyakārikā*) in three *quan*. Noting that it is incorrect to state, as these catalogues had done, that both titles are extant, he then justifies including such a non-Buddhist text in the canon:

> Despite the fact that this treatise and the *Shengzong shijuyi lun* 勝宗十句義經 (*Vaiśeṣikadaśapadārtha-śāstra;* K. 1045) are not the Buddhadharma, all the non-Buddhist (*oedo* 外道) sects consider these two treatises of the Sāṃkhya and Vaiśeṣika [schools] to be superlative. Those who, through wide learning,

> wish to expunge the perverse and reveal the orthodox must first examine meticulously the positions of the heterodox schools; therefore, they have been translated and published, fearing that they otherwise would fall out of circulation and not be transmitted. It is for this reason alone that they have been entered into the canon.
>
> 此論及勝宗十句義論者, 非是佛法, 而諸外道宗以此數, 勝二論爲上. 欲令博學而破邪現正之者先須委悉異道之宗故譯出之. 恐其失而不傳故, 編入藏中耳. (K.1402.38:702a–b)

Apocryphal Scriptures

In one of the more interesting discussions appearing in his *Collation Notes*, Sugi describes the types of social pressures with which a cataloguer or editor must contend when evaluating a popular Buddhist text. Ignoring his own better judgment, Sugi is compelled to include in his canon a text that he knows to be an apocryphon (*weijing/wigyŏng* 偽經). His rationale for accepting this text is both intriguing and insightful. This text, the thirty-fascicle *Foming jing* mentioned above, was dismissed by both KYL and the *Zhenyuan xinding Shijiao mulu* 貞元新定釋教目錄 (T. 2157) as spurious and was forbidden from being entered into the canon. Sugi quotes the *Zhenyuan lu* 貞元錄, for example:

> This scripture mixes the words of the saints with the vulgar language of the common people. Although the scripture itself is authentic, due to its spurious admixtures, I have made this assessment and included it in the "roster of [texts in which] spurious and false are mixed with the authentic" (*weiwang luan zhen lu* 僞妄亂眞錄) and do not allow it to be entered into the canon. (貞元錄云, 此經乃以凡俗鄙語, 雜於聖言. 本經雖眞, 以有僞雜, 作此挍量, 編於僞妄亂眞錄中, 不得入藏; T.2157.55:837a23–25, quoted in K.1402.38:724b)

Sugi then begins his own adjudication by noting that the eighteen-*kwŏn Foming jing* mentioned previously had been excerpted from this text, with only minor differences. He mentions again the KYL's disdain for this text and its explicit dismissal of that scripture as one of the worst of spurious compositions. Sugi then asks, "If the cataloguers were so adamant about this, then how is it that the State edition recorded that [eighteen-*kwŏn* sūtra] in two different places?" (錄家懇囑如是. 國本如何二重重載; K.1402.38:724c). He finally relents:

> At any rate, this thirty-*kwŏn* scripture has been widely disseminated throughout this kingdom for a long time, and many of the common people of this kingdom rely on it to make merit. If I were now suddenly to proscribe it, that would be certain to arouse the enmity of the congregation. But if both [recensions] were retained, this also would be inappropriate.

> Finally, in accord with the sensibilities of the people, I delete that (i.e., the eighteen-*kwŏn* text) while retaining this (the thirty-*kwŏn* text). For this reason, I record the judgments of the ancients [on this scripture] in order to inform those gentlemen who are sophisticated and upright.
>
> 然此三十卷經, 本朝盛行, 行來日夊, 國俗多有倚此, 而作福者, 今忽刪之, 彼必衆怒. 若俱存之理, 亦未可. 且順人情存此而刪彼, 因書古人之意, 以告雅正君子. (K.1402.38:724c–725a)

Sugi then makes the following concession to the social exegencies of his age:

> Alas! Ānanda was a great sage. He was close to the Buddha, and compiled the repository of the scriptures. But even when he tried to correct one monk's *gāthā* [that mistakenly referred to] a water egret,[47] the monk ultimately would not accept it. Moreover, I am just an ordinary man and the Buddha's generation is long distant. During the protracted transmission of the sūtra teachings, this is a text that has long been disseminated through the whole kingdom. Were I suddenly to decide on my own to proscribe it and yet still have hope of avoiding the enmity of the congregation, it would be like a cicada or a centipede hoping to avoid being crushed by a cart that is about to run over its legs. But even this would be inadequate as a simile for my irresponsibility. In my heart I know [that this text] is spurious and false, but I do not have the power to make this right. This is one of the corruptions of the Dharma-ending Age.
>
> 嗚呼! 阿難大聖也. 距佛不遠也. 經藏所集也, 而欲正一僧水鶴之偈, 僧竟不從. 況我凡夫乎! 佛世已, 遠乎! 經法遙傳乎! 而於擧國盛行久遠之典, 忽獨起以刪之; 而欲衆情之不怒已. 如蒼螂之怒其臂以當車, 欲其不輾已也, 猶不足以譬其非分也. 心知僞妄, 力不能正, 末法之弊, 一至於此. (K.1402.38:725a)

Sugi's statements in this section offer a glimpse of a controversy that must have raged among his collaborators about whether or not to include this text in the canon. While clearly disposed to removing such an obviously spurious text, in the end Sugi relented to the substantial social pressure that was apparently brought to bear on him and his associates to include this text in the new edition.

IV. An Evaluation of Sugi's Editorial Standards

Even by modern standards of textual criticism, Sugi would qualify as a competent and intelligent editor. He avoided many of the errors that have befallen Western textual critics in the incipient stages of their art, and showed flexibility and intuition in applying his own editorial principles. His skill is even more remarkable when we consider that Sugi worked centuries before his counterparts in the West began even to become aware of the problems involved in publishing a critical edition of a sacred text.

While such classical scholars as Origen (184/185–253/254) and Jerome (ca. 347–420) were concerned with issues that would eventually lead to the development of the art of textual criticism, the discipline did not really start in the West until the invention of printing, which postdated by centuries the use of xylographic printing technologies in East Asia. The father of modern Western textual criticism is generally conceded to be Erasmus (1466–1536), but his edition of the New Testament has been discredited because of his faulty technique, as for example, in following the majority of the texts in deciding upon his readings. Sugi, who lived more than two centuries before Erasmus, was far more astute in establishing his text. It is thus not an overestimation to regard Sugi as one of the earliest known adherents of the formal art of textual criticism.

In his edition of the Koryŏ II canon Sugi managed to eschew fixed rules and, in A. E. Housman's terms, demonstrate the true textual critic's "apititude for thinking and willingness to think."[48] In many examples throughout his *Collation Notes,* Sugi rejects such discredited techniques as following the reading of the majority of manuscripts—as when he rejects the readings of both the Kaibao and Koryŏ I canons—or following uncritically the "best" manuscript, as in the cases where he rejects the reading of the Khitan edition. Even the editors of the modern Taishō canon were guilty of the latter mistake: in all cases where there was a Koryŏ II edition of a text, they mechanically copied that edition and merely footnoted alternate readings from other canons.

Sugi also avoided the pitfall of following the "oldest" manuscript, and indeed, his constant indictment of the Kaibao canon demonstrates that he hardly considered that to be a valid editorial principle. Finally, Sugi seems to have had little use for genealogy as a method of textual criticism. Though he recognizes the affinities between the Kaibao and Koryŏ I editions, he never relied on this knowledge in establishing textual recensions or correct readings.

In many ways, Sugi's task in compiling Koryŏ II was more akin to the work of Western editors of classical literature than of the Bible. Both had comparatively few manuscripts on which to draw in preparing their editions, and were consequently compelled to rely more on internal evidence, rather than on external manuscript affinities, in establishing readings. Of all the canons of textual criticism developed in Western scholarship over the last three centuries, Sugi most consistently follows the guiding principle of intrinsic probability—that is, he accepts the reading that seems to best fit the context. In such cases, Sugi clearly follows the equivalent of the first of Johann Jacob Griesbach's (1745–1812) fifteen canons of internal evidence, namely, *brevior lectio praeferenda verbosiori* ("the shorter reading is to be preferred to more verbose one") in his constant indictment of the repetitions of a canon, in particular the Kaibao. Indeed, the frequent dittographies in the Kaibao canon may indicate that its editors instead followed the opposite dictum, perhaps even conflating their text in order to include any and all possible readings, as is the case with the Syrian editions of the New Testament. Sugi comes close at times to engaging in "conjectural emendation" when he rejects the readings in all three canons and broaches possible corrections—a tendency that plagues the editors of the later Yuan and Ming Chinese canons. Yet even in these instances Sugi is invariably careful to add the concluding caveat that he "defers to later sages to resolve the issue," in order not to breach the fine line separating the emendable secular text from the unimpeachable sacred word of the Buddha.

All in all, then, Sugi qualifies as a sophisticated editor who adhered to the most basic canons of internal evidence used in modern textual criticism.[49] As one of the world's earliest known adherents of the formal art of textual criticism, Sugi deserves much wider recognition than he has heretofore received as one of the towering figures of the Korean intellectual tradition.

Beyond what his *Collation Notes* tells us about Sugi's editorial prowess, however, his compilation also offers strong indications of how other editors of East Asian Buddhist canons would have compiled their own scriptural collections. Sugi's information on the readings found in earlier canons allows us to extrapolate many of his techniques back to earlier canons. Thanks to his detailed testimony, we can ascertain that earlier East Asian Buddhist canons—certainly the Koryŏ I, Chinese Song, and Khitan Liao canons, but probably others as well—were produced following guidelines, and probably prompted by motivations, that were similar to Sugi's. His *Collation Notes* demonstrates, for example, that the editors of the first Koryŏ canon did not slavishly follow the readings of the Song Kaibao canon, despite the close relationship between the two canons. Rather, they made careful decisions about the readings appearing in the earlier canon and did not hesitate to follow different readings where warranted.

While no comparable compilation of collation notes from those earlier canons remain, Sugi's documentation of their different readings demonstrates that each was a unique record of the manuscript and xylographic traditions then current in their specific region of East Asia. This makes the *Collation Notes* all the more important as a record not only of the editorial decisions Sugi and his team made in compiling the second Koryŏ canon, but also of the decision-making processes that likely governed the compilation of all East Asian Buddhist canons.

Appendix
Works Treated in Sugi's *Collation Notes*

Sequential no. & title in Sugi's work (with putative Sanskrit)	K. no.	T. no.	pg. nos. in Sugi
1. *Jueding pini jing* 決定毗尼經 *Upālipariprcchā*	K. 35	T. 325	512a–513

There are three passages transposed in the Kaibao edition of the text: 487 Sinographs that belong in the first passage (T.325.12:39c27–40a27) and 517 Sinographs that belong in the last passage (T.325.12:40a27–40b29) have been transposed. This error has been repeated in the later Kaibao and Yuan editions, as the Taishō collation notes indicate (see T.325.12:39c, n. 20; 40a, n. 2, which show a 492- and 484-Sinograph discrepancy, respectively). Finally, Sugi shows that there has been dittography of 24 Sinographs in the second passage (T.325.12:39c28–29).

Sequential no. & title in Sugi's work (with putative Sanskrit)	K. no.	T. no.	pg. nos. in Sugi
2. *Xumoti pusa jing* 須摩提菩薩經 *Sumatidārikāpariprcchā*	K. 39	T. 334	513b–c

In his discussion of this text, the translation of which has been attributed to Dharmarakṣa, Sugi attempts to deal with the problems of variant translations and ascriptions to different translators. According to KYL, there were four translations made of this text, of which only three were extant; an earlier translation by Bodhiruci was lost. The Koryŏ I and Kaibao canons included the translations by Dharmarakṣa and the second of Bodhiruci's two renderings, but did not include the translation attributed to Kumārajīva. The Khitan canon does not include Bodhiruci's later translation but does include the translations made by Dharmarakṣa and Kumārajīva. However, Sugi finds that the text that the Khitan canon has labeled the "Kumārajīva translation" (T.335.12:79c–81c) is identical to the Dharmarakṣa translation in Koryŏ I and Kaibao canons (T. 334). Sugi thus concludes that the Khitan canon was wrong to have included both versions in its canon and he deletes the "Kumārajīva translation." (The text included in the Taishō canon is taken from the Chongning 崇寧 edition of the Song dynasty, with collation notes drawn from the Yuan and Ming editions.) Even a cursory comparison of the translation attributed to Kumārajīva (T. 335) with that of Dharmarakṣa (T. 334) will show the veracity of Sugi's statements: apart from a few minor textual variants, the two texts are indistinguishable. Sugi also indicts KYL for accepting the authenticity of the Kumārajīva attribution.

3. *Daji jing* K. 56 T. 397 514c–515c
大集經
[*Mahāvaipulyamahā*]*sannipāta-sūtra*
Sugi notes a discrepancy in the structure and division of this large collection between the Koryŏ I/Kaibao editions and the later Khitan edition. In the former two canons, the text is in 60 *quan*, with 17 chapters (*pin*), while the Khitan text has 11 chapters in 30 *quan;* these chapters are also differently organized in the different canons. After noting the variant accounts of the work in the *Sengyou lu* 僧祐錄 and KYL, Sugi attempts to correlate these with the extant recensions and notes six major discrepancies. After establishing the apparent relationship between the two recensions, he concludes that neither one can be shown to be unequivocably correct and the other false. As he cannot decide which of the two divisions is correct, Sugi finally defers to the tradition of the Korean Hwaŏm school and accepts its text, which was parallel in structure to the Koryŏ I and Kaibao editions.

4. *Daji jing* K. 56 T. 397 514c–515c
大集經
[*Mahāvaipulyamahā*]*sannipāta-sūtra*
Three passages in *quan* 59 and *quan* 60 of the Koryŏ I/Kaibao edition of the *Daji jing* have been transposed. These fascicles are missing in the Khitan version, however, and thus cannot be compared with another canonical edition. Sugi therefore collates them against a separate edition of the text as found in the *Mingdu wushi jiaoji jing* 明度五十校計經 (K. 411;

not included as separate sūtra in the Taishō canon), and finds that sections of 379 Sinographs in 27 lines and 376 Sinographs in 27 lines have been transposed (the passage in question is T.397.13:396a26–b19). This reading is noted in the Tenpyō 天平 manuscripts from the Sui and Tang periods as preserved at the Shōsō-in 總相院 in Nara (given in Taishō collation notes at T.397.13:396, nn. 3, 13).

5. *Banzhou sanmei jing* K. 67 T. 418 515c–516b
般舟三昧經
Bhadrapāla-sūtra
In the "two editions of East and North" there is a large section of the first *quan* (T.418.13:908a9–b12) that includes sixteen *gāthā*s and a prefatory prose section. The Kaibao edition included in place of this section a prose passage (*changhang* 章行) more than ten pages in length, which Sugi found to be virtually indistinguishable from one appearing in the "Wuzuo pin" and the "Sibi pin" of the second *quan*. Sugi assumes that the Kaibao edition wrongly entered the text of a different translation here, and thus deletes it "according to the two editions of East and North."

6. *Zheng fahua jing* K. 117 T. 263 516b–516a
正法華經
Saddharmapuṇḍarīka
Problems with the title and the text of the tenth chapter of the text (T.263.9:99a–102b) are discussed. The chapter title, "Yaowang rulai pin" 藥王如來品, appears in the Kaibao edition as "Fashi pin" 法師品, which Sugi considers to be an erroneous repetition of the immediately succeeding "Tan fashi pin" 歎法師品 (*pin* no. 18). The Kaibao edition deletes a long passage (six scrolls in length) from the text, which Sugi has added back into his canon, following the other editions.

7. *Puyao jing* K. 112 T. 186 518b–522b
普曜經
Lalitavistara
Sugi notes here that the Kaibao edition places chapter 3 at the end of the first *quan* of the text, and chapter 5 at the beginning of *quan* 2, omitting chapter 4. Sugi adds this fourth chapter ("Xiangshen chudai pin" 降神處胎品, T.186.3:489a–492c), a total of thirteen pages, following the Koryŏ I and Khitan editions.

8. *Yuedeng sanmei jing* K. 182 T. 640 522b–527a
月燈三昧經
This is the Khitan edition of *Yuedeng sanmei jing* (K. 182), in thirteen

pages, which is the Xiangong translation of the text. According to KYL, there were originally two separate translations of the text, one by An Shigao, which was no longer extant, and a second by Xiangong. Both were assumed to have constituted the seventh *quan* of the *Da yuedeng jing*. Sugi accepts that K. 182 is the authentic translation by Xiangong because the structure and size of the Khitan recension match the information on the text given in the headnote to the sūtra, as cited in KYL. Sugi notes, however, that there is a discrepancy in the KYL statement that this text derives from *quan* 7 of the longer text; his collation finds that it is instead taken from the first half of the sixth *quan*. He assumes either that the text was divided differently in the past, or that the KYL compiler mistakenly wrote "6" for "7." Note that in the edition of this text cited by Sugi in his collation note, the second line of the text (K.1402.38:522c19) has only has 13 Sinographs, rather than the standard 14. Might Sugi have done this to give an exact representation of the text as it was printed in the Khitan edition?

9. *Yuedeng sanmei jing* K. 183 T. 641 527a–c
月燈三昧經
Samādhirājacandrapradīpa-sūtra
This is the Kaibao and Koryŏ I edition of the text, in twenty-six pages. Since this recension does not include the alternate title of Xiangong's translation and as it is nearly twice the length of the text in KYL, Sugi concludes that the attribution here cannot be correct. Sugi suspects that this Kaibao edition was actually An Shigao's translation, which KYL had presumed lost. However, since there was apparently no translator cited in the headnote to the text they edited, they simply checked in the catalogues, found a listing for a *Yuedeng jing* as translated by Xiangong, and wrongly made the ascription. Sugi also notes again the KYL claim that this text comes from the seventh *quan* of the longer text, and finds instead that it comes from the latter half of the fifth *quan*.

10. *Mile xiasheng jing* K. 197 T. 453 527b–c
彌勒下生經
This is the Kaibao edition of the text (it has no Khitan counterpart), the translation of which is attributed to Dharmarakṣa by the Kaibao editors, although there is no reference in the bibliographical catalogues to Dharmarakṣa ever having made such a translation. Attempting to explain this discrepancy, Sugi first finds a reference in KYL to six alternate translations of the *Mile xiasheng jing* (K. 197), three of which were nonextant, and then another reference to a Dharmarakṣa translation of a *Mile chengfo jing*

彌勒成佛經 in its listing of nonextant scriptures. Sugi thought that these references might have provided the justification for the Kaibao ascription. This proved not to be the case: elsewhere in KYL, under the discussion for Kumārajīva's translation of *Mile xiasheng chengfo jing* (T. 454), there was a reference to an alternate translation by Dharmarakṣa. Sugi thus concludes that there was no catalogue evidence supporting the Kaibao claim of a Dharmarakṣa translation of the *Mile xiasheng jing*.

Sugi also cites structural evidence to prove that this text could not actually be one of those three nonextant works. Citing the *Jingang bore houxu* by Gushan Zhiyuan 孤山智圓 (981–1027), Sugi notes that scriptures were traditionally published in a format of 17 Sinographs per line, 25 lines per page. The notice to the nonextant translation of this text stated that it was seventeen pages long, which would total 7,222 Sinographs (*sic;* the correct number is 7,225); this sūtra, which has only 3,176 Sinographs, is not even half the length of that text. In the end, Sugi defers to "later sages" to determine the veracity of the Kaibao ascription of this recension to Dharmarakṣa.

11. *Mile xiasheng chengfo jing* K. 199 T. 455 527c–529c
彌勒下生成佛經
Maitreyavyākaraṇa[-*sūtra*]
Yijing's translation of this text appears only in the Khitan canon, and was not found in either the Kaibao or Koryŏ I canons. The text appears among the three extant recensions of the six translations made of this text, as noted in KYL.

12. *Shenri jing* K. 234 T. 535 529c–530a
申日經
Candraprabhakumāra[-*sūtra*]
This is the Kaibao edition of this text, which had no counterpart in the Khitan canon. Of its four translations one was said to be nonextant. According to KYL, among the translations by Dharmarakṣa there was a listing for a *Yueguang tongzi jing,* which had the alternate title *Shenri jing.* Complicating matters, however, the (Kaibao) canon already included a *Yueguang tongzi jing* by Dharmarakṣa (K. 219), so this *Shenri jing* must refer to yet another text by Dharmarakṣa. The KYL notes elsewhere that, among the translations of Zhi Qian, there is a reference to a *Shenri jing,* and Zhisheng's annotation said that this was simply a different translation of the *Yueguang tongzi jing;* the texts of the two scriptures were virtually identical. Sugi, noting that earlier canons had included a translation attributed to Zhi Qian of a *Shenri jing,* also known as *Yueguang tongzi jing,*

which was not included in any of the present canons, therefore suspects that K. 234 is actually the translation by Zhiqian, which has been mistakenly attributed to Dharmarakṣa. He also surmises that all four of the translations made of this text are actually extant, but as he cannot say this definitively he leaves it for "later sages" to determine.

13. *Liuzi shenzhou jing* K. 316 T. 1180 530a–b
六字神呪經
Ṣaḍakṣaravidyāmantra
The Kaibao and Koryŏ I canons included in their *cai/chae* case another translation of this *Liuzi shenzhou jing,* which was also attributed to Bodhiruci. This second translation was not found in the Khitan canon. According to KYL, this text is actually an alternate translation of the same work, the *Wenshushili pusa zhoufan* included in *quan* 6 of the *Tuoluoni ji jing* (K. 308), and of the *Liuzi tuoluoni,* which is included in the *Zhou wushou* 咒五首 (K. 312). Sugi corroborates this conclusion based on his own collation of these texts, but finds that there is no basis for attributing this text to Bodhiruci. He assumes that the Kaibao canon must have found the parallel text, the *Liuzi zhouwang jing* (K. 341), "by an anonymous translator, now appended to the *Liang lu*" that is included later in the *zhi/chi* case and—assuming that it was a different translation of this text—wrongly added Bodhiruci's name to it. Sugi rejects this ascription, again following the Khitan editors (who did not include this text in their canon), and deletes the text.

14. *Dongfang zuishengdengwang tuoluoni jing* K. 349 T. 1353 530c
東方最勝燈王陀羅尼經
Agrapradīpadhāraṇīvidyārāja
This is the Kaibao edition (K. 349) in six pages, including a spell that is three pages in length. The Khitan edition (K. 350) has a different title and its recension of the text is more than twice the length of the Kaibao edition. Sugi was therefore uncertain as to which text is the legitimate sūtra. The invocation to the Khitan edition indicates that it was the authentic translation of Jñānagupta. Based on the "archaic language and structure" (*ko ŏjil* 古語質) of the Kaibao edition, however, Sugi suspects that it could not have been translated by Jñānagupta. Nevertheless, as he cannot determine which is the authentic recension, he retains both, leaving it to "later sages" to determine which is correct, and enters K. 350 into the canon, following the Khitan editors.

15. *Dongfang zuishengdeng-wang rulai jing*	K. 350	T. 1354	530c–536c

東方最勝燈王如來經

Agrapradīpadhāraṇīvidyārāja

This is the Khitan edition of the preceding text, missing in the Kaibao canon. Sugi appends the entire text in his collation note, with no new discussion.

16. *Xuzhen tianzi jing*	K. 372	T. 588	536c–537a

須眞天子經

Suvikrānta[cintā]devaputraparipṛcchā

The Kaibao edition was in 4 *quan*, 3 *quan* in the Khitan. In place of the last two lines of the ninth page of the first *quan* (T.588.15:101b22–23), the Khitan edition gives a different passage of 38 lines; Sugi finds that this is an incorrect repetition of the final sections of *quan* 3 of the Kaibao edition and of chapter 8 of the third *quan*, the "Fenbie pin" 分別品, of the Khitan edition (T.588.15:108c12–109a20). He therefore deletes the passage from the Koryŏ II edition and bases his edition on the four-*quan* Kaibao version. This collation note is given at T.588.15:101b–c.

17. *Xianjie jing*	K. 387	T. 425	537a

賢劫經

Bhadrakalpita-sūtra

The [*Xianzai*] *Xianjie qianfo minghao jing* 現在賢劫千佛名號經 (viz. K. 392), included later in the *ki* 己 case, is an alternate translation of the chapter 20 of this text, "Qianfo minghao pin" 千佛名號品, included in *quan* 6 (T.425.14:45c–50b). For some unknown reason, however, the catalogues consistently include this text in the listings for single-edition translations, rather than recognizing that multiple translations were made.

18. *Suxiti jieluo gongyang fa*	K. 431	T. 894	537b
Suxiti jieluo jing	K. 432	T. 893	537b–584b

蘇悉地羯羅蘇悉地羯羅供養法

蘇悉地羯囉經

Susiddhikarapūjāvidhi

Susiddhikaramahātantrasādhanopāyikapaṭala[-sūtra]

K. 431 is the Koryŏ I/Kaibao edition of this text, which differs greatly from the Khitan recension (K. 432) both in title and content. Although there is no reference to such a *gongyang* 供養 scripture by Śubhakarasiṃha in KYL or in the *Zhenyuan lu*, Sugi rejects the notion that it was a spurious compilation and enters both recensions into the canon. The full text of the Khitan edition, K. 432, is then recorded.

19. *Moni jing* K. 463 T. 589 584c–593b
魔逆經
Mañjuśrīvikurvāṇaparivarta
KYL lists the *Moni jing* as a single-edition translation, done by Dharmarakṣa. While the Koryŏ I and Khitan editions are indistinguishable, the Kaibao edition is completely different in both wording and meaning, implying that there were actually two separate translations made. Through his collation, however, Sugi discovers that the Kaibao edition is identical to the *Wenshushili huiguo jing* (K. 538), also translated by Dharmarakṣa, which is included later in the *yŏm* 念 case. Recognizing that the Kaibao canon has wrongly titled it and reincluded it in the canon, Sugi rejects the Kaibao recension and retains the Koryŏ I and Khitan editions as the authentic sūtra.

20. *Dazhidu lun; quan* 4 K. 549 T. 1509 593c–594a
大智度論
Mahāprajñāpāramitā-śāstra
A passage of 306 Sinographs in 22 lines missing in the Kaibao edition is added from the Koryŏ I/Khitan recensions. For the passage in question, see T.1509.25:84c13–85c15. This passage is also missing in the "Old Song" (viz. Chongning 崇寧) and Japanese Tenpyō 天平 manuscripts, as indicated in the Taishō collation notes (T.1509.25:84, n. 51).

21. *Dazhidu lun; quan* 14 K. 549 T. 1509 594a–594b
大智度論
Mahāprajñāpāramitā-śāstra
A 7-line passage (see T.1509.25:164b5–19) missing in the Kaibao edition is added from the Koryŏ I and Khitan editions.

22. *Dazhidu lun; quan* 31 K. 549 T. 1509 594b–c
大智度論
Mahāprajñāpāramitā-śāstra
A 6-line passage (see T.1509.25:291b23–c20) missing in the Kaibao edition is added from the Koryŏ I/Khitan editions.

23. *Da baoji jing lun* K. 552 T. 1523 594c–607a
大寶積經論
Ratnakūṭasūtropadeśa
The first *quan* of the Kaibao edition is vastly different from that of the Koryŏ I and Khitan editions. Based on the KYL account of this commentary, Sugi discovers that this first *quan* is actually the text of the

Puming pusa hui 普明菩薩會, included as *quan* 112 of the *Da baoji jing* 大寶積經 (T.310.11:631c–638c). He therefore rejects the Kaibao recension and retains the Koryŏ I/Khitan edition.

24. *She dasheng lun shi* K. 590 T. 1595 607a
攝大乘論釋
Mahāyanasaṃgrahabhāṣya
In *quan* 9 of this text, a passage of 25 Sinographs (T.1595.31:214c25–26) from the *She dasheng lun* 攝大乘論 (K. 588), the text on which K. 590 comments, is missing "in all three state editions." From the context, this seems to be a reference to the Kaibao, Khitan, and Koryŏ I compilations, though some scholars have posited less plausibly that this is a reference to three independent Koryŏ editions. Sugi is therefore compelled to collate the text against the *She dasheng lun* (K. 588) itself, and adds this section from that text. This omission is noted also for the Three Editions and Chongning Song canons, as found in the Taishō collation note (T.1595.31:214, n. 2). This collation note appears at T.1595.31:220c.

25. *Juedingzang lun* K. 598 T. 1584 607a–609a
決定藏論
Three sections in *quan* 3 have been improperly transposed in the Kaibao edition, a mistake that has been corrected according to the Koryŏ I and Khitan editions; for the problematic passage, see T.1584.30:1032b18–1033b17.

26. *Baoxing lun* K. 600 T. 1611 609b–c
寶性論
[*Ratnagotravibhāga*]*Mahāyānottaratantra*
In *quan* 2, the Kaibao edition has incorrectly omitted a section of 338 Sinographs in 24 lines, which is added according to the other two editions. For the passage in question, see T.1611.31:825b5–27.

27. *Zhuanshi lun* K. 612 T. 1587 609c–611c
轉識論
Triṃṣikā[*-kārikā*]
The Kaibao edition has incorrectly omitted a section of 5 scrolls (*p'ok* 幅) and 13 lines. This is added according to the other editions and the edited passage is recorded. For the passage, see T.1587.31:62b29–63c18.

28. *Fajie wuchabie lun* K. 640 T. 1626 611c–614c
法界無差別論
This is the Khitan edition of the text, which Sugi accepts as Devaprajña's (d.u.) authentic translation of the *Fajie wuchabie lun*, because its format

corresponds to the information as given both in Fazang's 法藏 (643–712) commentary to the text and in KYL (see next entry). This collation note appears at T.1626.31:694a–b.

29. *Fajie wuchabie lun* K. 639 T. 1627 614c–615a
法界無差別論
This is the Kaibao and Koryŏ I edition of the text. This recension is also claimed to be Devaprajña's translation, but Sugi doubts the attribution. The verses of the preceding Khitan version are those explicated by Fazang (in T. 1838) and said by KYL to have been translated by Devaprajña. It is listed as a single-edition text, however, with no alternate translations made. Hence, the Koryŏ I/Kaibao recension must have been a translation made sometime after the compilation of KYL, but Sugi is unsure when or by whom such a translation would have been made. At any rate, it is clear to him that the attribution of this recension to Devaprajña is wrong. The collation note appears at T. 1627:31.896b.

30. *Zhong ahan jing; quan* 11 K. 648 T. 26 615b–616a
中阿含經
Madhyamāgama
The opening sūtra of this *quan*, the *Qibao jing* 七寶經, is omitted in the Koryŏ I and Kaibao editions, and is added into the text from the Khitan recension; see T.26:1.493a. In the following sūtra, the *Sanshi'er xiang jing* 三十二相經, the first 182 Sinographs are missing and are added from the Khitan edition; see T. 26:1.493a26–b7.

31. *Zhong ahan jing; quan* 15 K. 648 T. 26 616a–c
中阿含經
Madhyamāgama
The Koryŏ I and Kaibao editions omit a section of 490 Sinographs in 35 lines from the opening sections of the *Sanshiyu jing* 三十喻經; this corresponds to T. 26:1.518c8–519a13. The Khitan edition also misreads the title and mistakes *shi* ("time," in cursive form) for *sanshi* ("thirty"). Sugi accepts *sanshi* as correct.

32. *Za ahan jing; quan* 4 K. 650 T. 99 616c–625b
雜阿含經
Saṃyuktāgama
The Koryŏ I and Kaibao editions of this fascicle, 19 sūtras in 25 pages, are identical. The Khitan edition contains only 15 sūtras, but if these were copied in the 14 Sinographs per line format of the Kaibao edition, they would total 27 pages. The Khitan recension is also completely different

from that of the other two canons. When collating this *quan* against the complete text of the *Za ahan jing,* Sugi discovers that *quan* 4 of the Koryŏ I and Kaibao canons actually turns out to be identical to *quan* 42. He therefore rejects the Koryŏ I/Kaibao edition and adds this Khitan recension into the canon. For the section, see T.99.2:22b–29b. This collation note appears at T. 99:2.29b.

33. *Za ahan jing; quan* 34 K. 650 T. 99 625b–626a
雜阿含經
Saṃyuktāgama
A section of 516 Sinographs, from the end of sūtra 964 to the beginning of sūtra 965 in the *Za ahan jing,* is missing from the Kaibao edition and this elision obscures the end and beginning of the two scriptures. This missing section is added according to Koryŏ I and Khitan editions. For the passage in question, see T.99.2:247b21–c24.

34. *Bieyi za ahan jing* K. 651 T. 100 626a–631c
別譯雜阿含經
Saṃyuktāgama
Ten sūtras are missing from the end of *quan* 5 to the beginning of *quan* 6 in the Koryŏ I and Kaibao editions, and are found only in the Khitan recension. The elision obscures the division between *quan* 5 and *quan* 6. This same lack of *quan* division is corroborated in the Tenpyō manuscripts and in the Three Editions (see T.100.2:410, n. 3; T.100.2:411, n. 10). Sugi adds these sūtras (nos. 101–110), and divides the text into these two *quan.* For the section, see T.100.2:410a–414a. This collation note appears at T.100.2:411c.

35. *Qishi jing* K. 660 T. 24 631c
Qishi yinben jing K. 661 T. 25 631c
起世經
起世因本經
Qishi jing (K. 660) in the Koryŏ I/Kaibao edition is said to have been translated by Jñānagupta together with Dharmagupta, while the Khitan recension of the same text attributes it to Jñānagupta alone. *Qishi yinben jing* (K. 661) is attributed in Koryŏ I and Kaibao to Jñānagupta, while the Khitan recension names Dharmagupta instead. Sugi cites KYL, which gives the same attributions as the Khitan editors, and he accepts the Khitan recensions as correct.

36. *Daloutan jing* K. 662 T. 23 632a
大樓炭經
Fifteen lines of text in *quan* 1 are missing from the Kaibao and Khitan

editions, and are added according to the Koryŏ I edition. For the passage, see T.23.1:281b9–20.

37. *Zhongbenqi jing* K. 664 T. 196 632a–634a
中本起經
A six-page section omitted in the Kaibao edition is added from the Koryŏ I and Khitan editions. For the passage, see T.196.4:158a21–159b17.

38. *Shousui jing* K. 688 T. 50 634b–636b
受歲經
A text entitled *Shousui jing* (K. 688) is found in the Khitan canon but not in the Kaibao, while a *Shou xinsui jing* (K. 871) appears in the Kaibao canon but not in the Khitan. Both are said to have been translated by Dharmarakṣa. The titles are quite similar but the contents of the two texts are completely different. Using KYL, Sugi verifies that the *Shousui jing* was also translated by Dharmarakṣa, and has its parallel in a sūtra in the *Zhong ahan jing, quan* 23 (no. 89, T.26.1:571b–572c), which is included in the *chŏng/qing* 淸 case; therefore, the Khitan edition (K. 688) is correctly placed here. The Kaibao edition (K. 871) is completely different from the corresponding sūtra in the *Zhong ahan jing*. However, although the scripture differs somewhat from a similarly titled text included in the *chŏng* 淸 case, the *Xinsui jing* (K. 872), it is apparently a variant translation of that text. Sugi therefore decides to include *Shou xinsui jing* (K. 871) in the later case as well.

39. *Pinpisuoluowang yifo gongyang jing* K. 716 T. 133 636b–638b
頻毘娑羅王詣佛供養經
All three canons include a text with the same title, ascribed to the same translator. Although Koryŏ I and Kaibao are identical, they differ completely from their Khitan counterpart. According to KYL, this text is supposed to be a variant translation of a sūtra appearing in the *Zengyi ahan jing, quan* 26 (viz. K.649 [34.5]; T.125.2:694a–697a). The Koryŏ I/Kaibao edition is, however, identical to that text and is simply excerpted from the larger collection; it is not a variant translation. Sugi finally decides that that edition is a *chaojing/ch'ogyŏng* 鈔經 ("abbreviated sūtra") and therefore spurious. He accepts the Khitan edition as the legitimate recension and enters it into the canon.

40. *Sheweiguowang shimeng jing* K. 735 T. 147 638b
舍衛國王十夢經
K. 735 is the Khitan edition of this text and is a variant translation of a

sūtra appearing in the *Zengyi ahan jing, quan* 51 (T.125.2:829b–830b). The Koryŏ I and Kaibao editions of this text (K. 734) are virtually identical but their wording differs greatly from the Khitan recension. Since he cannot decide which of the two recensions is legitimate, Sugi retains both and leaves it to "later sages" to determine which is authentic.

41. *Si weizengyou fa jing* K. 748 T. 136 638c–639b
四未曾有法經

While the title and translator attribution for this text is identical in all three editions, the Koryŏ I/Kaibao edition differs considerably from the Khitan. The Koryŏ I/Kaibao edition discusses only the merit accruing from building stūpas, and only at the conclusion of the text does it even mention the "unprecedented dharmas" (*weizengyou fa* 未曾有法; Skt. *adbhūtadharma*) of the title. The Khitan edition, however, is chiefly concerned with the *weizengyou fa*, and conforms with the KYL statement that this text is a variant translation of sūtra no. 4 included in the *Zengyi ahan jing*, the "Banan pin" 八難品 (T.125.2:752c–753c). After collating the two editions, Sugi determines that the Koryŏ I/Kaibao edition is identical to the *Weizengyou jing* 未曾有經 (K. 237, T. 237) included in the earlier *hui* 毁 case, which is attributed to an anonymous translator of the Hou-Han 後漢 period, and he omits it here.

42. *Benshi jing* K. 803 T. 765 639c–646c
本事經
Itivṛttaka

The third *quan* of the Koryŏ I and Kaibao editions of this text are identical, but it differs greatly from the Khitan. Sugi details four major problems with the former edition and two points in favor of the Khitan recension, which prompt him to use the Khitan in preparing his own edition.

43. *Da anban shouyi jing* K. 806 T. 602 647a
大安般守意經
Mahāsmṛtyupasthāna-sūtra

Based upon both information in the preface to this sūtra and an examination of the actual text, Sugi suspects that a copyist has incorrectly entered the interlinear notes to the scripture into the main body of the text, thereby producing many sections that are difficult to construe. As he cannot resolve the problems with the text based on his collation, he leaves it for later scholars to resolve. This collation note is included at T.602.15:173a.

44. *Shou xinsui jing* K. 871 T. 61 647a
受新歲經
Pravāraṇa
This is the Kaibao/Koryŏ I edition of K. 688, discussed above. This text seems to be a variant translation of the *Xinsui jing* (K. 872): although the wording of the two texts is somewhat different, the sense is the same. The KYL seems to be wrong in considering the K. 872 version to be a single-edition translation (*danyi*).

45. *Hujing jing* K. 864 T. 748 647a–b
護淨經
An important section of 255 Sinographs missing in the Khitan edition is added from the Koryŏ I and Kaibao editions. For the passage, see T.748.17:565b12–28.

46. *Shisong lü* K. 890 T. 1435 647b–652a
十誦律
Sarvāstivāda-vinaya
Three sections missing in *quan* 5 of the Koryŏ I and Kaibao editions are added from the Khitan recension. For the passages, see T.1435.23:35b21–36b8, 36c7–37b23, 37c25–38c18.

47. *Genben shuoyiqie youbu bichuni pinaiye* K. 892 T. 1443 652a–653a
根本說一切有部苾芻尼毗奈耶
[Mūlasarvāstivāda]Bhikṣuṇīvinayavibhaṅga
In *quan* 20 of the Koryŏ I and Kaibao editions, a section of fifty-nine lines is missing, which is added from the Khitan; for the passage, see T.1443.23: 1018c23–1019b23.

48. *Mishase wufen jieben* K. 901 T. 1422 653a–664a
彌沙塞五分戒本
The Koryŏ I and Kaibao editions are identical; only the Khitan differs. After collating the different recensions with the actual Vinaya text, however, Sugi decides to accept the Khitan edition and enters it into the canon. The Kaibao edition turns out to be a copy of a text appearing in the *sui* 隨 case, the *Shisong biqiu poluotimucha jieben* 十誦比丘波羅提木叉戒本 (K. 902; T. 1436), translated by Kumārajīva, wrongly attributed to Buddhajīva (d.u.) in the Kaibao canon. While the Kaibao editions of K. 901 and K. 902 vary slightly, these variances are attributable to copyist errors rather than to anything more substantive.

49. *Mohesengqi biqiuni jieben* K. 900 T. 1427 663a
摩訶僧祇比丘尼戒本
The Khitan edition is vastly different from the Koryŏ I and Kaibao editions. Sugi collates the Khitan edition against the *Bhikṣuṇī* and *Bhikṣu* sections of the complete Vinaya of the Mahāsāṃghika school and discovers that it alone is legitimate. Sugi therefore enters the Khitan version in the canon.

50. *Shaminili jie wen* K. 912 T. 1475 663a–b
沙彌尼離戒文
**Śramaṇerīvinaya*
The Kaibao/Koryŏ I edition and KYL read the title as *Shaminili jie wen;* the Khitan gives instead *Shamini zajie wen.* Collating against the actual text of the scripture itself, Sugi believes that the title given in all three editions is wrong: the *li* of this translation is simply a different transliteration of the Sanskrit phoneme *ri,* which is represented by *ni* in the other editions. Hence, the correct title should be *Shamili jie wen.* However, as none of the three editions gives this title, Sugi does not dare to make the revision, and simply records his ideas to help later scholars resolve the discrepancy.

51. *Sifen biqiuni jiemo fa* K. 919 T. 1434 663c–677c
四分比丘尼羯磨法
Dharmaguptabhikṣuṇīkarman
The Kaibao and Koryŏ I editions are identical but differ from the Khitan recension. Sugi shows that there are six major errors in the Kaibao/Koryŏ I version, which reveal it as a "reckless abbreviation" (*nanch'o* 亂鈔) done by an unknown person of a later period. These include such mistakes of content as not specifying that a *bhikṣuṇī* must first obtain *upasaṃpadā* from the *bhikṣuṇī saṃgha* before requesting it from the *bhikṣu saṃgha* (the text implies that the ceremonies take place simultaneously). Also KYL states that this text was translated by Guṇavarman (367–431) during the Liu Kaibao period, but the translator colophon to Kaibao and Koryŏ I editions includes an alternate title for the text in place of the translator's name. For all these reasons, Sugi rejects the authenticity of the Kaibao and Koryŏ I editions and enters the Khitan recension into the canon.

52. *Binaiye* K. 936 T. 1464 678a–694b
鼻奈耶
The Koryŏ I and Khitan editions are in 10 *quan;* the Kaibao edition is only 8 *quan.* Sugi finds that the Kaibao edition has inadvertently omitted the fifth *quan* and designated the sixth *quan* as the fifth. In addition, it is

missing the seventh *quan* and designates the eighth *quan* as the seventh. Sugi therefore adds these two missing *quan* to the text from the Koryŏ I and Khitan editions.

53. *Apitan ba jiandu lun, quan* 6 K. 943 T. 1543 694c
阿毘曇八犍度論
[*Abhidharma*]*Jñānaprasthāna*
In this *quan* of the Kaibao edition a seventy-five–line passage has been incorrectly recopied from *quan* 5. Sugi omits it from the edition he enters into the canon. For the duplicated passage, see T.1543.26:793a25–c28.

54. *Apitan ba jiandu lun, quan* 8 K. 943 T. 1543 694c
阿毘曇八犍度論
[*Abhidharma*]*Jñānaprasthāna*
There is a thirty-five–line passage missing in the Khitan edition that is found in both the Kaibao and Koryŏ editions. The sense is not easily construed in the latter two editions, however, and Sugi finds that this passage is a dittography of one appearing later in the same *quan* of this text. Although that passage is somewhat abbreviated from the longer passage appearing later, it does not seem to be either a variant translation or another edition. Sugi examines Dao'an's preface to this text and discovers that the initial translation of this text by Zhu Fonian was said to have been full of misconstructions, which were corrected "over a forty-six–day period." Sugi therefore assumes that the first translation attributed to Zhu Fonian had both the initial, error-filled translation and a later revised one, either of which could have been the source for the wrongly recopied section in the Koryŏ I and Kaibao editions. Sugi therefore removes the passage, following the Khitan reading.

55. *Apidamo fazhi lun* K. 944 T. 1544 695a
阿毘達磨發智論
[*Abhidharma*]*Jñānaprasthāna*
A seventy-five–Sinograph section (T.1544.26:957a18–23) is misplaced in the Kaibao edition but is found in its correct position in the Khitan recension. The Koryŏ I edition, however, has conflated the text and includes the passage at both of the positions found in Kaibao and Khitan, hopelessly confusing its reading. The Kaibao misplacement of this passage is found also in the "Old Song" canon and the Tenpyō manuscripts, as mentioned in the Taishō collation notes (T.1544.26:957, nn. 1, 3).

56. *Apidamo jiyimen zu lun* K. 946 T. 1536 695a–696c
阿毘達磨集異門足論
[*Abhidharma*]*saṃgītīparyāya*
Three sections of text (T.1536.26:426a26–c25) are transposed in the Kaibao edition, making it difficult to construe. Sugi corrects the errors according to the readings in Koryŏ I and Khitan, and records the corrected passage. There then follows a section of 35 lines missing in the Koryŏ I and Kaibao editions, which is added from the Khitan edition. For the entire passage, see T.1536.26:427a24–b22.

57. *Apitan biposha lun* K. 951 T. 1546 696c–697a
阿毘曇毘婆沙論
[*Abhidharma*]*vibhāṣā*
A section of 455 Sinographs in *quan* 14 has been wrongly added in the Koryŏ I edition. Sugi omits it, following the Kaibao and Khitan readings. This annotation is included at T.1546.28:108b.

58. *Apitamo dabiposha lun, quan* 14 K. 952 T. 1545 697a–698a
阿毗達磨大毘婆沙論
[*Abhidharma*]*mahāvibhāṣā*
A sixty-eight–line passage omitted in the Kaibao edition is added following the other two editions; see T.1545.27:70b13–71c16. This annotation is included at T.1545.27:71c.

59. *Apitamo dabiposha lun, quan* 32 K. 952 T. 1545 698a–699b
阿毗達磨大毘婆沙論
[*Abhidharma*]*mahāvibhāṣā*
The Kaibao edition has transposed three sections; these are corrected according to the other two editions. Kaibao has also mistakenly written the Sinograph *xia* 下 ("below") for *bu* 不 ("not"). The Koryŏ I edition has also dittographed a section of twelve lines (starting at T.1545.27:164b23). This note is included at T.1545.27:164b23–165a25.

60. *Apitamo dabiposha lun, quan* 65 K. 952 T. 1545 699C
阿毗達磨大毘婆沙論
[*Abhidharma*]*mahāvibhāṣā*
There is a dittography of forty Sinographs in both the Kaibao and Koryŏ I editions. This is deleted according to the Khitan, and the correct reading is given. For the passage, see T.1545.27:339b1–4.

61. *Apitamo dabiposha lun, quan* 109 K. 952 T. 1545 699c–701a
阿毗達磨大毘婆沙論
[*Abhidharma*]*mahāvibhāṣā*
A seventy-two–line section missing in the Kaibao edition is supplied from the Koryŏ I and Khitan recensions. For the passage, see T.1545.27: 566b10–567a14.

62. *Apitamo dabiposha lun, quan* 199 K. 952 T. 1545 701a
阿毗達磨大毘婆沙論
[*Abhidharma*]*mahāvibhāṣā*
A section of 146 Sinographs wrongly copied in the Kaibao edition is deleted according to the Khitan and Koryŏ I editions and replaced by a section of 109 Sinographs. For the passage, see T.1545.27:998b19–26. This note is recorded at T.1545.27:998b–c.

63. *Apitamo dabiposha lun, quan* 200 K. 952 T. 1545 701a–b
阿毗達磨大毘婆沙論
[*Abhidharma*]*mahāvibhāṣā*
Several mistakes in the Kaibao edition are noted in this *quan.* First, a passage of eighty-five Sinographs is deleted according to the two other editions; this corresponds to T.1545.27:999a26–b2. Second, seventeen Sinographs omitted in the Kaibao edition are added according to the other two editions; see T.1545.27:1002b15–16. Third, seventeen Sinographs missing in the Kaibao edition are added following the readings of the other two canons; see T.1545.27:1002c18–19. Fourth, seventeen Sinographs are missing in the Kaibao edition; see T.1545.27:1002c22–23. Fifth, sixteen Sinographs are missing in the Kaibao edition; see T.1545.27:1003c6–7.

64. *Fenbie gongde lun* K. 973 T. 1507 701b–c
分別功德論
The Khitan edition is in 4 *quan,* a division corroborated in KYL, which also acknowledges variants of 3 and 5 *quan.* This text is a commentary to the *Zengyi ahan jing* (K. 649), *pin* 1–4; the translation is attributed to Gautama Saṃghadeva. The KYL attributes the translation of this commentary to Dharmarakṣa but other catalogues all ascribe it instead to an anonymous translator. Sugi accepts the latter judgment but, noting parallels between the passages cited in the commentary and the actual text itself, he suggests that the translator of these two texts was probably the same person. The

Sengyou lu, furthermore, states that the commentary was composed by the Indian monks Kāśyapa and Ānanda; Sugi rejects this claim.

65. *Shibabu lun* K. 976 T. 2032 701c
十八部論
Samayabhedoparacanacakra
The Kaibao edition has wrongly recopied the *Buyizhi lun* 部異執論 (*sic;* the correct title is *Buzhiyi lun* 部執異論; K. 975) and titled the recopied text *Shibabu lun.* Sugi enters the Koryŏ I edition into the canon, instead. Problems with translator attribution are then discussed. The cataloguers generally attribute the translation of the text to Paramārtha. Sugi, however, notes that the opening section of the text cites the *Wenshushili wen jing*, "Fenbu pin" (T.468.14:501a16–b29; quoted at T.2032.49:17b15–28) which includes at the conclusion of the quotation the note "compiled by Dharma Master Kumārajīva" (T.2032.49:17b29). However, as Sugi notes, the *Wenshushili wen jing* had not yet been translated during Kumārajīva's time. After showing that similar problems would remain even if the text were the product of an anonymous translator, Sugi then explores whether the *Wenshushili wen jing* might have been a retranslation by Paramārtha, which was then included in the *Shibabu lun.* Sugi notes that much of the phraseology derives from the Qin-period translations of Kumārajīva, and he concludes that all of the ascriptions concerning the translation of this treatise are suspicious. As he cannot resolve the issues, he leaves the problem for later scholars to resolve. This collation note also appears at T.2032.49:19c.

66. *Pusa benyuan jing* K. 988 T. 153 701c–702a
菩薩本緣經
In the first *quan* of the Khitan edition (T.153.3:53a, following line 3), there is a section of 412 Sinographs in 26 lines that is missing in Koryŏ I and Kaibao. Collating the texts, Sugi discovers that the Khitan edition has wrongly dittographed a passage appearing later in the second *quan* of this text, "Long pin" 龍品, no. 8 (T.153.3:68b29–c25), and he removes it. This same Khitan reading is followed in the Three Editions, as noted in the Taishō collation note to this passage (T.153.3:53, n. 2).

67. *Za baozang jing* K. 1001 T. 203 702a
雜寶藏經
The Khitan edition includes in *quan* 5 (T. 203:4.471b, following line 25) a section of six episodes (*yuan*) that are not found in the Koryŏ I and Kaibao editions. This section has been mistakenly recopied in the Khitan

edition from its earlier appearance in *quan* 4 (T.203.4:466c11–17). Sugi therefore does not follow it here.

68. *Jin qishi lun* K. 1032 T. 2137 702a–b
金七十論
Sāṃkhyakārikā
Sugi notes that in two catalogues, the *Changfang lu* 長房錄 and the *Neidian lu* 內典錄, there is a reference among Paramārtha's translations to both this text in 2 *quan* and a *Sengqie lun* in 3 *quan* (both render the Sanskrit title *Sāṃkhyakārikā*). Sugi remarks that it is incorrect to state that both titles are extant, as the catalogues had done. He justifies the inclusion of this non-Buddhist text in the canon due to its value in clarifying the viewpoints of the heterodox schools, which would help students articulate, by contrast, the correct positions of Buddhism on religious issues.

69. *Ji shenzhou sanbao gantong lu* K. 1069 T. 2106 702b–715c
集神州三寶感通錄
The first *quan* of the Kaibao edition of this text is completely different from that found in the other two editions. Collating the texts, Sugi discovers that the Kaibao edition has wrongly placed the *Daoxuan lüshi gantong* [*lu*] 道宣律師感通錄 (K. 1070) as the first *quan* of this text. This mistake is corrected according to the Khitan and Koryŏ I editions, and the correct text of this *quan* is recorded in full.

70. *Bianzheng lun* K. 1076 T. 2110 715c–716a
辯正論
A long section in an interlinear note is missing in *quan* 7 of the Kaibao edition of this text. The passages appearing in the Koryŏ I and Khitan recensions differ slightly, but these are collated and the edited passage is recorded in full. See T.2110.52:538b43–c33 (*sic*) for the passage in question.

71. *Putichang suoshuo yizi dinglunwang jing* K. 1290 T. 950 716a–720c
菩提場所說一字頂輪王經
Bodhimaṇḍanirdeśaikākṣaroṣṇiṣacakravartirāja-sūtra
K. 1290 is the Koryŏ I edition; Sugi did not have access to the Kaibao edition. In the first *quan* of the Koryŏ I edition there is a long passage in which three sections are transposed. These have been rearranged according to the Khitan recension and the edited passage recorded in full. For the passage in question, see T.950.19:194b17–197b10.

72. *Foshuo muhuan jing* 佛說木槵經	*shu* 孰 case	NA	721a

The Kaibao and Koryŏ I canons include in their *shu/suk* 孰 case a text entitled *Foshuo muhuan jing,* as translated by Amoghavajra. Sugi collates this against a text that appeared earlier in the *kyŏng* 竟 case, the *Muhuanzi jing* (木槵子經; K. 862) by an anonymous translator, included in the *Dongjin lu* (317–420 C.E.), and discovered that the two texts were identical. The phraseology of the text demonstrated that it was a translation of the Han-Jin 漢晉 period and correctly belonged in the *kyŏng* case. He therefore rejects the sūtra's placement in the *suk* case, and refers the reader to the earlier text.

73. *Genben shuoyiqie youbu pinaiye posengshi* 根本說一切有部毗奈耶破僧事 *Mūlasārvastivādavinaya-saṃghabhedakavastu*	K. 1390	T. 1450	721a–724a

An "earlier State edition" (*Kukchŏn pon*) and the Kaibao recension are missing two sections of 88 and 86 lines in the thirteenth *quan.* These are added according to a "later State edition" (*Kukho pon*) and the Khitan edition. For the passages, see T.1450.24:167a22–169b13.

74. *Foming jing* 佛名經	*hoe, han* 迴/漢 cases	NA	723c–724a

The *hoe* 迴 and *han* 漢 cases of the Koryŏ I canon included a *Foming jing* in 18 *quan.* Sugi discovers, however, that this text is identical to a text by the same title appearing later (K. 1404). He presumes that the difference in *quan* number led the Koryŏ I editors to assume, despite their similarities in content and wording, that these were independent texts, and he deletes it.

75. *Koryŏguk sinjo taejang kyojŏng pyŏllok* 高麗國新雕大藏校正別錄	K. 1402	NA	724a

In the Koryŏ I canon these cases had included an earlier scriptural catalogue, the *Yiqie jing yuanpin cilu* (*Ilch'e kyŏng wŏnp'um ch'arok* 一切經源品次錄) (*Sequential Listing of the Original Chapters of All the Scriptures*), in 30 *quan,* which had been compiled by the *śramaṇa* Congfan (Chongbŏm 從梵). (Given its placement, might this have been the table of contents of the Koryŏ I Canon? I have located no other references to this text or its compiler.) Because this catalogue was not relevant to the new Koryŏ compilation, Sugi deletes it, replacing it with his own *Collation Notes.*

76. *Foming jing* K. 1404 T. 441 724a–725a
佛名經

This text was dismissed as apocryphal in both KYL and the *Zhenyuan lu,* and was not allowed to be entered into the canon. In his own treatment of the text, Sugi first notes that the eighteen-*quan Foming jing* mentioned previously was excerpted from this text, with only minor differences. He notes again the KYL's disdain for this text and its rejection as one of the worst of spurious compositions. In the face of such strong evidence of the apocryphal nature of the text, Sugi wonders why the Koryŏ I editors would still have allowed it to be included in their canon, and in two different formats at that. He finally relents, however, and because of the text's popularity in Korea, he is willing to include the thirty-*quan* scripture in the canon but not the eighteen-*quan* recension.

Sugi corrects a few of the myriad textual problems that plague the scripture, especially its tendency to combine incorrectly two proper names into one. He lists only two such instances, however, lamenting that there are too many to record them all. Sugi's conclusion to this section indicates that a controversy must have raged among the editors of the canon as to whether or not to include this text. He is clearly disposed to remove it, but he and his associates must have been under considerable pressure to include the text in the canon in order to placate popular sentiment.

Acknowledgement: I am grateful to Ms. Sumi Lee, a doctoral student in Korean Buddhist Studies at the University of California, Los Angeles, for her assistance in preparing this chapter for publication.

Notes

1 See the summary in Paik Nak-choon (Paek Nakchun 白樂濬), "Tripiṭaka Koreana," *Transactions of the Korea Branch of the Royal Asiatic Society* 32 (1951): 67. Ikeuchi Hiroshi 池内宏 proposes a 1087 completion date for the Koryŏ I canon in "Kōraichō no daizōkyō" 高麗朝の大藏經 ("The Canon of the Koryŏ Dynasty"), *Tōyō gakuhō* 東洋學報 13 (1923): 331. Paik notes, however, that the year of completion is unknown.

2 Tsumaki Naoyoshi 妻木直良, "Kittan ni okeru daizōkyō chōzō no jijitsu o ronzu" 契丹に於ける大藏經彫造の事實を論ず ("Proof of a Carving of a Canon during the Khitan Liao Dynasty"), *Tōyō gakuhō* 東洋學報 2 (1912): 318–322; Ikeuchi Hiroshi, "Kōraichō no daizōkyō" 高麗朝の大藏經 ("The Canon of the Koryŏ Dynasty"), *Tōyō gakuhō* 東洋學報 14 (1924): 96.

3 Lewis R. Lancaster with Sung-bae Park, *The Korean Buddhist Canon: A Descriptive Catalogue* (Berkeley and Los Angeles: University of California Press, 1979). A. Charles Muller of Tokyo University has prepared a complete

digital version of this catalogue: www.acmuller.net/descriptive_catalogue/; accessed March 14, 2013.

4 This is a revised and expanded version of an earlier article, "Sugi's Collation Notes to the Koryŏ Buddhist Canon and Their Significance for Buddhist Textual Criticism," *The Journal of Korean Studies* 9/1 (Fall 2004): 129–184. I am grateful to *The Journal of Korean Studies* for permission to adapt the article here.

5 For Haeinsa's 海印寺 associations with the Koryŏ II canon, see Paik, "Tripiṭaka Koreana," p. 71. See also my article "Haein-sa: The Monastery of the Dharma Jewel," *Korean Culture* 10/1 (Spring 1989): 12–21.

6 For Sekino's reports, see Lancaster and Park, *The Korean Buddhist Canon,* p. xvi.

7 The Koryŏ canons are the subjects of an extensive secondary literature. Early work on the canon was done by Tsumaki in "Kittan ni okeru daizōkyō chōzō," in which he used the evidence of the Koryŏ II canon to prove the existence of a Khitan edition of the canon. Ikeuchi, in "Kōraichō no daizōkyō," made an extensive survey of the textual sources and historical background of the Koryŏ II canon; for other related articles by Ikeuchi, see the bibliography in Lancaster and Park, *The Korean Buddhist Canon,* p. 722. This Japanese scholarship was the basis for the account of these canons appearing in Paul Demiéville, "Sur les éditions imprimées du canon Chinois" ("On the Printed Editions of the Chinese Canon"), *Bulletin de l'École Française d'Extrême-Orient* 24 (1924): 190–207. Accessible summaries of these canons can be found in Paik, "Tripiṭaka Koreana," pp. 62–73; Daizōkai 大藏會, eds. *Daizōkyo: seiritsu to hensen* 大藏經: 成立と變遷 ("The Canon: Formation and Development") (Kyoto: Hyakkaen, 1964), pp. 36–394; Ahn Kai-hyon (An Kyehyŏn 安啓賢), "Publication of Buddhist Scriptures in the Koryŏ Period," in Chun Shin-yong (Ch'un Sinyŏng), ed., *Buddhist Culture in Korea* (Seoul: International Cultural Foundation, 1974), pp. 81–95. Catalogues of the Koryŏ II canon have been published by Yi Sŏn'gŭn 李瑄根, ed., *Koryŏ taejanggyŏng,* vol. 48: *ch'ongmongnok, haeje, saegin* 高麗大藏經: 總目錄·解題·索引 (*Catalogue to the Tripiṭaka Koreana*) (Seoul: Tongguk University Press, 1976); and Lancaster and Park, *The Korean Buddhist Canon.* For a comprehensive study of the Koryŏ canon, see Kim Yun'gon 金潤坤, *Koryŏ Taejanggyŏng ŭi saeroun ihae* 고려대장경의 새로운 이해 (*A New Understanding of the Koryŏ Taejanggyŏng* 高麗大藏經) (Seoul: Pulgyo Sidaesa, 2002).

8 Sugi's work appears in the *chun* 俊, *ye* 乂, and *mil* 密 cases of the xylographs of the Koryŏ canon. It has been reprinted in Yi Sŏn'gŭn, ed., *Koryŏ taejanggyŏng* 高麗大藏經 (Seoul: Tongguk University Press, 1976), vol. 38, pp. 512–725; it appears as K. 1402 in the reprint. There is also a digitized version available at kb.sutra.re.kr; the Hanmun passages translated here are taken from that edition. The text was also included in the *Pinqie dazangjing* 頻伽大藏經 (*The Pinqie Hermitage Edition of the Buddhist Canon*) (Shanghai: Pinqie Qingshe, 1909–1914), case *jie* 結, vols. 397–398, nos. 9–10. The Pinqie edition has the advantage of being a modern, typeset edition that includes punctuation.

9 See Pae Sanghyŏn, "'Koryŏguk Sinjo' taejang kyojŏng pyŏllok kwa Sugi" ("The *Collation Notes* and Sugi,") *Minjok munhwa nonch'ong* 17/1 (1997): 64–65.

I am grateful to Ms. Kim Sujung of Columbia University for bringing this information to my attention.

10 Its alternate title is *Sok P'ahan chip* 續破閑集 (*Continuation to Overcoming Idleness Collection*); cited in Tsumaki, "Kittan ni okeru daizōkyō chōzō," p. 320.

11 Quoted in Ikeuchi, "Kōraichō no daizōkyō" (1924), pp. 98–99.

12 None of these earlier canons have survived in their entirety, though substantial fragments have been discovered. The Kaibao canon is often called the Shu 蜀 edition, after the Szechwan 四川 region where it was carved. Following modern Chinese practice, however, I use the reign period during which the canon was published to distinguish it from the other Song canons. Sugi generally refers to this canon as the "Old Song edition" (*ku Songbon*); that usage should be distinguished from the "Old Song edition" mentioned in the Taishō collation notes, which apparently refers to another Song canon, the twelfth century Chongning 崇寧 canon (see Daizōkai, eds., *Daizōkyo*, pp. 43–46). Copies of the Song canon were sent to Koryŏ in 989, 991, 1019, and 1098–1100 and it served as the basis for the first Koryŏ carving. See the chart in Kim Sanggi 金庠基, "Songdae e issŏsŏ ŭi Koryŏbon ŭi yut'ong e taehayŏ" 宋代에 있어서의 高麗本의 流通에 對하여 ("The Transmission of Koryŏ Books in the Song Period"), *Asea yŏn'gu* 亞細亞研究 8/2 (1965): 273–274; see also the discussion in Ikeuchi, "Kōraichō no daizōkyō" (1923), pp. 311–319. Carrington Goodrich, in "Earliest Printed Editions of the Canon" *Visva-Bharati Quarterly* 19/3 (Winter 1953–1954): 3, gives only 991 and 1019.

For references to the Kaibao edition, see Demiéville, "Sur les éditions imprimées du canon Chinois," pp. 181–184; Kenneth K. S. Ch'en, "Notes on the Song and Yüan Canon," *Harvard Journal of Asiatic Studies* 14 (1951): 208–209, summarizing the work of Lo Zhenyu; Goodrich, "Earliest Printed Editions," pp. 2–3; Daizōkai, eds., *Daizōkyō*, pp. 29–33; Dao'an, *Zhongguo dazangjing fanyi keyin shi* 中國大藏經翻譯刻印史 ("A History of the Translation and Publication of the Chinese Canon") (Taipei: Lushan Chubanshe, 1978), pp. 28–29.

The Khitan canon is discussed in Kamio Ichiharu 神尾壹春, *Kittan bukkyō bunkashikō* 契丹佛教文化史考 (*Studies on the History of Khitan Buddhist Culture*) (Tokyo: Daiichi Shobō, 1982, reprint), pp. 78–97; its influence on the Koryŏ II canon is treated on pp. 136–151. Until recently, only one fragment of the Khitan canon was known to exist in Japan; twelve *quan* of the xylographs of this canon have now been discovered in Shanxi 山西 province, for which see the reports in Zhang Changgeng 張暢耕, "Shanxi Yingxian Foguan si mutanei faxian Liaodai zhengui wenwu" 山西應縣佛官寺木塔內發現遼代珍貴文物 ("The Precious Object from the Liao Period Discovered inside a Wooden Stūpa at Foguan Monastery in Yingxian, Shanxi"), *Wenwu* 文物 6 (1982): 1–8; Yan Wenru 閻文儒, Fu Zhenlun 傅振倫, and Zheng Enhuai 鄭恩淮, "Shanxi Yingxian Foguansi Shiqie ta faxian de Qidan zang he Liaodai kejing" 山西應縣佛官寺釋迦塔發現的「契丹藏」和遼代刻經 ("The Khitan Canon Discovered in the Śākyamuni Stūpa at Foguan Monastery in Yingxian, Shanxi, and the Carving of Scriptures during the Liao Period"), *Wenwu* 文物 6 (1982): 9–18.

For general background on East Asian Buddhist canons and their value for Buddhist studies, see Paul Pelliot, *Les débuts de l'imprimerie en Chine* (*The Debut of Printing in China), Oeuvres posthumes de Paul Pelliot* (Paris: Librairie d'Amérique et d'Orient, 1953), vol. 4, pp. 121–138; Kenneth K. S. Ch'en, *Buddhism in China: A Historical Survey* (Princeton, NJ: Princeton University Press, 1964), pp. 374–378; see also the extensive bibliography of works on the canons, pp. 538–539; Lewis R. Lancaster, "Buddhist Literature: Its Canons, Scribes, and Editors," in Wendy Doniger O'Flaherty, ed., *The Critical Study of Sacred Texts* (Berkeley: Graduate Theological Union, 1979), pp. 220–227, and "The Editing of Buddhist Texts," in Leslie Kawamura and Keith Scott, eds., *Buddhist Thought and Asian Civilization* (Berkeley: Dharma Press, 1977), pp. 146–150; Mizuno Kōgen 水野弘元, *Buddhist Sutras: Origin, Development, Transmission* (Tokyo: Kōsei Publishing Co., 1982), pp. 171–186.

13 There was doubt about the existence of the Khitan canon until Tsumaki's pioneering research in "Kittan ni okeru daizōkyō," which conclusively proved its authenticity; Tsumaki's work was the basis for the discussion of this canon in Demiéville, "Sur les éditions imprimées du canon Chinois," pp. 207–212. Sugi's work was also consulted by such earlier scholars as Tsumaki, "Kittan ni okeru daizōkyō," pp. 320, 333; Ikeuchi, "Kōraichō no daizōkyō" (1924), pp. 109–114; Demiéville, "Sur les éditions imprimées du canon Chinois," pp. 196–197; and Kamio, *Kittan bukkyō bunkashikō*, pp. 139–149.

14 See Daizōkai, eds., *Daizōkyo*, p. 105.

15 Quotations from Sugi's *Collation Notes* that are appended to specific texts in the Taishō are noted in the Appendix, in the listings of the works treated by Sugi.

16 Tsukamoto Zenryū 塚本善隆 previously suggested that the Liao-period lithic carvings at Fangshan were based on the lost Khitan canon, and an examination of those carvings would assist in the reconstruction of the lost Khitan readings; see Tsukamoto Zenryū, "Sekkei-zan Unkyo-ji to sekkoku daizōkyō" 石經山雲居寺と石刻大藏經 ("Yunju Monastery on Shijing Mountain and the Lithic Canon"), *Tōhō gakuhō* 東方學報 5 (1935): 1–245. Indeed, a close perusal of the Fangshan rock carvings with the Koryŏ II/Taishō readings reveals a remarkable similarity between the two editions. Although the complete collection of the Fangshan rubbings has yet to be published, samples have been reproduced in Zhongguo Fojiao Xiehui 中國佛教協會, eds., *Fangshan Yunjusi shijing* 方山雲居寺石經 (*The Lithic Scriptures of Yunju Monastery on Fang Mountain*) (Beijing: Wenwu Chubanshe, 1978). As one example, a xylograph from the first *quan* of the *Xianjie jing* (K. 387, T. 425), a Liao-dynasty block carved in 1093, is reprinted as plate no. 54 in the collection of Fangshan rubbings. This corresponds to one page of the Taishō canon (T.425.14:3c29–4c27), or approximately 1,479 Sinographs. Sixty-one alternate readings are noted in the Taishō collation notes to these pages, an extremely large number. Of these sixty-one alternate readings, however, only sixteen are followed in the Liao Fangshan carving (which also introduces three other alternate readings not corroborated in any other canonical recension), leaving forty-five readings that are identical in the Koryŏ and Taishō edition and the Liao Fangshan recension. While much more research needs to be done on the relationship between the Liao dynasty Fangshan carvings and the Khitan state canon, and thence with the Koryŏ II canon, this particular xylograph provides at least

one telling indication of the close affinities that seem to exist between the three recensions. The Koryŏ II canon is comparable to the Fangshan carvings in providing one of the largest and most reliable stores of Khitan readings now extant.

17 There is some variation between the use of such terms as "page" (*chang* 張) and "scroll" (*p'ok* 幅) in Sugi's work. This difference is especially apparent if one compares the text of *Collation Notes* itself with the actual note appended to the text in question in the Koryŏ II and Taishō canons.

18 See Tsumaki, "Kittan ni okeru daizōkyō chōzō," pp. 335–337, for information on the different organizational schemes used for the early canons.

19 Lancaster and Park, *The Korean Buddhist Canon;* Yi Sŏn'gŭn, *Koryŏ taejanggyŏng.*

20 Noted in Lancaster and Park, *The Korean Buddhist Canon,* p. 452.

21 This catalogue is mentioned in the *Xu Zhenyuan Shijiao lu* 續貞元釋教錄 (T.2158. 55:1052c22) as being thirty *quan* and 600 pages in length; see the discussion in Ikeuchi, "Kōraichō no daizōkyō" (1924), pp. 115–116.

22 Michael Rogers uses this phrase in his article "*P'yŏnnyŏn t'ongnok:* The Foundation Legend of the Koryŏ State," *The Journal of Korean Studies* 4 (1982–1983): 44. See the outline in Lancaster and Park, *The Korean Buddhist Canon,* p. xi, summarizing the earlier research of Paik, "Tripiṭaka Koreana," pp. 65–66. Ikeuchi's revisionist attempt to deny the national protection aspect of the carving of Koryŏ I has been conclusively countered by Lancaster and Park, *The Korean Buddhist Canon,* p. xi.

23 The word is used by Lancaster and Park, *The Korean Buddhist Canon,* p. xiii.

24 See Goodrich, "Earliest Printed Editions," p. 4.

25 An extreme example of a scholar's attempt to posit the role of Buddhist piety in motivating the production of the canon is found in Cho Myŏnggi 趙明基, *Koryŏ Taegak kuksa wa Ch'ŏnt'ae sasang* 高麗大覺國師와 天台思想 (*State Preceptor Ŭich'ŏn of Koryŏ and Ch'ŏnt'ae Thought*) (Seoul: Tongguk Munhwasa, 1964), p. 79.

26 The concern shown by the canonical editors regarding scholarly accuracy should have wider implications concerning the cult of the book in East Asian Buddhism.

27 Ikeuchi, "Kōraichō no daizōkyō" (1924), p. 111.

28 See Ikeuchi, "Kōraichō no daizōkyō"(1923), pp. 327–331, for the views of Ono and Murakami, and his rebuttal.

29 Demiéville, "Sur les éditions imprimées du canon Chinois," pp. 196–197. Demiéville is mistaken earlier where he says that the "State edition" means the "later State edition" (p. 196); it much more plausibly refers to the "earlier State edition."

30 Ikeuchi, "Kōraichō no daizōkyō" (1924), pp. 111–112. Ikeuchi also attempts to use the collation note to *Daloutan jing* (K. 662) as evidence for his view that "State edition" was used by Sugi to designate a single-edition text (p. 113). To differentiate Koryŏ I from these single editions, Sugi called the latter *Kukho pon.* Ikeuchi's argument is not convincing. It seems just as plausible that in

this entry Sugi was referring to Koryŏ I, and the differences between it and the Kaibao/Khitan recensions could have been due to editorial changes introduced by the Koryŏ I editors; see the Appendix, K. 662.

31 See Tsumaki, "Kittan ni okeru daizōkyō," pp. 321–322; Paik, "Tripiṭaka Koreana," p. 67; Lancaster and Park, *The Korean Buddhist Canon*, pp. xiii–xv.

32 See Ōya Tokujō 大屋德城, *Kōrai zokuzō chōzō kō* 高麗續藏彫造攷 (*Studies on the Carving of the Supplementary Canon of Koryŏ*) (Kyoto: Benridō, 1937), vol. 1, p. 55 ff; Cho, *Koryŏ Taegak kuksa*, p. 82, proposes the period of 1091–1100 for the production of Ŭich'ŏn's *Supplement*. Only fragments are extant; representative examples have been published in Ōya's *Kōrai zokuzō chōzō kō*, a rare copy of which may be found in the collection of the East Asiatic Library, University of California, Berkeley. Many of the plates included by Ōya were photographs of works included in the library of Songgwangsa, in South Chŏlla 全羅南道 province. Unfortunately, this library along with much of the rest of the monastery was burned to the ground during the Yŏsu-Sunch'ŏn Rebellion in October 1948, and all of the texts were lost forever, rendering Ōya's work all the more valuable. According to Cho, the *Supplement* was bound in scroll style, and followed the unusual format of 20 Sinographs per line, 30 lines per page (*Koryŏ Taegak kuksa*, p. 87). However, there was in fact considerable variation, ranging from 15 Sinographs per line (see Ōya, *Kōrai zokuzō chōzō kō*, vol. 2, p. 76), to 17 Sinographs per line (vol. 2, p. 41), 19 Sinographs (vol. 2, pp. 15, 72, 74), 20 Sinographs (vol. 2, pp. 13–15), 21 Sinographs (vol. 3, p. 125), and 22 Sinographs per line (vol. 2, p. 18).

33 This unusual feature of the canon was first noticed by Lewis Lancaster, to whom I am indebted for bringing it to my attention.

34 The *Zongjing lu* 宗鏡錄 (K. 1499) is 17 Sinographs per line; the *Chodang chip* (Ch. *Zutang ji*) 祖堂集 (K. 1503) is 18 Sinographs per line; the *Kŭmgang sammaegyŏng non* 金剛三昧經論 (K. 1501) is 20 Sinographs per line; the *Pŏpkyedo ki ch'ongsurok* 法界圖記叢髓錄 (K. 1502) varies from 20 to 24 Sinographs per line; the *Dazang yilan ji* 大藏一覽集 (K. 1504) and the *Sŏnmun yŏmsong chip* 禪門拈頌集 (K. 1505) are 21 Sinographs per line; the *Huayan jing tanxuan ji* 華嚴經探玄記 (K. 1513) is 18 Sinographs per line.

35 *Huayan jing helun* appears at Ōya, *Kōrai zokuzō chōzō kō*, vol. 2, pp. 43–48. The format of texts in the *Supplement* range from 15 Sinographs per line (vol. 2, p. 76), to 17 Sinographs per line (p. 41), 19 Sinographs (pp. 72, 74), 20 Sinographs (p. 16), 21 Sinographs (vol. 3, p. 125), and 22 Sinographs per line (vol. 2, p. 27, p. 18 ff.)

36 Quoted in Tsumaki, "Kittan ni okeru daizōkyō," p. 332; Tsumaki refers to Ch'ungji by his sobriquet Miram 密庵; see also Ikeuchi, "Kōraichō no daizōkyō" (1924), p. 114.

37 See Lewis R. Lancaster, "The Movement of Buddhist Texts from India to China and the Construction of the Chinese Buddhist Canon," in *Collection of Essays 1993: Buddhism across Boundaries—Chinese Buddhism and the Western Regions* (Sanchung, Taiwan: Fo Guang Shan Foundation for Buddhist and Cultural Education, 1999), pp. 517–544, especially pp. 540–542. Professor Fang

Guangchang's research notes that the term *dazangjing/taejanggyŏng* appears in the Dunhuang 敦煌 manuscripts Stein 3565, Pelliot 2987, and Pelliot 3846, all of which date from between 750 and 845. According to Professor Fang, Stein 3565 and Pelliot 2987 were composed between 750 and 845, and Pelliot 3846 likely appeared just after 845. See Fang Guangchang 方廣锠, *Zhongguo xieben dazang jing yanjiu* 中國寫本大藏經研究 (*Study on Copied Forms of the Chinese Buddhist Canon*) (Shanghai: Shanghai Guji Chubanshe, 2006), pp. 4–5. I am indebted to Professor Darui Long 龍達瑞 of the University of the West for this reference.

38 Sugi himself only covers up through K. 1404, while the case numbers end at K. 1498; there are 1,514 texts listed in the Koryŏ catalogues, with eighty-five supplementary works; see Lancaster and Park, *The Korean Buddhist Canon*, and Yi Sŏn'gŏn, *Koryŏ taejanggyŏng*.

39 Cf. Tsumaki, "Kittan ni okeru daizōkyō," p. 333; Demiéville, "Sur les éditions imprimées du canon Chinois," pp. 196–197; these two give slightly different figures.

40 The *Shi Moheyan lun*, as well as other scriptures, was added into the canon for the first time in the Khitan edition; see the discussion in Tsumaki, "Kittan ni okeru daizōkyō," pp. 326, 333–334.

41 Fei Changfang's penchant for entering false translator attributions into the *Lidai sanbao ji* has been discussed in Hayashiya Tomojirō 林屋友次郎, *Kyōroku kenkyū* 經錄研究 (*Studies on Scriptural Catalogues*) (Tokyo: Iwanami Shoten, 1941), pp. 62–65; cf. pp. 151–152, where Hayashiya calls attention to the uselessness of Fei's references for ascertaining textual origins. See also Kyoko Tokuno, "The Evaluation of Indigenous Scriptures in Chinese Buddhist Bibliographical Catalogues," in Robert E. Buswell, Jr., ed., *Chinese Buddhist Apocrypha* (Honolulu: University of Hawai'i Press, 1990), pp. 43–47.

42 *Kaiyuan Shijiao lu*, T.2154.55:587a23.

43 The Taishō editors repeated the mistake and included this text, following a later Song edition with collation notes drawn from the Yuan and Ming editions, in their canon.

44 I have been unable to trace Zhiyuan's *Jingang bore houxu* (*Postscript to the Vajracchedikā*).

45 The correct number is actually 7,225. Even if it were 14 Sinographs per line, 17 pages would only total 55,950 Sinographs.

46 For some reason, this *Liuzu shenzhou jing* is still included in the Koryŏ II canon in the *chae* case, and has not been deleted.

47 Sugi alludes here to an infamous story appearing in the *Mūlasarvāstivāda-vinaya-Kṣudrakavastu*, where a stubborn reciter has mistaken the term *udaya-vyaya* ("arising and ceasing") for *udakavayas* ("water bird" or "water egret," *suhak* 水鶴 in Chinese translation; cf. T.1451.24:408c–409a). Rather than reciting the verse correctly as "if a man were to live for a hundred years and not comprehend arising and ceasing . . . ," he instead gave it as "if a man were to live for a hundred years and not see a white water egret. . . ." Despite Ānanda's

attempts to correct him, the monk and his teacher refused to accept Ānanda's rendition and Ānanda, in despair, decided that he might as well go ahead into *parinirvāṇa.* See the discussion in John Brough, *The Gāndhārī Dharmapada* (London: Oxford University Press, 1962), pp. 45–48. I am grateful to Jan Nattier for first bringing this story to my attention.

48 A. E. Housman, "The Application of Thought to Textual Criticism," in J. Diggle and F. R. D. Goodyear, eds., *The Classical Papers of A. E. Housman* (Cambridge: Cambridge University Press, 1972), vol. 3, p. 1069.

49 These canons of textual criticism are cogently summarized in Edward Hobbs, "An Introduction to Methods of Textual Criticism," in Wendy Doniger O'Flaherty, ed., *The Critical Study of Sacred Texts* (Berkeley: Graduate Theological Union, 1979), pp. 16–26.

References

Ahn Kai-hyon (An Kyehyŏn 安啓賢). "Publication of Buddhist Scriptures in the Koryŏ Period," in Chun Shin-yong (Ch'un Sinyŏng), ed., *Buddhist Culture in Korea,* pp. 81–95. Korean Culture Series, vol. 3. Seoul: International Cultural Foundation, 1974.

Brough, John. *The Gāndhārī Dharmapada.* London Oriental Series, vol. 7. London: Oxford University Press, 1962.

Buswell, Robert E., Jr. "Haein-sa: The Monastery of the Dharma Jewel," *Korean Culture* 10/1 (Spring 1989): 12–21.

—. "Sugi's Collation Notes to the Koryŏ Buddhist Canon and Their Significance for Buddhist Textual Criticism," *The Journal of Korean Studies* 9/1 (Fall 2004): 129–184.

—. "Tripiṭaka Koreana," in Ainslie T. Embree, ed., *Encyclopedia of Asian History,* s.v. New York: Charles Scribner's Sons, 1988.

Ch'en, Kenneth K. S. *Buddhism in China: A Historical Survey.* Princeton, NJ: Princeton University Press, 1964.

—. "Notes on the Song and Yüan Canon," *Harvard Journal of Asiatic Studies* 14 (1951): 208–214.

Chikusha Masaaki 竺沙雅章. "Kittan daizōkyō shōkō" 契丹大藏經小考 ("A Brief Study of the Khitan Canon"), in *Toyōshi ronshū, Uchida Ginpū hakushi shōju kinen* 内田吟風博士頌壽記念: 東洋史論集 (*Essays on Oriental History, Uchida Ginpū Festschrift*), pp. 311–329. Kyoto: Dōhōsha, 1978.

Ch'oe Cha 崔滋 (1188–1260). *Pohan chip* 補閑集 (*Supplementing Idleness Collection*), in Yi Ch'unhŭi 李春熙, ed., *Koryŏ myŏnghyŏn chip* 高麗名賢集 (*Collection of Famous Writers of Koryŏ*), vol. 2, pp. 105–147. Seoul: Taedong Munhwa Yŏn'guwŏn, 1973.

Cho Myŏnggi 趙明基. *Koryŏ Taegak kuksa wa Ch'ŏnt'ae sasang* 高麗大覺國師와 天台思想 (*State Preceptor Ŭich'ŏn of Koryŏ and Ch'ŏnt'ae Thought*). Seoul: Tongguk Munhwasa, 1964.

Daizōkai 大藏會, eds. *Daizōkyō: seiritsu to hensen* 大藏經: 成立と變遷 (*The Canon: Formation and Development*). Kyoto: Hyakkaen, 1964.

Dao'an 道安. *Zhongguo dazangjing fanyi keyin shi* 中國大藏經翻譯刻印史 (*A History of the Translation and Publication of the Chinese Canon*). Taipei: Lushan Chubanshe, 1978.

Demiéville, Paul. "Notes additionnelles sur les éditions imprimées du canon bouddhique" ("Supplementary Notes on the Printed Editions of the Buddhist Canon"), in Paul Pelliot, *Les débuts de l'imprimerie en Chine* (*The Debut of Printing in China*), *Oeuvres posthumes de Paul Pelliot*, vol. 4, pp. 121–138. Paris: Librairie d'Amérique et d'Orient, 1953.

—. "Sur les éditions imprimées du canon Chinois" ("On the Printed Editions of the Chinese Canon"), *Bulletin de l'École Française d'Extrême-Orient* 24 (1924): 181–218.

Eda Toshio 江田俊雄. "Richō kankyō tokan to sono kankō butten" 李朝刊經都監と其の刊行佛典 ("The Office of Scriptural Publication During the Yi Dynasty and its Publication of Buddhist Texts"), in Eda Toshio, *Chōsen bukkyōshi no kenkyū* 朝鮮佛教史の研究 (*Studies in Korean Buddhist History*), pp. 293–319. Tokyo: Kokusho Kankōkai, 1977.

Fang Guangchang 方廣锠. *Zhongguo xieben dazang jing yanjiu* 中國寫本大藏經研究 (*Study on Copied Forms of the Chinese Buddhist Canon*). Shanghai: Shanghai Guji Chubanshe, 2006.

Goodrich, Carrington. "Earliest Printed Editions of the Canon," *Visva-Bharati Quarterly* 19/3 (Winter 1953–1954): 1–6.

Hayashiya Tomojirō 林屋友次郎. *Kyōroku kenkyū* 經錄研究 (*Studies on Scriptural Catalogues*). Tokyo: Iwanami Shoten, 1941.

Hobbs, Edward. "An Introduction to Methods of Textual Criticism," in Wendy Doniger O'Flaherty, ed., *The Critical Study of Sacred Texts*, pp. 1–27. Berkeley Religious Studies Series 2. Berkeley: Graduate Theological Union, 1979.

Housman, A. E. "The Application of Thought to Textual Criticism," in J. Diggle and F. R. D. Goodyear, eds., *The Classical Papers of A. E. Housman*, vol. 3, pp. 1058–1069. Cambridge: Cambridge University Press, 1972.

Ikeuchi Hiroshi 池內宏. "Kōraichō no daizōkyō" 高麗朝の大藏經 ("The Canon of the Koryŏ Dynasty"), *Tōyō gakuhō* 東洋學報 13 (1923): 307–362.

—. "Kōraichō no daizōkyō" 高麗朝の大藏經 ("The Canon of the Koryŏ Dynasty"), *Tōyō gakuhō* 東洋學報 14 (1924): 91–130.

Kamio Ichiharu 神尾壹春. *Kittan bukkyō bunkashikō* 契丹佛教文化史考 (*Studies on the History of Khitan Buddhist Culture*). (1937). Tokyo: Daiichi Shobō, 1982, reprint.

Kim Sanggi 金庠基. "Songdae e issŏsŏ ŭi Koryŏbon ŭi yut'ong e taehayŏ" 宋代에 있어서의 高麗本의 流通에 對하여 ("The Transmission of Koryŏ Books in the Song Period"), *Asea yŏn'gu* 亞細亞研究 8/2 (1965): 273–279.

Kim Yun'gon 金潤坤. *Koryŏ Taejanggyŏng ŭi saeroun ihae* 고려대장경의 새로운 이해 (*A New Understanding of the Koryŏ Taejanggyŏng* 高麗大藏經). Seoul: Pulgyosidaesa, 2002.

Koryŏ taejanggyŏng 高麗大藏經 (*Tripiṭaka Koreana*). Seoul: Tongguk University Press, 1976.

Lancaster, Lewis R. "Buddhist Literature: Its Canons, Scribes, and Editors," in Wendy Doniger O'Flaherty, ed., *The Critical Study of Sacred Texts*, pp. 215–229. Berkeley Religious Studies Series 2. Berkeley: Graduate Theological Union, 1979.

—. "Comparison of the Two Carvings of the Korean Buddhist Canon," *Korea Journal* 23/8 (August 1983): 34–39.

—. "The Editing of Buddhist Texts," in Leslie Kawamura and Keith Scott, eds., *Buddhist Thought and Asian Civilization*, pp. 145–151. Berkeley: Dharma Press, 1977.

—. "The Movement of Buddhist Texts from India to China and the Construction of the Chinese Buddhist Canon," in *Collection of Essays 1993: Buddhism across Boundaries—Chinese Buddhism and the Western Regions*, pp. 517–544. Sanchung, Taiwan: Fo Guang Shan Foundation for Buddhist and Cultural Education, 1999.

Lancaster, Lewis R., with Sung-bae Park. *The Korean Buddhist Canon: A Descriptive Catalogue*. Berkeley and Los Angeles: University of California Press, 1979.

Li Jung-hsi. "The Stone Scriptures of Fang-shan," *Eastern Buddhist* 12 (1979): 104–113.

Mair, Victor H. "Review of *The Korean Buddhist Canon: A Descriptive Catalogue*, by Lewis R. Lancaster," *Journal of the American Oriental Society* 103 (1983): 468–469.

Mizuno Kōgen 水野弘元. *Buddhist Sutras: Origin, Development, Transmission*. Tokyo: Kōsei Publishing Co., 1982.

Ōya Tokujō 大屋德城. *Kōrai zokuzō chōzō kō* 高麗續藏彫造攷 (*Studies on the Carving of the Supplementary Canon of Koryŏ*). Kyoto: Benridō, 1937.

Pae Sanghyŏn 裵象鉉. "Koryŏguk Sinjo taejang kyojŏng pyŏllok kwa Sugi" 高麗國新雕大藏校正別錄과 守其 ("The Collation Notes and Sugi"), *Minjok munhwa nonch'ong* 17/1 (1997): 57–83.

Paik Nak-choon (Paek Nakchun 白樂濬). "Tripiṭaka Koreana," *Transactions of the Korea Branch of the Royal Asiatic Society* 32 (1951): 62–73.

Pelliot, Paul. *Les débuts de l'imprimerie en Chine* (*The Debut of Printing in China*), in *Oeuvres posthumes de Paul Pelliot*, vol. 4. Paris: Librairie d'Amérique et d'Orient, 1953.

Pinqie dazangjing 頻伽大藏經 (*The Pinqie Hermitage Edition of the Buddhist Canon*). Shanghai: Pinqie Qingshe, 1909–1914.

Rogers, Michael C. "*P'yŏnnyŏn t'ongnok:* The Foundation Legend of the Koryŏ State," *The Journal of Korean Studies* 4 (1982–1983): 3–72.

Tokuno, Kyoko. "The Evaluation of Indigenous Scriptures in Chinese Buddhist Bibliographical Catalogues," in Robert E. Buswell, Jr., ed., *Chinese Buddhist Apocrypha*, pp. 31–74. Honolulu: University of Hawai'i Press, 1990.

Tsukamoto Zenryū 塚本善隆. "Sekkei-zan Unkyo-ji to sekkoku daizōkyō" 石經山雲居寺と石刻大藏經 ("Yunju Monastery on Shijing Mountain and the Lithic Canon"), *Tōhō gakuhō* 東方學報 5 (1935): 1–245.

Tsumaki Naoyoshi 妻木直良. "Kittan ni okeru daizōkyō chōzō no jijitsu o ronzu" 契丹に於ける大藏經彫造の事實を論ず ("Proof of a Carving of a Canon in the Khitan Liao Dynasty"), *Tōyō gakuhō* 東洋學報 2 (1912): 317–340.

Yang, T'ae-jin. "About the Tripiṭaka Koreana," *Korea Journal* 12/5 (1972): 43–48.

Yan Wenru 閻文儒, Fu Zhenlun 傅振倫, and Zheng Enhuai 鄭恩淮. "Shanxi Yingxian Foguansi Shiqie ta faxian de Qidan zang he Liaodai kejing" 山西應縣佛官寺釋迦塔發現的「契丹藏」和遼代刻經 ("The Khitan Canon Discovered in the Śākyamuni Stūpa at Foguan Monastery in Yingxian, Shanxi, and the Carving of Scriptures during the Liao Period"), *Wenwu* 文物 6 (1982): 9–18.

Yi Sŏn'gŭn 李瑄根, ed. *Koryŏ taejanggyŏng*, vol. 48: *ch'ongmongnok, haeje, saegin* 高麗大藏經: 總目錄·解題·索引 (*Catalogue to the Tripiṭaka Koreana*). Seoul: Tongguk University Press, 1976.

Zhang Changgeng 張暢耕. "Shanxi Yingxian Foguan si mutanei faxian Liaodai zhengui wenwu" 山西應縣佛官寺木塔內發現遼代珍貴文物 ("The Precious Object from the Liao Period Discovered inside a Wooden Stūpa at Foguan Monastery in Yingxian, Shanxi"), *Wenwu* 文物 6 (1982): 1–8.

Zhongguo Fojiao Xiehui 中國佛教協會, eds. *Fangshan Yunjusi shijing* 方山雲居寺石經 (*The Lithic Scriptures of Yunju Monastery on Fang Mountain*). Beijing: Wenwu Chubanshe, 1978.

Studies in *Dhāraṇī* Literature III: Seeking the Parameters of a *Dhāraṇī-piṭaka*, the Formation of the *Dhāraṇīsaṃgrahas*, and the Place of the Seven Buddhas

Ronald M. Davidson
Fairfield University

Lew Lancaster continually prodded his graduate students to investigate questions of canon, scripture, and related issues. I hope this *gurudakṣiṇā* is sufficient to repay his enthusiasm for these notoriously intractable problems.

In previous studies of *dhāraṇī* literature, I have attempted to wrestle with the questions of the semantic value of the term *dhāraṇī* and the historical pragmatics of actual *dhāraṇī* texts.[1] There is much more to be said on the linguistic issues, but these must be temporarily held in abeyance, for I now wish to look briefly at some of the questions around claims concerning a canon of *dhāraṇī* texts. In Buddhist studies literature, this has sometimes been referenced with the term *"Dhāraṇī-piṭaka,"* indicating a basket of texts containing coded phrases, said to have the power and performance of the entire Buddhist canon. At first glance, it might appear that this term is simply an extension of the placement of Buddhist documents in baskets in the ostensible manner of the other *piṭaka*s. Following this line of reasoning, the *Dhāraṇī-piṭaka* might be accepted as a newer one of these, analogous to the Abhidharma-*piṭaka* or the Bodhisattva-*piṭaka*. However, it should be evident that such claims are not uncomplicated, and tend to evaporate once light is cast on them. In part this is because the reality of the other *piṭaka*s in India is almost as conceptual as it is physical, and in part because the nomenclature for this new *piṭaka* was neither standardized nor well attested in our surviving documents.

This essay will argue that the *Dhāraṇī-piṭaka* was even more of an ideological chimera than previous *piṭaka*s, and that the very few notices we actually have suggest an image of an inexhaustible reservoir of coded phrases, one that served as a conceptual category for the production of new scriptures, and that theoretically could be accessed by advanced meditators. The indistinct parameters of this *piṭaka* appear in some measure a reflection of actual *dhāraṇī* collections, the various compendia generally known by the designation *Dhāraṇīsaṃgraha;* these collections preceded *Dhāraṇī-piṭaka* statements and seem to have provided a prototype for the new *piṭaka.* The early *Dhāraṇīsaṃgraha* in turn featured the collected spells of the seven buddhas, a fusion of early Buddhist ideas of lineage with the emerging *dhāraṇī* practices. Arguably, the most important version of the *dhāraṇīs* of the seven buddhas is delineated within the recensions of the *Saptabuddhaka,* a *dhāraṇī* text on the seven buddhas that was well attested from the sixth to the eighth centuries. Even after this, some form of text on the seven buddhas—however understood—was often included in *dhāraṇī* collections.

The *Piṭaka* Problem

It has been evident for some time that the several baskets of the Buddhist "canon" are not without problems of authority and authenticity, not the least being that their parameters were by no means fixed.[2] In all of the literature of Indian Buddhism we have no list of titles that would be recognizable as a Buddhist canon. Thus, Buddhist canons cannot be understood with the Semitic religions' use of Ptolemy's term *kanōn* to mean a closed, finite list of items, modeled to some degree on the star catalogue included in Ptolemy's *Almagest.* While there are thematic and functional similarities between the canons of the Semitic religions and those of Indian Buddhism—whether satisfying the sense of a sacred text that is revealed or utilizing a body of critical and exegetical literature to validate or invalidate the employment of specific texts—it cannot be said that Indian Buddhists absolutely closed their canon in the manner observable in the Fifth Theravāda Council under King Mingdon in 1871, when the Pāli Canon as recognized in Burma was literally inscribed on 729 slabs. This act constructed a hard boundary around the Tipiṭaka in a manner that cannot be located in India at any period of Buddhist history.

New scriptures thus consistently proposed themselves as the word of the Buddha (*buddhavacana*), but at the same time they were challenged to find a place in the preexistent taxonomies of the Tripiṭaka. In the case of *dhāraṇīs,* neither the well-known nine-branch nor the twelve-branch taxonomies of the word of the Buddha allow for the idea of a canon of incomprehensible coded messages, let alone their function as apotropaic or therapeutic spells. The fourth-century *Abhidharmasamuccaya*, written about the time when the production of *dhāraṇī* scripture was gaining momentum, defines the twelve-branch system in the following manner:[3]

1. *Sūtra* is that which is a prose text expressed [by the Buddha] through a method of [indirectly] expressing the intended goal (*yad abhipretārthaṃ sūcanākāreṇa gadyabhāṣitam*).

2. *Geya* is that which will be sung through verse at the middle or at the conclusion of the sūtras. Alternatively, it may constitute some implicative point (*neyartha*) that is expanded (*sūtrāṇāṃ madhye vā ante vā gāthayā yad gīyate / sūtreṣu anirūpito 'rtho vā yad vyākhāyate*).

3. *Vyākaraṇa* indicates the different prophecies given to the advanced noble disciples in the past about their different births and attainments in various places. Or it may mean the further expansion of a (definitive, *nītārtha*) point expressed in the sūtras, since there is the expansion of a meaning intended to be revealed (*tat sthāneṣu samatikrāntānām atītānām āryaśrāvakāṇāṃ prāptyutpattiprabhedavyākaraṇam / api ca sūtreṣu nirūptārthasya sphuṭīkaraṇam / vivṛtyābhisandhivyākaraṇāt*).

4. *Gāthā* is demonstrated in the sūtras by association with verse feet—either two, three, four, five, or six verse feet (*sūtreṣu pādayogena deśyate / dvipadī tripadī catuṣpadī paṃcapadī ṣaṭpadī vā*).

5. *Udāna* is that pronounced sometimes in the sūtras by the Tathāgata with joy (*sūtreṣu kadācit tathāgatena āttamanaskena yad udāhṛtam*).

6. *Nidāna* is that which [the Buddha] expressed because of an inquiry, or for setting forth some rule and its reason (*pṛṣṭena yad bhāṣitam / sotpattikaṃ śikṣāprajñaptikaṃ vā*).

7. *Avadāna* is that expressed [by the Buddha] in the sūtras with an example (*sūtreṣu sadṛṣṭāntakaṃ bhāṣitam*).

8. *Itivṛttaka* is that which teaches the previous worldly behavior of the noble disciples (*yad āryaśrāvakāṇāṃ pūrvalaukikaṃ vṛttaṃ deśayati*).

9. *Jātaka* is that which teaches the behavior associated with the canonical basket of the bodhisattva's activity (*yad bodhisattvacaritapiṭakasaṃprayuktaṃ vṛttaṃ deśayati*).

10. *Vaipulya* is that associated with the Bodhisattva-*piṭaka* (*bodhisattvapiṭakasaṃprayuktaṃ bhāṣitam*), because it is the establishment of the welfare and benefit of all beings and because it is the pronouncement of the sublime and deep Dharma (*sarvasattvānāṃ hitasukhādhiṣṭhānataḥ udāragambhīradharmadeśanātaś ca*). *Vaipulya* is also called *Vaidalya* because it splits apart all the veils (*sarvāvaraṇavidalanataḥ*); it is also called *Vaitulya* because it is without any equivalent among comparable teachings (*upamānadharmāṇāṃ tulanābhāvataḥ*).

11. *Adbhutadharma* is the demonstration of extraordinarily miraculous and wonderful teachings [in the behavior] of the *śrāvaka*s, bodhisattvas, and tathāgatas (*yatra śrāvakabodhisattvatathāgatānāṃ paramādbhutāścarya-dharmāṇāṃ deśanā*).

12. *Upadeśa* is the incontrovertible exegesis of the characteristics of all the deep and subtle phenomena (*śrāvakabodhisattvatathāgatānām aviparītaṃ vyākhyānam*).

These and the other definitions of the categories of scripture are most often promoted without any actual titles identified within the categories, and it may be argued that the *Jātaka* exhibits the closest correspondence between a specific document and its textual category. Even then, it is clear that most Buddhist scriptures could confidently be included in these taxons, but that is not the case for *dhāraṇī*s or similar spell-based ritual manuals. None of the standards of scriptural authenticity—they must be passed down through the Sūtra, reflected in the Vinaya, and not contradict reality (*sūtre 'vataranti vinaye saṃdṛśyante dharmatāñ ca na vilomayanti*)—can be easily applied to the *dhāraṇī* texts, especially as they contain nonlinguistic codings, the *mantra-dhāraṇī*s.[4]

The consequence is that the *dhāraṇī* practices initially seem to have floated around as textual orphans, outside the legitimate category of the word of the Buddha but with a compelling purpose in their own right. Little wonder that we so often see what amounts to freestanding *dhāraṇī* texts bundled with the authentically *vaipulya* materials of the Mahāyāna sūtras, as in the case of the *Karuṇāpuṇḍarīka*, the *Saddharmapuṇḍarīka*, and the *Suvarṇabhāsottama*, to mention but a few obvious examples. These appear to be attempts by the Mahāyāna authors to include *dhāraṇī*s in texts that are closer to the Mahāyāna norm, gaining legitimacy in the process. When we understand that the *dhāraṇī* chapter of the *Karuṇāpuṇḍarīka* was transmitted in a separate recension as the *Sarvajñātākāra-dhāraṇī*, and see rituals to Śrī and Sārasvatī transmitted outside the *Suvarṇabhāsottama*, then the association of *dhāraṇī*s with their *vaipulya* texts appears a bit more adventitious.[5]

Yet *dhāraṇī*s clearly fulfilled needs—whether expressed, implied, or inchoate—identified or felt by Indian monks, and the practices appear in some measure to be predicated on the models of domestic rituals found in caste India. Many domestic rituals were overseen by brahmans and so may be authentically called brahmanical by that right, but many more were found on the margins of brahmanical rites. Indeed, the porosity between the much larger ritual environment found in villages, among non-caste or *śūdra* Indians, tribal peoples, or other sources may be measured by the continual formation of mantras in the *gṛhya* ritual lineages. Sometimes these were captured in freestanding compendia—such as the *Mantra-brāhmaṇa* of the *Gobhila* and the *Kauthuma-śākhā*s of the *Sāmaveda*, or the *Mantrapāṭha* of the *Āpastamba-śākhā* of the *Kṛṣṇa Yājurveda*—or they were simply included and employed in the *gṛhya* sūtras of the many branches, especially notable in the *Yajurveda* traditions.[6]

The idea that somehow the mantras of the orthodox tradition were unchanging or without modification is an ideological position based in the theological structure of Brahmanism. This is actually contradicted by the texts themselves, which sometimes describe the manner in which new mantras are to be produced to include new gods in the domestic rituals, especially in cases of marriage or betrothal.[7]

As spells and coded texts became increasingly central to Buddhist identity, the idea of another basket to the canon becomes intermittently articulated—a *Dhāraṇī-piṭaka* or *Vidyā-piṭaka*. This was undoubtedly facilitated by the Mahāyāna presentation of its own Bodhisattva-*piṭaka*, a term that sometimes indicates individual texts, sometimes denotes the collective body of Mahāyāna scriptures, and sometimes identifies a separate section of the canon; the latter usage is occasionally associated with *dhāraṇī*s.[8] There are, however, many difficulties with the question of a "spell basket," beginning with the paucity of early sources (those that exist are mostly in Chinese), the diffuse nature of the scholarly propositions to date, and the inherent difficulties of the Indian evidence.

Early on, certainly, we find the idea of a *dhāraṇī* treasury (*dhāraṇī-nidhāna*) in the *Lalitavistara*, but this appears to mean a metaphysical potential for the realization of *dhāraṇī*s, one of eight treasuries obtained by a person who writes, memorizes, and propagates the *Lalitavistara*.[9] This may have been analogous to the use of *dhāraṇī-mukh*a (method of *dhāraṇī*s) as both a method and an attainment in the scriptures. The earliest mention of mantras in a section of the canon that I have been able to trace comes in a somewhat confusing mention in Saṅghavarman's 435 C.E. translation of the *Sarvāstivādavinaya-mātṛkā:*

> 復有如來四境界. 謂智境界. 法境界. 人境界. 神足境界. 此四境界中如來制戒. 謂智法人神足境界如是制毘尼. 制波羅提木叉. 修多羅. 阿毘曇. 呪術究竟. 毘尼集. 毘尼發露罪. (T.1441.23:608b2–6)

> Moreover, here are the four domains (**viṣaya*) of the Tathāgata, which are the domains of insight, of Dharma, of persons, and of miraculous powers (*ṛddhipāda*). With reference to these four domains, the Tathāgata institutes discipline. That is to say, insight, Dharma, persons, and miraculous powers

institute the Vinaya, institute the *Prātimokṣa,* the Sūtra, the Abhidharma, the conclusion of mantras (? **mantra-niṣṭhā*), the *Vinayasaṃgraha,* the Vinaya confession . . . (a lengthy list of other monastic texts follows).

The embedding of language about the conclusion of (or perhaps certainty about) mantras (*zhòushù jiūjīng,* 咒術究竟) in a list of canonical or paracanonical textual materials is intriguing, but it reveals very little of what is meant, especially since this may be the only appearance of this term in the available archive.

Statements attributed by Jízàng (吉藏; 549–623 C.E.) and later commentators to Paramārtha's (active ca. 545–569 C.E.) missing commentary to Vasumitra's well-known work on the origin of the Indian Buddhist sects are a bit clearer. Jízàng and others indicate that Paramārtha's comment on the development of the Dharmagupta order included a discussion of their canon in five baskets: beginning with the standard Sūtra, Vinaya, and Abhidharma, but continuing with a fourth basket of mantras (Mantra-*piṭaka; zhòuzàng,* 咒藏) and a fifth, the Bodhisattva-*piṭaka.*[10] While there is little reason to doubt that Paramārtha understood such a system to be in place in his time, there is equally little reason to believe that this was much earlier than the sixth century.

Certainly, in several places the Dhamaguptakas discussed the use of mantras in their Vinaya, but none of the versions of Vasumitra's text declare them to have a Mantra-*piṭaka,* and Bhavya's seventh-century treatise on the various understandings of the early schools leave out canonical groupings as well.[11] In this case, the intrusion of a *Bodhisattva-piṭaka* may reflect the Mahāyānization of that school somewhere, possibly Gandhāra, the Dharmaguptakas' zone of greatest early strength. The discovery of Gāndhārī versions of the *Aṣṭasahasrikā* and other texts reveals Gandhāra having a robust Mahāyāna at an early period.[12]

Elsewhere in the late sixth century, we increasingly find allusions to one or more separate spell baskets, reflecting the changing circumstances of the Nikāyas and the Mahāyāna in India. Both Candrakīrti and Bhavya (writing ca. 550–600 C.E.) refer to a *Sorcerers' Basket* (*Vidyādhara-piṭaka*), in the former case as a member of a Mahāyānized seven-basket system (it also includes a Bodhisattva-*piṭaka*) attributed to the Pūrvaśaila-Aparaśaila Nikāyas, and in the latter case identified as a component of the Mahāsāṃghika canon.[13] A notice focused on the Mahāsāṃghikas in Xuánzàng's 646 C.E. record of his travels includes a legend of an alternative recital by the Mahāsāṃghikas, since non-arhats were not included by Mahākāśyapa at Rājagṛha. In this note, the Mahāsāṃghika recitation was of a canon in five baskets; the fourth basket was a **Kṣudraka-piṭaka* (or **Saṃyukta-piṭaka; zájízàng,* 雜集藏), and the fifth was a Mantra-*piṭaka* (*jìnzhòuzàng,* 禁咒藏).[14] Reference to a Mahāyānist five-basket system occurs in a note found in Prajñā's 788 C.E. translation of the **Mahāyāna-naya-ṣaṭpāramitā-sūtra* (*Dàshèng lǐqū liùbōluómìduōjīng,* 大乘理趣六波羅蜜多經), which indicates much the same arrangement. Here, the fourth basket includes the Perfection of Insight scriptures and in the fifth basket the *dhāraṇī* entrance (*dhāraṇīmukha; tuóluóníмén,* 陀羅尼門); the former was collected and recited by Mañjuśrī, the latter by Vajrapāṇi.[15]

Shortly after the compilation of Xuánzàng's travel notes, the great compendium of Atikūṭa, the *Dhāraṇīsaṃgraha,* was put together in China and presented to the throne in 654 C.E. The introduction to this text, probably written by the monk who served as the scribe, Xuánkāi (玄揩), affirms that "This scripture comes from the *Vajramahāmaṇḍala-sūtra,* which is a small fraction of part of the *Mahāvidyā-piṭaka*" (此經出金剛大道場經. 大明呪藏分之少分也; T.901.18:785b–3). At the beginning of the eighth century the hermeneutical issue is raised in a entry by Yìjìng, describing the studies of another Chinese monk, Dàolín, in India. He said that Dàolín listened carefully to a Mantra-*piṭaka,* and that after founding an individual temple in Lāṭa (around the Nāramadā delta in Western India), he engaged seriously in the practice of spells (*vidyā*).[16] However, Yìjìng, in an explanatory note, writes that this phrase means that Dàolín had tried to teach the *Vidyādhara-piṭaka,* the *Sorcerers' Basket.*[17] Evidently, Yìjìng understood these to be synonymous, and goes on to specify that the compendium constituted about a 100,000 verses in Sanskrit, which would be approximately 300 rolls if translated into Chinese. Similar claims are made for another spell basket at the end of the *Cuṇḍīdevī-dhāraṇī,* translated by Divākara in 685 C.E., which says that it was abstracted from a *Mahāvidyā-piṭaka* (*dàmíngzhòuzàng,* 大明咒藏) of 60,000 verses.[18] From this time on, there are several allusions to a *Sorcerers' Basket* (*Vidyādhara-piṭaka*), as well as continuing mentions of Mantra-*piṭaka*s or *Vidyā-piṭaka*s, occasionally specifying the number of verses in the compendium, though the force of this specificity is diminished by an absence of agreement.[19]

As Yìjìng's record suggests, the passage from Mantra-*piṭaka* to *Dhāraṇī-piṭaka* to *Vidyā-piṭaka* to *Vidyādhara-piṭaka* was taken in relatively easy strides, but was there ever any actual referent to the designation? Despite Divākara's having given a value of 60,000 verses to a *Vidyā-piṭaka* and Yìjìng's attribution of 100,000 verses to a *Vidyādhara-piṭaka,* do we have any confidence that any spell collection of this size ever existed as a material item? The answer is: Probably not, at least not as a specific group of works that had specific titles or content and was limited to that material. Indian Buddhists have consistently resisted closure of the canon, and all of our canonical lists have been made outside of India, first by the Chinese, then by the Tibetans and others. Indians created elastic categories of scriptures—long, middle-length, short, enumerated, collected, scattered, extended, verse, and so forth, as we have seen. The *Sorcerers' Basket* was similarly conceptual, taking its place in the company of a number of other elastic rubrics. As such, the *Sorcerers' Basket* became an inexhaustible wish-granting gem of unlimited new scriptures, since new scriptures can be revealed in words, letters, atoms of the universe, or they can unfold in the minds of monks as the teachings of buddhas past.

When we turn from such spotty notices of a *Dhāraṇī-nidhāna* or a *Vidyā-piṭaka* to actual texts, we quickly run into the corollary of the ideology of a *piṭaka:* what are spell texts to be called, and in which *aṅga* or *piṭaka* do they belong? Texts sometimes termed *dhāraṇī* are otherwise called mantra, *hṛdaya,* or *vidyā.* More often, however, we find elaborate *dhāraṇī* or *vidyā* chapters in normative Mahāyāna sūtras already mentioned. Other texts, such as the *Ratnaketu-dhāraṇī,* may otherwise be understood to be chapters in a larger compendium, and so designated as the *Ratnaketu-parivarta.* Indeed, it appears to me that the majority of actual mantra-*dhāraṇī*s up to the sixth century were included as chapters or sections (*dhāraṇī-parivarta*) in texts that identify themselves solely or primarily as sūtras. Consequently, it is unclear to which taxonomic category these texts belong, a circumstance acknowledged as a problem by Dalton and van Schaik in their Dunhuang catalogue of *dhāraṇī*s and tantras, and which bedevils attempts at differentiating one category of scripture from the other.[20]

One way to gain insight into this seemingly intractable historical and taxonomic question is to examine actual texts or groups of texts that appear to be intentional aggregates of such *dhāraṇī*s to see if these might be of some assistance. That is, when we turn from the ideology of *dhāraṇī*s to the textual compendia that both represent their collective presence in Buddhist communities and actually have been employed, we may gain insight into the conceptual structures that promoted the affirmation of a *Dhāraṇī-piṭaka* in the first place. Often titled something like *Dhāraṇī-saṃgraha,* there are many such works, although they are quite diverse in both size and organization. Grounding our understanding of the nature of the mythic *Dhāraṇī-piṭaka* in the content of actual *Dhāraṇīsaṃgraha*s seems all the more cogent when we realize that the surviving compendia appeared long before any citation of a *Dhāraṇī*- or Mantra-*piṭaka*. The surviving *Dhāraṇīsaṃgrahas* thus have some claim to precedence and appear in some sense to have served as physical prototypes for the mythic *Dhāraṇī-piṭaka*.

Even though available *Dhāraṇīsaṃgrahas* have their own problems of boundary classification, making them almost as difficult to define as other canonical quandaries, they do offer some guidance in both their implicit ideology of *dhāraṇī* aggregation and the menu of *dhāraṇīs* actually aggregated. As in the case of some other Buddhist scriptural genres (Abhidharma, Vinaya), the *Dhāraṇīsaṃgrahas* may either contain elements abstracted from freestanding *dhāraṇī* scriptures to be compiled into documents of greater or lesser bulk, or they may bundle whole recensions of such texts together with different organizations and priorities. In the first instance, most often it is the bare-bones mantra-*dhāraṇīs* that are abstracted, so that in some texts (e.g., *Dhāraṇīsaṃgraha*, T. 901) we find lists of useful spells. Conversely, in case of the whole-text aggregation, there are grand compendia of *dhāraṇī* scriptures, each with their individual title, body, and conclusion, that are sometimes no different from their discrete appearance outside of a *dhāraṇī* collection, as if they were simply copied on the same material as other *dhāraṇīs* and bundled together for convenience.

Unfortunately, what we do not find in India is an individual text that articulates an index of *Dhāraṇīsaṃgraha* organization or a reason for the compilation; such works, like the canonical catalogues, are found outside of India.[21] The lack of definitive boundaries and the drift from one textual bundle to another—with the resulting questions of intention and meaning—frustrate the study of *dhāraṇī* compendia. So the *Mahāmāyūrī-vidyārājñī* aggregates previous *vidyā* and *dhāraṇī* materials into a compendium, even while its core narrative is also found bundled at the end of the *Bhaiṣajyavastu* of the Mūlasarvāstivāda vinaya, probably because it was involved in healing. Later, two versions of the *Mahāmāyūrī* will be bundled together toward the end of the Bower manuscript. Thus the boundaries between practices, coded phrases, texts, and textual bundles are very fluid, a point that is evident the more one looks into *dhāraṇī* materials.

Cult of the Seven Buddhas

This is not to suggest that *dhāraṇī* collections lack central foci. Indeed, one rather important thread in many, perhaps most, of these *dhāraṇī* collections is the lore of the seven buddhas as a collective group: Vipaśyin,

Śikhin, Viśvabhū, Krakucchanda, Kanakamuni, Kāśyapa, and Śākyamuni (in their Sanskritized names). This cult is an extremely important part of Indian Buddhist practice that has received relatively little investigation; most notices appear as subsets of other questions—as indeed this essay is but another example.[22] Yet there are few more important and well-attested specific cults in the history of Indian Buddhism. The cult of the seven buddhas is certainly on a par with some of the early arhat cults, and it seems to me that the later popularity of cult of the eight bodhisattvas is closely related to it and may even have been modeled on it. We will first briefly examine the earlier seven buddhas materials and then trace the extension of this practice into a fully developed *dhāraṇī* system.

As a group, the seven buddhas were certainly cobbled together from different sources, and it appears that the three names before Śākyamuni (Krakucchanda, Kanakamuni, and Kāśyapa) were figures identified with places in the early Buddhist zone, a fact already recognized by Alois Füher, George Bühler, Jean Philippe Vogel, and Jan Nattier. As is well known, one of Aśoka's minor pillar inscriptions, at Niglīvā near Lumbini, mentions the emperor enlarging or refurbishing the stūpa of Buddha Konākamana, presumably one of the variations on the name by which Kanakamuni was denoted.[23] The records of Făxiăn and Xuánzàng have led Füher and Alexander Cunningham to identify one specific mound with the *nirvāṇa-stūpa* of Krakucchanda, near Kapilavastu in the village of Goṭihvā in the Nepalese Terai, and another mound with the *nirvāṇa-stūpa* of Kāśyapa, near Śrāvastī in the village of Tandwā in Uttar Pradesh.[24]

It is doubtful, however, whether the mythic predecessors of the Buddha were initially understood to form a group, whether of four (as is sometimes inferred), seven, or twenty-four (as in the Pāli *Buddhavaṃsa*), let alone that they belong to the thousand buddhas of the *bhadrakalpa*.[25] Instead, the identification of mounds as the final resting place of a great sage/hero of uncertain origin was and is common enough, so I would presume these were inferred to be the predecessors of the Buddha at some early time. Führer notes that "The Buddhist origin of these ruins is quite forgotten, as the remains are ascribed by the villagers to Lori, the great *Ābhīra* or *Ahīr* hero."[26] Indeed, in modern India, the cult of the *bīr-bābā* is localized in a mound sometimes said to be his final resting place (*samādhi*), and it is probable that some cult sites of this more ancient form were appropriated by Buddhists for the purpose of legitimizing Śākyamuni's mythic antecedents.[27]

The earliest physical evidence for something like the seven buddhas as a group is from Bharhut (east of Jabalpur, Madhya Pradesh), where there are medallions representing all but the second buddha, Śikhin, carved on pillars that support the great railing that establishes the circumambulatory path of the Bharhut stūpa. Each of the buddhas identified are illustrated not as an icon but by their species of *bodhi* tree, according to the artist's understanding. Each is also given an inscription in late second-century Brahmi; for example, *bhagavato vipasino bodhi,* "the *bodhi* tree of Vipaśyin."[28] Cunningham indicates that the pillars had approximately 1'10½" (about 57 cm.) width available for the carving surface, so the medallions are not insignificant.[29] The arrangement he describes is quite curious, however, since the images were not collected in a group, as is seen in all other representations of the seven buddhas. As might be expected, Śākyamuni was given a position of prominence on the face of the entry gateway to the southern direction. However, the other five surviving medallions were scattered around in no particular order. Vipaśyin was located somewhere in the northwest quadrant, Viśvabhū in the southeast, Krakucchanda in the northwest, Kanakamuni in the southeast, and Kāśyapa in the southwest, and there was no buddha figure in the northeast. The pillars are extremely heavy so it is unlikely that they had been moved from their original location.

The oddness of the Bharhut arrangement is immediately evident when we observe that the other groupings most often exhibit the seven buddhas lined up together. Seldom do we find individuals from that set arranged in such isolated environments, with the exception of Śākyamuni and arguably Kāśyapa, Śākyamuni's immediate mythic predecessor and a figure who enjoyed something of an autonomous cult of his own.[30] In the Bharhut case, there are at least three possible explanations for the disconnection between the several buddhas. First, the seven buddhas may not have yet been codified as a group and so several previous buddhas were simply represented on their own; if this were the case, though, we might have expected to find different representations, perhaps Dīpaṃkara, another previous buddha of some importance. Second, it may be that at Bharhut we are not dealing with one grouping of the seven buddhas but several groupings, localized in the different directions; however, in the absence of any reduplicated figures, this is not a particularly compelling explanation. Third, perhaps a bit more plausible, the seven buddhas cult was relatively new and the medallions were placed after most of the railing pillars had already been carved, so that there were not seven pillars in a row still available to the artists when they were carved. The fact that Śākyamuni is carved on the gateway, which Mitra has argued is an addition to the railing made fifty years later,[31] would support a model that the other buddhas were added to available space on the railing. If this was the case, then we see an early moment in the emergence of a cultic system in the late second century B.C.E., and we may assume that Bharhut was in some proximity to the cult's origin.

What is certain is that by the end of the second century B.C.E. there was already in place some cultic awareness of the importance of the Buddha's predecessors, and that their representations were to be granted a place on the circumambulatory path. We have little sense that there is a standardized textual component as yet to this cult, and Bhagavānlāl Indraji has argued, followed by Heinrich Lüders,[32] that the Vipaśyin medallion does not depict the tree under which this buddha is said to have obtained his awakening (*pāṭali; bignonia suaveolens*) in the primary hagiography (*Mahāvadāna/Mahāpadāna*), but shows an *aśoka* tree (*saraca indica*) instead. As Indraji points out, the *aśoka* tree is associated with Vipaśyin in the *Mahāmāyūrī*, so there seems to be some relationship between the Bharhut medallion and the later text on *nāga* and *yakṣa* lore, a topic that is explored further below.

The dating of the next earliest representations, at Sāñchī, seems to confirm the early north-central India focus of the cult. At the top of the elevated gateways (*toraṇa*), the *nirvāṇa-stūpa*s of each of the seven buddhas are placed in proximity to the trees under which each buddha is said to have obtained awakening. The position of these at the gateways in the four directions would seem to validate their importance to their builders, and, as at Bharhut, these reliefs were certainly added after the initial construction of the stūpa. While it is difficult to claim that the importance of the seven buddhas would have been evident to visitors viewing the small reliefs from ground level, the same could be said of most of the other relief sculptures on the gateway, leading us to assume that there was a group of interpreters for pilgrims to the site. As in most instances of seven buddha representations, the buddhas' stūpas and trees are not labeled per se, requiring inferences on which belongs to whom.[33]

If the sculptors of neither Bharhut nor Sāñchī represented the seven buddhas in their iconic forms for ideological reasons (as is now generally accepted), then by the third or fourth centuries such reticence had been seemingly swept aside. There are representations of the seven buddhas in Gandhāra, Swat, Mathurā, Amaravati, in Ellora cave 12, and in the

Kanheri caves 2 and 3, to mention only the more important sites and areas.[34] Perhaps most noteworthy are the representations and inscriptions to all or part of the seven buddhas at Ajanta, in caves 10, 17, and 22. The refurbishment and subsequent additions to cave 10, which Walter Spink places in the "period of disruption" between 478 and 480,[35] includes an image of a standing buddha identified as "Vipaśvī," evidently a local spelling of Vipaśyin also attested in cave 22. In cave 17 there is an interesting seven buddha painting directly above a somewhat smaller panel with amorous (*maithuna*) figures, but it lacks a recorded inscription. Both the paintings and the inscription in cave 22 include an identification of the seven buddhas by name.[36] Most of these and other representations seen from the third century on feature the group of seven buddhas followed by Maitreya, the next buddha.[37] Consequently, there is a sense of continuity, where the past pattern of the Buddha's activity is reconstituted within the future pattern.

Figural representations of the seven buddhas continue on throughout the period of Buddhist activity in India, but one group is of particular interest. Around the seventh to eighth centuries a stūpa seems to have undergone repair in Sopārā, with the consequence that new relics were added to the relic chamber at that time.[38] In April 29, 1882, an archaeological team led by Bhagavānlāl Indraji opened the relic chamber, where they found a circular stone casket, 24 inches in diameter and 17½ inches high. Inside was a copper casket, which contained four more caskets of silver, stone, crystal, and gold, decreasing in size and embedded one in another. Eight images were nestled between the interior walls of the large stone casket and the copper reliquary; they depicted the seven buddhas and Maitreya, facing outward, with Vipaśyin in the northwest, then in regular order clockwise, ending with Maitreya facing west. The images are of copper; Maitreya is the largest at 5 inches, the others are approximately 3½ inches tall. While the relics inside the interior caskets are presumably older, it is believed that these images were added at the time of a repair or renovation of the stūpa.

What is so remarkable is not that there should be small copper images of the seven buddhas and Maitreya, but that they were placed in a *maṇḍala* pattern in the interior of a stūpa, as part of a relic deposit. From a relatively early period, buddha figures were represented on the outer faces of stūpas and relics were installed within images as well as within stūpas. But in first-century Gandhāra the Bīmarān casket appears to signal that images could be part of reliquaries, though examples of this are somewhat rare.[39] Whatever its background, the Sopārā reliquary signals both the sense of sacrality of the aggregate group of eight figures, and its acceptance as an essential relic of the tradition.

This sense of the essentialism of the pattern established by past buddhas is reinforced by the literary presentation of the seven buddhas' lives. The most important sources for the group are the recensions of the *Mahāvadāna-sūtra* and related scriptures in Pāli, Sanskrit, and Chinese, and these have been primarily subject to textual discussions rather than examining the seven buddhas' position in the larger epic structure.[40] In the *Mahāvadāna* text, the dominant thread is framed through Vipaśyin's narrative, with all the other buddhas understood to be subsequent iterations of that story. Only their details—the kind of *bodhi* trees associated with each, the length of their lives, their family designations, the durations of their Dharmas, etc.—differentiate them, as we see in the Bharhut and Sāñchī representations.

Outside of their aggregate status, one or another of the seven buddhas had a parallel existence in *Jātaka, Avadāna,* and Vinaya literature. Bhikkhu Anālayo's recent study of the path of the bodhisattva is a welcome divergence from a narrowly philological focus, and he explores the intersection of the Gautama and Kāśyapa narratives of the previous lives of the Buddha. He proposes that the literature reflects three stages in their encounter: first, "Gautama is simply identified with a young Brahmin who goes forth under the Buddha Kāśyapa"; second, "this meeting inspires the bodhisattva to take a vow to become a Buddha"; and third, "the bodhisattva's meeting with the Buddha Kāśyapa serves to reconfirm his impending Buddhahood through a prediction."[41]

If Kāśyapa is foregrounded in early Buddhist literature, he is by no means the only previous buddha given an independent narrative.[42] Not only are there other episodes featuring one of the other five buddhas, but other buddha figures such as Dīpaṃkara also find literary and artistic expression, part of a larger movement to the statements of aspiration and prediction that will be so fruitful.[43] Indeed, narratives of the buddhas other than Śākyamuni continue to develop in literary form as Śākyamuni's hagiography evolves; Étienne Lamotte opines that the Śākyamuni story took elements from the Vipaśyin myth, rather than vice versa.[44] Whatever the circumstances, it certainly appears that there was an interweaving of mythic elements between the present Buddha and past and future buddhas.

So, if these figures are so important to be represented through art, literature, and (as we shall see) ritual, the obvious question is: Why?

Why did the seven buddhas carry such great social and psychological weight as to require such extensive representation of their several stories? Different theories have been proposed, most of which revolve around the model that the seven buddhas epitomized the Buddhist response to the precedent of the seven *ṛṣi*s of Vedic literature or the twenty-four *tīrthaṅkara*s of the Jains.[45] The latter example has more resonance with the twenty-four buddhas of the *Buddhavaṃsa*, but since the last six of this grouping are the first six of the seven buddhas, it would appear that the earlier six buddhas plus Śākyamuni constitute the primary form.[46] Moreover, as Katherine Harper has so eloquently shown, any simple affirmation of seven as invariably leading to the *ṛṣi*s would seem to ignore the very fertile field of sets of sevens in early Indian religions, for example, seven rivers, seven mothers, seven sisters, seven stars, etc.[47]

I believe that the most potent objection to a simplistic imitative model, however, may be framed in a question I have discussed before, with reference to the later forms of the *siddha*s: Is the grouping important for lineage purposes or for the *siddha*s' simultaneous potency? In the case of the early use of the seven buddhas, the literature is clear that they are the predecessors; their simultaneous appearance occurs in *dhāraṇī* literature, long after their value has already been established. So it would seem that the presentation of a collective lineage of ancestral figures is the principal reason for their formulation, and I would further suggest that the line of the seven buddhas is patterned after the ideology of ancestral authority, associated with caste, as understood by early Buddhists.

Consequently, in brahmanical terms, the previous buddhas were understood primarily as metaphorical ancestors (*pitṛ*) rather than perceived as metaphorical scripture revealers (*ṛṣi*). In other words, they acted as predecessors whose model of activity is inherited over generations, rather than an aggregation of saints who revealed a specific body of scripture still employed. It is fair to say, however, that the difference between these two concepts is a bit muddied even in the brahmanical world by the claims of some families to descend from *ṛṣi*s; still, there is a consistent distinction between ancestor/clan (*pitṛ/gotra*) on the one hand and revealer/Vedic lineage (*ṛṣi/pravara*) on the other.

Overall, there are two indicators of the closeness of the seven buddhas with ancestral ideology: the understanding of caste genealogy found in the scriptures and the *Dharma-śāstra*s on the one hand, and the position of the *Prātimokṣa* in both the ideology of the seven buddhas and the statement of lineal representation in the *Mahāparinirvāṇa-sūtra* and the *Milinda-pañha* on the other. The primary evidence for the first of these, the Buddhist perception of caste genealogy, comes from a standard trope found in several early Buddhist scriptures, usually in the context of a dispute between the Buddha and different brahmans over their respective claims to superiority. In the *Vāseṭṭha-sutta*—found in both the *Suttanipāta* and the *Majjhima-nikāya*—the brahman Vāseṭṭha Bhāradvāja, when asked what constitutes a brahman, replies with his definition:

> *bhāradvājo māṇavo evam āha: yato kho bho ubhato sujāto hoti mātito ca pitito ca saṃsuddhagahaṇiko yāva sattamā pitāmahayugā akkhitto anupakkuṭṭho jātivādena ettāvatā kho brāhmaṇo hotīti* (*Suttanipāta*, p. 115)

Norman translates this:

> The young brahman Bhāradvāja replied: "When one is well-born on both the mother's and the father's side, and is of pure descent for seven generations, uncriticised and irreproachable with reference to birth, to such an extent one becomes a brahman."[48]

Virtually identical language is given in the *Soṇadaṇḍa-sutta* and the *Kūṭadaṇḍa-sutta* in the *Dīgha-nikāya*, and is found in the *Dīrghāgama* as well, but in the *Soṇadaṇḍa-sutta* the tables are turned. We are told that 500 brahmans visiting Campā espoused this same criterion as the validating source of brahmanical superiority, and used it to restrain Soṇadaṇḍa from visiting the Buddha. Soṇadaṇḍa retorts that if brahmans are pure through seven generations, then Gautama also comes from a family similarly pure through seven generations.[49] This standard of ancestral integrity is, to be sure, acknowledged as difficult to maintain. In the *Assalāyana-sutta* the Buddha relates a story about a *ṛṣi* named Asita Devala who refuted the brahmanical posturing of seven *ṛṣi*s by asking if brahmans knew for a fact that their grandmothers or grandfathers back to the seventh generation had only had sexual congress with brahmans (MN II.156: *jānanti pana bhonto yā janīmātu mātā yāvā sattamā mātāmahayugā brāhmaṇaṃ yeva agamāsi no abrāhmaṇan ti. no hidaṃ bho . . . jānanti pana bhonto yo janīpitu pitā yāva sattamā pitāmahayugā brāhmaṇiṃ yeva agamāsi no abrāhmaṇin ti*), a claim clearly impossible to verify.

Moreover, such questions of lineage are extended to questions of lines of teachers in the early canon, so that the Buddha's challenge to brahmanical authority becomes extended to confidence in a lineage of understanding, not just of descent. In both the *Tevijja-sutta* and the *Subha-sutta* brahmans are questioned about whether their teachers for seven generations have either seen Brahma (*Tevijja-sutta*) or could say that they themselves have seen the result of their practices (*Subha-sutta*).[50] In most of these episodes of brahmanical claims to authenticity, the standard of seven generations is taken as the *sine qua non.*

While the Buddhist representation is not exactly the same as seen in the *Dharma-śāstras*, it is close enough to understand that both shared some common suppositions and a broad understanding of lineal relationships. Given that the seven buddha documents are not very early, the Buddhist socialization into Sanskritic legal and ritual standards would have facilitated a common basis for that understanding, especially as it was ritually reinforced in the quotidian instances of caste marriages and funerals. For their part, the *Dharma-śāstras* align the idea of seven generations with three basic concerns: ancestral descent, purity of lineage, and inheritance. The first is certainly reflected in the Buddhist sphere, and it is seen in such works as the *Mānava-dharma-śāstra* as well, which considers how to deal with questions of normative and forbidden marriage. In the case of normative marriage, a straightforward statement in the *Baudhāyana-dharma-sūtra* explains: "Common ancestry among those making common ritual offerings lasts until the seventh generation" (1.5.11.2: *sapiṇḍatā tv ā saptamāt sapiṇḍeṣu*). The *Viṣṇusmṛti* reinforces this limit: "Common ancestry ceases with the seventh generation" (Olivelle's translation; *Viṣṇusmṛti* 22.5: *sapiṇḍatā ca saptame puruṣe nirvartate*).[51]

As this and other similar rules make clear, this is about the all-important *sapiṇḍa* relationship, a technical term with two different interpretations. Vijñāneśvara's commentary to the *Yājñavalkyasmṛti* 2.135 understands the term "element" (*piṇḍa*) as a part of the person's physical body, inherited from the ancestors; marital prohibitions thus work to keep apart those with a shared, inherited physicality.[52] In distinction, Jīmūtavāhana perhaps more convincingly argues that *sapiṇḍa* indicates the commonality of ancestors up to the seventh generation to whom one makes offerings of a rice ball (*piṇḍa*).[53] Whatever its actual etymology, marriage within the *sapiṇḍa* relationship is prohibited, as seen in this rule by Nārada:

> *ā saptamāt pañcamād vā bandhubhyaḥ pitṛmātṛtāḥ /*
> *avivāhyāḥ sagotrāḥ syuḥ samānapravarās tathā* / / 12.7

> There should be no marriage to relatives within the seven generations on the father's side or five on the mother's, or within the same clan or Vedic lineage.

And yet the ancestral heritage may, in specific circumstances, serve to redefine the lineage of caste in some sense, particularly in the case of intercaste marriage. So the *Mānava-dharma-śāstra* allows that

śūdrāyāṃ brāhmaṇāj jātaḥ śreyasā cet prajāyate /
aśreyāñ chreyasīṃ jātiṃ gacchatyā saptamād yugāt // 10.64
śūdro brāhmaṇatām eti brāhmaṇaś caiti śūdratām /
kṣatriyāj jātam evaṃ tu vidyād vaiśyāt tathaiva ca // 10.65

> If an offspring of a Brahmin man from a Śūdra woman were to bear children from a superior partner, within seven generations the inferior attains the superior caste; a Śūdra thus attains the rank of a Brahmin, and so does a Brahmin the rank of a Śūdra—one should understand that this rule holds good also for offspring born from a Kṣatriya or a Vaiśya man.[54]

Similar rules are found in the *Gautama-dharma-sūtra* (4.22) and the *Yājñavalkyasmṛti* (1.96); consequently, it appears there was some consensus that familial purity can be gained by the seventh generation, and it is applied in cases of intercaste marriage. Finally, the question of inheritance is also tied to the *sapiṇḍa* relationship. As *Āpastambīya-dharma-sūtra* 2.6.14.3 explains, if there is no son, then the nearest *sapiṇḍa* is to inherit (*putrābhāve yaḥ pratyāsannaḥ sapiṇḍaḥ*).[55] Consequently, the process of inheritance is closely connected with an ideology of descent and offering to the ancestors up to the seventh generation.

The relationship between this model of lineal descent and the seven buddhas' mythology hinges on the peculiar position of the *Prātimokṣa* in the *Mahāvadāna* and related texts. In the hagiography of Vipaśyin—the paradigmatic hagiography related in these works—he gains awakening, decides to teach, instructs on the four truths, and sends the various monks and arhats out to preach. However, every six years the entire group of 84,000 monks are to return to Vipaśyin's home in Bandhumatī to recite the *Prātimokṣa* together. This is the only text that is so identified in the *Mahāvadāna* narrative. Why the *Prātimokṣa*? Because it was relatively clear to some early communities that they were held together by the ritual recitation and confession associated with that text; it was also the emblem of division between the various Vinaya lineages, so its centrality was unmistakable.

The importance of the *Prātimokṣa* is highlighted in the *Mahāparinirvāṇa-sūtra*, in which Ānanda requests that the Buddha appoint a successor so that the teaching will not languish without an appointed head. The Buddha's response is that "the teaching" will be the teacher, and by implication function as his successor. While the Pāli text simply indicates "the teaching" by a general designation of the *dhamma* and the *vinaya*, the Sanskrit version is explicit: the *Prātimokṣa* text, which had been taught by the Buddha every fortnight, was to be followed as the supreme teacher and preceptor (§41.2 *yo vo mayānvardhamāsaṃ p[r]ā[t]i-[mokṣa uddeśitaḥ sa vo 'dyāgr]eṇa śās[tā] sa ca v[o niḥsaraṇam]*).[56] Thus, the *Prātimokṣa* was viewed in some communities as the lineal successor of the Buddha and the basis of the dispensation.

The missing piece here is the attitude toward the *Prātimokṣa* held by at least some communities in North India. It is common to refer to this extremely important text as noncanonical, but this designation is based on the Pāli understanding of canon and should be reassessed. It clearly enjoyed pride of place in its Sanskrit composition, followed by its canonical status in the various Chinese translations and in the Tibetan ones as well. Even in some Pāli records the text has an authoritative voice, exemplified in the *Milinda-pañha* by the question given to Nāgasena about why the recitation of the *Prātimokṣa* is hidden (*paticchanna*) from the laity's witness of the rite.[57] Nāgasena's answer presents three reasons for such restrictions: it is the time-honored familial custom of all the previous buddhas, it is out of respect to the Dharma, and furthermore it is based on consideration of the monks' position.

The first rationale is the most interesting: Nāgasena indicates that the *Prātimokṣa* is in reality the proprietary speech of the Buddhist order, passed down through the authority of the Buddha's family (*vaṃsavasena*). Once the ritual boundary (*sīmā*) has been closed prior to the recitation of the rules, no one not already admitted by monastic membership should be included. He likens this peculiar form of ritual practice to the secret strategies of a dynasty (*khattiyamāyā*) that is their familial culture occluded to other *kṣatriya*s in the world. Likewise occluded to the world are the technical vocabulary, jargon, argot, and secret usages (*rahasya*) found among wrestlers, jugglers, dancers, athletes, augurs of the gods and goddesses of good and bad fortune, and others, whose family-based caste activities require proprietary vocabulary and initiates' significations for their peculiar needs.

The Vinaya in general, and the *Prātimokṣa* in particular, thus belongs to the family of the buddhas, to the monks and nuns who constitute the sons and daughters (*śākyaputra, śākyaduhitā*) of Śākyamuni. That this accords honor to the Dharma and the condition of the monk (*bhikṣubhūmi*) is of added benefit in the real-world requirement that clergy are accorded greater status than those who are not invested with both the authority and the responsibility for its maintenance. Nāgasena's assessment accords well with the position of the seven buddhas in the surviving non-Pāli *Prātimokṣa* texts. In almost every other surviving *bhikṣu* and *bhikṣuṇī*

Prātimokṣa, the position of the seven buddhas as the source of the text is made abundantly clear. This is done at the conclusion of the text, after the final *uddāna* summary of the several *Prātimokṣa* rule sections, where we find a series of verses attributed to the seven buddhas.[58] Presented here is a reconstructed form of the final verses of a Sarvāstivāda *Prātimokṣa,* based on the Kumārajīva Chinese translation and the surviving Sanskrit manuscripts.[59]

> *vipaśyī nāma bhagavān [tathāgataḥ saṃyaksambuddho dvāṣaṣṭaśatasahasrabhikṣuparivāra idam prātimokṣam adeśayat /]*
>
> Vipaśyin, the Lord, the Tathāgata, the complete Buddha, with a retinue of 6,200,000 monks taught this *Prātimokṣa:*
>
> > *kṣānti[ḥ] paramaṃ tapas titīkṣā nirvāṇam paramaṃ vadanti buddhā[ḥ] /*
> > *na hi pravrajita[ḥ pa]ropat[āp]ī śramaṇo bhavati parā[n] viheṭhayānaḥ / /*
> > (= *Udānavarga* 26.2)
> >
> > Patience, the highest ascesis, is forebearance. Buddhas have proclaimed nirvana (marked by patience) to be supreme.
> > It is not the case that a renunciant who harasses or bothers others may be considered [a real] ascetic.
>
> *Śikhī [nāma bhagavān tathāgataḥ saṃyaksambuddho 'ṣṭaśatasahasrabhikṣuparivāra idam prātimokṣam adeśayat /]*
>
> Śikhin, the Lord, the Tathāgata, the complete Buddha, with a retinue of 800,000 monks taught this *Prātimokṣa:*
>
> > *cakṣuṣmān viṣamānī[va] vidyamāne parākrame[t] /*
> > *paṇḍito jīvaloke 'smi[n] pāpāni [parivarjayet / /]*
> > (= *Udānavarga* 28.13)
> >
> > As a normal sighted person overcomes impediments before him
> > So the learned man would reject sins in this world of the living.
>
> *[Viśvabhūr nāma bhagavān tathāgataḥ saṃyaksambuddho śatasahasrabhikṣuparivāra idam] prātimokṣam adeśa[yat] /*
>
> Viśvabhū, the lord, the Tathāgata, the complete Buddha, with a retinue of 100,000 monks taught this *Prātimokṣa:*
>
> > *[nopavā]d[ī] nopaghātī prātimokṣe ca saṃvaraḥ /*
> > *mātrajñatā ca bhakteṣu prāntam ca śayanāsanam /*
> > *adhicitte samāyoga etad buddhasya ś[āsa]nam / /*
> > (= *Udānavarga* 31.50)[60]

In the *Prātimokṣa,* the discipline is that one neither accuses others nor assaults them,
But understanding restraint toward food, and having a secluded bed and sitting place,
Applying oneself to subtle intelligence—that is the dispensation of the Buddha!

[*Krakucchando nāma bhagavān tathāgataḥ saṃyaksambuddho catvāriṃśatsahasrabhikṣuparivāra idam prātimokṣam adeśayat* /]

Krakucchanda, the Lord, the Tathāgata, the complete Buddha, with a retinue of 40,000 monks taught this *Prātimokṣa:*

yath[*ā*]*pi bhramaraḥ puṣpād varṇagandhāv aheṭhayan* /
paraiti rasam ādāya tathā grāmāṃ muniś caret / /
na pareṣāṃ vilomāni na pareṣāṃ kṛtākṛtam /
ātmanas tu samīkṣeta samāni viṣamāni ca / /
(= *Udānavarga* 18.8–9)

As the honeybee takes nectar from a flower without harming either its color or fragrance,
So the sage wanders in villages and departs, having taken only the nectar.
Not rubbing others the wrong way, or [pointing out] something [they have] done or not done,
But he should examine himself, both his agreeable and disagreeable ways.

[*Kanakamunir nāmo bhagavān tathāgataḥ saṃyaksambuddho triṃśatsahasrabhikṣuparivāra idam prātimokṣam adeśayat* /]

Kanakamuni, the Lord, the Tathāgata, the complete Buddha, with a retinue of 30,000 monks taught this Prātimokṣa:

adhicet[*a*]*s*[*i*] *mā p*[*ra*]*madyata pratataṃ maunapadeṣu śikṣata* /
śokā na bhavanti tāyino hy apaśāntasya sadā smṛtātmanaḥ / /
(= *Udānavarga* 4.7)

Don't be indolent toward subtle learning, but continually train in the ascetic conditions.
There are no forms of distress for the well-pacified religious who is always self-recollected.

Kāśyapo [*nāmo bhagavān tathāgataḥ saṃyaksambuddho viṃśatisahasrabhikṣuparivāra idam prātimokṣam adeśayat* /]

Kāśyapa, the Lord, the Tathāgata, the complete Buddha, with a retinue of 20,000 monks taught this *Prātimokṣa:*

sarvapāpasākaraṇaṃ kuśalasyopasaṃpadaḥ /
sucittaparyavadanam etad buddhasya śāsanam //
(= *Udānavarga* 28.1)

Refraining from all sin, but accomplishing all benefit,
Purifying one's own mind—that is the dispensation of the Buddha.

Śākyasiṃho [nāmo bhagavān tathāgataḥ saṃyaksambuddho ardhatrayodaśaśata-bhikṣuparivāra idam prātimokṣam adeśayat /]

Śākyasiṃha, the Lord, the Tathāgata, the complete Buddha, with a retinue of 1,250 monks taught this *Prātimokṣa:*

kāyena saṃvaraḥ sādhu sādhu vācā ca saṃvaraḥ /
manasā saṃvaraḥ sādhu sādhu sarvatra saṃvaraḥ /
sarvatra saṃvṛto bhikṣu[ḥ] sarvaduḥkhāt pramucyate //
(= *Udānavarga* 7.11)

vācānurakṣī manasā susaṃvṛtaḥ
kāyena caivākuśalam na kuryāt /
etām śubhām karmapathām viśodhaya[nn]
ā[rādhay]en [mārga]m ṛṣipraveditam //
(= *Udānavarga* 7.12)

Discipline of body is excellent; excellent is discipline of speech.
Discipline of mind is excellent; excellent is discipline in all aspects.
Disciplined in all aspects, the monk is released from distress.

Protecting his speech, well disciplined in his mind,
He should not perform any unwholesomeness with his body.
Purifying the excellent karmic pathways;
He should propitiate the path attained by the sages.

[ākruṣṭena na pratyākroṣṭavyam /
roṣitena na pratiroṣitavyam /
bhaṇḍitena na pratibhaṇḍitavyam /
tāḍitena na pratitāḍitavyam //][61]

Abuse should not be returned with abuse.
Anger should not be returned with anger.
Quarreling should not be returned with quarreling.
Assault should not be returned with assault.

We can see that in the several recensions the verses are by and large in agreement, with minor differences. The fact that all but the last verse can be located in the Sanskrit *Udānavarga* is a reminder of the central position that the homilies of this text played in northern Buddhist communities, and the final verse is treated as a well-known statement in Sanskrit Buddhist literature. As a group, then, the seven buddhas are understood to be the sources of *Prātimokṣa* declarations that survive outside of the Pāli tradition, and the relative uniformity of the materials provides confidence that the seven buddhas were collectively seen to be the source of the *Prātimokṣa* itself long before they were seen to utter *dhāraṇīs*.

Charles S. Prebish argues that for the Mahāsāṃghika *Prātimokṣa,* the term "*Prātimokṣa*" in the framing statement to each of the concluding verses appears to denote the particular verse attributed to each of the buddhas rather than the entire *Prātimokṣa* text, so that each concluding verse would be that Buddha's *Prātimokṣa.*[62] In distinction, as he notes, in the case of the Mūlasarvāstivāda *Prātimokṣa* there is a summary verse implicating the entire text for all seven buddhas, and the verses are not each assigned to individual buddhas. Kumārajīva's text, similar to the Mahāsāṃghika *Prātimokṣa* in affirming individual verses to specific buddhas, seems to imply an analogous denotation to the term *Prātimokṣa* in the introductory attribution. But we then find the Mūlasarvāstivāda *Prātimokṣa*-related omnibus statement in Klaus T. Schmidt's Sanskrit Sarvāstivāda *Prātimokṣa* manuscripts:[63]

> *saptabhir lokanāyakair buddhavīrair mahātmabhiḥ /*
> *prātimokṣaḥ samuddiṣṭo nirdiṣṭaś ca maharṣiṇā / /*

> The *Prātimokṣa* has been conferred by the seven Leaders of the World,
> The Heroic Buddhas, the great beings, and also taught by the Great Ṛṣi [Śākyamuni].[64]

It would thus appear that the several *Prātimokṣa* texts, and even recensions, had somewhat different positions on this idea. Certainly the verse and its placement in the Tarim manuscripts of the Sarvāstivāda *Prātimokṣa* marks a position closer to the Mūlasarvāstivāda text in that regard, and both are explicit in affirming that each of the seven buddhas taught the whole *Prātimokṣa.*[65] Given the ambiguous sense of the other *Prātimokṣa* texts, as well as their Chinese translations, in some instances the concluding verses may have been understood to be the *Prātimokṣa* teaching of an individual buddha that somehow encapsulated the larger *Prātimokṣa.*

It would seem, then, that in various ways the nascent cult of the seven buddhas, as it began to take form, became associated with the ideology of ancestry, legacy, inheritance, paternity, family ritual, and filial piety. Each of the buddhas was born, had a lifetime, obtained awakening under a tree specific to each, turned the wheel of the Dharma in a common manner, and required their disciples to assemble for the recitation of the *Prātimokṣa* prior to their demise, to be interred in a specific stūpa. Outside of their individual episodes with disciples reincarnating through time, as a group the previous six buddhas served as models for the buddha of the present. They also stood as the paradigm for Maitreya, who quickly assumed an iconographical and representational, if not textual, alliance with the ideology of the seven buddhas, and Maitreya eventually assumes his position as the eighth figure at the end of the line of the seven buddhas. Such a direction eventually expanded, of course, with the twenty-four past buddhas in the *Buddhavaṃsa,* and eventually forward into the future through the literary agency of the thousand buddhas of the *bhadrakalpa.*

The Seven Buddhas and *Dhāraṇī* Literature

There is much more to be said for the various permutations of the seven buddha cultus in both Indian Buddhism and normative Mahāyāna, but for now we may turn to a distinctive branch of seven buddha lore: that found within *dhāraṇī* texts. If the seven buddhas were important for their collective expression of ancestral lineage in the world of early Buddhism, they were reorganized in the emerging *dhāraṇī* literature as an important aspect of the *dhāraṇī* coalescence.

The literature of the seven buddhas in the *dhāraṇī* scriptures specifies two interesting and distinctive developments. First, they were taken to authenticate *dhāraṇī* collections that operated as ubiquitous apotropaic or therapeutic tools for any problem that might be encountered in monastic life. Second, in this capacity, neither the individual narratives of the seven buddhas nor their lineal order were of importance. They performed the function of the revelation of mantra-*dhāraṇī*s as a group, appearing at the same time and in the same place. In this regard, we see the seven buddhas in *dhāraṇī* texts occupy the other side of the ledger—while the earlier seven buddha literature tended to treat them as *pitṛ*s for their ancestral legacy, the *dhāraṇī* texts distinguished them as authentic *ṛṣi*s or *vidyādhara* sorcerers for their revelation of magical phrases.

This process may have begun much earlier than otherwise suspected; there are tantalizing signs even back in Bharhut, where we find not only the earliest representations of the seven buddhas but also the earliest inscription featuring a sorcerer: *vijapi vijadharo,* "the sorcerer Vijapi."[66] Barua and Sinha interpreted this obscure inscription as alluding to the *Samuggajātaka* (*Jātaka* 436),[67] where a trickster sorcerer (*vidyādhara*) seduces the wife of an *asura* and escapes by magic. At best, however, this connection is circumstantial. A somewhat more secure connection between the seven buddhas and spell literature happens in the *Khandha-vatta-jātaka* (*Jātaka* 203). This narrative is closely connected with other stories about protection from snakebite by means of spells or prayers and loving-kindness: the *Mahāmāyūrī*, the *Upasena-sūtra*, the *Nāgaropama-sūtra*, the *Āṭānāṭika-sūtra*, the recently recovered spell text to the *nāgarāja* Manasvin, to mention only the most important of this extensive class of works.[68] At the end, the *Khandha-vatta-jātaka* includes a canonical verse that reads:

> *katā me rakkhā katā me parittā paṭikkamantu bhūtāni*
> *so 'haṃ namo bhagavato namo sattannaṃ sammāsambuddhānan 'ti*
> *Jātaka* v. 105: *Jātaka-aṭṭhakathā* II.147

> My protection is complete, my defense has been done; may creatures move away.
> So homage to the Lord, and to the Seven Buddhas!

This appears to be the only instance in the *Jātaka* verses where the seven buddhas are mentioned, and it is interesting that they are specifically given a place in the protection from serpents. If this verse is not datable, it nonetheless has some claim to antiquity and is likely to be the earliest surviving association of the seven buddhas and spell literature.

There is some possibility that a text conveying mantras of the seven buddhas circulated in India in the third century, if not before. The 695 C.E. catalogue of Míngquán affirms that there was such a single-roll text, entitled simply the *Sūtra of the Seven Buddhas' Mantras* (*Qīfó shénzhòujīng*, 七佛神呪經), translated by Zhīqiān (active 229–252 C.E.), no longer extant; the attribution to Zhīqiān is dubious.[69] Given that this text seems to be lost, it will be difficult to determine the legitimacy of such an early translation. In any event, the title is included in the *Scripture in Homage to the Buddhas' Names* (*Fóshuō fómíngjīng*, 佛說佛名經), said to have been translated during the Liáng dynasty (502–557 C.E.).[70] The 515 C.E. *Chū sānzàng jìjí* lists four separate entries for spell texts associated with the seven buddhas: two are entitled the *Seven Buddha Knotted Sesame Oil Mantra* (?) (*Qīfó suǒjíe máyóu shùzhòu*, 七佛所結麻油述呪), and the other two are entitled the *Sūtra of the Seven Buddhas' Mantras*—all of which Sengyou affirms are different works.[71] Other catalogues, such as the 597 C.E. *Lìdài sānbǎojì*, lend support to a relatively early translation of some variety of text articulating mantras for the seven buddhas.[72]

The relationship of a missing *Sūtra of the Seven Buddhas' Mantras* to the extant *Great Dhāraṇī Sūtra of the Seven Buddhas and Eight Bodhisattvas* (*Qīfó bāpúsà suǒshuō dàtuóluóní shénzhòujīng*, 七佛八菩薩所說大陀羅尼神呪經,

T. 1332) is obscure—the former is given in catalogues as consisting of a single roll and the latter as four rolls—but in his *Kāiyuán shìjiàolù* Zhìshēng attributes to Míngquán the position that the latter is a retranslation of the former.[73] Whatever the truth, the *Great Dhāraṇī Sūtra of the Seven Buddhas and Eight Bodhisattvas* is a collection of *dhāraṇī*s that was reputedly translated in the period of the Eastern Jìn (317–420 C.E.), which is possible but not uncomplicated. It is made the more complex because of its systematic intertextuality with the *Dhāraṇīsaṃgraha*, T. 1336. Much of this *Dhāraṇīsaṃgraha* text (and all of the seven buddhas and eight bodhisattvas material) contains components derived from slightly different recensions of the same text. The chart below shows the systematic correspondence between the two works.

Content	**T. 1332**	**T. 1336**
Seven buddhas *dhāraṇī*s	536b14–538b7	580c21–582c3
Eight bodhisattvas *dhāraṇī*s	538b10–541a10	582c4–585b8
Ānanda *dhāraṇī*	541c24–542a11	585c21–586a9
Avalokiteśvara leprosy *dhāraṇī*	542a20–b4	614b7–b15
Samantabhadra *dhāraṇī*-sūtra	542a12–a19	586a10–a19
Mañjuśrī *dhāraṇī*	543a10–b2, 545c27–546b9	586a20–b13/b29
Jífǎyuè shěkǔ tuóluóníjīng[74]	544b5–c26	631a4–b27
*Samādhivaśirāja Bodhisattva *dhāraṇī*	545b10–c12	586c1–587a3
*Sunetrarāja Bodhisattva *dhāraṇī*	545c13–c28	587a4–a18
*Puṇyālaṃkāra Bodhisattva *dhāraṇī*	545c28–546a26	587a19–b17
*Suparikīrtita-nāmadheya Bodhisattva *dhāraṇī*	546a27–b20	587b18–c8
*Ratnacandraprabhā Bodhisattva *dhāraṇī*	546b12–c23	587c9–588a9
*Dhruva (? Buddha) *dhāraṇī*	546c23–547b3	588a10–b16
Bṛhaspati *dhāraṇī*	547b4–c10	588b17–c22
*Aṅgāraka *dhāraṇī*	547c10–548a12	588c23–589a25
Mahābrahmā-devarāja *dhāraṇī*	548a13–b12	589a26–b25
Maheśvara-devarāja *dhāraṇī*	548b13-c9	589b26–c22
Sunirmita-devarāja *dhāraṇī*	548c10-549a14	589c23–590a27
Tuṣita-devarāja *dhāraṇī*	549a15–b12	590a28–b24
Yāma-devarāja *dhāraṇī*	549b13–29	590b25–c11
Trāyastriṃśa-devarāja *dhāraṇī*	549c1–21	590c12–591a4
Maheśvara-devarāja *dhāraṇī*	549c28–550b10	591a16–b27
*Aṣṭabhuja-nārāyaṇa *dhāraṇī*	550b11–c20	591b28–592a8

Mahāśrīdevī *dhāraṇī*	550c21–551a17	592a9–b5
Eight *nāgarāja dhāraṇīs*	551a18–554c12	592b6–595c25
Eight bodhisattva *dhāraṇīs* restated	554c19–555b20	595c26–596b27
Verses by bodhisattvas, gods, and *nāgarājas*	555b21–556c27	596b28–598a6
Assorted demons' identities	557c13–561b8	619a24–623a16

The overwhelming majority of the *Great Dhāraṇī Sūtra of the Seven Buddhas and Eight Bodhisattvas* (T. 1332) is thus contained in the text of the *Dhāraṇīsaṃgraha* (T. 1336). Most important, this means that T. 1336 built on the earlier work, and probably represents a slightly different textual genealogy from the current T. 1332 text replicated in the Taishō Tripiṭaka. This assessment is reinforced by the presence of a *dhāraṇī* to Āṭavika (T.1332.21:543c12–544b3) that is not contained in the *Dhāraṇīsaṃgraha* (T. 1336). The distinction between T. 1332 and the actual source text for the *Dhāraṇīsaṃgraha* (T. 1336) is also observable in the confused pattern of the separately titled Mañjuśrī *dhāraṇī,* which is twice iterated in T. 1332 but only once in the *Dhāraṇīsaṃgraha* (T. 1336).

The seven buddhas section in both texts, the material of greatest interest to us, has a formulaic pattern, similar to that exhibited within the succeeding sections addressing the bodhisattvas, gods, and subsequent figures. Each of the buddhas is said to declare a *dhāraṇī* "named" such-and-such; each is represented in a form understood to be the logographs providing the pronunciation of an Indian word, for which a Chinese translation in miniscule characters is provided. Then the actual *dhāraṇī* is given, followed by a concluding section indicating the application and benefits of the *dhāraṇī.*

A clear understanding of the text is inhibited by the propensity of the author/compiler to abbreviate what may have been seen by the Chinese as a list of meaningless sounds. So the first three buddhas' names have been contracted: Vipaśyin is *wéi-wéi* (維衛; T. 1336: 惟越), Śikhin is *shì* (式), and Viśvabhū becomes *suí-yè* (隨葉). In distinction the last four buddhas' names are relatively more common renderings. The predisposition to contraction or abbreviation extends to the names of their *dhāraṇīs* as well, with the result that they can hardly be recovered with any confidence. Vipaśyin's *dhāraṇī* is named *sū-lú-dū-hē* (穌盧都呵, ? *śrauta* something?), glossed as "certainty in the melodious speech" (*fànyīn juédìng,* 梵音決定, ? perhaps *brahmasvaraniścaya*). Śikhin's *dhāraṇī* is *hú-sū-dūo* (胡穌多), glossed as "eliminating all burning afflictions" (*chúyìqiè zhēngrèn-nǎo,* 除一切欝蒸熱惱, perhaps *sarvadāhanakleśaparihāna*). The *dhāraṇī* of

Viśvabhū is *mì-qí-dōu* (蜜耆兜, ? *mṛdaṅga*), glossed as a drum or gong (*jīngŭ*, 金鼓). Krakucchanda's *dhāraṇī* is translated rather than transcribed; it must have been something close to *vajradhvaja-* or *vajraketu-samādhi* (*jīngāngchuáng sānmèi*, 金剛幢三昧). The *dhāraṇī* of Kanakamuni is *bì-zhĕ-a-nóu* (畢者阿[少/兔]), "sound shaking the ten directions" (*shēng-zhèn shífāng*, 聲振十方). Kāśyapa's is *chū-mó-lí-dì* (初摩梨帝), glossed as "aiding living beings" (*zhĕngjì qúnshēng*, 拯濟群生). Finally, Śākyamuni's *dhāraṇī* is named *wū-sū-qí-nì-dūo* (烏穌耆晝膩多), glossed somehow as "golden brilliance" (*jīnguāng zhàoyào*, 金光照曜). For the most part, the glosses must provide the preponderance of significance, but it is true that Mahāyāna scriptures described *dhāraṇī*s by name, much as they had done with *samādhi* designations. Unfortunately, the surviving lists are of little assistance in this case.[75]

Similar problems afflict the comprehension of the eight bodhisattvas, who were enumerated following the seven buddhas in the above texts. The names of several of the eight bodhisattvas are quite irregular and it is difficult to assess their pattern in conjunction with more normative lists of eight bodhisattvas. Specifically, the names for Mañjuśrī (no. 1), Ākāśa-garbha (no. 2), Avalokiteśvara (no. 3), and Mahāsthāmaprāpta (no. 7) are clear; no. 5 may refer to [Samanta]bhadra (*báduóhé*, 跋陀和), and no. 6 may mean Mahābala (*dàshìzhì*, 大勢至), but it is not clearly the case. The other two names, no. 4, "seeking liberation" (*jiùtuō*, 救脫) and no. 8, "firm heroism" (*jiānyŏng*, 堅勇), are difficult to associate with names in standard lists; the latter is attested here and in *Dhāraṇīsamgraha* T. 1336, indicating its status as a hapax legomenon for the underlying *dhāraṇī* scriptures. However, this list is reiterated later in both texts, as a list and in the bodhisattva verses, so there can be no doubt it was somehow understood to be essential to the overall textual and ritual architecture, whatever Indic name it may have represented. The fact that there are multiple lists of eight bodhisattvas in the Buddhist archive (e.g., as found in the *Aṣṭabuddhaka* / *Maṅgalāṣṭaka* texts, T. 427–431) provides some sense of the complexity of the "eight bodhisattva" situation.

The ritual applications of most of these early seven buddhas' *dhāraṇī*s are quite modest: they are to be recited over a knotted string, which is placed either around the neck or, in the case of a illness or affliction, on the afflicted part. Most of the sections in the text following each *dhāraṇī* are dedicated to a hyperbolic description of the power of the *dhāraṇī*—they can reduce mountains to rubble, dry up oceans, cause the world systems to tremble in six ways, etc.

In one instance, after the *dhāraṇī* of Viśvabhū, there is a description of performing a ritual on the sixteenth day of the fourth month. One circumambulates a stūpa eighty times in a day, beginning from the eastern direction. Then the ritualist sits below the western wall of the stūpa and, facing east toward it, he recites the *dhāraṇī* twenty-four times. He maintains wakefulness for seven days, and then offers seven sesame oil lamps in the four directions. Then he is to dress in fresh clothing and come for a day and night, after which Viśvabhū will send a great light before that person; he will stroke the top of his head with his hand and bestow on him discernment (*júe,* 決; *avadhāraṇa*). The ritualist's karmic obscurations (*karmāvaraṇa*) will be eliminated without residue.

Having but glossed over the many problems of the *Great Dhāraṇī Sūtra of the Seven Buddhas and Eight Bodhisattvas* and its closely related *Dhāraṇī-saṃgraha,* we may note that they were by no means the only *dhāraṇī* texts from the fourth to sixth centuries that discussed the seven buddhas. Perhaps best represented are the several recensions of the *Mahāmāyūrī-vidyārājñī,* which, as already mentioned, survives in an early version in the *Bhaiṣajyavastu,* an independent Sanskrit recension, in two versions in the Bower manuscript, seven Chinese translations, and the Tibetan version.

The textual history of this work is complicated, but the *Bhaiṣajyavastu* version—possibly the earliest—has no mention of the seven buddhas, nor does one of the Chinese translations attributed to the Qín period (T. 986, 350–431 C.E.). The latter translation appears to be a rendering of a fragment rather than the entire text, as the core narrative of Svāti and his snakebit toe is not mentioned, and the pericope is primarily concerned with a few mantra-*dhāraṇī*s and the *ṛṣi*s rather than *nāga*s or *yakṣa*s. The other ostensible Qín translation mentions the seven buddhas simply to pay homage to them as a group, rather than providing them individual identities or other factors (T.987.19:479a6, 481a26–7), and a similar citation is found in the translation attributed to Kumārajīva (T.988.19:483a4). The connection between the seven buddhas and the early *Mahāmāyūrī* recensions is thus as tenuous as it was in the *Khandha-vatta-jātaka* (*Jātaka* 203) noted above.

This situation changes from the early sixth century on, where the 502–520 C.E. translation attributed to Samghabhāra begins to approximate the received Sanskrit text.[76] There we find the two most important seven buddha statements encountered in the received text: the description of each of the buddhas and the tree under which they obtained awakening, and the individual mantras pronounced and approved by each of the buddhas.[77] The description of the buddhas is the introductory part of a long mantra-*dhāraṇī*, immediately prior to the *tadyathā* interjection speech marker that precedes the nonreferential phonemes.

aśokam āśritya jino vipaśyī / śikhī jinaḥ puṇḍarīkasya mūle /
śālasya mūle upagamya viśvabhūt / śirīṣamūle krakucchanda-brāhmaṇaḥ /
buddhaś ca kanakamunī udumbare / nyagrodhamūle upagamya kāśyapaḥ /
aśvatthamule muni śākyapuṅgavaḥ / upetya bodhiṃ samavāpya gotamaḥ /
eteṣu buddheṣu maharddhikeṣu / yā devatāḥ santi atiprasannāḥ /
tā devatā muditamanā udagrāḥ / kurvantu śāntiṃ ca śivaṃ ca nityaṃ /

The Victor Vipaśyin, relying on the *aśoka* [tree], and Śikhin at the root of a *puṇḍarīka,*
Viśvabhū approached the root of the *śāla,* and Krakucchanda the brāhmin at a *śiriṣa* root,
Buddha Kanakamuni at an *uduṃbara,* Kāśyapa approached the *nyagrodha* root,
The Śākya hero approached the root of an *āśvattha;* he, Gotama, attained awakening.
Those gods who are filled with clear faith at these miraculous buddhas,
May they—joyful and delighted—make peace and eternal blessedness.

This text preserves the association of Vipaśyin and the *aśoka* tree that is displayed in the Bharhut medallion, not the *pāṭali* tree with which he is otherwise associated (*Mahāpadāna* DN II.4)

The *mantra-dhāraṇī*s for the seven buddhas in the *Mahāmāyūrī* fall within the general form observed for many of the other mantra-*dhāraṇī*s of that text, seemingly with a strong influx of Dravidian phonetics, which is recognized in the work. The seven buddhas' mantra-*dhāraṇī*s are no exception; they include claims of Dravidian phonetic influence and appear different from the other seven buddhas' mantra-*dhāraṇī*s. The latter quality, however, seems to define the mantra-*dhāraṇī*s of the seven buddhas overall. None of the three early texts—the T. 1332/T. 1336 group, the *Mahāmāyūrī,* and the *Saptabuddhaka*—agree on the mantras assigned to the seven buddhas. To give one example, the mantra of Śikhin Buddha, the second of the seven, reads:

T.1332.21.536c5: 陀摩帝那 遮波兜帝那 奢副奢副帝那 烏穌多烏穌多帝那
tuó mó dì nà zhē bō dōu dì nà shē fù shē fù dì nà wū sū duō wū sū duō dì nà
浮浮奢浮浮奢帝那 阿輸帝阿踰帝帝那 尼梨遮尼梨遮帝那 支波晝支波晝帝那
fú fú shē fú fú shē dì nà ā lún dì ā yú dì dì nà ní lí zhē ní lí zhā dì nà zhī bō zhùo zhī bō zhùo dì nà
穌呵兜穌呵兜帝那 耶無奢耶無奢帝那 奢波不帝那 漚奢不帝那

sū hē dōu sū hē dōu dì nà yé wú shē yé wú shē dè nà shē bō bù dì nà où shē bù dì nà
穌奢不帝那 奢破不帝那 莎呵
sū shē bù dì nà shē bò bù dì nà sūo hé

Mahāmāyūrī, p. 43: *iḍi miḍi khire vikhire hili hili hili mili mili tumūle ambare ambarāvati dumbe dumbe hili hili hili kuvi kuvi kuvi muci muci muci svāhā /*

Saptabuddhaka, To. 512 (fol. 23a1): *namo buddhāya / namo dharmāya / samaḥ saṃbhāya / oṃ paca paca pācaya pācaya / sarvabhūtānāṃ / cchindhaya / kīlaya / paravidyānāṃ svāhā /*

This example is representative of similar differences seen in all the other mantras, so I have not given all their individual statements here. The differences between these mantras are quite curious, and reveal a fluidity in mantra production in the communities of the early *dhāraṇī* texts that belies suppositions of uniformity. Tentatively, I believe we may safely conclude that the cult of the seven buddhas was sufficiently widespread so that, once mantra-*dhāraṇī*s were understood to be desirable, the different sites produced their own mantra-*dhāraṇī*s, along with their individual *dhāraṇī* texts presenting their coded phrases.

The *Saptabuddhaka* and Related *Dhāraṇī*s and *Stotra*s

Perhaps the most important and best developed of the early seven buddhas *dhāraṇī* texts is the one known in some catalogues as the *Saptabuddhaka-nāma-mahāyāna-sūtra.* This text survives in three Chinese translations, ostensibly from the early sixth to the late tenth centuries, and in a Tibetan translation.[78] The title *Saptabuddhaka* is probably not its original designation, given the titles reflected in the various translations. The earliest translation is an anonymous one in T. 1333, attributed to the Liáng (502–557 C.E.); it is translated as if it were entitled **Ākāśagarbha-paripṛcchā-saptabuddha-dhāraṇī-sūtra* (*Xūkōngzàng púsàwèn qīfó tuóluóní-zhòujīng* 虚空藏菩薩問七佛陀羅尼呪經), reflecting the centrality of Ākāśagarbha as its interlocutor. The 587 C.E. translation, T. 1334, attributed to Jñānagupta appears as though entitled **Tathāgata-upāyakauśalya-mantra-sūtra* (*Rúlái fāngbiàn shànqiǎo zhòujīng* 如來方便善巧呪經), perhaps reflecting the ideology of the narrative frame in which the buddhas pronounced mantra-*dhāraṇī*s in response to a problem. By the time of the 984 C.E. rendering, T. 1147, by Fǎtiān (法天), the translation seems to be entitled *Ārya-Ākāśagarbha-bodhisattva-dhāraṇī-sūtra* (*Shèng xūkōngzàng púsà tuóluóníjīng* 聖虚空藏菩薩陀羅尼經), returning to the earlier form. Most of these alternative titles reflect the tension in the text between Ākāśagarbha, who operates as a central organizing figure in the various revelations, and the seven buddhas who appear and pronounce the methods for ameliorating the problems invoked.

The status of this text as a *dhāraṇī* is furthermore complicated by its title, which indentifies it as a sūtra, and the catalogues reflect this divided assessment. The Chinese translations, as they often do, carry both designations—mantra or *dhāraṇī* sūtra—while the Tibetan translation affirms its position as a sūtra. In the modern Chinese canon, all three translations are found in two of the four volumes of the Taishō given to esoteric materials, even if the older catalogues do not necessarily reflect this same thematic organization. In the royal dynastic Tibetan catalogues, the *lDan-dkar-ma* lists the text in the sūtra section rather than in the *dhāraṇī* section, but the *'Phang-thang-ma* lists it as a *dhāraṇī*.[79] This mildly conflicted response continues through the xylographic printings of the Tibetan canon and is probably the source of the versions we find with very minor differences: To. 270 is the *Saptabuddhaka* in the mDo-sde section of the *sDe-dge bka'-'gyur,* whereas To. 512 is found in the tantric section; there is also the version (To. 852) found in the *dhāraṇī* collection (*gzungs-'dus*). The differences between these versions are relatively minor and can be attributed to scribal corruption rather than differences in translation, but they also suggest the possibility of the texts having had separate transmissions in various collections of sūtras, tantras, and *dhāraṇī*s, a point in need of further clarification.

All four translations of the *Saptabuddhaka* (taking this as a shorthand for the contested title) reveal the probability of very similar source texts that had not undergone substantial modification in the period between the early sixth and late tenth centuries. This is not to say that all the translations are the same; the earliest one stands out in particular. T. 1333, the translation attributed to the Liáng period (502–557 C.E.), is undoubtedly the most interesting of the four translations, as it is the longest. The material in the introduction is slightly expanded, as are some of the seven buddha sections at the beginning and end. The translator has taken greatest license in the material on Viśvabhū, and to a lesser extent Krakucchanda and Kanakamuni. In these areas, the ritual application of the mantra has been enlarged, judging by both the style of the rituals and the absence of such details in all the other versions. In distinction, T. 1147, the latest translation attributed to Fǎtiān (984 C.E.), appears to be the most abbreviated and many ritual details are missing. We will first go quickly through the text and then examine a rite illustrating the differing state of the texts.

The *Saptabuddhaka* begins in a manner that is closer to the Vinaya than to standard sūtras. Śākyamuni is in residence with his entourage of 500 monks and 500 bodhisattvas in a forest on the peak of Kailāsa, not too distant from "*Ṛṣis*' practice," evidently understood as a place name. Suddenly, two *bhikṣus* stand up and begin to act in a peculiar manner, possessed by some spirit.

> 時一比丘爲鬼所持. 形體裸露不自覺知. 擧手叫喚言語麁獷. 更一比丘著邪背佛. 在虛空中嗚呼出聲不得自在. (T.1334.21:565a12–14)

> Then, one of them, possessed by a spirit, exposed his body, unconscious of his nakedness, raised his hands in the attitude of prayer, and began to curse volubly with crude language. The other monk displayed contempt, turning his back to the Buddha, and toward the air he yelled "*wū-hū!*" with no ability to control himself.

Buddhists consistently had to deal with the problem of spirit possession, a topic that is ubiquitous in Indian religious praxis. Not only do the Vinayas address the treatment of those so possessed (sometimes as insane: *unmatta*), but some even offer some latitude for monks suffering from states of spirit possession to suspend certain rules. In one instance, a monk who was afflicted by "non-humans" (*amanussikābādho*) ran to a hog-slaughterer, gobbling up the raw flesh and drinking the blood of pigs (*so sūkarasūnaṃ gantvā āmakamaṃsaṃ khādi, āmakalohitaṃ pivi*).[80] The Buddha was said to have allowed the ingestion of these substances as medicine in the case of possession (*anujānāmi bhikkhave, amanussikābādhe āmakamaṃsaṃ āmakalohitaṃ*), for Indian medicine tended to treat possession as a disease. The dissonance in Buddhist opinion on the nature of such behaviors comes to the fore in the *Saptabuddhaka,* where the Buddha, in diagnosing the monks' problems, tends to vacillate between declaring them to be either diseased or possessed.[81] Ākāśagarbha, apparently wanting to be certain that all bases are covered, then inquires how disease might be cured and possession averted.

As is usual in such instances, the substance of the Buddha's reply (in the form of a ritual treatment) begins with a miraculous revelation that provides the overall structure of the text. Suddenly appearing altogether in the sky, the six past buddhas assemble, with Śākyamuni then assuming his position as the seventh. Each buddha acknowledges the problem of disease and possession, utters his mantra, and then instructs Ākāśagarbha—and, of course, the putative reader/listener—in the many benefits and uses of the mantra. The paragraphs defining the mantra's benefits and uses also provide short ritual applications (*vidhi*) for the recitation of the mantra, including brief *homa* ceremonies, identifying a few of the many items that will come to be well represented in later *homa* texts. While these rites are not, in the Chinese translations at least, explicitly described with words like *homa* or *huta*, nonetheless they are recognizable as such in the Tibetan and follow the pattern of such ritual activities in the *gṛhya*-sūtra systems of domestic rituals.

As an example of the manner in which these are stated, and to demonstrate the expansive properties of the Liáng Chinese translation, at the end of the Viśvabhū section there is a short ritual for counteracting poison. We will first look at the Tibetan translation:

> *dug mi gdug par byed par 'dod pas sangs rgyas kyi spyan sngar seng ldeng gi thur ma ba'i lci bar smyugs pa brgya rtsa brgyad ming nas smos te sbyin sreg byas na dug mi gdug par 'gyur ro / gdon dang / srung ba dang / 'byung po la sogs pa'i las thams cad la yang sbyar bar byas na bde bar gnas par 'gyur ro //* (To. 270, fol. 15b2–3; To. 512, fol.24a1; sTog 472, fol. 18b4–6)
>
> One wishing to render a poison to be nonpoisonous will smear 108 small sticks of sandalwood with cowdung, and will perform before an image of the Buddha a *homa* saying the name [of the person afflicted], so that the poison will be rendered nonpoisonous. The same rite can be used in cases of possession by planets (*graha*), demons (*rakṣa*), or spirits (*bhūta*), etc.; if it is applied in all such cases, then the person will become comfortable.

In distinction, the "same" ritual is described in the Liáng translation as follows:

> 若復有人被毒藥者. 須紫橿木寸截之如筋大作一千八段. 以牛糞塗之. 在於像前然火. 取木一段呪之一遍. 擲著火中一千八遍. 然後乃止. 稱病人名. 我爲彼人除其藥毒即得除愈. 此呪功能説不可盡. 若心中所欲作事者. 依此呪法無不成就. (T.1333.21:562c27–563a4)
>
> If there is a person oppressed by poisonous medicine, then you should take inch-sized pieces of purple Japanese blue oak, cut to be as thick as a tendon, making 1,008 in all. Smear them with cowdung. Then before an image, kindle a fire. Take a piece of wood, and with each piece say the [Viśvabhū] mantra one time—completing the full 1,008 pieces. Then after you have stopped, call out the name of the person [saying], "On behalf of this person, I remove the medical poison, so that he just obtains remission and healing." It is not possible to explain the benefits of this mantra. If there is something in your heart you wish to accomplish, then based on this mantra-method (**mantravidhi*) it is impossible that it will not come to pass.

While a rigorous comparison of the various versions of the *Saptabuddhaka* is well beyond the scope of this article, we can see that the

Liáng translator tended to render his source text liberally, probably incorporating various practical instructions as he would have received them either in India or from Indians. Overall, the earliest translation seems to provide a specific interpretive program, one that seeks the completion of the material written in the text, lending us the sense—obvious in the Tibetan instance—that the written text was taken to be a shorthand version of the implied ritual system. One simply cannot perform the ritual given in the Tibetan version without many questions about ritual order and performative details. The Liáng version is much more complete, and we also see the elevation of the level of practice, by stipulating 1,008 *homa* sticks rather than the 108 of most other versions.[82] The translator is filling in the details, taking the text as a starting place for the ritual instruction rather than as a self-contained scriptural event, as is sometimes presumed by those with incomplete experience in the manner that texts have been traditionally employed in India, or generally elsewhere for that matter.[83]

To return to the example at hand, the 984 C.E. Sōng translation has no such poison ritual, the only translation in which this instruction is lacking. Other rituals are also missing from this version, whereas the mantra-*dhāraṇī* benefit statements and the sotereological elements appear to be highlighted. Both the Liáng and Sōng translations are more distinctive versions of textual editing than is seen in the other *Saptabuddhaka* renditions, and the argument could be made that, overall, these *dhāraṇī* ritual texts appear to have been understood more as works in progress than as codified texts with sanctified readings. Indeed, we see traces of textual expansion, deletion, manipulation, and floating pericope throughout the history of Indian Buddhism, from the early Gandhāran materials to the latest tantric texts.

The *Saptabuddhaka* evidently had a relatively short active ritual life. Achieving its heyday in the fifth to seventh centuries, it was eventually eclipsed in many of the *dhāraṇī* collections by other texts. Within the later *dhāraṇī* collections found in Nepal, the major work that replaced the *Saptabuddhaka* appears to have been the *Saptabuddhastotra*, a slightly more elaborate versified summary of the lives of the seven buddhas said to be abstracted from the *Sugatāvadāna*, itself a late *avadāna*.[84] Its closest companion is the *Saptajinastava* or *Saptatathāgatastava;* these texts add Maitreya to the list as the buddha of the future, and reflect a return to the earlier language of the *Mahāvadāna-sūtra* and other repositories of seven buddhas lore in the Mahāyāna sūtras. These works do not include a mantra-*dhāraṇī*, nor do we find specific ritual instructions about offerings.

Instead, they are panegyrics that summarize the respective buddhas' lives, and so operate as vignettes of their hagiographies.

A few tentative observations might be suggestedconcerning the replacement of the *dhāraṇī* form by the panegyric to the seven buddhas in the later collections, even acknowledging the complex factors that must have been involved. Nevertheless, at the top of the list should be the diminution of interest in the *dhāraṇī* genre with the emergence of mature esoteric Buddhism. True, *dhāraṇī*s continued to be recited, and *dhāraṇī*s continued to be composed, but I believe it is fair to say that the speed of their production and the intensity of interest in Mahāyānist *dhāraṇī*s per se lessen over time. *Dhāraṇī*s certainly continued to be employed in the consecration of stūpas, images, and specific sites; they continued to be recited in apotropaic and healing rituals. But their soteriological imperative seems to have become less compelling than it once was. During and after the eighth century, the tantras become the grand soteriological vehicles, assessed as the true conveyers of the path of mantras, while *dhāraṇī*s, when they were considered at all, became relegated to the status of "ritual scriptures" (*kriyā*) and were in some measure displaced by the lengthy rites of the mature tantric scriptures.

Second, the replacement of longer *dhāraṇī*s by shorter verses of homage (*stotra, stava*), which were included among *dhāraṇī* collections, suggests that when faced with the rising tide of esoteric materials, some among the conservative Mahāyānists retreated to the idea that *dhāraṇī*s could still represent the comprehensible encryption of meaning. That is, much as the earlier exclamations that *dhāraṇī*s were the encoding of the entire scripture into lesser texts, as the shorter Prajñāpāramitā scriptures could encode the longer ones, the intermittent inclusion of straightforward verses of homage within *dhāraṇī* compendia would suggest that the later Mahāyāna partially reformulated this same idea. Thereafter the soteriological force and value of *dhāraṇī*s could be found within abbreviated comprehensible statements rather than solely within nonlinguistic sounds.

By the sixth century there is an acceleration of works identified by the designation *dhāraṇī* but for which there is no mantra-*dhāraṇī* at all, such as the *Avikalpraveśa-dhāraṇī* or the *Vajramaṇḍa-dhāraṇī*. True, the composition of such texts may have been partially in response to the widespread fascination with mantras or a reaffirmation of a basic Buddhist mistrust of nonreferential (*anarthaka*) sounds (as some said the Vedas were), or may even represent a desire to appropriate the *dhāraṇī* designation for more sophisticated doctrinal statements. Yet a redirection of the term *dhāraṇī* from its emphasis on the nonconceptual/nonreferential and returning it to the possibility of a conceptual format seems to have served the purposes of the intellectuals in the monasteries by bringing the *dhāraṇī* designation to the philosophical table. The apparent replacement of the *Saptabuddhaka* by the *Saptabuddhastotra* would suggest that, in some areas at least, the effort to divert *dhāraṇī* ritual toward a conceptual-referential format met with modest success.

The Other Seven Buddhas among the *Dhāraṇī*s

It appears that by the mid-seventh century the seven buddhas of the past themselves became peripheral to the emerging esoteric program; there is no mention of the seven buddhas as a group in Atikūṭa's 654 C.E. *Dhāraṇīsaṃgraha* (T. 901). While this does not mean that the seven buddhas were no longer important, it suggests that in the later period they lost their previous centrality. It appears that the explosion of new "buddha" figures in the esoteric pantheon—Vairocana, Tejorāśi, the *vidyārājas*, etc.—eclipsed in some measure the emphasis on the seven buddhas as revealers of the *Prātimokṣa* and secret spells. Even in *dhāraṇī* literature, their position was eroded by the emerging emphasis on the eight bodhisattvas, who were to become an important part of several esoteric *maṇḍalas*, and by the buddhas of the pure lands.

Much of the attraction of the pure land buddhas and the eight bodhisattvas was that they were mythically contemporary rather than resident only as memories of an ancient past. Both groups were understood to be living realities available to great saints and those with sufficient faith, and both could provide bridges between normative Mahāyāna and the newer systems. Mahāyāna scriptures had long before articulated the significance of Akṣobhya and Amitābha, but the designation as a pure land buddha was extended to other figures, particularly a group of eight buddhas in the east, a mark of the Indian emphasis on the eastern direction as intrinsically holy. Several related texts—variously identified as the *Aṣṭamaṇḍalaka*, the *Aṣṭabuddhaka*, the **Aṣṭamaṅgala*, the *Maṅgalāṣṭaka*, etc.—described revelations of buddhas in the eastern direction who were assembled in an eightfold pattern.[85] So far as I have been able to ascertain, none of the names of these buddhas provided in the several texts are precisely the same, and most of the lists have only modest overlap. Yet most of them have a very similar structure of revelation and are observably part of the same overall program of expressing the importance of contemporary buddhas and the centrality of reciting their names.

In later texts such as the Tibetan *Aṣṭabuddhaka* (To. 271) we find the sudden appearance of the buddhas on lion thrones atop eight lotuses, but there is no detectible circular organization nor are these buddhas assigned specific directions relative to each other or to a center. Nor do the texts provide mantra-*dhāraṇīs* for the buddhas, although at least two works (T. 427 and T. 428) identify themselves as "mantra scriptures" (*shénzhòujīng*, 神呪經) in the version of their titles recognized in later catalogues. But earlier catalogue entries provide no such description and the history of these texts is overall obscured by the Tang Dynasty catalogue attributions.[86]

The absence of directional assignments or identifiable mantras is different from what is seen in two later texts, the *Daśabuddhaka* (*Ten Buddhas*) and *Dvādaśabuddhaka* (*Twelve Buddhas*), both of which are assiduous in giving directional assignment; the latter text also includes a mantra-*dhāraṇī* to be employed.[87] Even with this change, in all these works the emphasis is decidedly on recitation of the buddhas' names, recollecting them at death, and the benefits to be accrued from their names. The buddhas are represented as having pure buddha fields, devoid of the problems of this Sahā world system, and the *Daśabhuddhaka* explicitly references the cult of Amitābha in Sukhāvatī as the standard against which other buddhas and their pure lands are compared.[88]

Partially based on the organization of these eight-, ten-, or twelve-buddha texts is another seven-buddha work, the *Saptatathāgatapūrva-praṇidhāna-viśeṣavistāra-sūtra,* the *Detailed Description of the Previous Aspirations of Seven Tathāgatas.* However, this *Seven Tathāgatas* scripture integrates other sources as well, especially much of the *Bhaiṣajyaguru-vaidūryaprabharāja-sūtra* in the last half of the text. The 707 C.E. Chinese translation (T. 451) of the *Seven Tathāgatas* is attributed to Yìjìng, the well-known traveler to India, and there seems little reason to call this attribution into question; the canonical Tibetan translation appears in both the surviving Tibetan royal dynastic catalogues as well.[89]

The *Seven Tathāgatas* articulates the current residence, prior aspirations, and practices of seven buddhas: *Suparikīrtitaśrīrāja, *Ratnacandrapadma-vibhūṣita-kuśalatejonirghoṣa-rāja, *Suvarṇabhadra-vimalaratnaprabhāsa-vrata-siddha, *Aśokottamaśrī, *Dharmakīrtisāgaraghoṣa, *Dharmasāgarā-gramativikrīḍitābhijñārāja, and Bhaiṣajyaguru-vaidūrya-prabharāja. While these largely reconstructed names, based on the Tibetan translation, may not be exact in all details, my rendering is guided by the occurrence of names very similar to these within the received text of the *Śikṣāsamuccaya* and in the iconographical workof lCang-kya.[90] The entire Yìjìng text has been translated into English[91] so there is little point in revisiting the work here, other than to indicate that the ideology of currently existing buddhas, living and preaching in real time, is the driving function of this and the eight-, ten-, and twelve-buddha materials. Recitation of their names remains the primary method of interacting with these distant buddhas, though a few *dhāraṇīs* have been placed in the text, even augmenting the Bhaiṣajyaguru cultus in this regard.

If measured by the number of ritual manuals, the *Seven Tathāgatas* exhibited a degree of popularity, especially evident in the surviving Tibetan translations, and we may surmise that rituals based on this text were employed with some frequency. At least three separate works were written to invoke these seven buddhas (To. 3132–3144), and, if the modifications in the Dunhuang version of the *Method of Reading the Seven Tathāgatas* is any guide, rituals focused on these figures were employed in actual praxis, not only in theory.[92] As much of the *Seven Tathāgatas* text is actually a restatement and reformulation of the Bhaiṣajyaguru scripture, it certainly augmented the status of that buddha and marked the popularity of healing rituals in the seventh through tenth centuries.

Conclusion

In his extended citation and discussion of the problem of the Bodhisattva-*piṭaka,* Ulrich Pagel concludes:

> To sum up: Initially, the term Bodhisattvapiṭaka was probably used to designate sūtras that dealt in particular with the bodhisattva training. At a later stage, or in some other region, its application widened to embrace not only bodhisattva sūtras, but to include Mahāyāna sūtra literature in its entirety.[93]

While I do not disagree with this learned estimation, I would add that the evidence here also suggests that the better-known Bodhisattva-*piṭaka* was, like the *Dhāraṇī-* or *Vidyā-* or Mantra-*piṭakas*, something of an imaginary construct of a container that never existed. Schools were represented as having such compendia, but the precise nature of what constituted the *Bodhisattva-piṭaka*—even though it was much better represented than the *Dhāraṇī/Vidyā*[*dhara*]-*piṭaka* in literary citations—still was vague enough to be something of a category for all seasons, so long as the topic was somehow understood to be the Mahāyāna or the bodhisattva path.

As in the case of the Bodhisattva-*piṭaka,* the *Dhāraṇī-piṭaka* was an imaginary container acting as an infinite reservoir of possibilities, but it was much more limited in its actualities. Little wonder that the *Dhāraṇī-piṭaka* was such "a mass of foam, a bubble, an illusory city, a dream," to use the language of the Mahāyānist scriptures, as the individual *dhāraṇī* texts are continually treated as fluid entities, to be changed, adapted, modified, increased, and decreased at will. The numerical values ascribed to the *piṭaka*—60,000 verses, 100,000 verses, etc.—were literary gestures designed both to bring the abstract potential into physical dimensions and to serve as verbal homages to the predisposition of Indian Buddhists to provide expansive numbers whenever possible. Positing the spectra of immense repositories of vast scriptures, the unspoken goal behind the statements seems to have been to impress on the minds of Mahāyāna monks, laity, and patrons that the charismatic Dharmabhāṇakas and Mahāyāna bodhisattvas had at their command an infinite wealth of technical resources that could overcome all obstacles, from the banal to the cosmic.

The *Dhāraṇīsaṃgraha*s, the only compendia for which we have physical iterations, must have acted as the basis for such imaginary constructions, as they existed much earlier than any mention of a *piṭaka* of spells. As such, they were also grist for the conceptual mill of Buddhist canonical categories, so that the mention of the mythic *Dhāraṇī*- or Mantra- or *Vidyā-piṭaka*s (whatever these may have meant) were in some way based on the collections of *dhāraṇī* texts that were carried in cloth-covered bundles of manuscripts from one place to the next. These actual compendia were evidently declared to be only small fragments of their imaginary source basket, a construct that served to amaze the audience, promote the message, and provide legitimacy for whatever teaching was being communicated. The surviving *Dhāraṇīsaṃgraha*s suggest an attitude of fluid overcoding, utilizing text, practice, instruction, and inspiration, all mixed together in the moment. New *dhāraṇī*s would replace previous ones, new cults could be promoted, and new needs were engaged as the opportunity presented itself.

Central to the early articulation of the *dhāraṇī* procedure (*dhāraṇīnaya*), the seven buddhas formed a bridge from the early ideology of Śākyamuni's predecessors through the *Prātimokṣa* revelation in the Vinaya, into the Mahāyāna scriptures and the *dhāraṇī* pronouncements. After all, they were the ancestors, the progenitors of the ancestral *Prātimokṣa* that survived even when the buddhas themselves did not. The *Prātimokṣa,* as the textual embodiment of the seven buddhas, contained the codes, the behaviors, and the legal fundamentals of the Buddhist dispensation. Taking pride of place at the head of the early *Dhāraṇīsaṃgraha*s, the seven buddhas effected a softening of the disjuncture between the *Prātimokṣa* expressions of restricted behavior, the stūpa cults of South Asia, the *avadāna* literature of the earlier exploits of the seven buddhas and the various bodhisattvas, and the imperatives of the new therapeutic spells. These were both a response to and a reaction against the ailments of possession, accidents, and disease, so that the seven buddhas of the past moved effortlessly from the ancestor Śākyamuni to the *ṛṣi*s as agents of healing in service of a populace adrift in the Indian medieval world.

The *dhāraṇī*s they offered were individually and collectively considered to be methods of health, powerful agents of change, signa of moral rectitude, and balms for the oppressed. *Dhāraṇī*s cured the five sins of immediate retribution, obliterated the obscurations of past karma and emotional imbalance, and yielded salvation in one's lifetime; they were to be distributed to all and sundry, and they could shake the foundation of the world or cause the oceans to evaporate—powerful indeed. Their efficacy was in their promise, their mythic background, having been pronounced by all the buddhas of the past and affirmed by the buddhas yet to come. Brought together into the *Dhāraṇīsaṃgraha*s, they became the foundations for a new basket of the word of the Buddha, to be unfolded as needed. This was the emptiest basket of all, one that could contain and reveal all the phonemes of the world without being limited by them.

Notes

1 Ronald M. Davidson, "Studies in *Dhāraṇī* Literature I: Revisiting the Meaning of the Term *Dhāraṇī*," *Journal of Indian Philosophy* 37/2 (2009): 97–147; "Studies in *Dhāraṇī* Literature II: Pragmatics of *Dhāraṇī*s," in Michael Willis, ed., *Mantra and Dhāraṇī in the Religious Traditions of Asia,* special issue of the *Bulletin of the School of Oriental and African Studies* 77/1 (2014): 5–61.

2 The literature on the Buddhist canon is extensive but not all of it is applicable to the problems of Indian canon conceptualization; Steven Collins, "On the Very Idea of the Pali Canon," *Journal of the Pali Text Society* 15 (1990): 89–126, remains particularly useful.

3 *Abhidharmasamuccaya,* pp. 78–79; To. 4048, fol. 100b7–101b4; T.1605.31:686a21–b24; *Abhidharmasamuccayabhāṣya,* pp. 95–96; Étienne Lamotte, *History of Indian Buddhism: From the Origins to the Śaka Era* (Louvain-La-Neuve: Peters Press, 1988), pp. 143–191; this corrects my previous clumsy and incorrect use of the *Abhidharmasamuccaya* in "Canon and Identity in Indian Esoteric Buddhism as the Confluence of Cultures," in Volkhard Krecht and Marion Steinicke, eds., *Dynamics in the History of Religions between Asia and Europe: Encounters, Notions, and Comparative Perspectives, Dynamics in the History of Religions,* vol. 1. (Leiden: Brill, 2011), pp. 321–341.

In terms of meaning, suffice it to say that the Tibetan and Chinese translations do not agree with one another on the exact significance of some terms. Compare also the bewilderingly different definitions found in Śrāvakabhūmi Study Group, ed., *Śrāvakabhūmi: Revised Sanskrit Text and Japanese Translation, The First Chapter* (Tokyo: The Sankibo Press, 1998), pp. 226–232.

[4] On these standards and their sources, see my articles "Studies in *Dhāraṇī* Literature I" and "An Introduction to the Standards of Scriptural Authenticity in Indian Buddhism," in Robert Buswell, ed., *Chinese Buddhist Apocrypha* (Honolulu: University of Hawai'i Press, 1990), pp. 291–325.

[5] Issi Yamada, *Karuṇāpuṇḍarīka: The White Lotus of Compassion* (London: School of Oriental and African Studies, 1986), vol. 2, pp. 2–3, argues that the *Sarvajñtākāradhāraṇī* was abstracted from the *Karuṇapuṇḍarīka,* based on the difference with the Chinese translation of the third *dhāraṇī*. I believe this needs a bit more investigation. The Śrī rituals of the *Suvarṇabhāsottama* were included into Atikūṭa's 654 C.E. *Dhāraṇīsaṃgraha,* T.901.18:874b25–876a5.

[6] See in particular, Jan Gonda, *The Ritual Sūtras. A History of Indian Literature* (Wiesbaden: Harrasssowitz, 1977), vol. 1, fasc. 2, p. 571:

> Rather than on the ancient *saṃhitās* and *brāhmaṇas* the domestic rites and mantras are generally speaking based on a tradition of their own and on autonomous collections which are not identical with the four well-known *samhitās.* Relations with these basic works are of course not lacking but in many cases limited to stray citations and the occurrence of formulas that may or may not be the result of direct or indirect borrowing, the ṛgvedic *sūtras* drawing, for instance, from the *Ṛgveda-Saṃhitā.* Or, to express myself otherwise, the *gṛhya* formulas are in all probability based on collections which maintain various, more or less close, occasional or secondary, relations with the *śrauta* tradition.

[7] E.g., *Śāṅkhāyanagṛhyasūtra* I.9.18:

> In the case of gods required [to be included in the ceremony] but whose mantras are not handed down in *śruti,* then one should sacrifice saying 'to this [god] *svāhā,* to that [god]! *svāhā'* to be done by the pure addition of *svāhā* (*anāmnātamantrāsvādiṣṭadevatāsu amuṣyai svāhā 'muṣyai svāhā iti juhuyāt svāhākāreṇa śuddhena* /).

[8] Ulrich Pagel's proposal, in his "Introduction" to Jens Braarvig and Ulrich Pagel, "Fragments of the Bodhisattvapiṭakasūtra," in Jens Braarvig, ed. *Buddhist Manuscripts Volume III* (Oslo: Hermes Publishing, 2006), pp. 21–30, especially p. 29, will be considered in the conclusion.

[9] *Lalitavistara,* p. 440.18; T.187.3:616b21–22.

[10] *Sānlùnxuányì* 三論玄義; T.1852.45:9c23; Paul Demiéville, "L'origine des sectes bouddhiques d'après Paramārtha," *Mélanges chinois et bouddhiques* 1 (1932): 61.

[11] On the original text, see Jiryo Matsuda, "Origin and Doctrine of Early Indian Buddhist Schools," *Asia Major* 2 (1925): 1–78. Vasumitra's authorship is capable of being questioned; Bhavya's commentary is the *Nikāyabhedavibhaṅgavyākhyāna,* To. 4139.

[12] The robustness of early Mahāyāna in Gandhāra has been recently demonstrated by Mark Allon and Richard Salomon, "New Evidence of Mahayana in Early Gandhāra," *Eastern Buddhist* 41/1 (2010): 1–22; and by Ingo Strauch, "More Missing Pieces of Early Pure Land Buddhism: New Evidence for Akṣobhya and Abhirati in an Early Mahayana Sutra from Gandhāra," *Eastern Buddhist* 41/1 (2010): 23–66.

[13] Per K. Sorensen, *Triśaraṇasaptati: The Septuagint on the Three Refuges* (Vienna: Arbeitskreis für Tibetische unde Buddhistische Studien, 1986), p. 53; and

Tarkajvālā, To. 3856, fol. 175b1, noted by Peter Skilling, "The *Rakṣā* Literature of the *Śrāvakayāna*," *Journal of the Pali Text Society* 16 (1992): 114, n. 3.

14 *Dàtángxīyùjì* 大唐西域記; T.2087.51:923a8; Samuel Beal, *Si-Yu-Ki: Buddhist Records of the Western World* (London: Kegan Paul, Trench, Trübner & Co, 1869), vol. 2, p. 165. Beal's rendering of this phrase as *Dhāraṇī-piṭaka* has caused much confusion, as it seems to have been followed by Thomas Watters, *On Yuan Chwang's Travels in India, 629–645 A.D.* (London: Royal Asiatic Society, 1904), vol. 2, p. 160; Demiéville, "L'origine des sectes bouddhiques d'après Paramārtha," p. 61; André Bareau, *Les sectes bouddhiques du petit véhicule* (Saigon: École Française d'Extrême-orient, 1955), p. 56; and Étienne Lamotte, *History of Indian Buddhism: From the Origins to the Śaka Era* (Louvain-La-Neuve: Peters Press, 1988), p. 139. There also seems to be a difference of opinion on the rendering of *zájízàng* 雜集藏 as to whether this indicates Saṃyukta-*piṭaka* (Bareau, *Les sectes bouddhiques du petit véhicule*, p. 56; Lamotte, *History of Indian Buddhism*, p. 139), or *Kṣudraka-piṭaka* (Beal, *Si-Yu-Ki: Buddhist Records of the Western World*, vol. 2, p. 164). This problem was noted in Louis de la Vallée Poussin, "The Vidyādharapiṭaka," *Journal of the Royal Asiatic Society of Great Britain and Ireland* (1895): 433–436.

15 **Mahāyāna-naya-ṣaṭpāramitā-sūtra*; T.261.8:868b29–c24.

16 *Dàtáng xīyù qiúfǎ gāosēngchúan* 大唐西域求法高僧傳; T.2066.51:6c16, 21; Latika Lahiri, *Chinese Monks in India: Biography of Eminent Monks Who Went to the Western World in Search of the Law During the Great T'ang Dynasty* (Delhi: Motilal Banarsidass, 1986), pp. 64–68, renders mantra-*piṭaka* (*zhòuzàng* 咒藏) as *dhāraṇī-piṭaka*, continuing the problems initiated by Beal.

17 *Dàtáng xīyù qiúfǎ gāosēngchúan* 夫明呪者梵云毘睇陀羅必得家. 毘睇譯爲明呪. 陀羅是持. 必得家是藏 (T.2066.51:6c22–23): "Now, *vidyā* in the Sanskrit language is *'vidyādharapiṭaka.' Vidy*ā is translated as a spell; *dhara* means to hold; and *piṭaka* is a treasury."

18 *Cuṇḍīdevīdhāraṇī*; T.1077.20:186b2. The same claim is not made at the end of either of the other Chinese versions, T. 1075–1076, or the anonymous Tibetan translation, To. 613.

19 E.g., *Śikṣasamuccaya*, p. 142: *imām api vidyām anantajātismarahetuṃ mahāprabhāvāṃ saptapañcāśadakṣarāṃ vidyādharapiṭakōpanibaddhāṃ sarvabhayarakṣārthaṃ prayuñjīta / /*; *Subāhuparipṛcchā*, To. 805, fol. 136a4: *lha dang lha min mi la phan gdags phyir / gsang sngags rig sngags rnam pa sna tshogs dang / 'bum phrag lnga dang bye ba phrag gsum dag / rig 'dzin sde snod bshad par rgyal bas gsungs /*.

20 Jacob Dalton and Sam van Shaik, *Tibetan Tantric Manuscripts from Dunhuang* (Leiden and Boston: Brill, 2006), pp. xxi–xxiii. As we will see in the literature of the seven buddhas, textual sections may easily drift through the categories of sūtra and vinaya, or vinaya and *śāstra*, so that the idea of scriptural texts strongly differentiated by category or even from non-scripture is difficult to validate.

21 The earliest work known to me is the *gLegs bam gyi dkar chags* of Grags-pa rgyal-mtshan; see my *Tibetan Renaissance: Tantric Buddhism in the Rebirth of Tibetan Culture* (New York: Columbia University Press, 2005), pp. 356–360.

22 The only dedicated study known to me is Jean Philippe Vogel, "The Past Buddhas and Kāśyapa in Indian Art and Epigraphy," in Johannes Schubert and Ulrich Schneider, eds., *Asiatica: Festschrift Fredrich Weller* (Leipzig: Harrassowitz, 1954), pp. 808–816; many of his items will be revisited here. Jan Nattier also gives a short notice on the seven buddhas in her larger article on "Buddha(s)" in Robert E. Buswell, ed., *Encyclopedia of Buddhism: A–L, Volume 1* (New York: Macmillan Reference USA, 2004), p. 72.

23 Alois Führer, *Monograph on Buddha Sakyamuni's Birth-Place in The Nepalese Tarai* (Allahabad: The Government Press, N.-W. P. and Oudh, 1897), pp. 22–25, describes the pillar as he discovered it. E. Hultzsch, *Inscriptions of Aśoka* (Oxford: Printed for the Government of India at the Clarendon Press, 1925), p. 165, has the following edition:

> *devānaṃpiyena piyadasina lājina codasavasā[bh]i[si]t[e]n[a] budhasa konākamanasa thube dutiyaṃ vaḍhite . . . sābhisitena ca atana āgāca mahīyite . . . pāpite.*
>
> When King Devānāṃpriya Priyadarśin had been anointed fourteen years, he enlarged the Stūpa of the Buddha Konākamana to the double (of its original size). And when he has been anointed [twenty] years, he came himself and worshipped (this spot) [and] caused [a stone pillar to be set up].

Cf. George Bühler, "The Asoka Edicts of Paderia and Nigliva," *Epigraphia Indica* 5 (1898–1899): 6, who translates *dutiyaṃ* as "for a second time," thus bringing into question whether Aśoka or someone else had enlarged it. Hultzsch, *Inscriptions of Aśoka*, p. 165, n. 7, defends his translation. Harry Falk, "The Diverse Degrees of Authenticity of Aśokan Texts," in Patrick Olivelle, ed., *Aśoka In History and Historical Memory* (Delhi: Motilal Banarsidass, 2003), pp. 5–17, does not call into question the authenticity of the Niglīvā pillar edict.

24 Führer, *Monograph on Buddha Sakyamuni's Birth-Place*, pp. 16–21; Alexander Cunningham, *Archaeological Survey of India: Four Reports Made During the Years 1862–63–64–65* (Simla: Government Central Press, 1871), pp. 348–349, and *Report on Tours in the Gangetic Provinces from Badaon to Bihar, in 1875–76 and 1877–78* (Calcutta: Office of the Superintendent of Government Printing, 1880), pp. 70–78. On Fǎxiǎn's and Xuánzàng's records of these sites, see Max Deeg, *Das Gaoseng-Faxian-Zhuan als religionsgeschichtiliche Quelle* (Wiesbaden: Harrasowitz, 2005), pp. 322–327.

Krakucchanda's *keśanakhastūpa* is a topic of conversation in *Avadānaśataka* 87, vol. 2, p. 100, and presumably the same one is found in *Divyāvadāna* 27, p. 271. André Bareau, "La construction et le culte des stūpa d'après les *Vinayapiṭaka*," *Bulletin de'l'École Française d'Extrême-Orient* 50/2 (1962): 229–274, has taken the narrative of the construction of Kāśyapa's stūpa as paradigmatic for the overall development of the stūpa cult. Both his methods and conclusion have been disputed by Gregory Schopen, "Two Problems in the History of Indian Buddhism: The Layman/Monk Distinction and the Doctrines of the Transference of Merit," *Studien zur Indologie und Iranistik* 10 (1985): 9–47, although Schopen's position would be questionable as an improvement over Bareau's, as it argues that a single data point is to be privileged over multiple data points.

25 John Marshall and Alfred Foucher, *The Monuments of Sāñchī* (London: Probsthain, 1940), vol. 1, p. 390, discuss an offering inscription to the "place

where *(the images of)* the four Buddhas are seated," *caturbuddhāsane;* they explain: "The 'four Buddhas' are the four images in the *pradakṣiṇa-patha* adjoining the ground balustrade, one opposite each entrance."

[26] Führer, *Monograph on Buddha Sakyamuni's Birth-Place in The Nepalese Tarai,* p. 19.

[27] On the *bīr-bābā* sites in general, see Diane Coccari, "Protection and Identity: Banaras's Bīr Babas as Neighborhood Guardian Deities," in Sandra B. Freitag, ed., *Culture and Power in Banaras: Community, Performance and Environment, 1800–1980* (Berkeley: University of California Press, 1989), pp. 130–146, and "The Bir Babas of Banaras and the Deified Dead," in Alf Hiltebeitel, ed., *Criminal Gods and Demon Devotees: Essays on the Guardians of Popular Hinduism* (Albany, NY: State University of New York Press, 1989), pp. 251–269. The convergence of heroes and saints in the divinity of death is explored in Lindsey Harlan, *The Goddesses' Henchmen: Gender in Indian Hero Worship* (Oxford: Oxford University Press, 2003), although this narrative thread goes back to before the Buddha was given the alternative identity as a potential *cakravartin* and continues on through the position of Bhiṣma in the Śāntiparvan of the *Mahābhārata,* and into the present.

[28] Heinrich Lüders, *Bhārhut Inscriptions* (New Delhi: Director General, Archaeological Survey of India, 1963), pp. 82–86, plates XXXIII, XXXVII; Alexander Cunningham, *The Stūpa of Bharhut: A Buddhist Monument Ornamented with Numerous Sculptures Illustrative of Buddhist Legend and History in the Third Century B.C.* (London: Wm. H. Allen and Co., et al., 1879), pp. 45–46, 107–108, plates XXIX, XXX. The early Buddhist use of the term *bodhi* was a well-known abbreviation for the tree under which a buddha obtained awakening.

[29] Cunningham, *The Stūpa of Bharhut,* p. 10.

[30] Vogel, "The Past Buddhas and Kāśyapa in Indian Art and Epigraphy."

[31] Debala Mitra, *Buddhist Monuments* (Calcutta: Sahitya Samsad, 1971), p. 95.

[32] Bhagavānlāl Indraji, *Antiquarian Remains at Sopārā and Padaṇa* (Bombay: Education Society's Press, 1882), pp. 28–29; Lüders, *Bhārhut Inscriptions,* p. 83.

[33] Marshall and Foucher, *The Monuments of Sāñchī,* vol. 1, pp. 199–200; F. C. Maisey, *Sánchi and Its Remains* (London: Kegan Paul, Trench, Trübner & Co, 1892), pp. 18–66; a useful introduction to the layout of the gateways is in M. D. Dhavalikar, *Monumental Legacy: Sanchi* (New Delhi: Oxford University Press, 2003), pp. 18–81.

[34] There are too many individual items to list, but a representative sampling would include: from Gandhāra, Alfred Foucher, *Les Bas-reliefs Gréco-Bouddhiques du Gandhâra* (Paris: Imprimerie Nationale, 1905), p. 257, fig. 134; John Huntington, "The Iconography and Iconology of Maitreya Images in Gandhara," *Journal of Central Asia* 7/1 (1984): p. 166, fig. 1. Several items in the British Museum would seem to be candidates; see W. Zwalf, *A Catalogue of the Gandhāra Sculpture in the British Museum* (London: British Museum Press, 1996), vol. 2, pls. 117, 118, 290, 385–386, and vol. 1, p. 34, n. 22. From Swat, the Victoria and Albert Museum has a relief slab of the seven buddhas with Maitreya (V&A: IM.71–1939). From Mathurā, there is at least one frieze slab with the seven buddhas, apparently the one referenced by Christian Luczanits,

"The Bodhisattva with the Flask in Gandharan Narrative Scenes," *East and West* 55 (2005): 180, n. 45. The group from Ellora is illustrated in Mitra, *Buddhist Monuments*, pl. 116. From Amaravati, Robert Knox, *Amaravati: Buddhist Sculpture from the Great Stūpa* (London: British Museum Press, 1992), pp. 112–113 (nos. 52 and 53, third century C.E.). From Kanheri, Shobhana Gokhale, *Kanheri Inscriptions* (Pune: Deccan College Post Graduate and Research Institute, 1991), p. 25.

35 Walter Spink, *Ajanta: History and Development. Vol. 2: Arguments about Ajanta* (Leiden: Brill, 2006), pp. 167–173, 204-220; *Ajanta: History and Development. Vol. 4: Painting, Sculpture, Architecture* (Leiden: Brill, 2009), pp. 96–105; *Ajanta: History and Development. Vol. 5: Cave by Cave* (Leiden, Brill, 2005), pp. 135–140.

36 Richard Cohen, "Ajanta's Inscriptions," Appendix in Spink, *Ajanta: History and Development. Vol. 2*, inscriptions 58 and 91, pp. 303–304; James Burgess and Bhagwanlal Indraji Pandit, *Inscriptions from the Cave-Temples of Western India. Archaeological Survey of Western India* (Bombay: Government Central Press, 1881), inscriptions 17 and 30, pp. 85, 88.

37 On Maitreya images and their association with the seven buddhas, see Luczanits, "The Bodhisattva with the Flask in Gandharan Narrative Scenes," pp. 182–183.

38 Indraji, *Antiquarian Remains at Sopārā and Padaṇa;* Mitra, *Buddhist Monuments*, pp. 188–189.

39 Juhyung Rhi, "Images, Relics, and Jewels: The Assimilation of Images in the Buddhist Relic Cult of Gandhāra—or Vice Versa," *Artibus Asiae* 65/2 (2005): 169–211, discusses the investiture of relics in buddha statues. There were certainly examples of images on the sides of stūpas, some of which were probably inspired by the seven buddhas; see John Marshall, *Taxila* (Cambridge: Cambridge University Press, 1951), vol. 3, pl. 104–107. Zwalf, *A Catalogue of the Gandhāra Sculpture in the British Museum*, vol. 1, pp. 348–350, gives an account of the scholarship on the Bīmarān casket to the mid-1990s.

40 Takamichi Fukita, *The Mahāvadānasūtra: A New Edition Based on Manuscripts Discovered in Northern Turkestan* (Göttingen: Vendenhoeck & Ruprecht, 2003), pp. xvii–xxii, reviews the philology of the text. A complete assessment of the seven buddhas remains a desideratum, for which this contribution will be but a part.

41 Bhikkhu Anālayo, *The Genesis of the Bodhisattva Ideal* (Hamburg: Hamburg University Press, 2008), pp. 71–93; quoted material from p. 88.

42 To give but a few examples of narratives of the buddhas independent of their status as one of the seven, an episode involving Vipaśyin and Śroṇakoṭiviṃśa is found in the *Saṅghabhedavastu*, vol. 2, pp. 147–149; he has an interaction with the Bodhisattva as Gaṇavācaka in *Bhaiṣajyavastu* 46–47; Śikhin is in the *Mahāvastu*, vol. 3, pp. 94-95; Krakucchanda has an episode in *Avadānaśataka* 75, vol. 2, pp. 29–30; and Kanakamuni appears in *Avadānaśataka*, vol. 2, pp. 34–35.

43 Junko Matsumura has recently proposed a useful classification of the many Dīpaṃkara narratives in "The Story of the Dīpaṃkara Buddha Prophecy in Northern Buddhist Texts: An Attempt at Classification," *Journal of Indian and Buddhist Studies* 59/3 (2011): 63–72.

44 Étienne Lamotte, "La légende du Buddha," *Revue de l'histoire des religions* 134/1–3 (1947): 37–71.

45 See Bhikkhu Anālayo, *A Comparative Study of the Majjhima-nikāya* (Taipei: Dharma Drum Publishing Corporation, 2011), vol. 1, p. 49, for some of the opinions; also Nattier, "Buddhas," p. 72; Vogel, "The Past Buddhas and Kāśyapa in Indian Art and Epigraphy," p. 816. Suuko Ohira, "The Twenty-Four Buddhas and the Twenty-Four Tīrthaṅkaras," in Nalini Blabir and Joachim K. Bautze, eds., *Festschrift Klaus Bruhn: zur Vollendung des 65. Lebensjahres* (Reinbek: Dr. Inge Wezler Verlag für Orientalistische Fachpublikationen, 1994), pp. 475–488, discusses the correlation of the two groups of twenty-four.

46 Yamada, *Karuṇāpuṇḍarīka*, vol. 1, pp. 121–126, has discussed some of these relationships.

47 Katherine Anne Harper, *Seven Hindu Goddesses of Spiritual Transformation: The Iconography of the Saptamatrikas* (Lewiston, NY: The Edwin Mellen Press, 1989), pp. 13–45.

48 Translated in K. R. Norman, *The Group of Discourses (Sutta-nipāta)* (Oxford: Pali Text Society, 1992), p. 69.

49 *Dīghanikāya* I.113, 115, 120–121, 123; *Dīrghāgama* T.1.1:94a24–25: 此婆羅門七世以來父母眞正. 不爲他人之所輕毀; 95a2–3: 沙門瞿曇. 七世已來父母眞正. 不爲他人之所輕毀; and 96a2. Similarly in the *Kūṭadanta*, DN I.130–131, but also applied to King Mahāvijita and his *purohita*, DN I.137–141; T.1.1:96c23, 97b11; T.1.1:96c23–4, 97b11–12, 97c7–8. The same phrase has been placed in the *Dīrghāgama* version of the *Ambaṭṭha-sutta*, T.1.1:82a12–13, 83b6–7. A similar discussion is found in the Pāli *Caṅkī-sutta*, MN II.165–66, 169–170; see Anālayo, *A Comparative Study of the Majjhima-nikāya*, vol. 2, pp. 557–563, especially p. 557, n. 144, where he discusses surviving published Sanskrit fragments.

50 *Tevijja-sutta; Dīghanikāya* I.238–43 passim: *kim pana, Vāseṭṭha. atthi koci tevijjānaṃ brāhmaṇānaṃ yāva sattamā ācariya-mahāyugā yena brahmā sakkhidiṭṭho ti. no h'idaṃ bho gotama;* T.1.1:105a1–2, 105a5–6. *Subha-sutta; Majjhimanikāya* II.199–200; the *Subha-sutta* versions in Chinese do not seem to contain this material: T.26.1:666c–670a, T.79; see Anālayo, *A Comparative Study of the Majjhima-nikāya*, vol. 2, pp. 572–579, on the different versions of the text.

51 Patrick Olivelle, *The Law Code of Viṣṇu: A Critical Edition and Annotated Translation of the Vaiṣṇava-Dharmaśāstra* (Cambridge, MA: Department of Sanskrit and Indian Studies, Harvard University, 2009), pp. 82, 287.

52 On this difference, see Panduranga Vamana Kane, *History of Dharmaśāstra: Ancient and Mediaeval Religious and Civil Law* (Poona: Bhandarkar Oriental Research Institute, 1930–1962), vol. II, part 1, pp. 452–478; *Dāyabhāga*, pp. 26–28.

53 *Gautama-dharma-śāstra* 4.23 also allows that some authorities recognize the fifth rather than the seventh generation.

54 Translated in Patrick Olivelle, *Manu's Code of Law: A Critical Edition and Translation of the Mānava-Dharmaśāstra* (Oxford: Oxford University Press, 2005), pp. 211, 823.

55 Similarly, *Baudhāyana-dharma-sūtra* 1.5.11.11–12; *Dāyabhāga* 11.6.12; on inheritance, see Kane, *History of Dharmaśāstra*, vol. III, pp. 733–765.

56 Ernst Waldschmidt, *Das Mahāparinirvāṇasūtra* (Berlin: Akademie-Verlag, 1951), § 41.2.

57 *Milindapañha,* pp. 190–192; Isaline B. Horner, *Milinda's Questions* (London: Luzac, 1963), vol. 1, pp. 271–272, provides notes that are valuable for some of the lexical peculiarities of this passage. I thank Steven Collins for his advice on some of the difficult terminology.

58 **Mahīśāsaka-prātimokṣa,* T.1422.22:206a6-b10; *Mahāsāṃghika-prātimokṣa,* W. Pachow and Ramakanta Mishra, *The Prātimokṣa-Sūtra of the Mahāsāṅghikās* (Allahabad: Ganganatha Jha Research Institute, 1956), pp. 42–45, T.1426.22.555b22–c28; **Mahāsāṃghika-bhikṣuṇī-prātimokṣa* T.1427.22:564c8–565a14; **Dharmaguptaka-prātimokṣa* T.1429.22:1022b11–c8; **Dharmaguptaka-bhikṣuṇī-prātimokṣa* T.1430.22:1030a11–b7, T.1431.22:1040b17–c15; *Mūlasarvastivāda-prātimokṣa,* Ankul Chandra Banerjee, "The Prātimokṣa-Sūtra," *Indian Historical Quarterly* 29 (1953): 376–377, T. 1454.24:507b27–c27, To. 2, fol. 20a4–b6; *Mūlasarvastivāda-bhikṣuṇī-prātimokṣa,* T.1455.24.517a7–b22, To. 4, fol. 24b3–25a6. Note that the arrangement and personality identification of the verses in Yìjìng's translation in both T. 1454 and T. 1455 is closer to the *Mahāsāṃghika-prātimokṣa* rather than either the surviving Sanskrit or the Tibetan, To. 2 or To. 4; this would suggest alternative recensions of the *Mūlasarvāstivāda-prātimokṣa,* much as is seen in the case of the *Sarvāstivāda-prātimokṣa.*

59 Material in brackets is reconstructed. Louis M. Finot and M. Édouard Huber, "Le Prātimokṣasūtra des Sarvāstivādins, texte Sanskrit par M. Louis Finot avec la Version Chinoise de Kumārajīva traduit en Français par M. Édouard Huber," *Journal Asiatique* (Novembre-Décembre 1913): 539–543; Klaus T. Schmidt, *Der Schlußteil des Prātimokṣasūtra der Sarvāstivādins: Text in Sanskrit und Tocharisch A verglichen mit den Parallelversionen anderer Schulen* (Göttingen: Vandenhoeck & Ruprecht, 1989), p. 73; Georg von Simson, *Prātimokṣasūtra der Sarvāstivādins* (Göttingen: Vandenhoeck & Ruprecht, 2000), pp. 259–263; T.1436.23:478b22–c26; von Simson notes that pp. 2–3 of Kumārajīva's recension follows the older "Gruppe A," as opposed to "Gruppe B," although neither recension provides the seven buddhas attribution in the manner of Kumārajīva. Finot's manuscript includes material attached to some of the seven buddhas, but most often in a manner that is dissimilar to the way they are described in T. 1436. To reconstruct the language of T. 1436 I have used the language of the *Mahāvadāna* (Fukita, *The Mahāvadānasūtra,* pp. 40–42) and of the *Saptabuddhastotra.*

60 *Udānavarga,* n. 50b, reads *prīti mokṣe ca,* but cf. Finot and Huber, "Le Prātimokṣasūtra des Sarvāstivādins," p. 541, n. 1; Schmidt, *Der Schlußteil des Prātimokṣasūtra,* p. 74, von Simson, *Prātimokṣasūtra der Sarvāstivādins,* p. 260; the Chinese clearly reads *prātimokṣa: rújìe suǒshuōxíng* 如戒所說行.

61 This verse is not recognized in the manuscripts edited and studied by Schmidt, *Der Schlußteil des Prātimokṣasūtra,* p. 74, and followed by von Simson, *Prātimokṣasūtra der Sarvāstivādins,* pp. 262–263. Instead, Schmidt provides six other verses that complete the text, one of which affirms that the *Prātimokṣa* derives from the seven buddhas, considered below. Extraordinarily, Finot and Huber matched the Chinese translation of the final verse presented here to

the material in *Mahāvyutpatti* 8709–8712; this statement, however, is well attested elsewhere in Sanskrit Buddhist literature: *Abhidharma-samuccayabhāṣya*, p. 104, *Bodhisattvabhūmi*, p. 170, *Kāśyapaparivarta*, p. 156 (§ 107), *Śrāvakabhūmi*, in Śrāvakabhūmi Study Group, ed., *Śrāvakabhūmi*, pp. 216.2–3, 288.9–10; *Śrāvakabhūmi*, in Karunesha Shukla, ed., *Śrāvakabhūmi of Ācārya Asaṅga* (Patna: K. P. Jayaswal Research Institute, 1973), pp. 130.2–5, 163.6–8, 378.15–17, etc.

62 Charles S. Prebish, *Buddhist Monastic Discipline: The Sanskrit Prātimokṣa Sūtras of the Mahāsāṃghikas and Mūlasarvāstivādins* (University Park, PA: Pennsylvania State University Press, 1975), p. 138.

63 Schmidt, *Der Schlußteil des Prātimokṣasūtra*, p. 74.

64 Schmidt, *Der Schlußteil des Prātimokṣasūtra*, p. 79, interpreted "Maharṣi" as Śākyamuni, whereas von Simson, *Prātimokṣasūtra der Sarvāstivādins*, p. 317, makes no such identification. Given the position of the term, Śākyamuni would seem the most likely identification.

65 von Simson, *Prātimokṣasūtra der Sarvāstivādins*, p. 4; Schmidt, *Der Schlußteil des Prātimokṣasūtra*, p. 93, v. 12, is the Mūlasarvāstivāda recension.

66 Lüders, *Bhārhut Inscriptions*, p. 154.

67 B. Barua and K. G. Sinha, *Barhut Inscriptions* (Calcutta: University of Calcutta, 1926), pp. 89–90.

68 Ingo Strauch, *The Bajaur Collection: A New Collection of Kharoṣṭhī Manuscripts—A Preliminary Catalogue and Survey*, 2008 (www.geschkult.fu-berlin.de/e/indologie/ bajaur/publication/index.html#Strauch2007), pp. 40–47.

69 *Dàzhōu kāngdìng zhòngjīng mùlù* 大周刊定衆經目録, T.2153.55:400b21–24. The corpus of Zhīqiān's translations have been considered in detail in Jan Nattier, *A Guide to the Earliest Chinese Buddhist Translations: Texts from the Eastern Han* 東漢 *and Three Kingdoms* 三國 *Periods* (Tokyo: The International Research Institute for Advanced Buddhology, Soka University, 2008), pp. 116–148.

70 *Fóshuō fómíngjīng* 佛說佛名經, T.441.14:197c5.

71 *Chū sānzàng jìjí* 出三藏記集, T.2145.55:31b11–14; it is curious that *taila* would be regularly translated by *má yóu* (麻油), which seems to mean hemp oil in China.

72 *Lìdài sānbǎojì* 歷代三寶紀, T.2034.49:74c6–7, 113c25–26, mentions both the titles given in the *Chū sānzàng jìjí*; see also T.2034.49:58b10.

73 This question is considered in Jonathan A. Silk, "The *Jefayue sheku tuoluoji jing*—Translation, Non-translation, Both or Neither?", *Journal of the International Association of Buddhist Studies* 31/1–2 (2010): 377–378; in his discussion, Silk presumes that a catalogue entry for *Qīfó shénzhòujīng* 七佛神呪經 in four rolls is "what appears to be this text (i.e., the *Qīfó bāpúsà suǒshuō shénzhòujīng* 七佛八菩薩所說神呪經) more or less" (pp. 376–377), a supposition I would question; *Kāiyuán shìjiàolù* 開元釋教録, T.2154.55:510a8; cf. *Dàzhōu kāngdìng zhòngjīng mùlù* 大周刊定衆經目録, T.2153.55:400b21–24.

74 Silk, "The *Jefayue sheku tuoluoji jing*."

75 Cf. Ulrich Pagel "The *Dhāraṇīs* of *Mahāvyutpatti* #748: Origin and Formation," *Buddhist Studies Review* 24/2 (2007): 151–191; and the studies of

mantra transcriptions by Paul Harrison and W. South Coblin, "The Oldest Buddhist Incantation in Chinese? A Preliminary Study of the Chinese Transcriptions of the Mantra in the *Druma-kinnara-rāja-paripṛcchā*," in John R. McRae and Jan Nattier, eds., *Buddhism Across Boundaries* (Philadelphia: Department of East Asian Languages and Civilizations, 2012), pp. 61–85; South W. Coblin, "Notes on Sanghabhara's Mahamayuri transcriptions," *Cahiers de linguistique—Asie orientale* 19/2 (1990): 195–251.

76 Coblin, "Notes on Sanghabhara's Mahamayuri transcriptions," has studied both this text and the transcription regimen employed.

77 *Mahāmāyūrī*, pp. 13–14, corresponding to T.894.19:449a19–25; and *Mahāmāyūrī*, pp. 43–44, corresponding to T.984.19:455b24–456a23.

78 There may be surviving Sanskrit texts: the German Manuscript Preservation Project lists a *Saptabuddha(nāma)dhāraṇī* in its electronic catalogue, reel E 1504/14, and a *Saptabuddhanāmadhāraṇī*, reel E1923/3. I do not have access to these texts at this time to determine their relationship(s) to the Chinese and Tibetan texts under discussion. I have located no other Sanskrit text with the same or a similar title.

79 *lDan-dkar-ma*, no. 202; *'Phang-thang-ma*, no. 330.

80 *Vinaya-piṭaka* I.202–203; on possession more generally in South Asia, see Frederick M. Smith, *The Self Possessed: Deity and Spirit Possession in South Asian Literature and Civilization* (New York: Columbia University Press, 2006).

81 The Buddha's diagnoses of the monks' problems are at T.1333.21:561b29–c2: 此一比丘爲惡病所持出是音聲. 又一比丘爲惡鬼所持露形而走; T.1334.21:565a20: 是一比丘惡鬼所捉. 復一比丘著於邪魅; T.1147.20:605a4–5: 彼二比丘疾病所纒部多所執是故裸形叫喚啼泣; To. 512, fol. 22a7: *'di ni nad kyis btab pa yin no / cig shos 'di yang nad kyis btab pa yin no.*

82 This specific ritual is missing from T. 1147, although generally it declares that it is capable of overcoming poison, as is also claimed by the other versions. The 984 C.E. text appears a bit more abbreviated than the others, and it is interesting that the longest and most explicit work is earliest while the shortest and apparently least complete is the latest.

83 Silk's article "The *Jefayue sheku tuoluoji jing*" would have been improved with a consideration of the way that ritual texts are more generally seen by Indians; for example, see Thomas B. Coburn, "'Scripture' in India: Towards a Typology of the Word in Hindu Life," *Journal of the American Academy of Religion* 52/3 (1984): 435–459. Silk could equally have profited from modern text-critical understandings, as in the case of form criticism or social scientific criticism; for an overview of form criticism, see Samuel Byrskog, "A Century with the Sitz im Leben: From Form-Critical Setting to Gospel Community and Beyond," *Zeitschrift für die neutestamentliche Wissenschaft und die Kunde der älteren Kirche* 98/1 (2007): 1–27. Silk indicates that the problem is observable in Tibet as well ("The *Jefayue sheku tuoluoji jing*," p. 371, n. 6), but does not mention the extensive discussions about this issue; for my perspective on what I have termed "gray" texts, see "Gsar ma Apocrypha: The Creation of Orthodoxy, Gray Texts, and the New Revelation," in Helmut Eimer and David

Germano, eds., *The Many Canons of Tibetan Buddhism* (Leiden: Brill, 2002), pp. 203–224; *Tibetan Renaissance*, pp. 117–249.

84 This text is edited in Janardan Shastri Pandey, *Bauddhastotrasaṃgraha* (Delhi: Motilal Banarsidass, 1994), pp. 249–250, and translated in Horace Hayman Wilson, "Notice of Three Tracts Received From Nepal," *Asiatic Researches* 16 (1828): 450–478. Matsunami's *A Catalogue of the Sanskrit Manuscripts in the Tokyo University Library* (Tokyo: Suzuki Research Foundation, 1965), pp. 330, 324, referencing mss. nos. 201, 276, 416, 418, and 420, indicates that five of the *dhāraṇīsaṃgraha* manuscripts at Tokyo University contain this text. Janak Lāl Vaidya and Prem Bahādur Kaṃsakār, *A Descriptive Catalogue of Selected Manuscripts Preserved at the Āśā Saphū Kuthī (Āśā Archives)* (Kathmandu: Cvasāpāsā, 1991), p. 187, identifies this text in ms. catalogue no. 480, *Dhāraṇī Saṃgraha.* My thanks to the late Prof. Min Bahadur Shakya for his assistance in obtaining this catalogue. Not all of the *dhāraṇīsaṃgraha*s, however, contain either the *Saptabuddhastotra* or the *Saptajinastava;* it is missing in both Jean Filliozat, *Catalogue du Fonds Sanskrit* (Paris: Adrien-Maisonneuve, 1941), pp. 31–57, and in the *dhāraṇīsaṃgraha* ms. described by Janardan Shastri Pandey, *Durlabha Bauddha Grantha Parichaya* (Sarnath: Central Institute of Higher Tibetan Studies, 1990), pp. 58–68.

85 These texts are To. 271, 277, 278; T. 427–431.

86 T.427.14:73a12 appears to use the term "mantra" to identify the buddhas' names. In the current Taishō edition, T. 427 (perhaps properly rendered as **Aṣṭamaṅgalaka; Bājíxiáng shénzhòujīng* 八吉祥神呪經) is identified as a translation by Zhīqiān, but this is apparently taken from the 695 C.E. catalogue of Míngquán (*Dàzhōu kāndìng zhòngjīng mùlù*, T.2153.55:390c8). Sēngyòu's *Chū sānzàng jìjí* provides no such attribution but instead records that the text was translated on the thirteenth day of Yúanjiā, in the area of Jīngzhōu (T.2145.55:12c22: 八吉祥經一卷元嘉二十九年正月十三日於荊州譯出), which corresponds to February13, 452 C.E., a much more satisfactory date. Likewise, the attribution of T. 428 to Dharmarakṣa is suspicious, as no early catalogue has it. In all likelihood, these are fifth- to sixth-century texts. For an overall survey of these catalogues and their attitude to indigenous scriptures, see Kyoko Tokuno, "The Evaluation of Indigenous Scriptures in Chinese Buddhist Bibliographical Categories," in Robert E. Buswell, ed., *Chinese Buddhist Apocrypha* (Honolulu: University of Hawai'i Press, 1990), pp. 31–74.

87 An apparently earlier **Daśamaṅgala,* T. 432, is phrased in much the same manner as the *Aṣṭabuddhaka/Maṅgalāṣṭaka* texts, and it does not include directional assignments for the buddhas named therein, other than mentioning they are all in the east.

88 *Daśabuddhaka,* To. 272, fol. 23b6: *ji ltar de bzhin gshegs pa dgra bcom pa yang dag par rdzogs pa'i sangs rgyas 'od dpag med kyi 'jig rten gyi khams bde ba can de 'dra ba'i sangs rgyas kyi zhing yon tan bkod pa rnams 'thob par 'gyur ro /*; also 24b4; T.310(34).11:565c5, c26.

89 *lDan-dkar-ma,* no. 147. The *'Phang-thang-ma* entry (no. 118) is for a *'Phags pa de bzhing gshegs pa bdun gyi smon lam,* of two *bam-po,* which is the same size as the *lDan-dkar-ma* text and our received version; while it is not absolutely clear

that *'Phang-thang-ma* 118 is our text, the likelihood is great, especially as it employs the same title, again apparently to reference the sūtra, that is in Dalton and Shaik, *Tibetan Tantric Manuscripts from Dunhuang,* IOL Tib J 433.

90 *Śikṣāsamuccaya,* p. 169; lCang-kya's text is integrated into Lokesh Chandra, *Tibetan-Sanskrit Dictionary,* 2 vols. (Kyoto: Rinsen Book Company, 1976), and *Tibetan Sanskrit Dictionary, Supplementary Volume* (Kyoto: Rinsen Book Company, 2009). Curiously, the many names found in *Karuṇāpuṇḍarīka,* vol. 2, pp. 159–161, scarcely overlap in this instance.

91 Raoul Birnbaum, *The Healing Buddha* (Boston: Shambhala Publications, 1989), pp. 173–217.

92 Dalton and Shaik, *Tibetan Tantric Manuscripts from Dunhuang,* no. 433, is a version of both part of the scripture and of To. 3134, whereas *'Phang-thang-ma* 944 appears to be To. 3133.

93 Pagel, "Introduction," p. 29.

References

Abbreviations

sTog Tadeusz Skorupski, *A Catalogue of the Stog Palace Kanjur.* Tokyo: International Institute for Buddhist Studies, 1985.

T. Takakusu Junjirō and Watanabe Kaikyoku, eds., *Taishō Shinshū Daizōkyō.* Tokyo: Daizōkyōkai, 1924–1935.

To. Hakuju Ui, et al., eds., *A Complete Catalogue of the Tibetan Buddhist Canons (BKaḥ-ḥgyur and Bstan-ḥgyur).* Sendai: Tōhoku Imperial University, 1934.

Primary Sources

Abhidharmasamuccaya. Pralhad Pradhan, *Abhidharma Samuccaya of Asanga.* Visva-Bharati Studies 12. Santiniketan: Visva-Bharati, 1950.

Abhidharmasamuccayabhāṣya. Nathmal Tatia, *Abhidharmasamuccaya-bhāṣyam.* Tibetan Sanskrit Works Series No. 17. Patna: Kashi Prasad Jayaswal Research Institute, 1976.

Āpastambīya-dharma-sūtra. George Bühler, *Āpastamba's Aphorisms on the Sacred Law of the Hindus.* Bombay Sanskrit Series, Nos. 44, 50. Bombay: Government Central Book Depot, 1932, third rev. ed.

Aṣṭabuddhaka-nāma-mahāyāna-sūtra, To. 271, 277; T. 427–428, 430–431.

Avadānaśataka. J. S. Speyer, *Avadānaçataka: A Century of Edifying Tales Belonging to the Hīnayāna.* Bibliotheca Buddhica III, 2 vols. St. Pétersbourg: l'Académie Impériale des Sciences, 1906.

Baudhāyana-dharmasūtra. E. Hultzsch, *Das Baudhāyana-Dharmasūtra. Abhandlungen für die Künde des Morgenländes,* Bd. 16. Leipzig: Brockhaus, 1922, second rev. ed.

Bhaiṣajyavastu, To. 1, vols. ka 277b6–ga, 50a7; T. 1448. Nalinaksha Dutt, *Gilgit Manuscripts,* vol. III/1. Srinagar: Research Department, 1947.

Bodhisattvabhūmi, To. 4037; T. 1579 (15), 1581, 1582. Unrai Wogihara. *Bodhisattvabhūmi: A Statement of the Whole Course of the Bodhisattva.* Tokyo: Sankibo Buddhist Book Store, 1971.

Chū sānzàng jìjí 出三藏記集, T. 2145.

Cuṇḍīdevīdhāraṇī, To. 613; T. 1075–1077.

Daśabuddhaka (= *Guṇaratnasaṅkusumitaparipṛcchā-sūtra*), To. 78, 272; T. 310 (34).

Dàtáng xīyùjì 大唐西域記, T. 2089.

Dàtáng xīyù qiúfǎ gāosēngchuán 大唐西域求法高僧傳, T. 2066.

Dāyabhāga. Judo Rocher, ed. and trans. *Jīmūtavāhana's Dāyabhāga: The Hindu Law of Inheritance in Bengal.* Oxford: Oxford University Press, 2002.

Dàzhōu kāngdìng zhòngjīng mùlù 大周刊定衆經目録, T. 2153.

Dhāraṇīsaṃgraha, T. 901.

Dhāraṇīsaṃgraha, T. 1336.

**Dharmaguptaka-bhikṣuṇī-prātimokṣa,* T. 1430, 1431.

**Dharmaguptaka-prātimokṣa,* T. 1429.

Dīghanikāya. T. W. Rhys Davids and J. Estlin Carpenter, *The Dīgha Nikāya,* 3 vols. London: Pali Text Society, 1890–1911.

Dīrghāgama, T. 1.

Divyāvadāna. Edward B. Cowell and Robert A. Neil, *The Divyāvadāna: A Collection of Early Buddhist Legends.* Cambridge: The University Press, 1886.

Dvādaśabuddhaka, To. 273, 511, 853; T. 1348–1349.

Fóshuō fómíngjīng 佛説佛名經, T. 441.

Gautama-dharmaśāstra. Umeśacandra Pāṇḍeya, *Gautamadharmasūtrāṇi Hindīvyākhyāvibhūṣita-haradattakṛta-mitākṣarāvṛti-sahitāni.* Vārāṇasī: Chaukhambha Samskrit Bhawan, 1966.

Jātaka-aṭṭhkathā. Viggo Fausbøll, *The Jātaka Together with its Commentary,* 6 vols. London: Trübner & Co., 1877–1896.

Kāiyuán shìjiàolù 開元釋教録, T. 2154.

Karuṇāpuṇḍarīka. Issi Yamada, *Karuṇāpuṇḍarīka: The White Lotus of Compassion,* 2 vols. London: School of Oriental and African Studies, 1986.

Kāśyapaparivarta. Baron A. von Staël-Holstein, *The Kāçyapaparivarta: A Mahāyānasūtra of the Ratnakūṭa Class.* Shanghai: Commercial Press, 1926.

Lalitavistara. S. Lefmann, *Lalita Vistara: Leben und Lehre des Çâkya-Buddha,* 2 vols. Halle a.S.: Buchhandlung des Waisenhauses, 1902–1908.

lDan-dkar-ma. Adelheid Herrmann-Pfandt, *Die lHan kar ma: Ein Früher Katalog der ins Tibetische übersetzten buddhistischen Texte.* Wien: Verlag der Österreichischen Akademie der Wissenschaften, 2008.

Lìdài sānbǎojì 歷代三寶紀, T. 2034.

Madhyamāgama, T. 26.

Mahāmāyūrī-vidyārājñī. Shūyo Takubo, *Ārya-Mahā-Māyūrī Vidyā-Rājñī.* Tokyo: Sankibo, 1972.

Mahāparinirvāṇa-sūtra. Ernst Waldschmidt, *Das Mahāparinirvāṇasūtra.* Abhandlungen der Deutschen Akademie der Wissenschaften zu Berlin, Klasse für Sprachen, Literatur und Kunst, Jahrgang 1950 Nr. 3. 3 Teile. Berlin: Akademie-Verlag, 1951.

**Mahāsāṃghika-bhikṣuṇī-prātimokṣa,* T. 1427.

Mahāsāṃghika-prātimokṣa, T. 1426. W. Pachow and Ramakanta Mishra, *The Prātimokṣa-Sūtra of the Mahāsāṅghikās.* Allahabad: Ganganatha Jha Research Institute, 1956.

Mahāvadāna. Takamichi Fukita, *The Mahāvadānasūtra: A New Edition Based on Manuscripts Discovered in Northern Turkestan.* Göttingen: Vendenhoeck & Ruprecht, 2003.

Mahāvastu. Émile Senart, *Le Mahāvastu: Texte Sanscrit,* 3 vols. Paris: Imprimerie Nationale, 1882–1897.

Mahāvyutpatti. Sakai Ryōzaburō, *Bon-Zō-Kan-Wa yon yaku taikō hon yaku myōgi taishū,* 2 vols. Tokyo: Suzuki Gakujutsu Zaidan, 1962.

**Mahāyāna-naya-ṣaṭpāramitā-sūtra,* T. 261.

**Mahīśāsaka-prātimokṣa,* T. 1422.

Majjhimanikāya. V. Trenckner, et al., *The Majjhima-Nikāya.* London: Pali Text Society, 1888–1925.

Mānava-dharma-śāstra, To. 278; T. 429. Patrick Olivelle, *Manu's Code of Law: A Critical Edition and Translation of the Mānava-Dharmaśāstra.* Oxford: Oxford University Press, 2005.

Maṅgalāṣṭaka, To. 278; T. 429.

Milinda-pañha. V. Trenckner, *The Milindapañho: Being Dialogues between King Milinda and the Buddhist Sage Nāgasena.* London: Williams and Norgate, 1880.

Mūlasarvāstivāda-bhikṣuṇī-prātimokṣa, T. 1455.

Mūlasarvāstivāda-prātimokṣa, To. 2; T. 1454. Ankul Chandra Banerjee, "The Prātimokṣa-Sūtra," *Indian Historical Quarterly* 29 (1953): 162–174, 266–275, 363–377.

Nāradasmṛti. Richard, W. Lariviere, *The Nāradasmṛti: Critically Edited with an Introduction, Annotated Translation, and Appendices,* 2 vols. Philadelphia: Department of South Asia Regional Studies, University of Pennsylvania, 1989.

Nikāyabhedavibhaṅgavyākhyāna, To. 4139.

Nirvikalpapraveśadhāraṇī. Kazunobu Matsuda, ed. and trans., "*Nirvikalpapraveśa-dhāraṇī*: Sanskrit Text and Japanese Translation," *Bulletin of the Research Institute of Bukkyo University (Bukkyō Daigaku Sōgō Kenkyūjo Kiyō)* 3 (1996): 89–113.

'Phang-thang-ma. Eishin Kawagoe, *dKar chag 'Phang thang ma.* Sendai: Tohoku Society for Indo-Tibetan Studies, 2005.

Qīfó bāpúsà suǒshuō dàtuóluóní shénzhòujīng 七佛八菩薩所說大陀羅尼神呪經. T. 1332.

Saṅghabhedavastu. Raniero Gnoli, *The Gilgit Manuscript of the Saṅghabhedavastu,* 2 vols. Serie Orientale Roma vol. XLIX. Rome: Istituto Italiano per il Medio ed Estremo Oriente, 1977.

Śāṅkhāyanagṛhya-sūtra. S. R. Sehgal, *Śāṅkhāyana Gṛhya Sūtram.* Delhi: Sri Satguru Publications, 1987.

Sānlùn xúanyì 三論玄義, T. 1852.

Saptabuddhaka, To. 270, 512, 852; Tog 472; T. 1127, 1333, 1334.

Saptabuddhastotra. Janardan Shastri Pandey, *Bauddhastotrasamgraha,* pp. 249–250. Delhi: Motilal Banarsidass, 1994. See also Horace Hayman Wilson, "Notice of Three Tracts Received From Nepal," *Asiatic Researches* 16 (1828): 450–478.

Saptajinastava, To. 1165. Janardan Shastri Pandey, *Bauddhastotrasamgraha,* p. 247. Delhi: Motilal Banarsidass, 1994.

Saptatathāgatapūrvapraṇidhānaviśeṣavistāra-nāma-mahāyāna-sūtra, To. 503; T. 449.

Sarvāstivāda-prātimokṣa. Louis M. Finot and M. Édouard Huber, "Le Prātimokṣa-sūtra des Sarvāstivādins, texte Sanskrit par M. Louis Finot avec la Version Chinoise de Kumārajīva traduit en Français par M. Édouard Huber," *Journal Asiatique* (Novembre-Décembre 1913): 465–558. Georg von Simson, *Prātimokṣasūtra der Sarvāstivādins.* Sanskrittexte aus den Turfan funden XI. Teil II. Göttingen: Vandenhoeck & Ruprecht, 2000. Klaus T. Schmidt, *Der Schlußteil des Prātimokṣasūtra der Sarvāstivādins: Text in Sanskrit und Tocharisch A verglichen mit den Parallelversionen anderer Schulen.* Sanskrittexte aus den Turfan funden XIII. Göttingen: Vandenhoeck & Ruprecht, 1989.

Sarvāstivādavinaya-mātṛkā, T. 1441

Śikṣasamuccaya. Cecil Bendall, *Çikshāsamuccaya: A Compendium of Buddhistic Teaching Compiled by Çāntideva.* Bibliotheca Buddhica I. St. Petersburg: l'Académie Impériale des Sciences, 1897.

Śrāvakabhūmi. Karunesha Shukla, *Śrāvakabhūmi of Ācārya Asaṅga.* Patna: K. P. Jayaswal Research Institute, 1973.

Subāhuparipṛcchā-tantra, To. 805.

Suttanipāta. Dines Andersen and Helmer Smith, *The Sutta-nipāta.* London: Pali Text Society, 1913.

Tarkajvālā, To. 3856.

Triśaraṇasaptati. Per K. Sorensen, *Triśaraṇasaptati: The Septuagint on the Three Refuges.* Vienna: Arbeitskreis für Tibetische unde Buddhistische Studien, 1986.

Udānavarga. Franz Bernhard, *Udānavarga,* 3 vols. Göttingen: Vandenhoeck & Ruprecht, 1965–1990.

Vajramaṇḍa-dhāraṇī, To. 139; T. 1344, 1345.

Vinaya-piṭaka. Hermann Oldenburg, *The Vinaya Piṭakaṃ: One of the Principal Buddhist Holy Scriptures in the Pâli Language,* 5 vols. London: Williams and Norgate, 1879–1883.

Viṣṇusmṛti. Patrick Olivelle, ed. and trans., *The Law Code of Viṣṇu: A Critical Edition and Annotated Translation of the Vaiṣṇava-Dharmaśāstra.* Harvard Oriental

Series, vol. 73. Cambridge, MA: Department of Sanskrit and Indian Studies, Harvard University, 2009.

Yājñavalkyasmṛti. Wāsudev Laxmaṇ Śāstrī Panśīkar, *Yādnyavalkyasmṛti of Yogīshvara Yādṇyavalkya With the Commentary Mitākṣarā of Vidnyāneshvara.* Bombay: Pāndurang Jāwaji, 1936, fourth ed.

Secondary Sources

Anālayo, Bhikkhu. *A Comparative Study of the Majjhima-nikāya,* 2 vols. Taipei: Dharma Drum Publishing Corporation, 2011.

—. *The Genesis of the Bodhisattva Ideal.* Hamburg: Hamburg University Press, 2008.

Andersen, Dines, and Helmer Smith. *The Sutta-nipāta.* London: Pali Text Society, 1913.

Banerjee, Ankul Chandra. "The Prātimokṣa-Sūtra," *Indian Historical Quarterly* 29 (1953): 162–174, 266–275, 363–377.

Bareau, André. "La construction et le culte des stūpa d'après les *Vinayapiṭaka,*" *Bulletin de l'École française d'Extrême-Orient* 50/2 (1962): 229–274.

—. *Les sectes bouddhiques du petit véhicule.* Saigon: École Française d'Extrême-orient, 1955.

Barua, B., and K. G. Sinha. *Barhut Inscriptions.* Calcutta: University of Calcutta, 1926.

Beal, Samuel. *Si-Yu-Ki: Buddhist Records of the Western World.* London: Kegan Paul, Trench, Trübner & Co, 1869.

Bendall, Cecil. *Çikshāsamuccaya: A Compendium of Buddhistic Teaching Compiled by Çāntideva.* Bibliotheca Buddhica I. St. Petersburg: l'Académie Impériale des Sciences, 1897.

Bernhard, Franz. *Udānavarga,* 3 vols. Göttingen: Vandenhoeck & Ruprecht, 1965–1990.

Birnbaum, Raoul. *The Healing Buddha.* Boston: Shambhala Publications, 1989, rev. ed.

Bühler, George. *Āpastamba's Aphorisms on the Sacred Law of the Hindus.* Bombay Sanskrit Series nos. 44, 50. Bombay: Government Central Book Depot, 1932, third rev. ed.

—. "The Asoka Edicts of Paderia and Nigliva," *Epigraphia Indica* 5 (1898-1899): 1–6.

Burgess, James, and Bhagwanlal Indraji Pandit. *Inscriptions from the Cave-Temples of Western India.* Archaeological Survey of Western India. Bombay: Government Central Press, 1881.

Byrskog, Samuel. "A Century with the Sitz im Leben: From Form-Critical Setting to Gospel Community and Beyond," *Zeitschrift für die neutestamentliche Wissenschaft und die Kunde der älteren Kirche* 98/1 (2007): 1–27.

Chandra, Lokesh. *Tibetan-Sanskrit Dictionary,* 2 vols. Kyoto: Rinsen Book Company, 1976.

—. *Tibetan Sanskrit Dictionary, Supplementary Volume.* Kyoto: Rinsen Book Company, 2009.

Coblin, South W. "Notes on Sanghabhara's Mahamayuri transcriptions," *Cahiers de linguistique—Asie orientale* 19/2 (1990): 195–251.

Coburn, Thomas B. "'Scripture' in India: Towards a Typology of the Word in Hindu Life," *Journal of the American Academy of Religion* 52/3 (1984): 435–459.

Coccari, Diane. "Protection and Identity: Banaras's Bīr Babas as Neighborhood Guardian Deities," in Sandra B. Freitag, ed., *Culture and Power in Banaras: Community, Performance and Environment, 1800–1980*, pp. 130–146. Berkeley: University of California Press, 1989.

—."The Bir Babas of Banaras and the Deified Dead," in Alf Hiltebeitel, ed., *Criminal Gods and Demon Devotees: Essays on the Guardians of Popular Hinduism*, pp. 251–269. Albany, NY: State University of New York Press, 1989.

Cohen, Richard. "Ajanta's Inscriptions," Appendix in Walter Spink, *Ajanta: History and Development. Vol. 2: Arguments about Ajanta*, pp. 273–339. Leiden: Brill, 2006.

Collins, Steven. "On the Very Idea of the Pali Canon," *Journal of the Pali Text Society* 15 (1990): 89–126.

Cowell, Edward B., and Robert A. Neil. *The Divyāvadāna: A Collection of Early Buddhist Legends.* Cambridge: the University Press, 1886.

Cunningham, Alexander. *Archaeological Survey of India: Four Reports Made During the Years 1862–63–64–65.* Archaeological Survey of India Annual Reports, vol. 1. Simla: Government Central Press, 1871.

—.*Report on Tours in the Gangetic Provinces from Badaon to Bihar, in 1875–76 and 1877–78.* Archaeological Survey of India Annual Reports, vol. 11. Calcutta: Office of the Superintendent of Government Printing, 1880.

—.*The Stūpa of Bharhut: A Buddhist Monument Ornamented with Numerous Sculptures Illustrative of Buddhist Legend and History in the Third Century B.C.* London: Wm. H. Allen and Co., et al., 1879.

Dalton, Jacob, and Sam van Schaik. *Tibetan Tantric Manuscripts from Dunhuang.* Leiden and Boston: Brill, 2006.

Davidson, Ronald M. "An Introduction to the Standards of Scriptural Authenticity in Indian Buddhism," in Robert Buswell, ed., *Chinese Buddhist Apocrypha*, pp. 291–325. Honolulu: University of Hawai'i Press, 1990.

—."Canon and Identity in Indian Esoteric Buddhism as the Confluence of Cultures," in Volkhard Krecht and Marion Steinicke, eds., *Dynamics in the History of Religions between Asia and Europe: Encounters, Notions, and Comparative Perspectives*, vol. 1, pp. 321–341. Leiden: Brill, 2011.

—."*Gsar ma* Apocrypha: The Creation of Orthodoxy, Gray Texts, and the New Revelation," in Helmut Eimer and David Germano, eds., *The Many Canons of Tibetan Buddhism*, pp. 203–224. Leiden: Brill, 2002.

—."Studies in *Dhāraṇī* Literature I: Revisiting the Meaning of the Term *Dhāraṇī*," *Journal of Indian Philosophy* 37/2 (2009): 97–147.

—."Studies in *Dhāraṇī* Literature II: Pragmatics of *Dhāraṇīs*," in Michael Willis, ed., *Mantra and Dhāraṇī in the Religious Traditions of Asia*, special issue of the *Bulletin of the School of Oriental and African Studies* 77/1 (2014): 5–61.

—.*Tibetan Renaissance: Tantric Buddhism in the Rebirth of Tibetan Culture.* New York: Columbia University Press, 2005.

Deeg, Max. *Das Gaoseng-Faxian-Zhuan als religionsgeschichtiliche Quelle.* Wiesbaden: Harrasowitz, 2005.

Demiéville, Paul. "L'origine des sectes bouddhiques d'après Paramārtha," *Mélanges chinois et bouddhiques* 1 (1932): 15-64.

Dhavalikar, M. D. *Monumental Legacy: Sanchi.* New Delhi: Oxford University Press, 2003.

Dutt, Nalinaksha. *Gilgit Manuscripts,* vol. III/1. Srinagar: Research Department, 1947.

Falk, Harry. "The Diverse Degrees of Authenticity of Aśokan Texts," in Patrick Olivelle, ed., *Aśoka In History and Historical Memory,* pp. 5–17. Delhi: Motilal Banarsidass, 2003.

Fausbøll, Viggo. *The Jātaka Together with its Commentary,* 6 vols. London: Trübner & Co., 1877–1896.

Filliozat, Jean. *Catalogue du Fonds Sanskrit.* Paris: Adrien-Maisonneuve, 1941.

Finot, Louis M., and M. Édouard Huber. "Le Prātimokṣasūtra des Sarvāstivādins, texte Sanskrit par M. Louis Finot avec la Version Chinoise de Kumārajīva traduit en Français par M. Édouard Huber," *Journal Asiatique* (Novembre-Décembre 1913): 465–558.

Foucher, Alfred. *Les Bas-reliefs Gréco-Bouddhiques du Gandhâra.* Paris: Imprimerie Nationale, 1905.

Führer, Alois. *Monograph on Buddha Sakyamuni's Birth-Place in The Nepalese Tarai.* Allahabad: The Government Press, N.-W. P. and Oudh, 1897.

Fukita, Takamichi. *The Mahāvadānasūtra: A New Edition Based on Manuscripts Discovered in Northern Turkestan.* Göttingen: Vendenhoeck & Ruprecht, 2003.

Gnoli, Raniero. *The Gilgit Manuscript of the Saṅghabhedavastu,* 2 vols. Serie Orientale Roma vol. XLIX. Rome: Istituto Italiano per il Medio ed Estremo Oriente, 1977.

Gokhale, Shobhana. *Kanheri Inscriptions.* Pune: Deccan College Post Graduate and Research Institute, 1991.

Gonda, Jan. *The Ritual Sūtras. A History of Indian Literature,* vol. 1, fasc. 2. Wiesbaden: Harrasssowitz, 1977.

Harlan, Lindsey. *The Goddesses' Henchmen: Gender in Indian Hero Worship.* Oxford: Oxford University Press, 2003.

Harper, Katherine Anne. *Seven Hindu Goddesses of Spiritual Transformation: The Iconography of the Saptamatrikas.* Lewiston, NY: The Edwin Mellen Press, 1989.

Harrison, Paul, and W. South Coblin. "The Oldest Buddhist Incantation in Chinese? A Preliminary Study of the Chinese Transcriptions of the Mantra in the *Druma-kinnara-rāja-paripṛcchā,*" in John R. McRae and Jan Nattier, eds., *Buddhism Across Boundaries,* pp. 61–85. Sino-Platonic Papers no. 222. Philadelphia: Department of East Asian Languages and Civilizations, 2012.

Herrmann-Pfandt, Adelheid. *Die lHan kar ma: Ein Früher Katalog der ins Tibetische übersetzten buddhistischen Texte.* Wien: Verlag der Österreichischen Akademie der Wissenschaften, 2008.

Horner, Isaline B. *Milinda's Questions,* 2 vols. London: Luzac, 1963–1964.

Hultzsch, E. *Das Baudhāyana-Dharmasūtra.* Abhandlungen für die Künde des Morgenländes, Bd. 16. Leipzig: Brockhaus, 1922, second rev. ed.

—. *Inscriptions of Aśoka.* Corpus Inscriptionum Indicarum 1. Oxford: Printed for the Government of India at the Clarendon Press, 1925.

Huntington, John. "The Iconography and Iconology of Maitreya Images in Gandhara," *Journal of Central Asia* 7/1 (1984): 133–179.

Indraji, Bhagavānlāl. *Antiquarian Remains at Sopārā and Padaṇa.* Bombay: Education Society's Press, 1882. Reprinted in *Journal of the Bombay Branch of the Royal Asiatic Society* 15 (1881–1881): 273–328 (pagination not replicated in the monograph).

Kane, Panduranga Vamana. *History of Dharmaśāstra: Ancient and Mediaeval Religious and Civil Law,* 5 vols. Poona: Bhandarkar Oriental Research Institute, 1930–1962.

Kawagoe, Eishin. *dKar chag 'Phang thang ma.* Sendai: Tohoku Society for Indo-Tibetan Studies, 2005.

Knox, Robert. *Amaravati: Buddhist Sculpture from the Great Stūpa.* London: British Museum Press, 1992.

Lahiri, Latika. *Chinese Monks in India: Biography of Eminent Monks Who Went to the Western World in Search of the Law During the Great T'ang Dynasty.* Buddhist Tradition Series, vol. 3. Delhi: Motilal Banarsidass, 1986.

Lamotte, Étienne. *History of Indian Buddhism: From the Origins to the Śaka Era.* Sara Webb-Boin, trans. Louvain-La-Neuve: Peters Press, 1988.

—. "La légende du Buddha," *Revue de l'histoire des religions* 134/1–3 (1947): 37–71.

Lariviere, Richard, W. *The Nāradasmṛti: Critically Edited with an Introduction, Annotated Translation, and Appendices,* 2 vols. Philadelphia: Department of South Asia Regional Studies, University of Pennsylvania, 1989.

la Vallée Poussin, Louis de. "The Vidyādharapiṭaka," *Journal of the Royal Asiatic Society of Great Britain and Ireland* (1895): 433–436.

Lefmann, S. *Lalita Vistara: Leben und Lehre des Çâkya-Buddha,* 2 vols. Halle a.S.: Buchhandlung des Waisenhauses, 1902–1908.

Luczanits, Christian. "The Bodhisattva with the Flask in Gandharan Narrative Scenes," *East and West* 55 (2004): 163–188.

Lüders, Heinrich. *Bhārhut Inscriptions.* Corpus Inscriptionum Indicarum, Vol. II, Part II. New Delhi: Director General, Archaeological Survey of India, 1963.

Maisey, F. C. *Sánchi and Its Remains.* London: Kegan Paul, Trench, Trübner & Co, 1892.

Marshall, John. *Taxila,* 3 vols. Cambridge: Cambridge University Press, 1951.

Marshall, John, and Alfred Foucher. *The Monuments of Sāñchī,* 3 vols. London: Probsthain, 1940.

Matsuda, Jiryo. "Origin and Doctrine of Early Indian Buddhist Schools," *Asia Major* 2 (1925): 1–78.

Matsuda, Kazunobu, ed. and trans. "*Nirvikalpapraveśadhāraṇī*: Sanskrit Text and Japanese Translation," *Bulletin of the Research Institute of Bukkyo University (Bukkyō Daigaku Sōgō Kenkyūjo Kiyō)* 3 (1996): 89–113.

Matsumura, Junko. "The Story of the Dīpaṃkara Buddha Prophecy in Northern Buddhist Texts: An Attempt at Classification," *Journal of Indian and Buddhist Studies* 59/3 (2011): 63–72.

Matsunami, Seiren. *A Catalogue of the Sanskrit Manuscripts in the Tokyo University Library.* Tokyo: Suzuki Research Foundation, 1965.

Mitra, Debala. *Buddhist Monuments.* Calcutta: Sahitya Samsad, 1971.

Nattier, Jan. *A Guide to the Earliest Chinese Buddhist Translations: Texts from the Eastern Han 東漢 and Three Kingdoms 三國 Periods.* Tokyo: The International Research Institute for Advanced Buddhology, Soka University, 2008.

—. "Buddha(s)," in Robert E. Buswell, ed., *Encyclopedia of Buddhism: A–L, Volume 1,* pp. 71–74. New York: Macmillan Reference USA, 2004.

Norman, K. R. *The Group of Discourses (Sutta-nipāta).* Oxford: Pali Text Society, 1992.

Ohira, Suzuko. "The Twenty-Four Buddhas and the Twenty-Four Tīrthaṅkaras," in Nalini Blabir and Joachim K. Bautze, eds., *Festschrift Klaus Bruhn: zur Vollendung des 65. Lebensjahres,* pp. 475-488. Reinbek: Dr. Inge Wezler Verlag für Orientalistische Fachpublikationen, 1994.

Oldenburg, Hermann. *The Vinaya Piṭakaṃ: One of the Principal Buddhist Holy Scriptures in the Pâli Language,* 5 vols. London: Williams and Norgate, 1897–1883.

Olivelle, Patrick, ed. *Aśoka In History and Historical Memory.* Delhi: Motilal Banarsidass, 2003.

—. *Manu's Code of Law: A Critical Edition and Translation of the Mānava-Dharmaśāstra.* Oxford: Oxford University Press, 2005.

—, ed. and trans. *The Law Code of Viṣṇu: A Critical Edition and Annotated Translation of the Vaiṣṇava-Dharmaśāstra.* Harvard Oriental Series, vol. 73. Cambridge, MA: Department of Sanskrit and Indian Studies, Harvard University, 2009.

Pachow, W., and Ramakanta Mishra. *The Prātimokṣa-Sūtra of the Mahāsāṅghikās.* Allahabad: Ganganatha Jha Research Institute, 1956.

Pagel, Ulrich. "Introduction" to Jens Braarvig and Ulrich Pagel, "Fragments of the Bodhisattvapiṭakasūtra," in Jens Braarvig, ed., *Buddhist Manuscripts Volume III,* pp. 11–88. Manuscripts in the Schøyen Collection. Oslo: Hermes Publishing, 2006.

—. "The *Dhāraṇī*s of *Mahāvyutpatti* #748: Origin and Formation," *Buddhist Studies Review* 24/2 (2007): 151–191.

Pandey, Janardan Shastri. *Bauddhastotrasamgraha.* Delhi: Motilal Banarsidass, 1994.

—. *Durlabha Bauddha Grantha Parichaya.* Rare Buddhist Text Series 3. Sarnath: Central Institute of Higher Tibetan Studies, 1990.

Pāṇḍeya, Umeśacandra. *Gautamadharmasūtrāṇi Hindīvyākhyāvibhūṣita-haradatta-kṛta-mitākṣarāvṛti-sahitāni.* Vārāṇasī: Chaukhambha Sanskrit Bhawan, 1966.

Panśīkar, Wāsudev Laxmaṇ Śāstrī. *Yādnyavalkyasmṛti of Yogīshvara Yādṇyavalkya*

With the Commentary Mitākṣarā of Vidnyāneshvara (sic). Bombay: Pāndurang Jāwaji, 1936, fourth ed.

Pradhan, Pralhad. *Abhidharma Samuccaya of Asanga*. Visva-Bharati Studies 12. Santiniketan: Visva-Bharati, 1950.

Prebish, Charles S. *Buddhist Monastic Discipline: The Sanskrit Prātimokṣa Sūtras of the Mahāsāṃghikas and Mūlasarvāstivādins*. University Park, PA: Pennsylvania State University Press, 1975.

Rhi, Juhyung. "Images, Relics, and Jewels: The Assimilation of Images in the Buddhist Relic Cult of Gandhāra—or Vice Versa," *Artibus Asiae* 65/2 (2005): 169–211.

Rhys Davids, T. W., and J. Estlin Carpenter. *The Dīgha Nikāya*, 3 vols. London: Pali Text Society, 1890–1911.

Rocher, Ludo, ed. and trans. *Jīmūtavāhana's Dāyabhāga: The Hindu Law of Inheritance in Bengal*. Oxford: Oxford University Press, 2002.

Sakai Ryōzaburō. *Bon-Zō-Kan-Wa yon yaku taikō hon yaku myōgi taishū*, 2 vols. Tokyo: Suzuki Gakujutsu Zaidan, 1962.

Schmidt, Klaus T. *Der Schlußteil des Prātimokṣasūtra der Sarvāstivādins: Text in Sanskrit und Tocharisch A verglichen mit den Parallelversionen anderer Schulen*. Sanskrittexte aus den Turfan funden 13. Göttingen: Vandenhoeck & Ruprecht, 1989.

Schopen, Gregory. "Two Problems in the History of Indian Buddhism: The Layman/Monk Distinction and the Doctrines of the Transference of Merit," *Studien zur Indologie und Iranistik* 10 (1985): 9–47.

Sehgal, S. R. *Śāṅkhāyana Gṛhya Sūtram*. Delhi: Sri Satguru Publications, 1987.

Senart, Émile. *Le Mahāvastu: Texte Sanscrit*, 3 vols. Paris: Imprimerie Nationale, 1882–1897.

Shukla, Karunesha. *Śrāvakabhūmi of Ācārya Asaṅga*. Patna: K. P. Jayaswal Research Institute, 1973.

Silk, Jonathan A. "The *Jefayue sheku tuoluoji jing*—Translation, Non-translation, Both or Neither?", *Journal of the International Association of Buddhist Studies* 31/1–2 (2010): 369–420.

Skilling, Peter. "The *Rakṣā* Literature of the *Śrāvakayāna*," *Journal of the Pali Text Society* 16 (1992): 109–182.

Skorupski, Tadeusz. *A Catalogue of the Stog Palace Kanjur*. Tokyo: International Institute for Buddhist Studies, 1985.

Smith, Frederick M. *The Self Possessed: Deity and Spirit Possession in South Asian Literature and Civilization*. New York: Columbia University Press, 2006.

Sorensen, Per K. *Triśaraṇasaptati: The Septuagint on the Three Refuges*. Vienna: Arbeitskreis für Tibetische unde Buddhistische Studien, 1986.

Speyer, J. S. *Avadānaçataka: A Century of Edifying Tales Belonging to the Hīnayāna*. Bibliotheca Buddhica III, 2 vols. St. Pétersbourg: l'Académie Impériale des Sciences, 1906.

Spink, Walter. *Ajanta: History and Development. Vol. 2: Arguments about Ajanta*. Leiden: Brill, 2006.

—. *Ajanta: History and Development. Vol. 4: Painting, Sculpture, Architecture.* Leiden: Brill, 2009.

—. *Ajanta: History and Development. Vol. 5: Cave by Cave.* Leiden, Brill, 2005.

Strauch, Ingo. *The Bajaur Collection: A New Collection of Kharoṣṭhī Manuscripts—A Preliminary Catalogue and Survey,* 2008. www.geschkult.fu-berlin.de/e/indologie/bajaur/publication/index.html#Strauch2007. Accessed March 3, 2009.

Takakusu Junjirō and Watanabe Kaikyoku, eds. *Taishō Shinshū Daizōkyō.* Tokyo: Daizōkyōkai, 1924–1935.

Takubo, Shūyo. *Ārya-Mahā-Māyūrī Vidyā-Rājñī.* Tokyo: Sankibo, 1972.

Tatia, Nathmal. *Abhidharmasamuccaya-bhāṣyam.* Tibetan Sanskrit Works Series No. 17. Patna: Kashi Prasad Jayaswal Research Institute, 1976.

Tokuno, Kyoko. "The Evaluation of Indigenous Scriptures in Chinese Buddhist Bibliographical Categories," in Robert E. Buswell, ed., *Chinese Buddhist Apocrypha,* pp. 31–74. Honolulu: University of Hawai'i Press, 1990.

Trenckner, V., et al. *The Majjhima-Nikāya.* London: Pali Text Society, 1888–1925.

—. *The Milindapañho: Being Dialogues between King Milinda and the Buddhist Sage Nāgasena.* London: Williams and Norgate, 1880.

Ui, Hakuju, et al., eds. *A Complete Catalogue of the Tibetan Buddhist Canons (BKaḥ-ḥgyur and Bstan-ḥgyur).* Sendai: Tōhoku Imperial University, 1934.

Vaidya, Janak Lāl, and Prem Bahādur Kaṃsakār. *A Descriptive Catalogue of Selected Manuscripts Preserved at the Āśā Saphū Kuthī (Āśā Archives).* Kathmandu: Cvasāpāsā, 1991.

Vogel, Jean Philippe. "The Past Buddhas and Kāśyapa in Indian Art and Epigraphy," in Johannes Schubert and Ulrich Schneider, eds., *Asiatica: Festschrift Fredrich Weller,* pp. 808–816. Leipzig: Harrassowitz, 1954.

von Simson, Georg. *Prātimokṣasūtra der Sarvāstivādins.* Sanskrittexte aus den Turfan funden XI. Teil II. Göttingen: Vandenhoeck & Ruprecht, 2000.

von Staël-Holstein, Baron A. *The Kāçyapaparivarta: A Mahāyānasūtra of the Ratnakūṭa Class.* Shanghai: Commercial Press, 1926.

Waldschmidt, Ernst. *Das Mahāparinirvāṇasūtra.* Abhandlungen der Deutschen Akademie der Wissenschaften zu Berlin, Klasse für Sprachen, Literatur und Kunst, Jahrgang 1950 Nr. 3. 3 Teile. Berlin: Akademie-Verlag, 1951.

Watters, Thomas. *On Yuan Chwang's Travels in India, 629–645 A.D.* Oriental Translation Fund New Series Vol. XIV. London: Royal Asiatic Society, 1904.

Wilson, Horace Hayman. "Notice of Three Tracts Received From Nepal," *Asiatic Researches* 16 (1828): 450–478.

Wogihara, Unrai. *Bodhisattvabhūmi: A Statement of the Whole Course of the Bodhisattva.* Tokyo: Sankibo Buddhist Book Store, 1971.

Yamada, Issi. *Karuṇāpuṇḍarīka: The White Lotus of Compassion,* 2 vols. London: School of Oriental and African Studies, 1986.

Zwalf, W. *A Catalogue of the Gandhāra Sculpture in the British Museum,* 2 vols. London: British Museum Press, 1996.

Affliction and Infestation in an Indian Buddhist Embryological Sutra[1]

Robert Kritzer
Kyoto Notre Dame University

Introduction

The *Garbhāvakrānti-sūtra* is a Buddhist text that describes the rebirth process in great detail. One of its purposes seems to have been to evoke disgust for samsara and to encourage its audience of monks to firmly maintain their renunciation of worldly life, and this aspect of the sūtra is the main focus of this paper. Another possible purpose may have been to present and preserve medical knowledge and notions, especially about obstetrics.

The sūtra begins by explaining the conditions necessary for conception and why a woman might fail to conceive. It then describes the Oedipal-like fantasies of the transmigrating being and its state of mind as it enters its mother's womb. The heart of the sūtra is a very detailed, week-by-week account of the thirty-eight weeks of gestation, which is followed by descriptions of both stillbirth and successful childbirth. The remainder of the work is devoted to the suffering that befalls the newborn, including infestation by worms, attack by demons, and affliction by many illnesses.

This sūtra is not extant in Sanskrit but there are six translations, three Chinese and three Tibetan.

Table 1. Translations of the *Garbhāvakrānti-sūtra*

Title	Translator	Date
Bāotāi jīng 胞胎經, T. 317	Dharmarakṣa (Zhú Fǎhù 竺法護)	281 or 303
Chùtāi huì = *Fó wéi Ànán shuō chùtāi huì* 佛爲阿難説處胎會 (*Ratnakūṭa-sūtra*, T. 310, no. 13)	Bodhiruci (Pútíliúzhì 菩提流志)	703–713

Mṅal du 'jug pa = Tshe daṅ ldan pa dga' bo la mṅal du 'jug pa bstan pa (translation of *Chùtāi huì*), Tohoku 58	Chos grub (Fǎchéng 法成)	ninth century
Rùtāi jīng = Fóshuō rù tāizàng huì 佛說入胎藏會 (*Ratnakūṭa-sūtra*, T. 310, n. 14, also found in *Mūlasarvāstivāda-vinaya-kṣudrakavastu*, T.1451:251a14–262a19)	Yìjìng 義淨	710
Mṅal na gnas pa = Dga' bo la mṅal na gnas pa bstan pa (translation of *Rùtāi jīng*), Tohoku 57	Unknown (perhaps Chos grub)	ninth century
Mṅal du 'jug pa źes bya ba'i chos kyi rnam graṅs (found in the Tibetan *Mūlasarvāstivāda-vinaya-kṣudrakavastu*), Tohoku 6	Vidyākaraprabha, Dharmaśribhadra, and Dpal 'byor	ninth century

There are basically two different short versions and two different long versions of the text. In this paper, I refer to the longest version, the one in the Tibetan *Mūlasarvāstivāda-vinaya-kṣudrakavastu*, Tohoku 6.

Table 2. Versions of the *Garbhāvakrānti-sūtra*

Short version	**Long version**
1. *Bāotāi jīng* 胞胎經 (about 4.6 Taishō pages)	1. *Mūlasarvāstivāda-vinaya-kṣudrakavastu* (about 28.6 folios in the Derge edition)
2. *Chùtāi huì* 處胎會 (about 4.3 Taishō pages)	2. *Rùtāi jīng* 入胎經 (about 7.3 Taishō pages)
2a. *Mṅal du 'jug pa* (about 11 folios [22 sides] in the Derge edition)	2a. *Mṅal na gnas pa* (about 21.3 folios in the Derge edition)

I have discussed elsewhere the accounts of conception, gestation, and miscarriage, and have shown how the sūtra employs the medical information available at the time for its own purposes, some of which are not at all the same as those of the Indian medical texts.[2] Although I do not dwell on this subject, there is perhaps a parallel here, albeit a contrast, with the way today's anti-abortion campaigners use scientific information concerning the development of the fetus for a religious purpose. The sūtra devalues worldly life by highlighting the suffering experienced by the fetus, while those opposed to abortion talk about "the miracle of life" and celebrate the growth of fetal life in the womb, which, as Karen Newman points out, they sometimes illustrate with romanticized images.[3]

I have also suggested a connection between the imagery in the sūtra and the classic Buddhist meditations on the body and on the unpleasant.[4] The repetition of descriptions of the womb and the vagina as filthy, uncomfortable places, subject to grotesquely numerous "faults"; the detailed anatomical descriptions of the fetus, including enumerations of the 200 major bones and of vast numbers of interwoven arteries and sinews, channels, and pores; the fancifully named winds that initiate developmental progress; the gruesome description of the dismemberment of a dead fetus—all create a pathological atmosphere designed to provoke aversion to the cycle of rebirth, to the process of birth, and to worldly life itself.

In this paper I suggest that enumerations and descriptions of worms, demons, and diseases are similarly used to evoke revulsion for the world. Regarding all three topics, the sūtra takes material from the medical discourse and embellishes it to a greater or lesser extent in order to horrify its listeners and hearers and to weaken their attachment to this life.

Worms

After the account of gestation that forms the core of the *Garbhāvakrānti-sūtra* (137a4–138a2), there is a description of the suffering of the infant just after leaving the womb. No matter how tenderly the baby is handled, it will experience unbearable suffering. Comparisons are made: the infant, received in the hands or in a cloth after birth, is like a flayed ox that, wherever he stands, is devoured by whatever creatures are nearby; the infant, when splashed with pleasantly warm water, is like a leper whose body, dripping and decayed, is struck with a whip. The rhetorical question is then asked: "What good is there in craving rebirth in samsara?" The sūtra then states that after a week has passed, 80,000 types of worms will take up residence in and feed on the child's body (138a2).

Reading the lengthy passage that follows, one might feel as though the text indeed mentions 80,000 types of worms, but in fact only seventy-eight are named (138a2–139a2). Still, this number is more than three times the number found in similar lists in the classical Indian medical texts, which typically give twenty worms. It is not the case that the list in the sūtra contains all twenty of these; only a very few of the worms mentioned in this text correspond with those described in the medical literature. Furthermore, I do not suggest that the sūtra relies directly on the extant medical texts I mention, which are not even necessarily older than the oldest version of the sūtra. Nevertheless, it seems clear that the authors of the sūtra were familiar with the medical knowledge of parasites and used it for their own purposes.

Kenneth Zysk sees a continuity between the discussions of worm infestation in medical texts such as the *Carakasaṃhitā* (original version finished by the second or third century C.E.) and the *Suśrutasaṃhitā* (original version finished by the end of the third century C.E.),[5] and those in the much earlier *Atharvaveda* (sometime between 1250 and 800 B.C.E.).[6] According to him, the worms in the *Atharvaveda* are generally described realistically, although the descriptions sometimes "border on the mythical," with names that are impossible to understand. There was some idea of treatment involving the ritual chanting of charms, as well as the ceremonial destruction of worms that were no longer inside the body. In a gradual process culminating in the Āyurveda, medical procedures were developed to treat infestation.[7]

The medical texts are more systematic than the sūtra in classifying the worms. They generally identify three different sources of worms: blood, phlegm, and feces. In addition, they identify the causes (for example, uncleanliness or diet), locations, and appearance of the worms, and they enumerate the symptoms caused by each group. The *Carakasaṃhitā* in particular contains elaborate recommendations for treatment by enemas and purgatives. However, as Gerrit Jan Meulenbeld suggests, it is often difficult to understand the names of the worms or to identify them with any precision, particularly when many of them may well be "imaginary creatures."[8]

The sūtra, unlike the medical texts, is not concerned about the causes of infestation or its treatment. It does not analyze the worms according to origin; it simply lists them and their location in the body, from the hair on the head down to the toes.

A few of the worms named in the sūtra seem to correspond with ones in the medical literature. Some of these are at least similar to parasites we know about today. The first worm mentioned in the text is called Hair-eater (*skra za ba*); this corresponds to *keśāda,* which is found in the lists of the *Caraka, Suśruta,* and *Aṣṭāṅgahṛdaya* (about 600 C.E.).[9] Hair-eater is said to live in and eat the hair; this descriptive pattern is repeated for of all the worms named in the sūtra. Other worm names in the text correspond to those in the medical texts. For example, the worm Hanging Down (*'phyaṅ ba*), which lives in the upper parts of the hands, resembles *lambarūpaka* (Pendulous) in the *Bheḷasaṃhitā,*[10] a text perhaps as old as the *Carakasaṃhitā.*[11] Needle Lips (*khab mchu*), which lives in the intestines, corresponds to *sūcimukha* (Needle Mouth) in the *Hārītasaṃhitā,* a considerably later text,[12] and may be what we call whipworm.[13] Leprosy (*mdze*), which lives in and eats the knees, has a name similar to *kuṣṭhaja*

(Produced by Leprosy) in the *Suśruta* (6.54.16).[14] This may be the larva of a fly, *Chrysomyia bezziana*, that breeds in living tissue.[15] Presumably the skin damage that it causes resembles the damage inflicted by leprosy.

Several worms with fanciful names in the sūtra correspond in their sites of infestation to ones with more prosaic names in medical texts, which usually name the worm according to the place where it lives. Honey Leaf (*sbraṅ rtsi 'dab ma*) lives in and eats the teeth, as does *dantāda* (Tooth-eater) in the *Suśruta*. Similarly, Angry One (*khon can*) and Big Angry One (*khon can chen po*), which live in the heart, resemble Heart-wanderer (*hṛdayacara*) in the *Caraka* (3.7.12)[16] and Heart-eater (*hṛdayadā*) in the *Aṣṭāṅgahṛdaya* (3.14.49).[17] According to the sutra, four types of worms live in the stomach: Lion (*seṅ ge*), Powerful (*stobs can*), Reed (*'dam bu*), and Holding a Flower (*me tog len*). There is a worm called *udarāda* (Stomach-eater) in the *Caraka* (3.7.12)[18] and *udarāveṣṭa* (Stomach-strangler) in the *Aṣṭāṅgahṛdaya* (3.14.49);[19] this may be a roundworm.[20]

Again, the sūtra mentions two worms that live in the intestines, Stable (*brtan pa*) and Nearly Stable (*ñe brtan*), while the *Caraka* (3.7.12)[21] and the *Aṣṭāṅgahṛdaya* (3.14.49)[22] include a worm called *antrāda* (Intestine-eating), which is perhaps a tapeworm.[23] Finally, the text says that four types of worms live in the anus, Unpleasant Sound (*sgra ṅan*), Big Unpleasant Sound (*sgra ṅan chen po*), Leader (*'dren byed*), and Possessing the Rotten (*'drul ldan*), while in the *Caraka* (3.7.12)[24] and the *Mādhavanidāna*[25] (about 700 C.E.)[26] there is a worm called *mahāguda* (Big Anus).

However, most of the worms named in the sūtra have no equivalent in the medical literature. One striking feature of the text is that most of the infested parts of the body are said to host more than one type of worm (some examples are mentioned above). This is obviously padding: worms with closely related names are said to infest a particular body part in order to increase the cautionary effect. So, as we have seen, the heart is eaten not only by Angry One but also by Big Angry One (*khon can chen po*). Similarly, the intestines are eaten by both Mixed Water (*chu 'dres*) and Big Mixed Water (*chu 'dres chen po*) and by Needle Lips (*khab mchu*) and Big Needle Lips (*khab mchu chen po*). Gradual Piercing (*rim 'bigs*), Former Piercing (*sṅar 'bigs*), Hard Piercing (*sra 'bigs*), and Abiding Piercing (*brtan 'bigs*) all eat the bones.

In the medical texts, the names are generally, although by no means always, at least somewhat naturalistic, either referring to the body part attacked by the worm (e.g., Stomach-eater) or describing the appearance of the worm, e.g., *Darbha* Flower, *darbhapuṣpa* (*Carakasaṃhitā* 3.7.12; *Suśrutasaṃhitā* 6.54.12)[27] or *darbhakusuma* (*Aṣṭāṅgahṛdayasaṃhitā* 3.14.49)[28]

On the other hand, most names in the sūtra seem to be products of imagination rather than of observation. Table 3 lists the names of all of the worms mentioned in the sūtra.

Table 3. Worm Names in the *Garbhāvakrānti-sūtra*

Body part	Worm name	Tibetan
hair	Hair-eater	*skra za ba*
head	Stick-holder	*dbyug pa can*
	Big Head	*mgo bo che*
eyes	Eye-eater	*mig zan*
brain	Running	*rgyug pa*
	Giving	*sbyin byed*
	Of Noble Birth	*rigs ldan*
	Entire	*gaṅ po*
ears	*Bsam* Leaf	*bsam lo*
nose	Treasury Door	*mdzod sgo*
lips	Throwing	*'phen byed*
	Placing	*jog byed*
teeth	Honey Leaf	*sbraṅ rtsi 'dab ma*
roots of the teeth	Wood Mouth	*śiṅ sgo*
tongue	Needle Lips	*khab mchu*
roots of the tongue	Sharp Lips	*mchu rnon*
palate	Having Hands	*lag can*
fingers	Water Net	*chu'i dra ba*
	Half-bent	*phyed sgur*
upper part of the hands	Hanging Down	*phyaṅ ba*
	Hanging Very Far Down	*rab tu 'phyaṅ ba*
arms	Arm	*dpuṅ ba*
	Near-arm (Forearm?)	*ñe dpuṅ*
throat	Digging	*rko ba*
	Digging Close	*ñe rko*
heart	Angry One	*khon can*
	Big Angry One	*khon can chen po*
flesh	Conch Shell	*duṅ*
	Conch Shell Water (Lips?)	*duṅ chu* (*mchu?*)
blood	Colored	*mdog can*
	Powerful	*stobs can*
tendons	Hero	*dpa' bo*
	Fragrance Mouth	*dri sgo*

spine	Low	*dma' ba*
	Face Down	*kha sbub can*
fat	Fat Color	*tshil mdog*
bile	Bile Color	*mkhris mdog*
spleen	Pearl	*mu tig*
kidney	Big Pearl	*mu tig chen po*
liver	Not Arrived	*oṅs miṅ*
intestines	Mixed Water	*chu 'dres*
	Big Mixed Water	*chu 'dres chen po*
	Needle Lips	*khab mchu*
	Big Needle Lips	*khab mchu chen po*
right side of the body	Moon	*zla*
	Moon Face	*zla gdoṅ*
	Moonlight	*zla 'od*
	Moonlight Face	*zla 'od gdoṅ*
	Vast	*rgya chen*
left side of the body[29]	Moon	*zla*
	Moon Face	*zla gdoṅ*
	Moonlight	*zla 'od*
	Moonlight Face	*zla 'od gdoṅ*
	Vast	*rgya chen*
bones	Gradual Piercing	*rim 'bigs*
	Former Piercing	*sṅar 'bigs*
	Hard Piercing	*sra 'bigs*
	Abiding Piercing	*brtan 'bigs*
channels	White	*dkar po*
	Nearly White	*ñe dkar*
	Robbing Power	*stobs 'phrog*
	Smelling	*snom pa*
stomach	Lion	*seṅ ge*
	Powerful	*stobs can*
	Reed	*'dam bu*
	Holding a Flower	*me tog len*
intestines	Stable	*brtan pa*
	Nearly Stable	*ñe brtan*
urethra	Worm Lips	*srin bu'i mchu*
	Mass Face	*phuṅ po'i gdoṅ*
	Net Mouth	*dra ba'i kha*
	Plow	*dral byed*
anus	Unpleasant Sound	*sgra ṅan*
	Big Unpleasant Sound	*sgra ṅan chen po*

anus (*continued*)	Leader	*dren byed*
	Possessing the Rotten	*drul ldan*
thighs	Mouth Disease	*kha nad*
	Terrifying	*jigs byed*
knees	Leprosy	*mdze*
	Near Leprosy	*ñe mdze*
lower legs	Root of Foolishness	*glen gźi*
toes	Black Head	*mgo nag*
tendons	Hero	*dpa' bo*
	Fragrance Mouth	*dri sgo*

It is difficult to understand the names precisely, since all we have are the Tibetan translations of Sanskrit words (or, in the case of translations of other versions of the text, different Tibetan translations, Chinese translations, and a fragment of a Tocharian translation). Nevertheless, one can clearly see that names like those of a pair of worms that infests the tendons, Hero (*dpa' bo*) and Fragrance Mouth (*dri sgo*), have nothing to do with their appearance or the part of the body they afflict.

Although we cannot reconstruct the original Sanskrit names of the worms nor fully appreciate the resonance of these names for the original audience, they clearly help to create a somewhat grotesque atmosphere in which the reader is threatened by the unremitting litany of strange names. Furthermore, the number "80,000" is obviously a stereotyped large number dramatizing both the vulnerability of the body and its disgustingness. The proliferation of worm names in this passage is another aspect of the close relation between the sūtra and the classic Buddhist meditations on the body and on the impure.

Demons

Just after the list of worms, the sūtra mentions thirty-one *graha*s or demons that will afflict the child (139a5–b1). Unfortunately, there are no explanations of what exactly each of these *graha*s does, what it looks like, or how to counteract it, although the commentary offers some very general information about some of them. Nevertheless, the composition of the list is interesting in itself as an illustration of the eclecticism of the sūtra.

Graha means "seizer," and the word has two relevant meanings: demons, especially ones that attack children; and planets, which are called *graha* because they affect the world of human beings. Dominik Wujastyk writes that there is no real connection between the demons and planets: "medical *graha*s are demons pure and simple."[30] However, as we shall see, the sūtra may be somewhat confused on this point.

There are a large number of sources for *graha*s, both medical and non-medical. The best-known account in the medical literature is found in the *Suśrutasaṃhitā,* which treats the topic twice in the *Uttaratantra.* In the section on pediatrics (*Kumāratantra*), nine *graha*s are named and the symptoms they cause in the child are described (6.27).[31] For example, the victim of the demon Śakuni

> has flaccid limbs, [a] bird's smell, is frightened, suffers from discharging wounds all around, and [its] body is covered with eruptive boils with burning sensation and suppuration. (6.27.10)[32]

The section on demons and mental illness (*Bhūtavidyātantra*) mentions eight groups of *graha*s, and remedies, generally ritual offerings, are prescribed (6.60).[33] There is no indication in this passage that these *graha*s specifically afflict children.

Similarly, the *Aṣṭāṅgahṛdayasaṃhitā* mentions demons in two places in its *Uttarasthāna:* ones specific to children in *Bālagrahapratiṣedha* (6.3)[34] and others in *Bhūtavijñānīya* (6.4).[35] The demons mentioned are nearly, though not completely, the same as those in the *Suśrutasaṃhitā.* Table 4, below, includes the names of all the demons mentioned in the sūtra with their Sanskrit equivalents, together with corresponding names found in the *Suśruta* and the *Aṣṭāṅgahṛdaya.* Names with asterisks indicate reconstructions; I have found no such demon names in extant Sanskrit sources.

Table 4. Demon Names in the *Garbhāvakrānti-sūtra and* in Two Medical Texts

Garbhāvakrānti-sūtra Tibetan	*Sanskrit	*Suśrutasaṃhitā* (k) = *Kumāratantra* (b) = *Bhūtavidyātantra*	*Aṣṭāṅgahṛdayasaṃhitā* (bg) = *Bālagrahapratiṣedha* (bv) = *Bhūtavijñānīyapratiṣedha*
lha'i gdoṅ	*devagraha*	(b) *deva*	(bv) *deva*
klu'i gdon	*nāgagraha*	(b) (*bhujaṅga*)	(bv) (*uraga*)
lha ma yin gyi gdon	*asuragraha*	(b) *daitya* (?)	(bv) *daitya* (?)
rluṅ lha'i gdon	*marutagraha*		
nam kha'i ldiṅ gdon	*garuḍagraha*		

dri za'i gdon	*gandharvagraha*	(b) *gandharva*	(bv) *gandharva*
mi 'am ci'i gdon	*kiṃnaragraha*		
lto 'phye chen po'i gdon	*mahoragagraha*		
gnod sbyin gyi gdon	*yakṣagraha*	(b) *yakṣa*	(bv) *yakṣa*
srin po'i gdon	*rākṣasagraha*	(b) *rakṣas*	(bv) *rākṣasa*
yi dags kyi gdon	*pretagraha*	(k, b) *pitṛgraha*	(bg) *pitṛ* (bv) *preta*
śa za'i gdon	*piśācagraha*	(b) *piśaca*	(bv) *piśāca*
byuṅ po'i gdon	*bhūtagraha*		
grul bum gyi gdon	*kumbhāṇḍagraha*		(bv) *kūṣmāṇḍa*
srul po'i gdon	*andhapūtana-graha*	(k) *andhapūtanā*	(bg) *andhapūtanā*
lus srul po'i gdon	*kaṭapūtanagraha*		
srul po lon bu'i gdon			
skem byed kyi gdon	*skandagraha*	(k) *skandagraha*	(bg) *skanda*
smyo byed kyi gdon	*unmādagraha*		
sgrib gnon gyi gdon	*chāyāgraha*		
rdul (rṅul ?) byed gyi gdon			
bya'i gdon	*śakunigraha*	(k) *śakunī*	(bg) *śakunigraha*
ri dags kyi gdon	**mṛgagraha*		
rnam gru'i gdon	*revatīgraha*	(k) *revatī*	(bg) *revatī*
phyugs bdag gi gdon	**paśupatigraha*		
ma mo'i gdon	**mātṛkāgraha*		
dzum byed kyi gdon			
rkaṅ bam gyi gdon	**ślīpadīgraha*		
ñams byed kyi gdon			

zla ba'i gdon	**candragraha (*somagraha?)*
ñi ma'i gdon	**ādityagraha (*sūryagraha?)*
rgyu skar gyi gdon	**nakṣatragraha*

Among the non-medical texts, the *Kumāratantra* of Rāvaṇa is the most noteworthy. It is devoted solely to descriptions of twelve demons that afflict children and rituals intended to make the demons desist. Although several of the demons correspond to those of the medical texts and those in the sūtra, for the most part they differ. In his study of the *Kumāratantra,* Jean Filliozat mentions many other texts containing lists of demons that differ to a greater or lesser extent. This is clearly a popular subject of rituals, and it is impossible to deal with the vast literature here.

However, in one ritual text, the *Sitātapatrā Dhāraṇī,* the list of demons corresponds particularly closely with that found in the sūtra. This includes twenty-one (or possibly twenty-two) of the same *graha*s that are found in the sūtra. As can be seen in Table 5, below, the Tibetan names in the text clearly correspond with the Sanskrit names in the *Sitātapatrā Dhāraṇī,* with the exception of the last item. The Tibetan *ma mo'i gdon* should translate *mātṛkāgraha,* but the *Sitātapatrā Dhāraṇī* gives the name as *mātṛnandigraha.*

Table 5. Demon Names in the *Garbhāvakrānti-sūtra* Corresponding to Names in the *Sitātapatrā Dhāraṇī*

Tibetan	*Sanskrit
lha'i gdon	*devagraha*
klu'i gdon	*nāgagraha*
lha ma yin gyi gdon	*asuragraha*
rluṅ lha'i gdon	*marutagraha*
nam kha'i ldiṅ gdon	*garuḍagraha*
dri za'i gdon	*gandharvagraha*
mi 'am ci'i gdon	*kiṃnaragraha*
lto 'phye chen po'i gdon	*mahoragagraha*
gnod sbyin gyi gdon	*yakṣagraha*
srin po'i gdon	*rākṣasagraha*
yi dags kyi gdon	*pretagraha*
śa za'i gdon	*piśācagraha*
byuṅ po'i gdon	*bhūtagraha*

grul bum gyi gdon	*kumbhāṇḍagraha*
srul po'i gdon	*pūtanagraha*
lus srul po'i gdon	*kaṭapūtanagraha*
skem byed kyi gdon	*skandagraha*
smyo byed kyi gdon	*unmādagraha*
grib gnon gyi gdon	*chāyāgraha*
bya'i gdon	*śakunigraha*
nam gru'i gdon	*revatīgraha*
ma mo'i gdon	**mātṛkāgraha* (*mātṛnandigraha* in the *Sitātapatrā Dhāraṇī*)

As can be seen in Table 6, below, in comparison with the *Sitātapatrā Dhāraṇī*, the *Suśruta* includes only twelve or thirteen of the same names as the sutra, while the *Aṣṭāṅgahṛdaya* includes thirteen or fourteen.

Table 6. Sūtra Demons Corresponding to Medical Demons

Garbhāvakrānti-sūtra Tibetan	*Sanskrit	*Suśrutasaṃhitā* (k) = *Kumāratantra* (b) = *Bhūtavidyātantra*	*Aṣṭāṅgahṛdayasaṃhitā* (bg) = *Bālagrahapratiṣedha* (bv) = *Bhūtavijñānīya-pratiṣedha*
lha'i gdoṅ	*devagraha*	(b) *deva*	(bv) *deva*
klu'i gdon	*nāgagraha*	(b) (*bhujaṅga*)	(bv) (*uraga*)
lha ma yin gyi gdon	*asuragraha*	(b) *daitya* (?)	(bv) *daitya* (?)
dri za'i gdon	*gandharvagraha*	(b) *gandharva*	(bv) *gandharva*
gnod sbyin gyi gdon	*yakṣagraha*	(b) *yakṣa*	(bv) *yakṣa*
srin po'i gdon	*rākṣasagraha*	(b) *rakṣas*	(bv) *rākṣasa*
yi dags kyi gdon	*pretagraha*	(k, b) *pitṛgraha*	(bg) *pitṛ* (bv) *preta*
śa za'i gdon	*piśācagraha*	(b) *piśaca*	(bv) *piśāca*
srul po'i gdon	*pūtanagraha*	(k) *pūtanā*	(bg) *pūtanā*
srul po lon bu'i gdon	*andhapūtana-graha*	(k) *andhapūtanā*	(bg) *andhapūtanā*
skem byed kyi gdon	*skandagraha*	(k) *skandagraha*	(bg) *skanda*
bya'i gdon	*śakunigraha*	(k) *śakunī*	(bg) *śakunigraha*
rnam gru'i gdon	*revatīgraha*	(k) *revatī*	(bg) *revatī*

It is not impossible that the sūtra reproduces a complete list of demons found in an older text, but I have not been able to find such a text. More likely is that the sūtra has assembled its list from a number of different sources. Table 7, below, shows that six of the demons in the sūtra can be found among the nine child-afflicting *graha*s in the *Suśrutasaṃhitā* and among the twelve in the *Aṣṭāṅgahṛdaya*.

Table 7. Sūtra Demons Corresponding to Pediatric Demons

Garbhāvakrānti-sūtra Tibetan	*Sanskrit	*Suśrutasaṃhitā* (*Kumāratantra*)	*Aṣṭāṅgahṛdayasaṃhitā* (*Bālagrahapratiṣedha*)
yi dags kyi gdon	*pretagraha*	*pitṛgraha*	*pitṛ*
srul po'i gdon	*pūtanagraha*	*pūtanā*	*pūtanā*
srul po'i lon bu'i gdon	*andhapūtana -graha*	*andhapūtanā*	*andhapūtanā*
skem byed kyi gdon	*skandagraha*	*skandagraha*	*skanda*
bya'i gdon	*śakunigraha*	*śakunī*	*śakunigraha*
nam gru'i gdon	*revatīgraha*	*revatī*	*revatī*

Of the demons shown in Table 8, seven or eight are found among the eight other *graha*s in the *Suśruta* and eight or nine among the fourteen in the *Aṣṭāṅgahṛdaya*.

Table 8. Sūtra Demons Corresponding to Demons in the Demonological Sections

Garbhāvakrānti-sūtra Tibetan	*Sanskrit	*Suśrutasaṃhitā* (*Kumāratantra*)	*Aṣṭāṅgahṛdayasaṃhitā* (*Bālagrahapratiṣedha*)
lha'i gdoṅ	*devagraha*	*deva*	*deva*
klu'i gdon	*nāgagraha*	(*bhujaṅga*)	(*uraga*)
lha ma yin gyi gdon	*asuragraha*	*daitya* (?)	*daitya* (?)
dri za'i gdon	*gandharvagraha*	*gandharva*	*gandharva*
gnod sbyin gyi gdon	*yakṣagraha*	*yakṣa*	*yakṣa*
srin po'i gdon	*rākṣasagraha*	*rakṣas*	*rākṣasa*
yi dags kyi gdon	*pretagraha*	*pitṛgraha*	*preta*
śa za'i gdon	*piśācagraha*	*piśaca*	*piśāca*
grul bum gyi gdon	*kumbhāṇḍagraha*		*kūṣmāṇḍa*

Table 9 lists the eighteen or nineteen *graha*s in the sūtra that have no correspondences in the medical texts.

Table 9. Demons in the Sūtra but Not in the Medical Texts

Tibetan	*Sanskrit
rluṅ lha'i gdon	*marutagraha*
nam kha'i ldiṅ gdon	*garuḍagraha*
mi 'am ci'i gdon	*kiṃnaragraha*
lto 'phye chen po'i gdon	*mahoragagraha*
byuṅ po'i gdon	*bhūtagraha*
lus srul po'i gdon	*kaṭapūtanagraha*
smyo byed kyi gdon	*unmādagraha*
grib gnon gyi gdon	*chāyāgraha*
rdul (rṅul?) byed gyi gdon	
ri dags kyi gdon	*mṛgagraha*
phyugs bdag gi gdon	*paśupatigraha*
ma mo'i gdon	*mātṛkāgraha*
dzum byed kyi gdon	
rkaṅ bam gyi gdon	*ślīpadīgraha*
ñams byed kyi gdon	
zla ba'i gdon	*candragraha* (*somagraha*?)
ñi ma'i gdon	*ādityagraha* (*sūryagraha*?)
rgyu skar gyi gdon	*nakṣatragraha*

Finally, Table 10 includes the nine or ten demon names found in neither the medical texts nor the *Sitātapatrā.* The last three of these seem to be *graha*s taken from the astrological literature.

Table 10. Demon Names Found Only in the *Garbhāvakrānti-sūtra*

Tibetan	*Sanskrit
rdul (rṅul?) byed gyi gdon	
ri dags kyi gdon	*mṛgagraha*
phyugs bdag gi gdon	*paśupatigraha*
dzum byed kyi gdon	
rkaṅ bam gyi gdon	*ślīpadīgraha*
ñams byed kyi gdon	

zla ba'i gdon	*candragraha* (*somagraha*?)
ñi ma'i gdon	*ādityagraha* (*sūryagraha*?)
rgyu skar gyi gdon	*nakṣatragraha*

Unlike the medical texts, which propose at least quasi-medical cures for the disorders caused by demons, or the ritual texts, which contain spells for the same purpose, the sūtra is not interested in the alleviation of suffering caused by the *graha*s. Instead, a long list seems to have been compiled from a variety of sources, again, as in the case of the worms, for the sole purpose of emphasizing the child's vulnerability (even though some of these demons are not known to single out children). As the text reads, "Since those sorts of demons arise in the body, what gain is there for the being dwelling in the mother's womb in seeking rebirth?"

Diseases

After the list of demons, the sūtra contains a brief sermon on the inescapability of suffering and the need to forego pleasure and engage in the religious life (139b1–140a1). This is one of the several occasions on which the cheerless message of the entire text is stated: even if the infant is cherished and well cared for, he will die shortly after birth or will live, at most, for a hundred years, half of which life span will be wasted in sleep. Once he is an adult, he will be rent with misery and mental distress, and he will also be afflicted with many hundreds of different types of bodily diseases. The interlocutor, Nanda, is then reminded that he will surely feel sorry in the end and will be deprived of everything that is desirable, agreeable, joyful, and pleasing. Brief explanations follow of the ten stages of life, the number of seasons, months, fortnights, and days in a lifetime, and the number of meals eaten in a lifetime.

After this, some forty-eight diseases that arise in the body of a fully developed person are named (140b2–5). Lists of diseases appear in a number of Buddhist texts, particularly in the Vinaya; for example, twenty-two in the *Mahāsāṃghika Bhikṣuṇīvinaya,* thirty-five in the *Bhikṣuṇīkarmavācanā,* thirty-nine in the *Karmavācanā,* thirty-eight in the *Upasampadājñapti,*[36] and forty-three in the Tibetan *Mūlasarvāstivāda-vinaya-vastu* (54b7–55a3). In addition, the *Śrāvakabhūmi* lists seventeen diseases (118.15–19), and the last eighty-two items (9483–9565) in the *Mahāvyutpatti* are names of diseases (607–610). Of course, classical Indian medical texts such as the *Caraka, Suśruta,* and *Aṣṭāṅgahṛdaya* name most of these diseases, as well as many more. However, the terse Buddhist lists do not match a specific Āyurvedic text.

Similarly, our sutra does not seem to have a single Āyurvedic source, nor does it seem to correspond to any of the Buddhist lists mentioned above. There are certainly similarities with vinaya lists. Many of the same diseases appear in the sūtra and, as in several of the vinayas, the sūtra list begins with a number of skin diseases and ends with several types of recurring fevers. However, the list in the sūtra is significantly longer than any of the other Buddhist lists, except for the one in the *Mahāvyutpatti,* which is significantly shorter. The contents of all of the lists differ somewhat, and the order of diseases is not identical in any of them. Still, it seems likely that the lists in the *Garbhāvakrānti-sūtra* have been more directly influenced by the vinaya than by the medical literature.

One might expect the sūtra list of forty-eight diseases to correspond most closely to the list of forty-three in the *Mūlasarvāstivāda-vinaya-vastu,* since the sutra is also found in the *Mūlasarvāstivāda-vinaya* and thus is also a Mūlasarvāstivāda text. However, the two lists have only about twenty-six items in common. By my count, only twenty-nine of the disease names in the Tibetan translation are listed in the *Mahāvyutpatti,* while twenty-five are found in the *Karmavācanā,* and fifteen in the *Śrāvakabhūmi.* However there are other names not found in either of these lists. In addition, I refer to the *Siddhasāra* (about 650 C.E.),[37] a medical text with a complete Tibetan translation,[38] which includes twenty-three of the diseases on the sūtra list. In Table 11 below, V, K, M, Śr, and Si are abbreviations for the *Mūlasarvāstivāda-vinaya-vastu,* the *Karmavācanā,* the *Mahāvyutpatti,* the *Śrāvakabhūmi,* and the *Siddhasāra,* respectively, while an asterisk indicates that I have not found an attestation of the Tibetan equivalence with the Sanskrit.

Table 11. Disease Names in the *Garbhāvakrānti-sūtra*

Tibetan		Sanskrit	English
mgo nad		**śiroroga*	head disease
mig nad	Si	*akṣiroga, akṣikopa, netrāmaya*	eye disease
rna ba'i nad		**karṇaroga*	ear disease
sna nad	Si	*ghrāṇa* (?)	nose disease
so nad	Si	**dantaroga*	dental disease
mgul nad		**kaṇṭharoga*	throat disease
sñiṅ nad		*hṛdroga*	heart disease
cham pa	Si	*pratiśyāya, pīnasa*	colds
śu ba	VKMŚrSi	*dadru, dardrū*	a skin disease, perhaps ringworm

g.yan pa	VKMŚrSi	*kaṇḍū, kacchū, pāmā*	a skin disease, some kind of itch
rkaṅ śu	KMŚrSi	*vicārcikā, vicarci*	a skin disease, perhaps eczema
mdze	VKMŚrSi	*kuṣṭha*	leprosy
'bras	VMŚrSi	*visphoṭa*	a skin disease, perhaps impetigo
'brum bu phra mo	VKMŚrSi	*kitibha, kitima*	a skin disease, perhaps psoriasis
śa bkra	VKMŚrSi	*kilāsa, svitra, sidhma*	a skin disease, perhaps leucoderma
brjed byed	VKMŚrSi	*apasmāra*	epilepsy
lhog pa	VKM	*lohaliṅga*	a boil filled with blood (anthrax?)
rkaṅ bam	VKMSi	*ślīpada*	elephantiasis
mtshan par rdol ba	VKMŚrSi	*bhagaṃdara*	fistulas
dmu rdziṅ	MSi	*dakodara, jalodara, udarāmaya*, etc.	dropsy
skyigs bu	VKMSi	*hikkā*	hiccups
skyug bro ba	VKMSi	*chardi* (*vami*)	vomiting
ser ga		*chidra*	fissures
khru ba	Si	*atisāra*	diarrhea
rims	VKMSi	*jvara*	contagious fever
rims drag po	VKM	*prajvara*	strong contagious fever
lud pa	KMŚrSi	*kāsa*	cough
dbugs mi bde ba	VKMSi	*śvāsa*	shortness of breath
skem pa	VKMSi	*śoṣa*	dessication, consumption
bkres ṅab	VKMŚr	*aṭakkara*	pathological hunger
skya rbab	VKMŚrSi	*pāṇḍūroga*	jaundice
skraṅ ba	VŚrSi	*śoṭha* (*śopha, śvayathu*)	swelling
tshil nad		(*medodoṣa*)	fat disease
mkhris nad	VM	*pittadoṣa*	bile disease
me dbal	MSi	*visarpa* (*vaisarpa*)	erysipelas
rims nad	VKMSi	*jvara* (*jvararoga*)	fever
rims ñin gcig pa	VKM	*ekāhika*	daily fever
(*rims*) *ñin gñis pa*	VKM	*dvaitīyaka*	every-other-day fever
(*rims*) *ñin gsum pa*	VKM	*traitīyaka*	every-third-day fever

(rims) ñin bźi pa	VKM	*cāturthaka*	every-fourth-day fever
rtags pa'i rims	VKMŚrSi	*pāṇḍūroga*	constant fever
yan lag tsha ba	VKM	**aṅgadāha*	fever in the limbs
rtsib logs tsha ba	VKM	*pārśvadāha*	fever in the ribs
sñiṅ tsha ba		*hṛddāha*	fever in the heart
yan lag na ba			ache in the limbs
rtsib logs na ba			ache in the ribs
sñiṅ na ba	Si	*hṛdāmaya, hṛcchula, hṛdgaḍa, hṛdroga*	ache in the heart
nam tshoṅ na ba			ache in the upper chest

Like the lists of worms and demons, the list of diseases in the sūtra seems to have been drawn from a variety of sources. The authors are clearly familiar with a great deal of medical information; none of the diseases appears to be an original creation. Immediately after the list, the text states that there are 404 diseases like these, 101 of which arise from an excess of each of the three *doṣa*s or humors, namely wind, bile, and phlegm, and another 101 are due to a combination of these. The theory that illness is the result of an imbalance of the *doṣa*s is commonplace in classical Indian medicine.

As in the case of worms and demons, however, the sūtra is not concerned with possible cures. The list of diseases, like the lists of worms and demons, is presented with a cautionary purpose. Its standpoint is that illness is basically incurable:

> This body becomes an illness; it becomes a tumor; it becomes a thorn. It is short-lived, subject to destruction, impermanent, suffering, empty, lacking in a self, possessed of enemies, insecure and subject to change for the worse. (140b6–7)

Conclusion

At this point, the sūtra is only about two-thirds finished. It continues to stay on message, and the reader can look forward to a list of afflictions, mainly punishments and various types of tortures (140b7–141a5); an explanation of why everything, including seemingly innocuous activities such as walking, standing, sitting, and lying down, is suffering (141a5–141b5); a reprise of the disgustingness of the vagina and womb (throughout the long section on the four types of *garbhāvakrānti* [142a5–147b1]); and a discourse on how, no matter how awful it is to be born as a human, it is even worse to be born as a god, hell-being, hungry ghost, or any of the various types of animals (147b1–148b6). Finally, readers are exhorted to practice diligently and to realize that the *skandha*s are impermanent; only this will free us from rebirth (150b5–151b5).

Much of the final portion of the sūtra, the exhortation to do good and to heed the Buddha's word, is taken directly from other Buddhist works, notably the *Mahāparinirvāṇa-sūtra* and the *Saṃyuktāgama.* To my perhaps jaded ear, this positive encouragement sounds rather half-hearted; certainly it lacks the vitality of the descriptions of the manifold horrors that befall those who fail to listen to the admonitions of the sūtra.

Notes

1 I am grateful to Elizabeth Kenney for her help, both in thinking about the topic and in improving the accuracy and readability of this article.

2 Robert Kritzer, "Life in the Womb: Conception and Gestation in Buddhist Scripture and Classical Indian Medical Literature," in Vanessa R. Sasson and Jane Marie Law, eds., *Imagining the Fetus: The Unborn in Myth, Religion, and Culture* (New York: Oxford University Press, 2009), pp. 73–89.

3 Karen Newman, *Fetal Positions: Individualism, Science, Visuality* (Palo Alto, CA: Stanford University Press, 1996).

4 Kritzer, "Life in the Womb," p. 80.

5 For these dates, see Gerrit Jan Meulenbeld, *The Mādhavanidāna and its Chief Commentary: Chapters 1–10: Introduction, Translation and Notes* (Leiden: E. J. Brill, 1974), pp. 404, 431. Meulenbeld discusses in great detail the dates of Caraka and Suśruta and their works in *A History of Indian Medical Literature* (Groningen: E. Forsten, 1999–2002), vol. IA, pp. 105–115, 342–344.

6 These dates are suggested for the Śaunakīya version in Gyula Wojtilla, "Agricultural Knowledge as it is Reflected in The Śaunakīya Atharvaveda," *Saṃskṛtavimarśaḥ* 6 (2012): 40–41.

7 Kenneth Zysk, *Religious Medicine: the History and Evolution of Indian Medicine* (New Brunswick: Transaction Publishers, 1993), pp. 64–69.

8 Meulenbeld, *The Mādhavanidāna and its Chief Commentary,* p. 623.

9 Meulenbeld, *The Mādhavanidāna and its Chief Commentary,* p. 425.

10 Meulenbeld, *The Mādhavanidāna and its Chief Commentary,* p. 291, n. 5.

11 Meulenbeld, *The Mādhavanidāna and its Chief Commentary,* p. 418.

12 Meulenbeld, *The Mādhavanidāna and its Chief Commentary,* p. 435.

13 Meulenbeld, *The Mādhavanidāna and its Chief Commentary,* p. 624.

14 Priya Vrat Sharma, ed. and trans., *Suśruta-saṃhitā: with English Translation of*

Text and Ḍalhaṇa's Commentary Along with Critical Notes (Varanasi: Chaukhambha Visvabharati, 2000–2001), vol. 3, p. 541.

15 Meulenbeld, *The Mādhavanidāna and its Chief Commentary,* p. 624.

16 Priya Vrat Sharma, ed. and trans., *Caraka-saṃhitā: Agniveśa's treatise refined and annotated by Caraka and redacted by Dṛḍhabala (Text with English Translation)* (Varanasi: Chaukhamba Orientalia, 1981), vol. 1, p. 342.

17 K. R. Srikantha, ed. and trans., *Vāgbhaṭa's Aṣṭāṅgahṛdayam* (Varanasi: Krishnadas Academy, 2000–2001, fourth ed.), vol. 2, p. 145.

18 Sharma, *Caraka-saṃhitā,* vol. 1, p. 342.

19 Srikantha, *Vāgbhaṭa's Aṣṭāṅgahṛdayam,* vol. 2, p. 145.

20 Meulenbeld, *The Mādhavanidāna and its Chief Commentary,* p. 623.

21 Sharma, *Caraka-saṃhitā,* vol. 1, p. 342.

22 Srikantha, *Vāgbhaṭa's Aṣṭāṅgahṛdayam,* vol. 2, p. 145.

23 Meulenbeld, *The Mādhavanidāna and its Chief Commentary,* p. 623.

24 Sharma, *Caraka-saṃhitā,* vol. 1, p. 342.

25 Meulenbeld, *The Mādhavanidāna and its Chief Commentary,* p. 288.

26 Meulenbeld, *The Mādhavanidāna and its Chief Commentary,* p. 21.

27 Sharma, *Caraka-saṃhitā,* vol. 1, p. 342; *Suśruta-saṃhitā,* vol. 3, p. 540.

28 Srikantha, *Vāgbhaṭa's Aṣṭāṅgahṛdayam,* vol. 2, 145.

29 Worms on the left side of the body are mentioned separately, but they have the same names as those on the right side.

30 Dominik Wujastyk, "Miscarriages of Justice: Demonic Vengeance in Classical Indian Medicine," in John Hinnells and Roy Porter, eds., *Religion, Health and Suffering* (London: Kegan Paul International, 1999), p. 259.

31 Sharma, *Suśruta-saṃhitā,* vol. 3, pp. 279–283.

32 Sharma, *Suśruta-saṃhitā,* vol. 3, pp. 281.

33 Sharma, *Suśruta-saṃhitā,* vol. 3, pp. 587–596.

34 Srikantha, *Vāgbhaṭa's Aṣṭāṅgahṛdayam,* vol. 3, pp. 27–37.

35 Srikantha, *Vāgbhaṭa's Aṣṭāṅgahṛdayam,* vol. 3, pp. 38–45.

36 Gustav Roth, ed., *Bhikṣuṇī-Vinaya: including Bhikṣuṇī-Prakīrṇaka and a Summary of the Bhikṣuṇī-Prakīrṇaka of the Ārya-Mahāsāṃghika-Lokottaravādin* (Patna: K. P. Jayaswal Research Institute, 1970), p. 34, n. 6.

37 R. E. Emmerick, ed. and trans., *The Siddhasāra of Ravigupta* (Wiesbaden: Steiner, 1980–1982), vol. I, p. 1.

38 I am grateful to Mauro Maggi, who, with the kind permission of Ann Emmerick, has given me access to materials prepared by the late R. E. Emmerick for Tibetan and Sanskrit glossaries to the *Siddhasāra.*

References

Primary Sources

Aṣṭāṅgahṛdayasaṃhitā. K. R. Srikantha, ed. and trans., *Vāgbhaṭa's Aṣṭāṅgahṛdayam.* Krishnadas Ayurveda Series 27. Varanasi: Krishnadas Academy, 2000–2001; fifth edition, vol. 1; fourth edition, vol. 2; third edition, vol. 3.

Carakasaṃhitā. Priya Vrat Sharma, ed. and trans., *Caraka-saṃhitā: Agniveśa's Treatise Refined and Annotated by Caraka and Redacted by Dṛḍhabala (Text with English Translation).* Jaikrishnadas Ayurveda Series 36. Varanasi: Chaukhamba Orientalia, 1981.

Garbhāvakrānti-sūtra. Mṅal du 'jug pa źes bya ba'i chos kyi rnam graṅs, in *'Dul ba phran tshegs kyi gźi,* Derge *'dul ba tha* 124b–153a.

Mahāvyutpatti. Sakaki Ryōsaburō, ed., *Mahāvyutpatti.* Tokyo: Suzuki Gakujutsu Zaidan, 1963.

Mūlasarvāstivāda-vinaya-vastu. 'Dul ba gźi, Derge *'dul ba ka.*

Śrāvakabhūmi. Shōmon ji Kenkyū-kai, ed. and trans., *Yuga ron shomon ji daiichi yugasho: Sansukurittogo tekisuto to wayaku* 瑜伽論声聞地 第一瑜伽処—サンスクリット語テキストと和訳— (*Śrāvakabhūmi: Revised Sanskrit Text and Japanese Translation, The First Chapter*). Tokyo: Sankibō busshorin, 1998.

Siddhasāra. R. E. Emmerick, ed. and trans., *The Siddhasāra of Ravigupta,* 2 vols. Wiesbaden: Steiner, 1980–1982.

Sitātapatrādhāraṇī. Dhīḥ 33 (2002): 147–154.

Suśrutasaṃhitā. Priya Vrat Sharma, ed. and trans., *Suśruta-saṃhitā: with English Translation of Text and Ḍalhaṇa's Commentary Along with Critical Notes,* 3 vols. Varanasi: Chaukhambha Visvabharati, 2000–2001.

Secondary Sources

Filliozat, Jean. *Le Kumāratantra de Rāvana et les textes paralléles indiens: tibétains, chinois, cambodgien et arabe.* Paris: Imprimerie Nationale, 1937.

Kritzer, Robert. "Life in the Womb: Conception and Gestation in Buddhist Scripture and Classical Indian Medical Literature," in Vanessa R. Sasson and Jane Marie Law, eds., *Imagining the Fetus: The Unborn in Myth, Religion, and Culture,* pp. 73–89. New York: Oxford University Press, 2009.

Meulenbeld, Gerrit Jan. *A History of Indian Medical Literature,* 5 vols. Groningen: E. Forsten, 1999–2002.

—. *The Mādhavanidāna and its Chief Commentary: Chapters 1–10: Introduction, Translation and Notes.* Leiden: E. J. Brill, 1974.

Newman, Karen. *Fetal Positions: Individualism, Science, Visuality.* Palo Alto, CA: Stanford University Press, 1996.

Roth, Gustav, ed. *Bhikṣuṇī-Vinaya: including Bhikṣuṇī-Prakīrṇaka and a Summary of the Bhikṣuṇī-Prakīrṇaka of the Ārya-Mahāsāṃghika-Lokottaravādin.* Patna: K. P. Jayaswal Research Institute, 1970.

Wojtilla, Gyula. "Agricultural Knowledge as it is Reflected in The Śaunakīya Atharvaveda," *Saṃskṛtavimarśaḥ* 6 (2012): 39–50.

Wujastyk, Dominik. "Miscarriages of Justice: Demonic Vengeance in Classical Indian Medicine," in John Hinnells and Roy Porter, eds., *Religion, Health and Suffering,* pp. 257–275. London: Kegan Paul International, 1999.

Zysk, Kenneth. *Religious Medicine: The History and Evolution of Indian Medicine.* New Brunswick: Transaction Publishers, 1993.

Alternative Configurations: Toward an Historiography of Practice[1]

Richard K. Payne
Institute of Buddhist Studies, Berkeley

Buddhism is basically a performing art.
—Stephan Beyer[2]

Over the last half century there has been a sea change in Buddhist studies, evident in the expansion of the field in various directions. One of the framing concepts employed by some scholars active in this process has been the dichotomous opposition between the study of texts and the study of what Buddhists actually do. Though this opposition has been productive, it seems to me that such a framing dichotomy is fundamentally flawed. It confuses theory and method—theory broadly understood as determining what topics are worthy of exploration, evident in the kinds of questions that scholars seek to answer. In contrast, method refers to the means by which those questions are answered. This essay, therefore, seeks to first untangle this confusion, and then suggest how an "historiography of practice" may be further developed.

I use the term "practice" here to refer to the range of specifically prescribed activities considered conducive to awakening in Buddhism.[3] This term is more broadly inclusive than the term "meditation." Thus, "practice" includes not only explicitly meditative practices, which may be grouped under the last two categories of the eightfold path, *smṛti* and *samādhi*, but also such practices as confession, pilgrimage, offering rituals (*pūjā*), chanting, sūtra recitation, devotional services, and so on. At the same time, practice is used here in a more limited fashion than in some works, where it is effectively equivalent to Pierre Bourdieu's *habitus*, what might also be identified as custom, habit, or tradition.[4] Given its definitional middle ground here—between the narrower category of meditation and the broader one of *habitus*—practice is not a category that can be sharply delineated. It is a "fuzzy" category, in the logically technical sense of that term, and it is employed as a term of art.

The historiography of religion has also seen changes over the last fifty years, analogous to those in Buddhist studies.[5] During this period some religious studies scholars have tried to problematize the field's otherwise largely unquestioned frame structure. That structure provided a common system for writing the history of religious systems[6] in terms of founders, their teachings, the texts that record their teachings, and the churches established by the founder (or his followers) with the goal of preserving and propagating the teachings. This frame structure has also been applied to the history of Buddhism since the nineteenth century, when Buddhism was hypostatized as an object of study in the scientific study of religion. As a specialized inquiry, Buddhist studies per se grew out of religious studies, and was largely modeled on Biblical studies.

Shifting to a study of practice highlights two problematic aspects of the modern Western interrogation of Buddhist texts. First is the tendency to examine texts for what they can tell us about doctrine, no matter what kind of texts are under examination. This leads to sifting through the text, like panning for doctrinal gold, while discarding all nondoctrinal "waste." Second, in the discussion of practice, the most common representation of Buddhism in popular religious culture is that of individual, silent, seated meditation, which has become normative for Buddhist identity. Similarly, academic studies of Buddhist practice are also commonly framed in terms of meditation. This presumption marginalizes the majority of Buddhists who may have never spent any time on a meditation cushion, and at the same time privileges as normative a practice that has, for most of Buddhist history, been engaged in solely by a monastic elite.

In this essay I begin by briefly examining the intellectual and historical framework in which Buddhist studies came to be dominated by an historiography of doctrine. Following this discussion, an argument regarding the importance of an historiography of practice as an alternative and complementary field is developed. Finally, I offer suggestions regarding the methodological consequences involved in developing a focus on practice.

History of the Historiography of Doctrine

In the field of religious studies, which was the intellectual home of Buddhist studies until its formulation as an independent specialization in the second half of the twentieth century, teachings are most frequently represented as doctrinal tenets. Doctrinal tenets are presented as central to understanding any religion, and all religions are defined in terms of their doctrinal tenets—a self-reinforcing dialectic. In this closed circle, greater focus is then given to those doctrinal tenets that can be considered unique, those that best serve to distinguish one religion from another. The unique and definitive status of such doctrinal tenets is further enhanced by their representation as the products of the founder's unique religious genius, itself informed by a unique transformative experience. Thus, we find that much of what passes as the history of religions is actually the historiography of doctrine—a complex mutually supportive network of concepts with doctrine at the center, and founder, texts, institutions, and practices serving as the outer nodes of the network.

An historiography of doctrine reflects the systematic priorities of Protestant Christianity. For much of Protestant theology, doctrine, in the form of proper belief (orthodoxy), is understood to be soteriologically essential. The sublation of this structuring focus on doctrine in the nineteenth century was a pivotal rhetorical move in the creation of the scientific study of religion, in which the field of study and its object exist in an epistemological polarity. In other words, the construction of religious studies (or comparative religion) was at the same time the construction of its object, religion as a distinct field of study. "Religion" was hypostatized as an entity autonomous from other social entities, such as economics, law, art, and literature. Having retained from comparative theology, its antecedent field, a tendency toward dehistoricized representations of eternal religious truths, "religious studies" could not conceptualize doctrine as historically contingent.

While doctrine provides the central, unifying theme for understanding Protestant Christianity, the idea that doctrine is the central, unifying thematic for all religions must be recognized as a theoretical presumption that has in fact not been established as a warranted generalization. Acting on this presumption distorts any religious system that does not consider doctrine salvific, and which is therefore not organized around doctrine as its central unifying theme. Despite this, for anyone standing inside the intellectual system that makes such a presumption, these distortions will be effectively invisible—the presumption is effective because it is naturalized, simply taken for granted as obviously the case, and therefore not subject to reflection, much less requiring justification. The very structuring of "religions" by religious studies, itself a system of discourse, means that all religious systems will be presented as doctrinal systems.[7] As a consequence, all of the instances considered within that intellectual system will focus on doctrine and therefore reinforce the foundational presumption.[8]

What does this mean for the study of the history of Buddhism/s? How do we step outside the bubble of the world religions view in order to even begin evaluating whether or not doctrine plays an equally important organizing role for Buddhism as it does for Protestant Christianity? At the same time, how can we avoid simply resorting to the pseudo-pragmatic discourse of Buddhist modernism that attempts to bifurcate doctrine from practice and claims that the latter exists independently of the former?

The alternative suggested here is an historiography of practice. Implementing an alternative historiography to that of doctrine has alternative methodological consequences. Specifically, the use of texts in relation to an historiography of practice relates to the general theme of this collection.[9] While an historiography of practice is as much dependent upon texts as is an historiography of doctrine, the two are distinguished by the kinds of questions that organize the inquiry, and those questions in turn lead to examination of a different range of texts. In other words, this does not mean abandoning philology as a central method for Buddhist studies. If we change the questions that are being asked, then we also change which texts are chosen for examination, and indeed, what counts as a text.

Despite nearly a half-century of work developed by a variety of other disciplinary approaches, the religious studies approach to Buddhism[10] continues to emphasize doctrine.[11] The scholastic tendency of modern Western academia continues to give primacy to doctrine, from the simplistic formulae of introductory textbooks to advanced studies.[12] While there has never been exclusive attention to doctrine, it has held long-standing dominance in the study of Buddhism. For example, John Holt notes the "comparative dearth of scholarly attention" paid to Vinaya studies, and suggests that the first reason for this is that

> pioneer buddhologists and historians of religions were extremely interested in central Buddhist doctrines that have been preserved in the Suttapiṭaka and Abhidhamma literature. Ostensibly, the Vinaya materials do not appear to be concerned with "higher thought."[13]

In the academy we seem to be like the metaphoric fish that doesn't know it is swimming in water. For our part, we swim in a discursive ocean that privileges doctrine in the understanding of religion, and, to shift metaphors, rarely are we disturbed in our doctrinal slumbers.

One striking example of the deeply pervasive character of this privileging of doctrine in the study of religion generally is a textbook surveying the world's religions[14] that I examined some years ago.[15] Organized on the stereotypical model of a catalogue of "world religions," the index revealed only one sustained discussion of ritual, which was found in the introductory chapter as a short subtopic under a discussion of "tribal" religion. Given such a formulation, any student reading this text could only conclude that ritual had in some fashion been left behind by the so-called "universal religions," a term placed in contrast to "tribal" religious belief and activity.[16] Such labeling is applied despite the evidence offered by even the most naïve bit of fieldwork that reveals a religious reality fully steeped in, organized by, and given existential significance[17] by ritual and ceremony.

Each of us can, no doubt, cite very important studies that are exceptions to the generalization that, compared with doctrine, ritual and practice continue to be relatively marginal undertakings in Buddhist studies.[18] I maintain, however, that any such studies are exactly that—exceptions. Despite noteworthy exceptions, the central organizing principle for the academic study of Buddhism continues to be doctrine, with founders and texts playing supporting roles.

This leads us to the current state of the field of Buddhist studies, which has two different dimensions that must be clearly delineated from one another. In addition to the centrality of doctrine as an organizing principle, there is also a corresponding methodological focus on textual studies, that is, philology understood in its expansive and inclusive sense. Just as doctrine functions as the central organizing principle for the contents of the field—the answer to the question of what it is that we study, which is theory—so philology serves as the organizing method—the answer to the question of how we go about the task of this study of Buddhism.

In other words, there is an important distinction to be made between the questions that are asked and the means by which answers to those questions are obtained. As obvious as this distinction may seem when so baldly stated, it is important to emphasize this point since the conflation of the two is deeply pervasive. This was evident during the discussion following the original presentation of this essay. An audience member dismissed my argument as obviously false on the grounds that, for example, the Japanese founders of Pure Land Buddhism, Hōnen, Shinran, and so on, paid a great deal of attention to texts. The (il)logic of the claim reveals how deeply the confusion of textual studies, which was not being addressed, with doctrinal studies, the actual topic under discussion, dominates the discourse in our field of study. Method (specifically, textual studies) is conflated with theory (specifically, doctrinal studies).

An instance of this conflation of method and theory is the otherwise deservedly famous essay by Gregory Schopen, "Archaeology and Protestant Presuppositions in the Study of Indian Buddhism."[19] Schopen first sets out a distinction between two kinds of source materials: texts and

> a large body of archeaological and epigraphical material, material which can be reasonably well located in time and space, material that is largely "unedited" and much of which was never intended to be "read."[20]

He then characterizes the textual material as "records of what a small atypical part of the Buddhist community wanted that community to believe or practice,"[21] while the archaeological and epigraphic material is characterized as recording or reflecting "at least a part of what Buddhists—both laypeople and monks—actually practiced and believed."[22] Although my critique here is unfair to the subtlety and sophistication, on balance, of Schopen's essay, I think it is not inaccurate to claim that for many readers this argument affirmed the opposition between studying texts and studying what Buddhists actually do, which is based on a confusion between theory (the question: What do Buddhists do?) and method (study of texts). This is admittedly how I initially read the essay, and mistakenly viewed it as supporting my assertion, made two and a half decades ago in my first attempt to articulate these ideas publicly, about the importance of the study of ritual for the future of Buddhist studies.

Expressed as a one-dimensional opposition, the text-versus-practice dichotomy has become an accepted formulation in the twenty-five years since Schopen's pioneering exposition of Protestant presuppositions. Margaret Gouin, discussing the history of the study of funerary practices in Buddhist studies, notes a longstanding evaluation of such practices as "abhorrently out of touch with the pure doctrine of Buddhism as it has been envisaged in the West." Having "been declared 'not Buddhist' by generations of Western scholars [funerary practices] therefore fail to register on the academic radar." She notes that in contrast,

> Since the late 20th century, more scholars have been going out into the field to study what is actually done in Buddhist cultures, rather than simply taking texts as normative.[23]

This evidences the same concern, shared by many who follow Schopen, that texts (a term usually employed without qualification, thus implicitly meaning *all* texts) cannot be relied upon as accurate descriptions of the past; rather they must be rendered under a hermeneutic of suspicion as idealizations.[24] This can be an epistemologically valid stance—depending on one's theoretical orientation, on what questions one seeks to answer. The questions many scholars ask today differ from those that motivated earlier inquiries. In other words, it is not that a more suspicious approach to texts necessarily means that we now have a more accurate understanding, but rather that different questions are being asked. And the texts that have tended to be selected as the focus of study in order to answer doctrinal questions are less able, if not incapable, of answering these different questions.

From the very origins of Buddhist studies in the mid-nineteenth century, it seems that the general assumption was that the questions worth asking—what one needs to know about Buddhism—had to do with its doctrine. Equally taken for granted was the belief that the way to answer such important questions about Buddhist belief was to study the "great sacred texts," the doctrinal treatises, of the tradition. Neither the theory nor the method are inherently wrong, but confusion/conflation of the two has led to an equally confused oppositional stance, in which the question "What do Buddhists do?" is identified with the study of sources other than the canon. The confusion of theory and method in the first instance seems to be the direct antecedent of the confusion of theory and method in the second.

As closely intertwined as the two dimensions of doctrine and philology have been in the history of Buddhist studies, they are not identical. In order to understand the intellectual history of the field, these two aspects will be discussed separately. I will first discuss the origins of the methodological focus on philology, then the origins of the thematic focus on doctrine.

It could be suggested that Buddhist studies is a bibliocentric project, at least as it has largely come down to us from its inception in the nineteenth century. This is a consequence of the fact that in the nineteenth century Christianity itself became much more bibliocentric, extending in a much more systematic and thoroughgoing fashion the textual criticisms initiated at the beginning of the Protestant Reformation by such scholars as Erasmus and Jacques Lefèvre d'Etaples.[25] The development of "Higher Criticism" in nineteenth-century Biblical studies set the standards of textual criticism to which Buddhist scholars working in the same intellectual milieux almost immediately aspired.

Just as command of the text of the Bible provided authority and rhetorical power, so also did command of Buddhist texts provide Western scholars with their own authority. In the eyes of a Western audience trained to textual authority,[26] independent command of texts is seen to be inherently superior to an authority that derives from living representatives of the tradition.[27] The religious dynamics behind this claim to authority are more complex, however, and understanding it is important for seeing the contemporary field of Buddhist studies as a continuation of concepts of religious scholarship dating from the time of the Protestant Reformation.

One of the factors motivating Buddhist scholarship's focus on texts is its basis in Protestant conceptions of religious history as a process of decay. Reform of the church was understood as requiring a return to the original and pure teachings as found in the book, the revealed text of the Bible. Clearly, the move to textual authority by leading figures of the Protestant Reformation was itself a strategic move to claim a higher authority than the authority of tradition and liturgy claimed by the Roman Church.[28] The primacy of texts as the source of authority then came to be a foundation stone of Western, specifically Anglophone, scholarship in the field of religious studies. Indeed, Francophone scholarship is generally much more interested in the study of ritual and practice, and this fact reflects differences in the religious cultures that inform Anglophone and Francophone intellectual traditions. Anglophone scholarship largely emerges from a Protestant religious culture, while Francophone emerges from a Catholic religious culture that during the Counter-Reformation resisted the Protestant rejection of the efficacy of the sacraments.

From a Protestant, Anglophone perspective, then, not only a colonialist assertion of power is involved in the rejection of the authority of living masters, but also an expression of the presumption of decay, which could be reversed by proper attention to the original teachings as preserved in the texts. This "proper attention" to the texts could be brought to the study by modern academics, not by traditional scholars who are themselves located within the contemporary Buddhist institution. In other words, temporal distance from the founder is presumed to result in decay of the teachings.[29] This distance can, however, be bridged by returning to the texts that record the founder's original revelation.[30]

We can see the problem with reading such a bibliocentric conception onto Buddhism when we consider an example that is not, in fact, hypothetical. Suppose a sincere Western scholar of religion, on learning that the Kegon school (華厳宗) was very influential in the formation of Japanese Buddhism, undertakes to read the *Avataṃsaka-sūtra*, the *Kegon-gyō* (華厳経). Upon completing this arduous task, however, what will he have learned about the role of Kegon in the formation of Japanese Buddhism? Perhaps how to "read" the Daibutsu in Nara, but very little beyond that. Indeed, based on exactly this kind of bibliocentric presumption, Japanese Buddhism is sometimes dismissed as not "serious"; the idea seems to be that Japanese Buddhists should work out their positions on various religious, philosophical, and moral issues on the basis of doctrinally foundational texts.[31] At least in my experience in Japan, most Buddhist priests, other perhaps than those who have been trained in Western conceptions of the authority of texts, do not read the sutras didactically. It was not the set of doctrinal claims made in the *Kegongyō* that was influential, and certainly not in the same sense in which the Bible stands as the ultimate arbiter of proper belief as the basis for proper action for much of contemporary Christianity. As much as it served as a source of doctrine, the *Avataṃsaka-sūtra* also served to provide a cosmic vision and an inspirational narrative of the path to awakening.[32]

In addition to the centrality of texts, contemporary religious studies scholarship reflects the prominence given to doctrine during the Protestant Reformation. Proper belief, orthodoxy, was promoted as salvific, contrasted with good acts, specifically the sacraments, the salvific efficacy of which was questioned. As the global reach of Protestant societies expanded in the "age of empire,"[33] so also did their exposure to a wider range of religions, which then motivated an increasingly zealous missionary project. The comparative study of religion was born in the nineteenth century as the handmaiden of evangelical Protestantism. The missionary impulse motivated the study of the beliefs and values of other peoples encountered in the process of imperial expansion. These beliefs and values were then selectively organized as "religions," a newly created category understood as an autonomous realm within a wider purview of society. Given the self-understanding of Protestantism, "religions" other than Christianity were naturally constructed so as to focus on their doctrinal systems, and these other doctrinal systems were to be proven wrong.[34]

As we find it at work today, this essentialist conception of religion involves a series of implicit philosophic assumptions. First, there is the "intellectualist presumption," the notion that thought causes action.[35] Add to this both the Protestant notion of the salvific power of orthodox belief (Martin Luther's *sola fide*), and the conception of proper thinking as axiomatic-deductive in character, what might be called the "Euclidean presumption." Under such a compounding of presumptions, beliefs become foundational—that is, axiomatic—and key not only as salvific but also as the basis from which other thoughts are systematically deduced, and finally as the basis for proper actions to be taken.[36]

From such a perspective, the question arises of how to determine which beliefs are proper—which beliefs can be safely taken as axioms? Christian theologians have generally turned to the Bible to address this question, treating it as the ultimate arbiter of belief, and consequently making its proper translation a critical issue.[37] Buddhist studies arose in the context of this nineteenth-century intellectual milieu, in which an emphasis on textual studies was closely intertwined with the primacy of doctrine, the first serving the second.

An historiography of doctrine forms Buddhism as an object of study by determining both what texts tend to be chosen for study, and what questions are asked of those texts that are studied. Since doctrine has served as the central organizing principle, sūtras and commentaries (broadly defined to include *śāstra*s and other similar works) have become the primary objects of study. These works are usually relied upon as the primary sources for our understanding of what Buddhism is, when we ask how to place Buddhism within a framework that conceives of "religions" primarily as doctrinal systems, or as worldviews[38] (in which "worldview" is itself understood as belief systems and the symbols that express those beliefs[39]). At the same time, the questions that are used to interrogate texts are often doctrinal in character, even when the texts are not themselves necessarily doctrinal treatises. Consider, for instance, the Pure Land texts and other sūtras that have a strongly visionary character, or tantras that are more oriented toward practice than doctrine.

The questions that we ask of texts presume a particular cognitive framework of concepts that we believe relate to the specific content of the text; but these concepts are themselves informed by our preapprehensions of what is important. Such an essentialist notion of religion as an axiomatic system of belief also interacts with yet another, not unrelated idea: the presumption that "original" is "authentic." From this understanding, the tenets of Pāli Buddhism have come to be widely treated, particularly in popular and introductory works, not simply as authentic but also as foundational and normative, becoming the standard of orthodox Buddhist thought and practice. Against this standard of the normative for Buddhism, such forms as tantra and Pure Land are likely to appear to be effectively non-Buddhist, and the orthodoxy of their doctrines, as much as the authenticity of their texts, is questioned. This situation derives from a specific set of generally unexamined preconceptions about the nature of religion that have developed over the last several centuries, and which have been received as the appropriate ways in which to structure the field of Buddhist studies.

An Alternative Historiography: The Importance of Studying Practice

As is well known, Buddhism did not arise in a vacuum but rather in the context of the Indic religious culture of Śākyamuni's time.[40] We need to keep in mind that Buddhism is originally an Indic religion—it did not arise *sui generis,* despite repeated representations focusing solely on the novel aspects of the founder's teaching. As Louis Renou, "the most prominent Sanskrit scholar of the twentieth century," notes: "Vedic religion is first and foremost a liturgy, and only secondarily a mythological or speculative system; we must therefore investigate it as a liturgy."[41] This "liturgical" understanding of what constitutes religion is the context for the rise of Buddhism.

Some may object that Buddhism is part of the *śramaṇa* movement that transformed Vedic religious culture on doctrinal grounds. Even more emphatically, Śākyamuni Buddha is often presented as a reformer who intended to purify religion of "empty ritualism." This interpretation of the Buddha (and of Indian religion of his time as corrupt) seems to derive from Protestant preconceptions of the history of religion as one of decadence requiring reform, and of religious leaders as reformers, as previously discussed. In this case, Śākyamuni is modeled either on Jesus cleansing the Temple in Jerusalem, or on Luther nailing his ninety-five theses to the doors of the Schlosskirche in Wittenberg.[42]

An argument about the relation between practice and doctrine is that practice and doctrine form a single, integrated whole. I have myself made this argument, which points to a relation between the two that ranges from very loose to very tight, though as this relation has generally been asserted, it is the result of interpretation rather than having been demonstrated historically. However, understood in a strong sense, a close bond between practice and doctrine suggests that there is a kind of isometric relation between the two. This isometry can be understood in different ways, such as that every practice is the expression of some doctrinal position (a view that implicitly privileges doctrine), or that all doctrines either originate from experiences arising from practice[43] or have been tested in practice, and found conducive to awakening (a view that implicitly privileges experience).[44] In this strong sense, isometry means that every practice is fully reducible to, or can be completely explained by, a particular doctrinal point; conversely, every doctrinal point is rooted in some particular of experience produced by practice.

However, as Geoffrey Samuel notes,

> the relationship between text and practice in the material is often oblique. I am sure, for example, that much of the writing of the Mahāyāna sūtras reflects visionary and meditative practices. This has become almost a cliché in writing about them in recent years. But it is often not easy to work out exactly what these practices might have been.[45]

Samuel goes on to give the example of the mandala of the *Suvarṇa-prabhāsa-sūtra.* While confident that the description of the mandala can be understood as reflecting "some kind of practice in which the four Buddhas were visualized and invoked," he notes that "precisely how and in what way remains obscure."[46]

A related tempting assumption is that present-day practices are simply continuous with those reflected in the text. However, the series of questions Samuel asks about the relation between the mandala description and any putative practice highlights the speculative nature of such an assumption.

> Was this purely a visualized procedure? Were there images set up in the four directions? Was there some kind of mediumship involved, in which communication from the Buddhas was invited? What was the role of the meditator[47] at the center? Was he or she taking on the role of the Buddha or of a fifth Buddha as in later Indian and Tibetan versions of that structure? Was this an elaborately scripted and liturgically defined practice, as it might be with the Tibetans today? Or was it a largely internal process in which the practitioners opened themselves up to a visionary state of some kind without much structure? All of these are open questions, and in fact there might also have been a range of different ways in which these practices were performed.[48]

Since a textual record may be less informative than we would like, such as the description of a mandala in Samuel's example, what other approach may be taken to augment our information? An appealing methodological solution might be to assume that contemporary practice can be employed to augment textual descriptions.[49] The question of Bodhidharma's "wall-examining" (*biguan,* 壁觀) provides an example of how problematic such assumptions actually are. At a very superficial level, familiarity with only the Japanese Sōtō Zen tradition would lead to the conclusion that Bodhidharma sat facing the wall, while someone familiar only with Rinzai practice would conclude that he had his face turned away from the wall. Similarly, those familiar only with Japanese styles of Zen practice would expect very rigid postural guidelines, while Korean Sŏn practice is much looser regarding posture. Such a simple but marked difference in styles of performing the "same" kind of meditation indicate that contemporary practice cannot be assumed to provide a sure model of earlier practices. Greater knowledge of the related textual tradition, however, serves only to further complicate the matter. Steven Heine has pointed out that the wall may be a literary trope.

> First, in terms of the issue of "facing the wall" or "being like a wall" while sitting, there are verbal images used by Song dynasty and later thinkers to the effect that the purity and clarity of a huge solid substance like a silver mountain or iron wall signifies equanimity achieved during meditation. But in the twelfth century even Dahui, who supposedly gave rise to contemporary Rinzai practice via Hakuin, did say that sitting should be done while facing a wall, even as he preached the shortcut method of contemplating the key-phrase that supposedly should not get bogged down in sitting for its own sake—so his message is complex and multifaceted.[50]

Samuel's summary that "the contexts of Yogic and Tantric practice vary over time and that they are often quite different from those of the traditions in today's world"[51] can be generalized as a caveat on the use of present-day practice to interpret texts. Each case needs to be approached as a unique methodological situation involving the interplay of specific textual material, present-day practice where it exists, and historical context.

Introducing a neologism, we can say that doctrine and practice are "semi-autonomous traditions."[52] Each has its own trajectory over time, and though they often interact, neither is completely independent of nor fully identical with the other. Fundamentally, the relation between doctrine and practice is always a matter of context and interpretation. There are times when doctrine runs off on its speculative own, and there are instances when practices are maintained simply out of institutional inertia.[53] We cannot, therefore, presume that there is any necessary connection between doctrine and practice, much less a one-to-one isometry. Such connections and isometric relations may be the case in some particular instances, but to establish them requires a case-by-case inquiry.

Finally, one of the issues raised in contemporary studies of ritual is that the realm of embodied experience for both those performing and those attending a ritual is not coterminous with the realm of concepts. Roy Rappaport insists that it is uncontroversial

> that ritual is not simply an alternative way to express any manner of thing, but that certain meanings and effects can best, or even *only*, be expressed or achieved in ritual.[54]

It is on this basis that Rappaport draws his distinction between canonical and indexical forms of communication in ritual (discussed below in relation to Jōkei's *kōshiki*), a distinction that maps roughly onto conceptual and experiential.

For our purposes here, this implies that practice cannot simply be reduced to its didactics, even when it is specifically created as an instructional device designed to convey doctrines, as discussed below in relation to the interplay of doctrinal exposition and performative experience in Jōkei's *kōshiki.*

Methodological Implications of an Historiography of Practice

As I have attempted to clarify, there is not an epistemologically significant opposition between text and practice. Despite the longstanding association between textual studies and doctrinal studies, the former is a method, while the latter is an organizing principle of the field of inquiry. Just as an historiography of practice does not displace doctrinal studies but adds to them, so also do the methods of the study of practice enhance textual studies. The study of practice, however, has not been developed to the same extent as have textual and doctrinal studies. Stephan Beyer's *The Cult of Tārā: Magic and Ritual in Tibet,* published thirty years ago, is indicative of this. This work still stands as one of the most detailed studies of ritual practices in Buddhism. Beyer opens his work by making the methodologically critical point that an historiography of practice depends upon detailed descriptions prior to any interpretive claims about the meaning, significance, or symbolism of the practices. He asserts that "we must first ask, simply, what the Tibetans are doing before we can go on to decide the 'real' reason they do it."[55] Beyer, however, does not provide us with any conclusion to his study, reflecting the need for more developed theory in the study of practice.

In order to develop an historiography of Buddhist practice, it is necessary to know what questions are important. For textual and doctrinal studies, the questions are sufficiently well established that they may be taken for granted. For the study of practice, however, there appears to be no consensus on what the important questions are, and most studies have borrowed from other ancillary fields of study, such as neuroscience[56] and anthropology.[57] These theoretically determined questions then provide guidance for the methodologies to be employed. Given the history of the field of Buddhist studies, in which a first approach to practice would be recourse to the texts, what do the texts actually tell us about practice? This approach is taken by Sarah Shaw, for example, in her study of meditation in the Pāli canonical and paracanonical literature.[58] She structures her study according to the forty meditative objects presented by Buddhaghoṣa in his *Visuddhimagga,* with additional material from other sources drawn in as commentary.

A necessary complement to textual studies of practice is personal observation. Even more preferable is actual participation in the practices being studied. Concerning meditation, Rod Bucknell and Chris Kang write that

> It is increasingly common for those doing research on meditation to be meditators themselves. Such people are far better equipped than non-meditator researchers to arrive at balanced and well informed conclusions. Textual scholars who meditate are in a position to interpret the textual accounts of meditation intelligibly and realistically, and perhaps to correlate otherwise obscure statements with actual meditative techniques and attainments. Psychologist-meditators, with their training in detached observation and their technical vocabulary, are in a position to formulate accurate and insightful descriptions and interpretations of what they experience in their meditation.[59]

As it stands, this claim, while pointing in the right direction, is not only overly sanguine in tone but epistemologically naive. The historical gaps discussed by Samuel are not so easily overcome; one cannot simply presume that one's present experience with practice corresponds to the textual record. Likewise, meditative experience is far from context-free—the culture in which meditation practice is undertaken unavoidably affects the character, understanding, and description of that experience.[60] Personal factors, such as a perhaps unconscious desire to confirm the value of a tradition, can influence experience in not so subtle ways. And psychological theory is not a neutral perspective for analysis and comparison but introduces its own presumptions and assumptions, values, and conditions of acceptable discourse.

This is not to say, however, that personal experience with practice is not a valuable method, only that it needs to be employed in a critically informed fashion. Critically employed experience may help to displace some of the popular preconceptions about practice. For example, there is a distinct gap between modernist rhetoric about Zen meditation, along the lines of "direct confrontation with the nature of mind," and the highly ritualized actuality of that practice.

Despite these limitations, Bucknell and Kang make the important point that for the historiography of practice, personal engagement is not simply a nice optional addition, something to fill out a textual study with a bit of decorative narrative about personal experience with the tradition. Nor is it solely for creating engaging narratives for use in the classroom, as important as pedagogical considerations are.[61] While it does not allay all of the concerns expressed in the preceding section, a researcher's actual experience with a practice may serve to dislocate some of his or her preconceptions. We can borrow from the discipline of anthropology some methods for the study of practice that complement textual studies. Though no single method solves all epistemological concerns, the participant-observer construct[62] can still provide a model for the study of religious practice. While this method has been critiqued in recent anthropological scholarship, the critiques do not invalidate the method per se but serve instead to correct it.[63]

At the same time, it is necessary to avoid the pointless politicized assertions of the superiority of "insider" experience over "outsider" study, or vice versa.[64] The partisan nature of conflicting assertions of superiority, outsider versus insider, constitute an impediment to scholarship. They are based on an overly reified and rigid dichotomous metaphor of religion as container, and under the entailments of this metaphor there is a sharp delineation between those who are inside and those who are outside the container.[65] Add to this conflicting claims of epistemological privilege: on the one hand, the outsider's superior knowledge is sometimes asserted because he or she is not deluded by religious commitments to a tradition. In contrast, the insider's claim to superior access to knowledge is based on the idea that only through personal lived experience can someone truly understand a religion. This results in the present impasse in the epistemology of religious studies, to the extent that it has largely accepted the insider-outsider dichotomy of "religion as container."

Instead of the dysfunctional pairing of insider vs. outsider as oppositional and mutually exclusive positions, each with their own epistemological privilege, a more useful epistemological model is that there are a variety of modes of engagement, different ways in which a person may engage a religious tradition. One mode of engagement is a person who engages the tradition through training in order to understand its history of practice. One senses on the part of some academics an almost visceral resistance to the ambiguities created by training in a tradition of practice as a methodologically intentional strategy. Yet, for the study of practice, depending on an exclusively textual methodology is confronted by four epistemologically critical limitations.

One such limitation is the presumption of familiarity. In the case of the Japanese Shingon tradition, for example, ritual texts exist and practitioners follow them. However, the manuals often use abbreviations or otherwise obscure allusions to ritual actions that the manual's author assumes are already familiar to the practitioner. This is why ritual manuals, even esoteric ones, can be freely purchased in contemporary Japan: the presumption of familiarity may make them less than perfectly transparent. Gudrun Bühnemann notes the same situation in India:

> Books sold on the roadside, in front of temples or by specialized books dealers attempt to guide the devotee in his *pūjā*. Often these books contain translations of the Skt. mantras into vernaculars. The explanations are usually brief; much is taken for granted as one can expect a Hindu reader to be familiar with the practice of worship.[66]

A second limitation is that a ritual manual may simply be a list of actions—first do this, then do that, then do this other, then recite this mantra so many times, and so on. One of the things that the syntactic study of rituals initiated by Frits Staal has made quite evident, however, is that rituals are not simply a linear sequence of actions. Actions are grouped and organized into larger units in a systematic and regular fashion. As I have discussed elsewhere, the purely formal analysis initiated by Staal can be further explicated by reference to an organizing metaphor. In the case of the Shingon *goma,* for example, the organizing metaphor is that of offering a feast to an honored guest.[67] As an organized activity, there is a systematic and regular internal structure to the ritual—a ritual syntax—that will probably not be evident in the linear sequence of actions revealed either by reading a ritual manual or by observation alone.

Situations in which there is a significant disconnect between texts and rituals constitute a third kind of limitation on an epistemological strategy of depending entirely on texts. For example, I understand from colleagues specializing in the study of south Indian Hindu tantra that it is not uncommon for ritual practitioners there to have a ritual manual in front of them while performing a rite. However, there may be no connection between the ritual described in the manual and the actual rite being performed. In such cases, even the most accurate translation of the manual will not yield an clear understanding of the tradition of practice. Here we also see that answering the question of what constitutes a text for the historiography of practice is different from the answer of what it might be for an historiography of doctrine. Rather than being a source of knowledge, or even a guide for action, a text may itself be treated as a ritual element, part of the requisite paraphernalia of a ritual.

Finally, there are practices that exist outside the textual tradition. In this regard we may consider that for the majority of the history of Buddhism, most practitioners were probably illiterate or only marginally literate. The textual tradition, for the most part, represents the culture of the literate monastic elite. Some scholars have speculated that some of the paintings of Sukhāvatī in Dunhuang were used for meditative visualization practices, yet they do not correspond to any particular Pure Land text.[68] In large part it is the intellectualist fallacy that action follows from thought, which leads us to presume that doctrines found in texts are primary, and that they serve necessarily as the source for practices as well as for religious artwork. It would be much more accurate to interpret all of these arenas—practice, art, and doctrine—as different traditions that are semi-autonomous in relation to one other.

The observer and participant modes of engagement do, however, have a significant methodological limitation when it comes to the history of ritual practice, the historical gap between practices as they are performed today and what was done in the past, discussed above. Based on the common cultural presumption that rituals are unchanging and rigidly conservative in nature, it is perhaps tempting to also assume that practices found today have been largely unchanged over the course of their history. As discussed above, however, such an assumption is unjustified as well as simply naïve. We cannot simply assume that contemporary Sōtō Zen practitioners in San Francisco or Shingon practitioners in Los Angeles are conducting practices in the same way that Dōgen and Kūkai learned them in China.[69]

Perhaps even more convincing examples are the use of mindfulness practice in entirely secular, psychotherapeutic settings, which certainly cannot be assumed to be the same practice that Śākyamuni employed, and similarly the practice of "Catholic Zen" cannot be assumed to be the same practice as that brought by Bodhidharma to China. These latter two examples also highlight the issues of context in the study of practice, and the more fundamental issue of the commensurability of practices as they are "translated" across cultural boundaries. Commensurability often appears to be simply presumed, rather than demonstrated. And a belief that supports this presumption is the modern idea that doctrine and practice are autonomous from one another, mentioned in relation to Buddhist Modernism above. In contemporary society this takes the form of a semiotics of technology, which treats practices such as meditation as a kind of context-free and value-neutral mental tool for self-improvement of one kind or another. In a recursive fashion, this technological conception is itself part of the contemporary cultural context. All of these are the kinds of issues that require further inquiry in the development of an historiography of practice.

Given these methodological issues, I think that we can take Stephan Beyer's claim that Buddhism is a performing art as a serious metaphoric expression of a theoretical orientation to practice. This would allow us to see practices such as *sādhanas* and *pūjās* as creative projects, performance art working within a highly structured set of fixed tropes. Consider, for example, the ritual devotions (*kōshiki*, 講式) of Jōkei (貞慶, 1155–1213). James Ford clearly explains the complexity of Jōkei's performances:

> *Kōshiki* incorporate a variety of Buddhist devotional forms and aims, including hymns of praise (Jp. *kada;* Sk. *gāthā;* one of twelve types of scripture in metrical verse), ritual offerings (*dengu*), communal obeisance (*sōrei*), merit transference (*ekō*), and pronouncements of intent (*hyōbyaku*). The *kō* of *kōshiki* might best be rendered as reading, since it involves a fixed liturgy, in contrast to a more normal, unconstrained sermon (*sekkyō*). The text, which generally praises the virtues of a particular Buddha, bodhisattva, patriarch, or sūtra, provides the framework for a performance that takes place before an image of the object of devotion (*honzon*). In some cases, the focus may even be on an important Buddhist concept as, for example, Jōkei's *Dōshinki kōshiki* and the *Hosshin kōshiki,* which highlight the importance for arousing the aspiration for enlightenment (Sk. *bodhicitta;* Jp. *bodaishin*). In any case, part of the *kōshiki* usually clarifies a text or texts closely connected to the object for the average listener.[70]

Jōkei's ceremonies integrated a variety of traditional ritual elements, while at the same time working at the interface of practice and doctrine. A *kōshiki* engages in two levels of communication: doctrinal exposition and ritual performance, analogous to Rappaport's canonical and indexical forms of communication.

Highlighting the important function of performative ritual is not to say that religion can be reduced to theater, but rather that an irreducible aspect of religion is its performativity.[71] The fact that we make aesthetic judgments about a given religious tradition—the quality of the chanting, the beauty of an altar, the colors of the brocade robes, the style with which ceremonial actions are performed—itself indicates that we inherently recognize religion's performative qualities.[72] Is the difference between the loose sitting style of Korean Sŏn and the rigid style of Japanese Zen actually functional, or is it, whether largely or in part, an aesthetic variation?

In addition to the aesthetics of performance, there is also the ability of performance to communicate in a nondiscursive fashion, giving a different kind of significance to doctrinal claims. Rappaport refers to the former as "canonical" and the latter as "indexical," noting that

> in all liturgical rituals, and most clearly *in all religious rituals, there is transmitted an indexical message that cannot be transmitted in any other way and, far from being trivial, it is one without which canonical messages are without force, or may even seem nonsensical.*[73]

We may paraphrase this by emphasizing the experience of embodied participation in the performance as essential to comprehending the doctrinal meaning. This also indicates why the disjunction of meditation from doctrine leads not to some "pure" direct meditative experience of reality but rather to the integration of meditation into a different doctrinal system.[74]

For these reasons—presumptions of familiarity, gaps between text and practice, the need to understand the syntax of practices, and the experiential, embodied, and performative dimensions of practice—the textual study of practice must be complemented both by observation and participation, and preferably by some training in the tradition itself. Whether identified as "indexical communication," as Rappaport calls it (employing terminology from Charles S. Peirce), or as embodied experience, in fact only through such participation in performances can the nondiscursive dimension of practice can be apprehended and appreciated as part of the way in which the tradition has been propagated over time and across cultural boundaries.[75]

This approach cannot, however, be considered a panacea; it does not resolve the issues of historical and cultural distance discussed above. But no single method can be expected to address all theoretical questions. This is therefore an instance of matching theory, the questions one wants to answer, and method, the means by which those questions can be answered.

Summary: Toward an Historiography of Practice

Given the range of issues in the history and methodology of Buddhist studies discussed briefly in this essay, the points most salient for the development of an historiography of practice can be summarized here. An examination of the intellectual milieux in which Buddhist studies developed highlights the bibliocentric context and the centrality of doctrine formative for Buddhist studies scholars in establishing the field in the last half of the nineteenth century, and which continued to define it well into the last half of the twentieth century. However, the intellectual and scholarly frameworks that developed out of the history of Christianity cannot simply be accepted by default as appropriate for the study of Buddhism.

The study of practice (as a general category, as well as of specific practices) entangles a variety of epistemological concerns. One is the problem of historical distance: it is difficult for us today to reconstruct what specific practice a text may have intended. Similarly, authors of texts that present practices either purposely or unavoidably presumed shared knowledge with the original intended audience, to which we today do not have immediate access—that is, the presumption of familiarity. While direct experiential familiarity with the practice being studied cannot overcome all of the problems of historical distance, it can provide both a better understanding of how the practice is structured and of the allusive qualities outside the didactic content.

An historiography of practice must also be critically reflective toward received representations, perhaps most importantly the exclusive identification of Buddhist practice with silent, seated meditation. Equally problematic is the modern tendency to create a dichotomy of meditation and ritual. Meditation tends to be loaded with the positive valence of the Romantic epistemology of direct, unmediated experience, while ritual is still negatively viewed as an unthinking, uncreative, and mindlessly repetitive mode of praxis. This overlooks the experiential nature of ritualizing meditative practices that contributes to their efficacy in changing a person's self-conception.[76]

Finally, doctrine and practice are semi-autonomous traditions, each with its own historical trajectory, presumptions, and values, despite their interaction at various points in those trajectories. Both have the character of a *bricolage,* integrating found elements from the religious cultures within which they have developed. In his study of *dhāraṇī* and Chinese material culture, Paul Copp writes:

> Scholars have long known that ritualists and the authors of scriptures and tales in medieval China (as elsewhere) composed religious forms out of what was at hand and held to be potent in their cultures, mixing religious frameworks, concepts, and objects into new forms, which were then themselves later incorporated into yet newer forms—and on and on in history.[77]

It was in just this fashion that Buddhist practitioners of tantra in India integrated the *homa* ritual, and Buddhist authors of medieval doctrinal texts integrated aspects of Nyāya logic. In the case of both doctrine and practice, the pre-Buddhist history, as well as the religious cultures within which Buddhist thinkers and practitioners worked, must be understood.

The meta-theoretical shift from an historiography of doctrine to an historiography of practice does not mean abandoning philology as a central method. Rather, it entails adding complementary methods appropriate to the study of practice. It is worth repeating that these include participation on the part of the researcher in order to gain a better understanding of how the practice is organized. Such experience is important both for opening up the allusive qualities of practice to the researcher, and also to provide access to information about the practice that would not be available through textual study alone. While many researchers have begun to report on their experiences in the practice of Buddhist studies, a scholar's personal engagement with the practices of Buddhism is still considered suspect in many quarters, much less recognized as an important primary source for their research.

What counts as a text appropriate for study also changes with the shift of focus from doctrine to practice. Instead of the authoritative canonic doctrinal texts, ritual manuals employed in performance now also fall within the purview of research.[78] As texts, however, these also require all the philological skills that scholars in the field can bring to bear.

Conclusion

The question of what questions we ask of Buddhism is a self-reflective inquiry. A self-consciously reflective scholarship recognizes that the questions we ask say more about us, what we presume the world to be like, and what we value than they do about Buddhism, and that the way we ask these questions constructs the Buddhism that we find in answer. This is simply to reiterate in more general terms a point made many years ago by Walter Liebenthal, in his study of Sengzhao's *Zhaolun*.[79] Liebenthal discussed the difference between the epistemological questions that orient Indian religious philosophy and the ontological questions that serve the same function in China. He pointed out that the Chinese were interrogating Buddhist texts for answers to their own ontological questions, and in doing so they determined the answers they received. This idea—that the person who formulates the question determines the nature of the answer—is key to a self-reflective scholarship. Self-reflection may help us see that our own questions, whether they are asked about doctrine or practice, are not the only possible or important ones that may be asked.

To suggest the value of an historiography of practice should not be understood as positing that practice is somehow more central, more essential to Buddhism than doctrine—an argument that is already all too familiar in Buddhist Modernism. Rather, my thesis is that it makes just as much sense to think of the history of Buddhism as much a history of practice—ritual, meditation, visualization, debate, devotional, ceremonial—as it is a history of doctrinal positions. The choice of what to foreground in our understanding of Buddhism is in fact just that—a choice, our choice. As such, it depends on the criteria we choose as most relevant to the issues and questions that are of concern to us.

No religion, including Buddhism, is in any way a "natural object" existing in the external, objective world, available for mutual, interpersonal observation and social agreement based on its natural characteristics. All religions, including Buddhism, are social constructs, intersubjective objects, created in the realm of discourse. These objects are themselves created in the way that we talk about them, including the social status that attaches to those to whom we attribute authority[80] for defining them. At the same time, this is not to say that there is no pool of resources out there with which we may engage. But what we think of as Buddhism is an intersubjectively constructed object, one that has been created in a dialectic between questions arising in the present and the resources, whether people, texts, or institutions, that are queried.

Since the very questions that we ask simultaneously elicit answers and construct the Buddhism we find in answer, it is very important to take responsibility for those questions that we do ask. An historiography of practice allows us at least to ask new questions, and we will then look differently at the textual and institutional resources we employ to construct our understanding of the history of Buddhism. New dimensions of this history that are otherwise made invisible may thereby be uncovered.

Notes

1 The earliest expression of the ideas formalized here was at the twentieth anniversary celebration of the Buddhist Studies program (established in 1972) at the University of California, Berkeley. I was honored by Lew's invitation to participate in a panel of graduates of the program. We were asked to share our thoughts on the future of Buddhist studies. I made two suggestions at the time: first, that the future of studying Buddhist tantra would depend upon placing that study in close relation to the equally rapidly expanding field of Hindu tantric studies. The expansion of Hindu tantric studies, particularly the influential role of Alexis Sanderson's publications on the subject of the relation between Buddhist and Śaiva tantras, feels like full vindication for this suggestion. Second, I suggested that there should be more academic attention to the study of ritual. One of the questions raised by the audience members was whether this meant moving away from the study of texts. The conflation of textual and doctrinal studies evident in the question produced further reflection. Eventually, these ideas were further mediated by presenting them in a much fuller and more formal version at the "Text, Translation, and Transmission" conference, part of the twentieth-anniversary celebration of the establishment of the Numata Chair program, held at the University of California, Berkeley, October 18–20, 2007. Further reflection and revisions led to the present form of this essay. I wish to thank Lew for welcoming me, a student cross-registering from the Graduate Theological Union, into his seminars. Memories of working with those who are now my colleagues, many of whom are represented in this collection, in Lew's office on the second floor of Durant Hall, translating the "same" text from Sanskrit, Tibetan, and Chinese versions, was one of the most memorable learning experiences of my life. My thanks also go to all of you.

2 Stephan Beyer, *The Cult of Tārā: Magic and Ritual in Tibet* (Berkeley, Los Angeles, and London: University of California Press, 1978), p. xii.

3 Regarding the term "Buddhism," I use it here to refer to the object of academic study, that is, as a category of historical phenomena. What that object is supposed to represent, however, is not a unity—in many discursive contexts it is more appropriate to speak of "Buddhisms." A discussion of parallel constructs in the study of the relations between Christianity and paganism can be found in Guy G. Stroumsa, *The End of Sacrifice: Religious Transformations in Late Antiquity* (Chicago and London: University of Chicago Press, 2009), p. 2, where he writes, "we have learned that 'neither' paganism nor even 'Christianity' can be reduced to a fractious unity that represents anything."

4 See, for example, David D. Hall, ed., *Lived Religion in America: Toward a History of Practice* (Princeton, NJ: Princeton University Press, 1997), especially Hall's introduction to the collection.

5 Since the Buddhism section was established as part of the American Academy of Religion (AAR) in 1981, discourses on religious studies have provided a context for Buddhist studies, though not in a closely determinative sense, rather that this created a venue for the development of approaches to the study of Buddhism that may well have been impossible in other academic venues.

6 I take care in my use of terminology here, distinguishing between "religion" as a general singular category, and "religions" as instances of "religion." As such, the two are meant to identify the almost Platonic conception of the field of religious studies as it originated in the nineteenth century, in which the ideal form, "religion," was to be approached through its various manifestations, "religions." For lack of a better marker, "religious systems" will be used to identify specific historically, culturally, and socially delimited phenomena. In this usage, therefore, Buddhism is a religion, while Sōtōshū Zen in Meiji-era Japan is a religious system. There is no attempt to impose a consistent standard of what constitutes an appropriate level of delimiting, only that the limits be explicit. This reflects the interlayering inherent in a systems approach.

7 In his study of the early Perfection of Wisdom literature, *Dawn of the Bodhisattva Path: The Early Perfection of Wisdom* (Berkeley: Institute of Buddhist Studies and BDK America, Inc., 2014), p. 112, Gil Fronsdal notes:

> Having initially started my study of the *Daoxing jing* with the understanding that it is a philosophical text, I was surprised to discover how much of the text is not concerned with philosophical issues. Most of the sūtra consists of discussions of a variety of religious practices and attitudes, including meditation, acquiring merit, transformation of merit, devotion, prediction, writing, reading, reciting, memorizing, preaching, listening, studying, making vows, and giving. Even the passages that discuss *prajñāpāramitā* do so in the context of religious practice, including cultivating attitudes or perspectives of the nonapprehension of various conceptual phenomena (dharmas) The text also gives instruction on how to relate to other bodhisattvas and to the *prajñāpāramitā,* and how to avoid being influenced by Māra.

8 The apparent circularity here is itself a consequence of attempting to explain a dialectical relation.

9 This should not be confused with the academic vs. practitioner dichotomy. The opposition between the academic study of Buddhism, particularly as the study of texts, and the actively engaged practice of Buddhism, in particular meditation, that is still frequently found in popular Buddhist discourse is a false dichotomy.

10 On issues resulting from the increasing role of the AAR for Buddhist studies specialists, see Malcolm David Eckel, "The Ghost at the Table: On the Study of Buddhism and the Study of Religion," *Journal of the American Academy of Religion* 62/4 (1994): 1085–1110.

11 The work of anthropologists has been particularly important in this regard.

12 This is not to imply that there are not similar kinds of scholasticism informing the Buddhist tradition, as well. Rather, the implicit scholasticism of Western academia taken together with the explicit scholasticism of the Buddhist tradition tend to overdetermine a doctrinal reading of the tradition.

13 John Clifford Holt, "Ritual Expression in the Vinayapiṭaka: A Prolegomenon," *History of Religions* 18/1 (August 1978): 42.

14 Similarly, despite many publications critical of this kind of formulation, the

"world's religions" model, or something fundamentally similar to it, remains the dominant academic format, entrenched in textbooks, curricula, and faculty appointments.

15 Denise Lardner Carmody and John Carmody, *Ways to the Center: An Introduction to World's Religions* (Belmont, CA: Wadsworth Publishing, 1981). This work remains in print: Denise Lardner Carmody and T. L. Brink, *Ways to the Center: An Introduction to the World's Religions* (Belmont, CA: Wadsworth Publishing, 2013, seventh ed.). The reprint edition shows little improvement in its treatment of ritual.

16 The term has been employed by some scholars seeking a defining characteristic to highlight that some "religions" are only open on the basis of birth, while others are open universally to all humans.

17 Citing John Blacking's work on women's initiations among the Venda, Camilla Powers, in "Old Wives' Tales: The Gossip Hypothesis and the Reliability of Cheap Signals," in James R. Hurford, Michael Studdert-Kennedy, and Chris Knight, eds., *Approaches to the Evolution of Language: Social and Cognitive Bases* (Cambridge: Cambridge University Press, 1998), p. 124, writes:

> Women long afterwards recalled the difficulties of co-ordinating dance movements, the physical contact, closeness and excitement when the dances went well, rather than the spoken instruction in the sophisticated associated symbolism. Clearly the physical aspect of the rituals nurtured strong emotional and affective bonds.

18 See, for example, Anne M. Blackburn, "Looking for the Vinaya: Monastic Discipline in the Practical Canons of the Theravāda," *Journal of the International Association of Buddhist Studies* 22/2 (1999): 281–309; she indicates that the goal of her distinction between formal and practical canons is to allow "scholars of the Theravāda to write histories of Buddhist practice with greater precision" (p. 281).

19 Gregory Schopen, "Archaeology and Protestant Presuppositions in the Study of Indian Buddhism," *History of Religions* 31/1 (August 1991): 1–23.

20 Schopen, "Archaeology and Protestant Presuppositions," pp. 1–2.

21 Schopen, "Archaeology and Protestant Presuppositions," p. 3.

22 Schopen, "Archaeology and Protestant Presuppositions," p. 2.

23 Margaret Gouin, "Funeral Practices," *Oxford Bibliographies,* sv. Buddhism; www.oxfordbibliographies.com/ (forthcoming).

24 I suspect that Paul Ricoeur's work, such as *Freud and Philosophy: An Essay on Interpretation* (Ithaca, NY: Yale University Press, 1970), has had an important formative effect for many Buddhist studies scholars, whether or not they are aware of it. While they may have never studied Ricoeur directly, the intellectual milieu in which they were educated imbued attitudes in keeping with his hermeneutics.

25 Mack P. Holt, *The French Wars of Religion, 1562–1629* (Cambridge: Cambridge University Press, 2005), pp. 13–16.

26 This training of the Western intellect is textualized not only religiously but also legalistically, the two being closely interlinked in the history of Western

thought. The very distinction between religion and politics is revealed as a modern artifice when one considers the function of "charter myths."

27 This is basic in much of the struggle to define Christianity in the Reformation, in which the institutional authority of priests deploying the sacraments was set against the individual authority of the believer deploying his, or rarely her, reading of the Bible. This background also informs the distinct differences between Anglophone and Francophone study of ritual.

28 See Desmond M. Clarke, *Descartes: A Biography* (Cambridge: Cambridge University Press, 2006), p. 4.

29 Similar rationales have also been employed by Buddhists. The theme of the decline of the Dharma has been employed to justify certain claims in Pure Land Buddhism, while reformers have employed the rhetoric of a return to original purity, as established in the Vinaya.

30 We should note, however, that despite the apparent similarities (see note 28, above) this is not the same as Buddhist notions of the decay of the Dharma, inherited from the broader Indic cosmogony. In the Buddhist case, greater emphasis is placed on the degradation of human beings' capacity to comprehend and correctly apply the teachings.

31 Interpreting a religious tradition's texts to determine an authoritative position vis-à-vis some contemporary issue is, loosely speaking, the project of theology. Not only is it problematic to universalize this project as either explicitly or implicitly mandatory for all religions, but is itself fundamentally problematic as simply an exercise in dueling claims of authority. What I have called "the indefinite malleability of doctrine" means that textually justified claims regarding the authority of some doctrinal assertion can be deployed for quite opposed ethical positions. See Richard K. Payne, "Traditionalist Representations of Buddhism," *Pacific World: Journal of the Institute of Buddhist Studies,* 3rd series, no. 10 (Fall 2008): p. 191.

32 See Shunshō Manabe, "The Development of Images Depicting the Teaching of the *Avataṃsaka-sūtra,*" in Robert Gimello, Frédéric Girard, and Imre Hamar, eds., *Avataṃsaka Buddhism in East Asia: Huayan, Kegon, Flower Ornament Buddhism Origins and Adaptation of a Visual Culture* (Wiesbaden: Harrasowitz Verlag, 2012), pp. 205–222; Makio Takemura, "Kūkai's Esotericism and *Avataṃsaka* Thought," in Gimello, Girard, and Hamar, eds., *Avataṃsaka Buddhism in East Asia*, pp. 339–376.

33 See Erich J. Hobsbawm, *The Age of Empire: 1875–1914* (New York: Pantheon Books, 1987).

34 See Fronsdal, *Dawn of the Bodhisattva Path*, p. 49. On the motivation for the comparative study of religion in relation to the goals of missionary work, see Eric Sharpe, *Comparative Religion* (London: Gerald Duckworth, 1975).

35 Although she herself did not use the phrase "intellectualist fallacy," the idea presented here is primarily informed by Catherine Bell's discussion of the thought–action dichotomy. See Catherine M. Bell, *Ritual Theory, Ritual Practice* (New York: Oxford University Press, 2009), Chapter 1: "Constructing Ritual,"pp. 19–29.

36 This view is instantiated not only in the religious realm but also in our contemporary legal system, where the same crime can be punished more or less severely depending on the criminal's intent. In a more extreme form, some forms of thinking have been effectively criminalized as well.

37 This impulse continued into the recent scholarly past with the search for "Q," (standing for the German *quelle,* meaning "source"), the hypothetical source text for the four gospels. The quest for Q was motivated by the idea that this source would meet two distinct though clearly interrelated goals—both an authoritative body of teachings and an accurate biography of the historical Jesus. The project seems to have foundered on the determination that there is no biographical source text, while the only teachings that can be determined to be common to all four gospels are a set of epigrammatic sayings that create the image of Jesus as teaching a kind of Stoicist ethics. See Burton L. Mack, *The Lost Gospel: The Book of Q and Christian Origins* (San Francisco: HarperSanFrancisco, 1993).

38 See Ninian Smart's proposals for revisioning the field of comparative religions in this regard, expressed most fully in *Worldviews: Crosscultural Explorations of Human Beliefs* (New York: Scribner, 1983).

39 Manuel A. Vásquez, in *More than Belief: A Materialist Theory of Religion* (Oxford and New York: Oxford University Press, 2011), p. 106, critiques Smart's idea of broadening the focus of religious studies to worldviews:

> Smart's stress on beliefs and symbols and his quest to explore the deep structure of consciousness ends up reinforcing the mind-body, internal-external dualism. Smart assumes a mentalist perspective that gives the symbolic, ideational, and axiological dimensions of religion privileged agency.

40 The significance of such contextual considerations continues to be a matter of discussion. See, for example, Jens Schlieter, "Did the Buddha Emerge from a Brahmanic Environment? The Early Buddhist Evaluation of 'Noble Brahmins' and the 'Ideological System' of Brahmanism," in Volkhard Krech and Marion Steinicke, eds., *Dynamics in the History of Religions between Asia and Europe: Encounters, Notions, and Comparative Perspectives* (Leiden and Boston: Brill, 2012), pp. 137–148.

41 Louis Renou, *Religions of Ancient India* (London: The Athlone Press, 1953), p. 29, cited in Frits Staal, "Theories and Facts on Ritual Simultaneities," in Kevin Schilbrack, ed., *Thinking Through Rituals: Philosophical Perspectives* (London and New York: Routledge, 2004), p. 178. It is worth pointing out here, in connection with the previous discussion regarding the difference between Francophone and Anglophone scholarly attitudes toward ritual, that Louis Renou was French.

42 Another modernizing interpretation is that the Buddha rejected all ritual but this is an overreach. What the Buddha rejected was Vedic sacrificial ritual that involved the death of animals. See Phyllis Granoff, "Other People's Rituals: Ritual Eclecticism in Early Medieval Indian Religions," *Journal of Indian Philosophy* 28/4 (2000): 399.

43 This is the central claim in Stephan Beyer, "Notes on the Vision Quest in Early Mahāyāna," in Lewis Lancaster, ed., *Prajñāpāramitā and Related Systems: Studies*

in Honor of Edward Conze (Berkeley: University of California, Berkeley and Institute of Buddhist Studies, 1977), pp. 329–360.

44 Is this the presumption of the great architectonics of path literature, *lam rim*?

45 Geoffrey Samuel, "The Writing of The Origins of Yoga and Tantra," *International Journal of Hindu Studies* 15/3 (2011): 308.

46 Samuel, "The Writing of The Origins of Yoga and Tantra," p. 308.

47 Note the default to "meditator" to describe the ritual practitioner; in my estimation, the latter descriptor is a better and more accurate term.

48 Samuel, "The Writing of The Origins of Yoga and Tantra," pp. 308–309.

49 My familiarity with the pitfalls of such a presumption follows from the fact that I have employed it myself in the past.

50 Steven Heine, personal communication, July 31, 2012.

51 Samuel, "The Writing of The Origins of Yoga and Tantra," p. 311.

52 This idea applies to all the different aspects frequently subsumed under the category of "religion." Thus, the relation of music or art to religious teachings is semi-autonomous. Music and art, like other components, have their own ways of formulating expressions that are not fully determined by religious doctrines.

53 We may, of course, speculate that within the Buddhist context such situations would eventually be "corrected" (?!)—the utility of doctrines for practice questioned, or the doctrinal foundations for a practice constructed.

54 Roy Rappaport, *Ritual and Religion in the Making of Humanity* (Cambridge: Cambridge University Press, 1999), p. 30.

55 Beyer, *The Cult of Tārā*, p. 3.

56 See, for example, B. Alan Wallace, *Contemplative Neuroscience: Where Buddhism and Neuroscience Converge* (New York: Columbia University Press, 2007).

57 See, for example, Gananath Obesesekere, *The Cult of the Goddess Pattini* (Chicago and London: University of Chicago Press, 1984).

58 Sarah Shaw, *Introduction to Buddhist Meditation* (London and New York: Routledge, 2008); see also Shaw, *Buddhist Meditation: An Anthology of Texts from the Pāli Canon* (London and New York: Routledge, 2006).

59 Rod Bucknell and Chris Kang, *The Meditative Way: Readings in the Theory and Practice of Buddhist Meditation* (London and New York: Routledge, 1997), p. 2.

60 In other words, they fail to consider crosscultural incommensurability. See Xinli Wang, *Incommensurability and Cross-Language Communication* (Aldershot, England, and Burlington, VT: Ashgate, 2007). See also Emily Apter, *Against World Literature: On the Politics of Untranslatability* (London: Verso, 2013).

61 This is not to say that scholars should not produce engaging narratives. A compelling case for the pedagogic value of "personal vignettes about our fieldwork, travels, or the context" of our studies is made by John S. Harding and Hilary Rodrigues in their introduction to John S. Harding, ed., *Studying Buddhism in Practice* (London and New York: Routledge, 2012), pp. 3–4.

62 This is the approach taken by Harding in compiling the essays for his *Studying Buddhism in Practice*.

[63] I am thinking here of the now-outdated notion that the participant-observer is able to enter into a social grouping without changing it. An example for the study of Buddhist practice would be what happens when a Japanese Zen temple begins to host scholar students from the U.S.—suddenly the temple no longer exists solely in the cultural horizon of Japan but also within an international horizon.

[64] Intellectually, such claims are rooted in the highly problematic epistemological distinction between understanding and explanation made by Wilhelm Dilthey, though in fact its roots are in the thought of Giambattista Vico. See Rudolf A. Makkreel, *Dilthey: Philosopher of the Social Sciences* (Princeton, NJ: Princeton University Press, 1992), and Isaiah Berlin, *Three Critics of the Enlightenment: Vico, Hamann, Herder* (Princeton, NJ: Princeton University Press, 2000).

[65] It is arguably the case that the pervasive character of the religion-as-container metaphor in contemporary religious studies is itself rooted in the formative role of Christian theology for religious studies. The majority of theology seems to be strongly exclusive, as exemplified perhaps most clearly by Calvinistic notions of the saved and the damned as mutually exclusive and predetermined categories.

[66] Gudrun Bühnemann, *Pūjā: A Study in Smārta Ritual* (Vienna: Institut für Indologie der Universität Wien, Sammlung De Nobili, 1988), p. 43.

[67] The metaphor of a feast reveals the historical continuity between contemporary Japanese Buddhist practice and Vedic ritual predating the time of Śākyamuni Buddha. This is equally true of contemporary Hindu *pūjā*. See Bühnemann, *Pūjā: A Study in Smārta Ritual*, p. 30, referring to Paul Thieme.

[68] See Nobuyoshi Yamabe, "The Sūtra on the Ocean-like Samādhi of the Visualization of the Buddha: The Interfusion of the Chinese and Indian Cultures in Central Asia as Reflected in a Fifth Century Apocryphal Sūtra," Ph.D. dissertation, Yale University, 1999.

[69] It might seem safe to assume that the process of transmitting practices from teacher to disciple is an inherently conservative one, and further that the very nature of religion is conservative. An example of the latter assumption is that some scholars have claimed that the highly stable character of pre-Vedic Indus Valley civilizations shows that they were a highly religious cultures. This rhetoric of passivity and activity appears in Friedrich Schlegel (1772–1829), who nostalgically equated the stability of medieval Europe and India, and contrasted that stability with the upheavals in Europe from the Renaissance through the Reformation and on to the French Revolution; Roger-Pol Droit, *L'oubli de l'Inde: Une amnésie philosophique* (Paris: Éditions du Seuil, 2004, reprint), p. 139. The underlying assumption here is that religion is conservative, while secular cultures are dynamic, a characterization rooted in the rhetorics of modernity. Not only is this in danger of becoming a circular argument—religion is conservative and resists change, therefore conservatives and those resistant to change are religious, which demonstrates that religion is conservative and resistant to change—but it is also simply prejudicial. What

we see at work here is not an historically informed generalization but an anticlerical prejudice, itself formed in the fires of the Reformation.

70 James L. Ford, *Jōkei and Buddhist Devotion in Early Medieval Japan* (Oxford and New York: Oxford University Press, 2006), pp. 74–75.

71 While performance theory per se is heuristically useful in the study of religious ceremony and ritual, it leaves out a great deal. It is, after all, simply another metaphor that may help to reveal aspects of ritual that would not be visible when examined in the light of different metaphoric understandings.

72 The importance of the aesthetic aspect of ritual was already noted by Xunzi in the third century B.C.E. See Howard J. Wechsler, *Offerings of Jade and Silk: Ritual and Symbol in the Legitimation of the T'ang Dynasty* (New Haven and London: Yale University Press, 1985), pp. 26–27.

73 Rappaport, *Ritual and Religion,* p. 58. Emphasis in original.

74 The putative successes of a medicalized mindfulness does not demonstrate that Buddhist meditation is a value- and context-free mental hygienics, as it has increasingly come to be viewed. Rather, this is simply a case of one set of contextualizing factors replacing another. The notion that technology is value- and context-free is perhaps a core concept for global capitalism, allowing the export not only of telephones or banking systems but of the value system necessary to support their adoption and use.

75 The importance of the experiential dimension lies in appreciating its function and power, not in any presumption that it opens up a universal dimension free from cultural and historical constraints.

76 An important examination of this efficacy outside the framework of religious studies is found in Dorinne S. Kondo, *Crafting Selves: Power, Gender, and Discourses of Identity in a Japanese Workplace* (Chicago: University of Chicago Press, 1990).

77 Paul Copp, "Manuscript Culture as Ritual Culture in Late Medieval Dunhuang: Buddhist Talisman-Seals and their Manuals," *Cahiers d'Extrême-Asie* 20 (2011): 199.

78 Christian Lee Novetzke, "Divining an Author: The Idea of Authorship in an Indian Religious Tradition," *History of Religions* 42/3 (February 2003): 213–242.

79 Walter Liebenthal, *Chao lun: The Treatises of Seng-chao* (Hong Kong: Hong Kong University Press, 1968).

80 As an example of this latter point, for most Buddhists the Pope's description of Buddhism is not authoritative, while for most Catholics it is.

References

Apter, Emily. *Against World Literature: On the Politics of Untranslatability.* London: Verso, 2013.

Bell, Catherine M. *Ritual Theory, Ritual Practice.* New York: Oxford University Press, 2009.

Beyer, Stephan. "Notes on the Vision Quest in Early Mahāyāna," in Lewis Lancaster, ed., *Prajñāpāramitā and Related Systems: Studies in Honor of Edward Conze*, pp. 329–360. Berkeley: University of California, Berkeley and Institute of Buddhist Studies, 1977.

—. *The Cult of Tārā: Magic and Ritual in Tibet.* Berkeley, Los Angeles, and London: University of California Press, 1973.

Blackburn, Anne M. "Looking for the Vinaya: Monastic Discipline in the Practical Canons of the Theravāda," *Journal of the International Association of Buddhist Studies* 22/2 (1999): 281–309.

Bucknell, Rod, and Chris Kang. *The Meditative Way: Readings in the Theory and Practice of Buddhist Meditation.* London and New York: Routledge, 1997.

Bühnemann, Gudrun. *Pūjā: A Study in Smārta Ritual.* Publications of the De Nobili Research Library, vol. XV. Vienna: Institut für Indologie der Universität Wien, Sammlung De Nobili, 1988.

Carmody, Denise Lardner, and John Carmody. *Ways to the Center: An Introduction to World's Religions.* Belmont, CA: Wadsworth Publishing, 1981. Reprint: Denise Lardner Carmody and T. L. Brink. *Ways to the Center: An Introduction to the World's Religions.* Belmont, CA: Wadsworth Publishing, 2013, 7th ed.

Clarke, Desmond M. *Descartes: A Biography.* Cambridge: Cambridge University Press, 2006.

Copp, Paul. "Manuscript Culture as Ritual Culture in Late Medieval Dunhuang: Buddhist Talisman-Seals and their Manuals," *Cahiers d'Extrême-Asie* 20 (2011): 193–226.

Droit, Roger-Pol. *L'oubli de l'Inde: Une amnésie philosophique* (1989). Paris: Éditions du Seuil, 2004, reprint.

Eckel, Malcolm David. "The Ghost at the Table: On the Study of Buddhism and the Study of Religion," *Journal of the American Academy of Religion* 62/4 (1994): 1085–1110.

Ford, James L. *Jōkei and Buddhist Devotion in Early Medieval Japan.* Oxford and New York: Oxford University Press, 2006.

Fronsdal, Gil. *Dawn of the Bodhisattva Path: The Early Perfection of Wisdom.* Berkeley: Institute of Buddhist Studies and BDK America, Inc., 2014.

Gouin, Margaret. "Funeral Practices," *Oxford Bibliographies*, sv Buddhism; www.oxfordbibliographies.com/ (forthcoming).

Granoff, Phyllis. "Other People's Rituals: Ritual Eclecticism in Early Medieval Indian Religions," *Journal of Indian Philosophy* 28/4 (2000): 399–424

Hall, David D., ed. *Lived Religion in America: Toward a History of Practice.* Princeton, NJ: Princeton University Press, 1997.

Harding John S., ed. *Studying Buddhism in Practice.* London and New York: Routledge, 2012.

Hobsbawm, Erich J. *The Age of Empire: 1875–1914.* New York: Pantheon Books, 1987.

Holt, John Clifford. "Ritual Expression in the *Vinayapiṭaka:* A Prolegomenon," *History of Religions* 18/1 (August 1978): 42–53.

Holt, Mack P. *The French Wars of Religion, 1562–1629.* New Approaches to European History, no. 36. Cambridge: Cambridge University Press, 2005, 2nd ed.

Kondo, Dorinne S. *Crafting Selves: Power, Gender, and Discourses of Identity in a Japanese Workplace.* Chicago: University of Chicago Press, 1990.

Liebenthal, Walter. *Chao lun: The Treatises of Seng-chao.* Hong Kong: Hong Kong University Press, 1968.

Manabe, Shunshō. "The Development of Images Depicting the Teaching of the *Avataṃsaka-sūtra,*" in Robert Gimello, Frédéric Girard, and Imre Hamar, eds., *Avataṃsaka Buddhism in East Asia: Huayan, Kegon, Flower Ornament Buddhism Origins and Adaptation of a Visual Culture,* pp. 205–222. Wiesbaden: Harrasowitz Verlag, 2012.

Novetzke, Christian Lee. "Divining an Author: The Idea of Authorship in an Indian Religious Tradition," *History of Religions* 42/3 (February 2003): 213–242.

Obesesekere, Gananath. *The Cult of the Goddess Pattini.* Chicago and London: University of Chicago Press, 1984.

Power, Camilla. "Old Wives' Tales: The Gossip Hypothesis and the Reliability of Cheap Signals," in James R. Hurford, Michael Studdert-Kennedy, and Chris Knight, eds., *Approaches to the Evolution of Language: Social and Cognitive Bases,* pp. 111–129. Cambridge: Cambridge University Press, 1998.

Rappaport, Roy. *Ritual and Religion in the Making of Humanity.* Cambridge Studies in Social and Cultural Anthropology, no. 110. Cambridge: Cambridge University Press, 1999.

Ricoeur, Paul. *Freud and Philosophy: An Essay on Interpretation.* Denis Savage, trans. Ithaca, NY: Yale University Press, 1970.

Samuel, Geoffrey. "The Writing of The Origins of Yoga and Tantra," *International Journal of Hindu Studies* 15/3 (2011): 305–312.

Schlieter, Jens. "Did the Buddha Emerge from a Brahmanic Environment? The Early Buddhist Evaluation of 'Noble Brahmins' and the 'Ideological System' of Brahmanism," in Volkhard Krech and Marion Steinicke, eds., *Dynamics in the History of Religions between Asia and Europe: Encounters, Notions, and Comparative Perspectives,* pp. 137–148. Leiden and Boston: Brill, 2012.

Sharpe, Eric. *Comparative Religion.* London: Gerald Duckworth, 1975.

Shaw, Sarah. *Buddhist Meditation: An Anthology of Texts from the Pāli Canon.* London and New York: Routledge, 2006.

—. *Introduction to Buddhist Meditation.* London and New York: Routledge, 2008.

Smart, Ninian. *Worldviews: Crosscultural Explorations of Human Beliefs.* New York: Scribner, 1983.

Staal, Frits. "Theories and Facts on Ritual Simultaneities," in Kevin Schilbrack, ed., *Thinking Through Rituals: Philosophical Perspectives,* pp. 177–193. London and New York: Routledge, 2004.

Stroumsa, Guy G. *The End of Sacrifice: Religious Transformations in Late Antiquity.* Susan Emanuel, trans. Chicago and London: University of Chicago Press, 2009.

Takemura, Makio. "Kūkai's Esotericism and *Avataṃsaka* Thought," in Robert Gimello, Frédéric Girard, and Imre Hamar, eds., *Avataṃsaka Buddhism in East Asia: Huayan, Kegon, Flower Ornament Buddhism Origins and Adaptation of a Visual Culture,* pp. 339–376. Wiesbaden: Harrasowitz Verlag, 2012.

Vásquez, Manuel A. *More than Belief: A Materialist Theory of Religion.* Oxford and New York: Oxford University Press, 2011.

Wallace, B. Alan. *Contemplative Neuroscience: Where Buddhism and Neuroscience Converge.* New York: Columbia University Press, 2007.

Wang, Xinli. *Incommensurability and Cross-Language Communication.* Aldershot, England, and Burlington, VT: Ashgate, 2007.

Wechsler, Howard J. *Offerings of Jade and Silk: Ritual and Symbol in the Legitimation of the T'ang Dynasty.* New Haven, CT and London: Yale University Press, 1985.

Assessing Shinran's *Shinjin* from an Indian Mahāyāna Buddhist Perspective: With a Focus on *Adhimukti* in Tathāgatagarbha Thought

Kenneth K. Tanaka
Musashino University

Preface

Shinran (1173–1263), the founder of Jōdo Shinshū Buddhism, is well known for his doctrine of *shinjin* (信心; faith, true entrusting, faith-mind, etc.) rooted in the absolute other-power of Amida Buddha. *Shinjin* plays a central role within his doctrinal framework, so it is crucial that it be correctly understood. This task is not as simple as it may seem, however, because *shinjin* is multivalent in meaning. Shinran defined it as truth, reality, sincerity, fullness, ultimacy, accomplishment, reliance, reverence, discernment, distinctness, clarity, and faithfulness. Contemporary scholars have taken a particular dimension of the meaning and rendered it into English in such terms as "faith," "faith-mind," "true entrusting," and "awareness," but no single term can do true justice in capturing the whole range of the meaning of *shinjin.*

Arriving at an accurate understanding has been further complicated in the West as many writers have sought to understand the meaning of *shinjin* from a comparative perspective, referencing the teachings of prominent Western theologians and philosophers. For example, *shinjin* has been compared to the doctrines of "faith only" (*sola fidé*) of Martin Luther or to the "leap of faith" of Søren Kierkegaard, among others. "Faith" has thus become the primary lens for a Western understanding of *shinjin.*

Further, Shinran's paradoxical rejection of *shinjin* as an efficient path to spiritual awakening or enlightenment has reinforced the perception of it as representing a very different mode of seeking than the rigorous spiritual practices demanded in many other Buddhist traditions. Consequently, *shinjin* is often perceived as being "merely" devotional in nature, rooted in a dualistic and polarized relationship involving, on the one hand, Amida Buddha, a buddha of infinite capacity, and on the other hand a seeker (a term I will use for a human being who seeks enlightenment) who has no capacity whatsoever to perform effective practice. This merely devotional *shinjin* is seen as devoid of any element of wisdom (*prajñā*), which is required for realizing ultimate enlightenment. *Shinjin* is not seen as being in the same league as wisdom.

This Western misconception has led some to regard Shin Buddhism as not authentic Buddhism, or, in its extreme, goes so far as to regard Shin teachings as an aberration of Buddhism. For example, in 1936 Albert Schweitzer commented, "Of course the doctrine of Shinran is an outrage on Buddhism."[1] More recently, the scholar of Buddhism Heinz Bechert remarked, "It takes the ideas of the Buddha and, in a way, twists them into their opposite. The most radical spokesman for this approach is Shinran Shonin. . . ."[2]

Given the existence, albeit extreme, of this kind of assessment, particularly within the contemporary Western context, I have embarked on a project to reevaluate and clarify the nature of *shinjin* from a broader Buddhist perspective. There have been numerous studies of *shinjin* within the traditional Shin sectarian studies (*shūgaku*, 宗学) framework, but given its narrow approach and limited reach beyond Shin studies, this scholarship has done little to refute such criticism as exemplified by the above quotes. In contrast, the works of Takamaro Shigaraki and Kōtatsu Fujita have overcome the shortcomings of sectarian studies and have introduced a deeper and more accurate understanding of *shinjin* to a wider readership.[3] Building on the valuable findings of their research, I hope to focus on some of the areas not addressed in their studies.

As the first step in my overall project, in this paper I examine a particular text from an Indian Tathāgatagarbha tradition, the *Ratnagotravibhāga* (*Baoxinglun* 宝性論, hereafter RGV) to examine its understanding of terms that can be rendered as "faith," particularly *adhimukti* (信, 信解, 勝解; *mos-pa*).[4] I am not aware of any substantial study relating the topic of *shinjin* in Shinran's thought to the topic of faith in Tathāgatagarbha thought.[5] It is my hope that the findings from this examination will help cast a new light on our understanding of *shinjin*.

Tathāgatagarbha Thought and Pure Land Buddhism

In order to begin to address the above-stated objective, I will focus on earlier Mahāyāna thought, referred to as Tathāgatagarbha ("buddha womb" or "embryo," or in a broader sense, "buddha-nature"). Tathāgatagarbha thought refers to a constellation of ideas found in a group of Mahāyāna sūtras and treatises that date back to as early as the second century C.E. This includes such sūtras as the *Tathāgatagarbha-sūtra,* the *Lankāvatāra-sūtra,* the *Avataṃsaka-sūtra,* the *Nirvāṇa-sūtra,* and the *Srimāladevī-sūtra,* as well as treatises such as the *Ratnagotravibhāga* and the *Awakening of Faith.*[6]

One reason for taking up Tathāgatagarbha thought in relation to Shinran's *shinjin* is that there are quite a number of references to Amitābha within Tathāgatagarbha literature, a fact that probably would be surprising to many contemporary readers. For example, in the *Ratnagotravibhāga,* a concluding verse on the merits accrued from authoring the treatise reads (chapter 5, verse 25, italics added here and in following quotes from RGV):

> By the merit I have acquired through this,
> May all living beings come to perceive
> *The Lord Amitāyus* endowed with infinite light,
> And, having seen him, may they, owing to the arising,
> Of the immaculate vision of the Doctrine in them,
> Obtain the Supreme Enlightenment.[7]

A similar thought is found in the concluding passage of the *Awakening of Faith* (*Dachengqixinlun* 大乘起信論), in which seekers are encouraged to contemplate Amituo (阿弥陀, Amitāyus/Amitābha) Buddha and transfer the merit they have accrued toward birth in the Western Pure Land.

Further, a number of eminent Japanese scholars, including Ui Hakuju, Takemura Shihō, Hirakawa Akira, and Takasaki Jikidō, have pointed out the parallels between Tathāgatagarbha and Pure Land thought. For example, Ui points out that both the *Avataṃsaka-sūtra* and the *Mahāyana-sūtra-ālaṃkara* (in Paramārtha's translation) conclude with a passage that states that to witness Amitābha becomes the basis for one's full enlightenment. Ui concludes, "It is customary for Tathāgatagarbha-related [texts] to show a close relationship with the [teachings of] birth in the Pure Land through *nembutsu* (念仏)."[8] Hirakawa goes even further, suggesting a possible historical connection:

> In summarizing the above, it is possible to regard the *Sutra of the Buddha of Immeasurable* [*Light and Life*] as having been compiled as a result of the Tathāgatagarbha thought being synthesized with the concepts of "transcendent realms" and "realms of extreme bliss."[9]

Although there has been no evidence to substantiate Hirakawa's suggestion, there is sufficient evidence for a doctrinal affinity between Amitābha Pure Land teachings and Tathāgatagarbha thought.

The second and more substantive reason for taking up Tathāgatagarbha thought in relation to Shinran's *shinjin* lies in the extremely important role that faith plays in the overall doctrinal framework of Tathāgatagarbha thought. This point has been made by other researchers, notably Jikidō Takasaki and Kōshō Mizutani, whose works on faith in the *Ratnagotravibhāga* provided the doctrinal insights necessary for my pursuit of research on the theme of this paper.[10]

The Text: *Ratnagotravibhāga*

The full title of this text is *Ratnagotravibhāga-mahāyānottaratantra-śāstra,* and it is the most systematic treatise extant on Indian Tathāgatagarbha thought. This work is available in Chinese and Tibetan translations as well, and it has played a particularly important role in Tibetan Buddhism.[11] No author is identified in the Sanskrit text, but the Chinese text attributes the authorship to Sāramati (Shaluomodi 沙羅末底, Jianhui 堅慧). As for the Tibetan text, Maitreya is said to have composed the verses and Asaṅga is said to have composed the prose section. It is thought that the Sanskrit text was compiled sometime between the late fifth and early sixth centuries, since it was translated into Chinese in 511.[12]

The *Ratnagotravibhāga* is comprised of five chapters: (1) *Tathāgatagarbha,* (2) Englightenment (*bodhi*), (3) Properties (*guṇa*) of the Buddha, (4) Acts (*kṛtyā*), and (5) Merits of Faith (*adhimuktyanuśaṃsa*). The text sets out to examine the seven adamantine subjects: the Three Jewels of Buddha, Dharma, and Sangha, plus *tathāgatagarbha,* enlightenment, properties, and acts. The last four subjects correspond to the topics of the first four chapters of the text, respectively. The fifth and final chapter is devoted to the importance of faith (*adhimukti*) and, as noted earlier, ends by encouraging the reader/practitioner to take refuge in Amitāyus Buddha.

I find it extremely interesting that in the opening section of the *Ratnagotravibhāga* the author consciously sets out to rectify what he sees as the shortcomings associated with the doctrine of emptiness as taught in the Prajñapāramitā sūtras. He describes these shortcomings as having a depressed mind (*līnam cittam*) and contempt for those who are judged as inferior; clinging to unreal things; speaking ill of truth; and having affection for oneself. It then concludes, "[The teaching about *tathāgatagarbha*] has been taught in order that those who are possessed of these defects might get rid of them."

The Importance of Faith in the *Ratnagotravibhāga*

I would like to begin discussing the role of faith in this treatise by introducing passages that extol the virtues of faith, which, at times, is said to surpass even devotional, ethical, and meditative practices. The second verse in Chapter Five, entitled "The Merits of Faith" (*adhimukty-anuśaṃsa*), sets the tone of the entire chapter by praising the advantages of faith:

> Buddha's realm, Buddha's enlightenment, Buddha's dharmas, and Buddha's action are inconceivable even to those of the purified mind (*śuddhasattva*), being the exclusive sphere of the Leaders (i.e., Buddhas).
> (chapter 5, verse 1)
>
> But the wise one, whose intellect
> *Accepts faith* (*adhimuktabuddhi*)
> In this exclusive sphere of the Buddha,
> Becomes a receptacle of the whole collection of properties,
> And being possessed [of] the desire [to obtain]
> The inconceivable properties of the [Buddha],
> He surpasses the abundance of merits of all living beings.
> (chapter 5, verse 2)

In this verse a person with faith is praised even more highly than those who possess a "purified mind." While there is no direct explanation of who are those "of purified mind" (*śuddhasattva*), it is safe to regard them as practitioners who are at higher levels on the Buddhist path (*mārga*), including bodhisattvas. A person of faith is thus valued as much as, if not more, than some bodhisattvas (who may lack proper faith), for the person of faith may obtain numerous positive qualities, including the motivated desire to realize the inconceivable properties of the Buddha.

The text goes on to compare the merits of faith (*adhimukti*) with those who engage in making offerings, keeping ethical purity, and attaining mystic absorption, respectively.

> Suppose there is one who, being anxious to obtain enlightenment,
> Would offer golden lands, constructed by jewels
> As innumerable as the sand in the Buddha's lands,
> To the Lord of Doctrine, always, day after day;
> Another if he hears but one word of this teaching,
> After hearing of it, *would have faith in this Doctrine* (*śrutvādhimucyet*);
> The latter would reap merits far more than the merits of offerings.
> (chapter 5, verse 3)

Suppose a wise man, being desirous of the highest enlightenment,
Would maintain pure moral conduct of his body, speech, and mind,
Without effort, in the course of innumerable eons;
Another, if he hears but one word of this teaching,
After hearing of it, *would have faith in this Doctrine* (*śrutvādhimucyet*);
The latter would reap merits far more than the merits of morality.
(chapter 5, verse 4)

Suppose one would give himself up to mystic absorption,
Which suppresses the fire of defilements in the three worlds,
And, having been transferred to the abode of Brahman in heaven,
Would be irreversible from the means of enlightenment;
Another, if he hears but one word of this teaching,
After hearing of it, *would have faith in this Doctrine* (*śrutvādhimucyet*);
The latter would reap merits far more than even the merits of mystic absorption.
(chapter 5, verse 5)

As these three verses argue, the merit of a person who has faith in the doctrine of *tathāgatagarbha* surpasses even that of those who make generous offerings, uphold strict precepts, or engage in strenuous meditative *samādhi* practices.

Further, faith is one of the four causes of purification along with wisdom (*prajñā*), meditation (*dhyāna*), and compassion (*karuṇā*). Faith is referred to as "the practice of faith in the teachings of Mahāyāna" (*mahāyānadharmādhimukti-bhāvanā*) and is regarded as an antidote to the enmity some people harbor toward Mahāyāna teachings (*mahāyānadharma-pratigha*). It works by rectifying people's aversion to the Mahāyāna teachings (i.e., *tathāgatagarbha*), a quality found in its extreme form among the *icchantikas*.

The other three practices of the four causes of purification—wisdom, meditation, and compassion—are also seen as antidotes to the following three obstructions, respectively: conception of the self, fear of suffering, and aversion or indifference to the benefits to sentient beings. And each of the four causes of purification, are identified respectively with the analogies of seed (faith), mother (wisdom), womb (meditation), and nursing mother (compassion).

Those whose seed is the faith in the Mahāyāna teachings,
Whose mother is the transcendental wisdom,
On account of the origination of Buddha's teachings:
Whose abiding womb is the blissful meditation

And whose nursing mother is called compassion;
They are the sons, the after-comers of the Buddhas.
(chapter 1, verse 34, p. 207)

The importance of faith is further expressed in a passage in which the truth of the teachings of *tathāgatagarbha* is upheld as true whether or not the Tathāgata appears in the world:

This essence itself is not accessible to imagination or to discrimination. It is accessible only to faith (*adhimoktavya*).
(chapter 1, p. 296)

The text then goes on to claim:

The highest truth of the buddhas
Can be understood only by faith
Indeed, the eyeless one cannot see
The blazing disk of the sun.
(chapter 1, verse 153, p. 296)

The "eyeless one" includes ordinary beings, *śrāvaka*s, *pratyekabuddha*s, and bodhisattvas who have recently entered the bodhisattva path (or gotten on the bodhisattva vehicle). Even some bodhisattvas are unable to understand the teachings of *tathāgatagarbha;* thus, the text explains that for all four categories of people who are deemed blind or "eyeless," faith is their only path to realizing the truth. This is consistent with RGV's position that "even bodhisattvas of the tenth *bhūmi* cannot fully see *tathāgatagarbha*" (*daśabhumisthitā bodhisattvas tathāgatagarbham īṣat paśyantīty uktam*).

Three Terms of Faith

We have so far looked at and confirmed the importance of faith in RGV. There are, however, three Sanskrit terms in this work that carry the meaning of the English word "faith," which are commonly rendered into Chinese as *xing* (信) or its derivatives (e.g., 信心, 净心, 信行, 信解, 勝解): *śraddhā, adhimukti,* and *prasāda.* Since *prasāda,* with only two occurrences, does not figure prominently in the thesis of this paper, it will not be dealt with here.

The terms *śraddhā* and *adhimukti* reveal clearly differing qualities. Each occurrence of these terms will be examined in the context of (1) its Chinese rendering, (2) its object, (3) the type of seeker or person exhibiting faith, (4) practices that accompany faith, and (5) the level or kind of attainment that result from faith and attendant practices.

Table 1. *Śraddhā* Faith

Term (Skt., Ch.)	Object	Seeker	Attendant practices	Attainment
1. *śraddhā*, 信	Tathāgata	ordinary beings *śrāvakas*, *pratyeka-buddhas*		*tathāgatagarbha*, *dharmakāya*, etc.
2. *śraddhā*, 信	Tathāgata	ordinary beings, *śrāvakas*, *pratyeka-buddhas*		*tathāgatagarbha*, *dharmakāya*, etc.
3. *śraddhā*, 信	Tathāgata	*śrāvakas*, *pratyeka-buddhas*		*tathāgatagarbha*, etc.
4. *śrāddhā*, 信 (adj.)	Buddhist teachings (Three Jewels)	non-traditional Buddhists and Pudgalavādins		
5. *śraddhā*, 信	自在者	ordinary beings, *śrāvakas*, *pratyeka-buddhas*, new bodhisattvas		affirmation 順知 of *tathāgatagarbha*
6. *śraddhā*, 信	(Buddha)	sentient beings	limit desire, raise vow, precepts, charity, etc.	see the 32 and 80 marks and realize a *bodhi* level with some desires left
7. *śraddhā*, 信	(Buddha)	sentient beings	(same as above)	(same as above)
8. *śraddhā*, 信	words of the Buddha 仏語	one with wisdom		confirmation of the Four Noble Truths
9. *śraddhen-drya*, 信根	all sentient beings			heightened purity of mind
10. *śraddhā-dhiṃukitas*, 信	the teaching that the realm of Tathāgatas exists, can be attained, and has virtues	a person with wisdom	*adhimukti*	become Buddha's child with *bodhi-citta* and in a state of nonretro-gression

Based on the above ten occurrences, we can make the following observations about *śraddhā:*

1. The objects of *śraddhā* are all either a person, invariably the Tathāgāta or the Buddha, or his teachings. One thus directs *śraddhā* not to the teaching itself but to the person who delivers the teachings on the strength of one's trust in that person.

2. In these occurrences the seekers include a wide range of beings, from "all sentient beings" to "one with wisdom." However, we can make the case that the seekers are mostly those who are not advanced or even those who are not considered exemplary Mahāyāna Buddhists, such as *śrāvakas*, *pratyekabuddhas*, "ordinary beings," "non-traditional Buddhists" and Pudgalavādins. The tenth type, *śraddhādhimukitas*, is somewhat of an exception and it will be dealt with later in this essay.

3. In most examples, the act of *śraddhā* is not attended by any other practices, and when it is attended by other practices those practices are ethical in nature, as in numbers 6 and 7. In number 9, it appears that *śraddhā* leads the seeker to cultivate wisdom—if not immediately, then further along the path. Number 10, as noted above, is anomalous.

4. As for the attainments connected to *śraddhā,* the seekers attain most of the traditional Buddhist goals; the most prominent, as would be expected, is *tathāgatagarbha.* However, it should be emphasized that *śraddhā* by itself does not directly lead to these attainments.

Based on the above observations, it is safe to say that *śraddhā* does not entail any qualities of insight or wisdom. It is faith in the teacher as a person, and its object is the Buddha.

Table 2. *Adhimukti* Faith

Term (Skt./Ch.)	Object	Seeker	Attendant practices	Attainment
1. *adhimucya*	*dharmas* are illusion	bodhisattva		(1) not be lethargic toward the Dharma, (2) possess insight, (3) awaken to the true nature of *dharmas*
2. *adhimoktavya,* 信	Dharma-nature			(observation of mind; purification of mind)
3. *adhimoktum,* 信	undefiled realm	young ordinary beings		

4. *adhimucyet*, 信	如来蔵, 性, 菩提, 諸功徳, 業	others (bodhisattva)	聞	attain benefits 布施 superior to those of 戒 or 禅定
5. *adhimucyet*, 信	如来蔵, 性, 菩提, 諸功徳, 業	others (bodhisattva)	聞	attain benefits superior to those of 布施, 戒, or 禅定
6. *adhimucyet*, 信	如来蔵, 性, 菩提, 諸功徳, 業	others (bodhisattva)	聞	attain benefits superior to those of 布施, 戒, or 禅定
7. *trayādhimuktāṃs*, 信	三供養	信解者		
8. *karādhimuktān*, 信	offerings to Buddha	信解者 (equal to bodhisattva)		
9. *karādhimuktān*, 信	offerings to Dharma	信解者 (equal to *pratyekabuddhas*)		
10. *karādhimuktān*, 信	offerings to Sangha	信解者 (equal to *śrāvakas*)		
11. *adhimuktānām*, 信	因縁法	*pratyekabuddhas*		
12. *anadhimukta*, 不信	第一義諦	non-Buddhists within 仏法		
13. *anadhimukto*, 不信	空性	non-Buddhists within 仏法		
14. *adhimuktānām*, 信心	四処 (如来性)	(菩薩)		benefits of 信解
15. *adhimukta*, 信	四処 (如来性)	有智慧者 (菩薩)		(1) receiver of benefits; (2) superior to benefits from other acts
16. *dharmadhimukti*, 信	大乗法	bodhisattva	般若, 三昧, 大悲	(*tathāgatagarbha*)
17. *adhimuktyādaya*, 信	大乗法	bodhisattva	般若, 三昧, 大悲	overcomes *icchantikas*' faults and four

				kinds of barriers, and realize *tathāgatagarbha*
18. *adhimuktibhāvanā,* 信	大乗法	bodhisattva	般若, etc.	overcomes *icchantikas*' faults
19. *adhimuktyādīn,* 信	大乗法	bodhisattva	般若, etc.	realize *dharmakāya,* be Dharma prince in Buddha's home
20. *agrayānādhimuktiyādīn,* 信	最乗法	(bodhisattva)	般若, etc.	be Buddha's child
21. *adhimuktyādayaś,* 信	大乗法	bodhisattva	般若, etc.	benefits of *parāmitā*'s purity, selfhood, bliss, permanency
22. *adhimuktibhāvanāyāh,* 信	大乗法	bodhisattva	般若, etc.	pure *parāmitā*
23. *adhimukti,* 信	大乗法	bodhisattva	般若, etc.	pure *parāmitā,* utmost Dharma realm
24. *adhimuktibhāvanāyāh,* 信	大乗最上法	bodhisattva	般若, etc.	utmost purity, utmost Dharma realm
25. *adhimukti,* 信心	one of three vehicles	*icchantika*	see buddha-nature	見
26. *adhimuktibhāvanā,* 信	大乗法	bodhisattva	realize 仏性	purity of *dharmakāya*
27. *adhimuktibhāvanāyā,* 信	大乗法	bodhisattva	realize 仏性	(purity of *dharmakāya*)
28. *adhimuktau,* 信				
29. *adhimuktau,* 信		衆生		
30. *visayādhimukti,* 信	仏の境界	those who doubt and misunderstand Buddha's unconditional conduct 自在		elimination of misunderstanding and doubt

31. *adhimuk-titas,* 信	実有性・	具智者 可能性・(bodhisattva) 有功徳性		qualification to eventually attain buddhahood, i.e., *bodhicitta,* and nonretrogression
32. *dhiyādhi-muktyā,* 信受		bodhisattva	善業	
33. *adhimukti,* 信	白法（大乗）	(who slander the Dharma)		
34. *śraddhā-dhimuktitaḥ,* 勝智	勝者の不可思議界	有智者 (bodhisattva)	信	become Buddha's child endowed with *bodhicitta* and nonretrogression

From these thirty-four occurrences, we are able to make the following observations about *adhimukti:*

1. The objects of *adhimukti* are not Buddha himself, as in the case of *śraddhā,* but the teachings themselves. The most numerous occurrences are "Mahāyāna teachings," which include *tathāgatagarbha,* emptiness, and various other terms pointing to the realm of enlightenment.

2. The seekers in virtually all occurrences are bodhisattvas. Thus, they are further advanced on the path compared to those seekers in the case of *śraddhā.*

3. In most occurrences, *adhimukti* is attended by other practices at a much higher rate than with *śraddhā.* The most frequently cited attendant practices are the cultivation of wisdom, *samādhi,* and great compassion. In these examples, *adhimukti* is in a category of practices that require more rigorous effort and realization.

4. As for the attainments connected to *adhimukti,* the seekers in most of the examples attain realms associated with enlightenment, expressed by such terms as *pāramitā, dharmakāya,* and *tathāgatagarbha.* Noteworthy are numbers 31 and 34, in which *adhimukti* on its own, without any attendant practices, leads to attainment that includes generating *bodhicitta* and the state of nonretrogression.

The generation of *bodhicitta* is of special interest, as it reinforces one of the other features associated with *adhimukti*—that the seekers often exhibit a desire to aspire with greater zeal. This can be further seen in other occurrences where *adhimukti* is part of an integral set of practices serving as a starting point or a seed for deepening one's cultivation of wisdom, *samādhi,* and great compassion.

The differences between the two kinds of faith have already become more apparent. While *śraddhā* exhibits traits that are devotional in nature, *adhimukti* requires from the seeker a higher level of insight and an enhanced motivation to aspire to enlightenment.

Analysis of *Adhimukti*

Based on the basic characteristics of *śraddhā* as faith and *adhimukti* as faith, derived from the analysis of their occurrences within the text, I now wish to examine a passage in which both types of faith are found (item number 10 in *śraddhā* and number 34 in *adhimukti*). The passage reads:

> The person of insight (*youzhizhe* 有智者) *has become full of faith* (*adhimukti*)
> With regard to its existence (*aṣṭitva*), potentiality (*śaktatva*), and virtue (*guṇavattva*).
> Therefore, he immediately attains the potentiality
> To acquire the state of Tathāgata.
>
> (chapter 5, verse 8)
>
> Indeed, as he is *full of devotion and faith* (*śraddhādhimuktitaḥ*)
> That there "exists" this inconceivable sphere,
> That it "can" be realized even by someone like him, and
> That this he would be "endowed with such virtues"
> Once it is attained.
>
> (chapter 5, verse 9, pp. 382–383)

In verse 9, the object of the compound of *śraddhā* and *adhimukti* is that "it" exists, has potentiality, and has virtues. "It" here refers to the "realm of the buddhas."[13] In verse 8, the person of insight is said to exhibit *adhimukti* with regard to the three qualities of the realm of the buddhas, i.e., its existence (*aṣṭitva*), potentiality (*śaktatva*), and virtues (*guṇavattva*).

Previous studies by Takasaki and Mizutani have shown that this particular passage is based on a very similar passage found in earlier texts, particularly in Yogācāra texts, such as the *Vijñaptimātratā-triṃśika-bhāṣya*[14] and the *Cheng wei shi lun* 成唯識論.[15] Of great interest to us is that RGV has undergone a change from the Yogācāra passages: it reordered the latter two of the three qualities of existence, virtues, and potentiality to read existence, potentiality, and virtues.

Both Takasaki and Mizutani have interpreted this switch as evidence of RGV's greater emphasis on the seeker's potentiality to realize the realm of the buddhas. Mizutani, in particular, feels that the Yogācāra passage is ambiguous as to whether the potentiality resided in the object (i.e., the realm of the buddhas) or in the subject (the seeker) who displays *adhimukti.* However, this RGV passage makes clear that the potentiality lies with the seeker (the subject) rather than with the realm of the buddhas (the object). The seeker thus comes to experience an enhanced sense that he or she is capable of realizing the realm of the buddhas, for he knows that it exists within himself and that he will be endowed with its virtues once it is realized. This highlighting of the seeker's potentiality is consistent with the overall emphasis of Tathāgatagarbha thought on the enhanced potentiality of seekers to realize full enlightenment based on the view that all beings essentially possess the same quality as the buddhas.

Takasaki provides an explanation for what he regards as one of the reasons for this enhanced potentiality. It is found in the buddhas' actions (*ye* 業) to benefit others out of their compassion for sentient beings. These actions have the power to instill in the seeker a greater sense that he or she has the potential to realize buddhahood. The key to this line of thinking is the view that the buddhas actually possess the power or capacity to have an impact on the seeker by instilling in them an enhanced sense of potentiality to realize full enlightenment.

This shift in understanding is also made possible in the RGV, in its view that buddhas and seekers are in essence the same. The apparent difference between the two lies in the simple fact that buddhas are those who have realized the qualities of wisdom and compassion, while seekers are those who have not yet realized their qualities of wisdom and compassion. The two groups are essentially the same, the only distinction being that the buddhas have attained the results while the seekers have simply not yet attained them. This view that the two groups are essentially not two but one can be seen in the following RGV passage:

> The multitudes of living [beings] are included
> In the Buddha's wisdom.
> Their immaculateness is nondual by nature,
> Its result manifests itself on the Nature of the Buddha;
> Therefore, it is said: all living beings
> Are possessed of the embryo of the Buddha.
>
> (chapter 1, verse 27, p. 197)

In regard to the first sentence, "the multitudes of living [beings] are included in the Buddha's wisdom," the commentary clarifies: "Its meaning is that the *dharmakāya* of the Buddha penetrates everywhere" (*tathāgatadharmakāya-parispharaṇārtha*). This idea is said to be based on the well-known metaphor of "the one dust includes the entire three thousand–great thousand worlds" found in the chapter on the "Arising of the Tathāgata" in the *Avataṃsaka-sūtra* (*Huayanjing xingqipin* 華厳経性起品).

I wish now to unpack the meaning of the use of the two kinds of faith (*śraddhādhimukti*) in the passage under examination. Takasaki translates this compound as "devotion and faith," and adds that they have essentially the same meaning. However, based on our examination of the nature of these two types of faith (*śraddhā, adhimukti*), we arrive at a different and a more nuanced understanding.

Given what we learned above about the nature of *śraddhā,* it would more likely be the case that the seeker exhibits a sense of trust or reliance on the Buddha as a person, but that there would not yet be a personal understanding of the teachings. The examples above show that in the act of *śraddhā* the seeker cannot vouch for the veracity of the teachings based on his own understanding but finds the teacher and his message to be trustworthy. In contrast, *adhimukti* entails a higher level of understanding about the doctrine that is being taught, and is usually manifested by someone with a higher level of insight.

The passage above, then, would better interpret the two terms as describing two different modes of action on the part of the seeker. In the act of *śraddhā* the seeker trusts that the words of the teacher are true, or, at the very least, worth investigating. At a later stage of the process, what we can call *adhimukti* kicks in. After one has taken the first step in *śraddhā,* he gradually matures in his understanding of the teachings and comes to be impacted by the workings of Buddha's action (*kṛtyā*) in some form of spiritual encounter, as expressed in the passage cited above, ". . . the *dharmakāya* of the Buddha penetrates everywhere." Human beings may experience a sense of being penetrated by the *dharmakāya* of the Buddha in the process of their spiritual development, and this experience confirms for the seeker that the teaching is indeed true. We can therefore see in *adhimukti* the following qualities of the seeker: (1) deepening insight, (2) encountering the Buddha's workings, and (3) confirmation of the truth of the teachings.

The compound *śraddhādhimukti* is thus better rendered as "entrusting and realization." The term *adhimukti* involves personal insight and spiritual realization. *Adhimukti* confirms to a greater degree the veracity of the teaching to which the seeker had earlier entrusted himself, in his act of *śraddhā.* Moreover, this realization is made possible by the workings of the Buddha's action, which empowers the seeker to generate an enhanced level of aspiration to realize full enlightenment. This is the potentiality emphasized in the RGV, in keeping with the overall thrust of Tathāgatagarbha thought. Finally, that *adhimukti* entails a higher level of personal insight or realization is supported by the fact that the passage describes the seeker as "the person of insight" (*youzhizhe* 有智者).

Conclusion: Implications for *Shinjin* in Shinran's Thought

I would like to close with some brief remarks about the implications of these findings on our understanding of Shinran's view of *shinjin*. For Shinran, it is clear that *shinjin* entails elements of wisdom. He talks about the "wisdom of *shinjin*" (*shinjin no chie* 信心の智慧) in his *Hymns of the Dharma Ages:*

> Through the compassion of Śākyamuni and Amida,
> We have been brought to realize the mind that seeks to attain buddhahood.
> It is by entering the *wisdom of shinjin*
> That we become persons who respond in gratitude to the Buddha's benevolence.[16]

Shinran explains the phrase "wisdom of *shinjin*" by noting next to the verse, "Know that since Amida's Vow is wisdom, the emergence of the mind of entrusting oneself (i.e., *shinjin*) to it is the arising of wisdom." Other similar terms such as "*shinjin* of supreme wisdom" (*mujōchie no shinjin* 無上智慧の信心) and "*shinjin* of wisdom" (*chie no shinjin* 智慧の信心) are also found numerous times throughout his writings. It should be mentioned at this point that this wisdom is not the product of the seeker's cultivation through self-power but is the outcome of the workings of Amida's Vow, which is none other than the expression of Amida's wisdom. Nevertheless, I maintain that the seeker realizes in *shinjin,* if not wisdom, some level of personal insight into one's own nature (as an ordinary, foolish being) as well as of the nature of Amida, even if the source of this insight derives ultimately from Amida's Vow.

Further evidence of the wisdom element in Shinran's understanding of *shinjin* is seen in the level of attainment by "persons of *shinjin*." Shinran states that *shinjin* invariably leads the seeker to the stage of joy, which he sees as being equal to the first fruit in the path of the sages:

> Thus, when one attains the true and real practice and *shinjin,* one greatly rejoices in one's heart. This attainment is therefore called the *stage of joy.* It is likened to the first fruit: the sages of the first fruit, . . . [17]

Not only does the person of *shinjin* attain the stage of joy, this stage is equal to the first level of the sages, which entails some level of wisdom. Another value of attaining this realization is that the seeker no longer retrogresses or, stated differently, is assured of realizing buddhahood. In explaining this level, Shinran quotes the words of Nāgārjuna ("immediately enter the stage of the group of the truly settled") and Danluan ("enter the group of the truly settled").

Thus, we see that Shinran's *shinjin* includes both wisdom and being empowered by Buddha's working, the same elements found in *adhimukti* in the RGV. While Shinran may not have explicitly stated his indebtedness to Indian Tathāgatagarbha thought for his doctrinal formulation, I believe that studying the concept of *adhimukti* in a key Mahāyāna text provides the basis for a more complete understanding of Shinran's *shinjin*. We can then go on to clarify the meaning of *shinjin* within the context of contemporary Buddhist studies and interreligious dialogue.

In closing, I end with a passage quoted by Shinran from the *Nirvāṇa-sūtra* in his *Kyōgyōshinshō:*

> Buddha-nature is great *shinjin*. Why? Because through *shinjin* the *bodhisattva-mahāsattva* has acquired all the *pāramitā*s from charity to wisdom. All sentient beings will without fail ultimately realize great *shinjin*. Therefore it is taught, "All sentient beings are possessed of Buddha-nature." Great *shinjin* is none other than Buddha-nature. Buddha-nature is Tathāgata.[18]

Notes

1 Albert Schweitzer, *Indian Thought and Its Development* (Boston: The Beacon Press, 1957, reprint), p. 154.

2 Hans Küng, et al., *Christianity and the World Religions* (Maryknoll, NY: Orbis Books, 1986), p. 373.

3 Takamaro Shigaraki, *Jōdokyō ni okeru shin no kenkyū* (Tokyo: Nagata bunshodo, 1975); Kōtatsu Fujita, *Genshi jōdo shisō kenkyū* (Tokyo: Iwanami shoten, 1970). These works have not been translated into a Western language, limiting their wider circulation among scholars beyond Japan.

4 I am aware of the criticism by the proponents of so-called Critical Buddhism that Tathāgatagarbha cannot be considered authentic Buddhism, but this is not the place to address this issue. I find these assertions unwarranted.

With regard to the use of the term "faith," I have elected to use this as a term that refers to a wide range of Buddhist terms, including *adhimukti*. "Faith" is required in this paper as an overarching category to not only compare the various Sanskrit terms of "faith" but also to enable participation in a wider discussion about this key psychological and religious phenomenon.

5 Kōshō Mizutani, "Nyoraizō to shin," in Akira Hirakawa, Yūichi Kajiyama, and Jikidō Takasaki, eds., *Kōza daijō bukkyō* (Tokyo: Shunjūsha, 1982), pp. 117–149. Mizutani refers to the affinity of the two schools of thought (Tathāgatagarbha and Pure Land) but focuses on Shinran's *shinjin.*

6 Based on Takasaki's views, expressed in his numerous writings on the subject.

7 Jikidō Takasaki, *A Study on the Ratnagotravibhāga (Uttaratantra) Being a Treatise on the Tathāgatagarbha Theory of Mahāyāna Buddhism,* S.O.R. 33 (Rome: Istituto Italiano per il Medio ed Estremo, 1966), pp. 389–390.

8 Hakuju Ui, *Indo-tetsugaku-shi* (Tokyo: Iwanami-shoten, 1965), p. 395.

9 Akira Hirakawa, "Nyoraizō to shite no hōzōbosatsu," in *Etani Sensei Koki Kinen: Jōdokyō no Shisō to Bunka* (Tokyo: Dōbōsha, 1972), p. 1303.

10 Jikidō Takasaki, "Nyoraizō-setsu ni okeru shin no kōzō," *Komazawa daigaku bukkyōgakubu kenkyū kiyō* 11 (1964): 86–109. For the article on Mizutani, see above.

11 The Chinese title is *Jiujingyichengbaoxinglun* 究竟一乗宝性論; the Tibetan is *Theg-pa chen-po rgyud bla-mahi bstan-bcos.*

12 Jikidō Takasaki, "On Hōshō-ron," in *Butten Kaidai Jiten* (Tokyo: Shunjūsha, 1966), pp. 144–145.

13 This realm of the buddhas is further described as having four features: the buddhas' nature or realm (*dhātu*), enlightenment (*bodhi*), dharmas (*dharmāḥ*), and action (*kṛtyā*).

14 Text edited by Sylvain Lévi, *Vijñaptimātratāsiddhi: deux traités de Vasubandhu* (Paris: H. Champion, 1925), p. 26.

15 T.31:29b.

16 Verse 34, adapted from Dennis Hirota, et al., eds., *The Collected Works of Shinran* (Kyoto: Jōdo Shinshū Hongwanji-ha, 1997), vol. 1, p. 407.

17 *Kyōgyōshinshō,* Hirota, et al., eds., *The Collected Works of Shinran,* p. 54.

18 *Nirvāṇa-sūtra,* Hirota, et al., eds., *The Collected Works of Shinran,* p. 99.

References

Fujita, Kōtatsu. *Genshi jōdo shisō kenkyū.* Tokyo: Iwanami shoten, 1970.

Hirakawa, Akira, "Nyoraizō to shite no hōzōbosatsu," in *Etani Sensei Koki Kinen: Jōdokyō no Shisō to Bunka,* pp. 1287–1306. Tokyo: Dōbōsha, 1972.

Hirota, Dennis, et al., eds. *The Collected Works of Shinran,* 2 vols. Kyoto: Jōdo Shinshū Hongwanji-ha, 1997.

Küng, Hans, et al. *Christianity and the World Religions.* Maryknoll, NY: Orbis Books, 1986.

Lévi, Sylvain. *Vijñaptimātratāsiddhi: deux traités de Vasubandhu.* Paris: H. Champion, 1925.

Mizutani, Kōshō. "Nyoraizō to shin," in Akira Hirakawa, Yūichi Kajiyama, and Jikidō Takasaki, eds., *Kōza daijō bukkyō,* pp. 117–149. Tokyo: Shunjūsha, 1982.

Schweitzer, Albert. *Indian Thought and Its Development* (1936). Translated by Mrs. Charles E. B. Buswell. Boston: The Beacon Press, 1957, reprint.

Shigaraki, Takamaro. *Jōdokyō ni okeru shin no kenkyū.* Tokyo: Nagata bunshodo, 1975.

Takasaki, Jikidō. *A Study on the Ratnagotravibhāga (Uttaratantra) Being a Treatise on the Tathāgatagarbha Theory of Mahāyāna Buddhism,* S.O.R. 33. Rome: Istituto Italiano per il Medio ed Estremo, 1966.

—."Nyoraizō-setsu ni okeru shin no kōzō," *Komazawa daigaku bukkyōgakubu kenkyū kiyō* 11 (1964): 86–109.

—."On Hōshō-ron," in *Butten Kaidai Jiten,* pp. 144–145. Tokyo: Shunjūsha, 1966.

Ui, Hakuju. *Indo-tetsugaku-shi.* Tokyo: Iwanami-shoten, 1965.

On Justifying the Choice of Mahāyāna among Multiple Paths in Buddhist Teachings: Based on the *Prajñāpāramitā-sūtras*

Yao-ming Tsai
National Taiwan University

Introduction

This paper takes as its central concern the Buddhist paths of cultivation. The so-called paths of cultivation are not what are usually known as religious denominations, groups, sects, or schools; rather, they are mainly about setting and approaching religious goals through constant and vigorous cultivation. The approach is not unlike walking on an ordinary pathway where one needs to first identify the destination. Then one will continue following the chosen path in order to progressively reach the destination.

Browsing through Buddhist scriptures, one quickly notices that there seems to be more than one way of Buddhist cultivation. As can be found in Buddhist scriptures in their broadest sense, the goals of cultivation include liberation from cyclic life and death and all-encompassing and thorough enlightenment. Among these, the cultivation of becoming liberated from cyclic life and death, the *vimukti-mārga,* can be further differentiated into the *śrāvakayāna,* which aims at *śrāvaka* nirvana, and the *pratyekabuddhayāna,* which aims at *pratyekabuddha* nirvana. If one aims at all-encompassing and thorough enlightenment while helping sentient beings and contributing to the purification of the world along the way, then the *mahāyāna, bodhisattvayāna, buddhayāna,* or *samyaksaṃbuddhayāna* can be categorized as the *bodhi-mārga* or *bodhi-patha.*

On the surface, Buddhism provides two paths of cultivation, the *vimukti-mārga* and the *bodhi-mārga,* or three paths, the *śrāvakayāna, pratyekabuddhayāna,* and *bodhisattvayāna.* Since Buddhism claims to be a religious teaching system, at the very least the following two clarifications must be given regarding the choice to be made among these multiple paths of cultivation. On the one hand, from the standpoint of an educator, two aspects need explanation in terms of education, especially in achieving the goals: the propriety of the multiple paths of cultivation, and the intrinsic reasoning involved in each path. On the other hand, from the standpoint of a practitioner-to-be or an active practitioner, when facing multiple choices certain issues require clarification: How can one gain a wider perspective? How does one make a proper decision? And how does one maintain proper relationships with other practitioners who choose to take other paths? If these two major concerns are not addressed, the instructor might be accused of teaching some things that are internally contradictory, or of teaching in an entirely haphazard manner. As a result, this could cause unnecessary difficulty to the practitioners and leave them baffled. Of these two major concerns, I have dealt with the former elsewhere;[1] the latter issue is the focus of this paper.

There are many possible ways to obtain a wide spectrum of understanding of the multiple paths of cultivation. One approach most worth attempting is to focus on Buddhist scriptures to determine what has been said regarding the multiple paths of cultivation. Obviously, the number of Buddhist scriptures is not small, and each text focuses on particular aspects or major themes. There are different discourses and guiding principles on how to take different paths of cultivation, such as how practitioners stay on their own paths, or how they get along with each other. A thorough reading of relevant texts will uncover various statements on the issues mentioned above, yet an underlying thorough rationale can be found in the discussions and their principles.

In order to focus more closely on textual studies of Buddhist doctrines, this paper will mainly rely on two texts, the *Aṣṭasāhasrikā* and the *Suvikrāntavikrāmi-paripṛcchā* in the Prajñāpāramitā sūtras translated by Xuanzang from 660 to 663.[2] While these two texts expound the issue of the paths of cultivation in great detail, due to space limitations this paper will examine only the opening sections of both texts. The number of pages analyzed in this study is significantly small in comparison to the entire scripture. However, the opening sections of the two texts are quite representative, even of the whole Prajñāpāramitā sūtras and, consequently, the main points presented in this paper cannot be accused of overemphasis or bias.[3]

To sum up, this paper focuses on the issues of how to perceive, choose, and abide in the paths elucidated in the *Aṣṭasāhasrikā* and the *Suvikrāntavikrāmi-paripṛcchā* of the Prajñāpāramitā sūtras. The perceived clues, guiding principles, and main doctrinal themes found in the texts contribute to understanding why Buddhism offers a beacon for so many pathways for cultivation. In addition, it will also provide useful references for those who encounter diverse modern adaptations of Buddhism and various religious advocates.

The paper is organized into four sections. The first section is the introduction. The second and the third sections focus respectively on the *Aṣṭasāhasrikā* and the *Suvikrāntavikrāmi-paripṛcchā* to discuss the basic principles to be followed when choosing from multiple Buddhist paths. The last section is the conclusion of this paper.

On How to Choose from Multiple Buddhist Paths as Expounded in the *Aṣṭasāhasrikā*

The *Aṣṭasāhasrikā* is also referred to as the *Perfection of Wisdom in 8,000 Lines,* or the *Short Prajñāpāramitā.*[4] The text begins with Śākyamuni Buddha asking Venerable Subhūti to explain *prajñāpāramitā* to bodhisattvas so that bodhisattvas can embark on and promote the cultivation of the *prajñāpāramitā.* This request made by Śākyamuni entails a series of profound discourses: the core of the *prajñāpāramitā* assembly is the cultivation of the *prajñāpāramitā,* which is the main task of bodhisattvas; Śākyamuni and all other buddhas have already completed their cultivation of the *prajñāpāramitā,* while Ven. Subhūti is a *śrāvaka* in terms of Buddhist cultivation. Therefore, the text reports that a *śrāvaka* was requested to explain *prajñāpāramitā,* the most central practice of bodhisattvas, to bodhisattvas by the Buddha, one who had completed the full course of the practice in question.

If the professional identities of *śrāvaka*s and bodhisattvas are of two different categories, then the request made at the beginning of the *Aṣṭasāhasrikā* represents a cross-category performance. This would not have been surprising if explicating *prajñāpāramitā* was the speciality of *śrāvaka*s. But what has been requested—that the most celebrated skill of bodhisattvas will be delivered by a *śrāvaka*—is very unusual. Such a seemingly contradictory situation cannot be explained simply with superficial guesswork. It will require a detailed textual reading to inquire into the relationship among the *prajñāpāramitā* that allows practitioners to access other categories and all possible paths, as well as the choices that *śrāvaka*s have when choosing from multiple paths of cultivation.

Four Quotes from the *Aṣṭasāhasrikā*

As briefly described above, after being asked by Śākyamuni Buddha, Ven. Subhūti began to explore the *prajñāpāramitā* in four aspects. For the sake of clarity, the passages are listed below, followed by analysis and further discussion.

> 1. Whether one wants to train on the level of disciple, *pratyekabuddha,* or bodhisattva, one should listen to this perfection of wisdom, take it up, bear it in mind, recite it, study it, spread it among others, and in this very perfection of wisdom one should be trained and exert oneself. In this very perfection of wisdom all dharmas that constitute a bodhisattva, and in which he should be trained and exert himself, are indicated in full detail.[5]
>
> 2. Those, however, who are certain that they have gotten safely out of this world (i.e., arhats who have reached their last birth) are unfit for full enlightenment [because they are not willing to go, out of compassion, back into birth-and-death.] And why? The flood of birth-and-death hems them in. Incapable of repeated rebirths, they are unable to aspire to full enlightenment. And yet, if they also will aspire to full enlightenment, I confirm them also. I shall not obstruct their wholesome root. For one should uphold the most distinguished dharmas above all others.[6]
>
> 3. Whatever the Lord's disciples teach, all that is to be known as the Tathāgata's work. For in the dharma demonstrated by the Tathāgata they train themselves, they realize its true nature, they hold it in mind. Thereafter nothing that they teach contradicts the true nature of dharma. It is just an outpouring of the Tathāgata's demonstration of dharma. Whatever those sons of good family may expound as the nature of dharma, they do not bring that into contradiction with the actual nature of dharma.[7]
>
> 4. This is the Lord's Absolute, the essence of the disciples who are without any support, so that, in whatever way they are questioned, they find a way out, do not contradict the true nature of dharmas, nor [do they] depart from it. And this is because they do not rely on any dharmas.[8]

In the spirit of doctrinal reasoning, the following analysis will start with the first quotation. The focus of this quote is the cultivation of *prajñāpāramitā,* which not only welcomes but also accommodates practitioners from the *śrāvakayāna, pratyekabuddhayāna,* or *bodhisattvayāna.* In other words, all practitioners cultivating any of these paths can benefit from practicing *prajñāpāramitā* and they will progressively reach their intended destinations on their chosen paths.

An analysis of the second quotation leads to the following four points. First, when practitioners on the *śrāvakayāna* or *pratyekabuddhayāna* attain *samyaktva-niyāma,* they achieve a state so far beyond the novice level that they are assured of continual progress on the right path. As a result, on the one hand, even though one is still in the cycle of birth and death, the entrances to the lower three realms of the cycle of birth and death are closed. On the other hand, at this point, as long as one continues to practice he or she will be certain, beyond a shadow of a doubt, to be heading toward their planned destination.[9]

Second, since there is no chance of falling into the lower three realms of the cycle of birth and death, with the help of constant practice one will with certainty eventually be free from the cycle of birth and death. As a result, on a pragmatic basis, there is no need for *śrāvaka*s or those on the way to become a *pratyekabuddha* to switch to another path. Consequently, it does not seem to be necessary to set an intention to achieve utmost, right, and perfect enlightenment, which is required to enter the bodhisattva path.

Third, for lofty practitioners who aim high, the more advanced practice should be undertaken.[10] Therefore, even after having obtained *samyaktva-niyāma*, *śrāvaka*s or those on the way to becoming a *pratyekabuddha* can still set an intention to achieve utmost, right, and perfect enlightenment. Finally,the intention to achieve utmost, right, and perfect enlightenment will still arise in the minds of those *śrāvaka*s or those on the way to becoming a *pratyekabuddha* who have already obtained *samyaktva-niyāma*. Ven. Subhūti says that this would not cause any trouble to their practice at all, and he feels happy for them from the bottom of his heart.

The third quotation is not unlike a narrative uttered by Ven. Subhūti, which unfolds the following three points. First, Ven. Subhūti has been listening to Śākyamuni Buddha's teachings and practicing vigorously. As a result, it is fair to say that he has realized reality as it really is (*tāṃ dharmatāṃ sākṣāt-√kṛ*). Second, after realizing reality as it really is, he is then qualified to talk to the assembly about *prajñāpāramitā* and is able to connect with the Buddha's majesty (*buddhānubhāvena*) without going against the Dharma. Third, as a disciple of the Buddha, Ven. Subhūti is modest and claims that his skillful utterance is the effect of the Buddha's majesty rather than his own eloquence.

The fourth quotation works closely with the third to emphasize that Ven. Subhūti is not the only exception in which a *śrāvaka* may expound the *prajñāpāramitā*. In fact, all disciples of the Buddha, in principle, can discuss and answer any question regarding *prajñāpāramitā*, regardless of their upbringing or the current path of practice they have taken. As long as they fulfill all the prerequisites of practice—not to rely on (*a-niśrita*) any conception of or attachment to any dharma, not to contradict (*na vi-√rudh*) the nature of reality, not to depart from (*na vy-ati-√vṛt*) the nature of reality—they can do exactly as Ven. Subhūti did and expound the *prajñāpāramitā.*

Summary of the Basic Points

To summarize the above four quotes from the learner's point of view, the basic principles in choosing from multiple paths of cultivation are as follows:

1. The bodhisattva path that employs cultivation of the *prajñāpāramitā* as the main focus, and is also is known as the *mahāyāna,* i.e., the great path of cultivation, encompasses all the practices of the *śrāvakayāna, pratyekabuddhayāna,* and *bodhisattvayāna.* In addition, it welcomes any practitioner who chooses to practice any of the three paths.

2. If one's goal is to be liberated from the cycle of birth and death, then it is perfectly fine to choose to practice the *śrāvakayāna* or the *pratyeabuddhayāna.* After studious practice, once one reaches a junction where he or she must follow either the *śrāvaka-samyaktva-niyāma* or the *pratyekabuddha-samyaktva-niyāma,* they will not fall into the lower three realms in their future process of life and they will eventually be free of the cycle of birth and death. After a certain period of practice, and having already achieved a certain level of cultivation, this promise of nonretrogression can be considered as a guarantee from a certain aspect. To switch to another path of practice at this point might be considered by some sentient beings as a bad choice or one that creates unnecessary trouble.

3. The practice of the bodhisattva path is not limited to liberation from the cycle of birth and death—it goes beyond this. There are so many advanced goals in life, such as unfolding limitless wisdom until one ultimately becomes a buddha, providing unconditional liberation to sentient beings, and contributing one's efforts and ability to make this world better, to name but a few. Consequently, at the junction of obtaining either the *śrāvaka-samyaktva-niyāma* or the *pratyekabuddha-samyaktva-niyāma,* one might wish to achieve a greater goal, beyond mere liberation from the cycle of birth and death. In this case, the higher and more advanced aspiration will entail setting the intention to achieve utmost, right, and perfect enlightenment. After reaching the turning point of setting this intention there will be no difficulty in switching one's cultivation from the *vimukti-mārga* to the *bodhi-mārga.*

4. All disciples of the Buddha, including those who have switched from the *vimukti-mārga* to the *bodhi-mārga,* will be able to continue practicing on the bodhisattva path to fulfill all kinds of required cultivation, such as learning, practicing vigorously, and realizing the nature of reality.

In addition, they will construct an interconnected system of cultivation manifested by the paths, dharmas, buddhas, bodhisattvas, and sentient beings to make extended contributions such as teaching, explaining, or discussing *prajñāpāramitā* in Buddhist assemblies.

To sum up, from the learner's point of view, the three different paths of cultivation in Buddhist teachings offer various practitioners different learning choices, institutions, or systems, rather than a single one-size-fits-all solution. In addition, it is possible to switch to other paths during one's course of practice, not unlike transferring to another school while pursuing higher education. In other words, this mechanism is not at all rigid—no one has to remain stuck in the path on which he or she started.

With great convenience, learners or researchers may respond with one of the following two different approaches. The first involves a thorough understanding of all the different paths in Buddhist cultivation so that one can make a good decision when the time comes, whether it is choosing a path or seriously evaluating all the pros and cons before switching to another path. However, this mechanism does not provide a standardized answer that is appropriate for everyone. On the contrary, each segment in the whole process will challenge the reasoning, aspirations, and decisions of the learners or researchers.

An alternative response might be haphazard and may throw one into disarray. The practitioner might grasp some fragmented appearances of the three paths of cultivation and then proudly hold on to those fragments, without any doubts. Or one might even stir up quarrels, fractious disputes, or confrontations among followers of different paths. One can use this mechanism to reflect on oneself, especially on how average beings mistake, abuse, waste, or miss the opportunity to choose from multiple paths of cultivation.

On Choosing from Multiple Paths of Cultivation in the *Suvikrāntavikrāmi-paripṛcchā*

The *Suvikrāntavikrāmi-paripṛcchā*, the *Questions of Suvikrāntavikrāmin*, also known as the *Prajñāpāramitā-sūtra in 2,500 Lines*, is the last but certainly not least assembly in the Prajñāpāramitā sūtras, and it is indeed the high point of the *prajñāpāramitā* teachings.[11] The *Suvikrāntavikrāmi-paripṛcchā* is essential to understanding how profound the *prajñāpāramitā* teachings can be. However, the main theme of this paper is not the profundity of the *prajñāpāramitā* but the inquiry of how to recognize multiple paths of cultivation and how to choose the most suitable path once one has decided to embark on Buddhist practice.

Four Passages from the *Suvikrāntavikrāmi-paripṛcchā*

The text begins with a series of questions asked by Suvikrāntavikrāmin Bodhisattva on the practice of the *prajñāpāramitā*.[12] Before replying to the bodhisattva, Śākyamuni Buddha asks him about the reasoning behind the series of questions.[13]

Suvikrāntavikrāmin Bodhisattva seems to be well prepared and gives a long and detailed answer, which reveals the characteristics of the expected reader of this text and even of the entirety of the Prajñāpāramitā sūtras. On the one hand, there is the issue of what kind of sentient beings attend *prajñāpāramitā* assemblies. On the other hand, the text also specifies the kind of sentient beings who are capable of embarking on the earnest practice of the systematic cultivation unfolded in the *prajñāpāramitā* assemblies. Suvikrāntavikrāmin's answer addresses exactly the focus of this paper, so it will be the reference for the contextual analysis and interpretation of this section.

Suvikrāntavikrāmin's response can be essentially divided into four parts. The first part provides an outline of how the *prajñāpāramitā* teachings encompass the education of all the *śrāvakayāna*, *pratyekabuddhayāna*, and *bodhisattvayāna* paths of cultivation. The second part points out the mentalities that are not suitable for practicing *prajñāpāramitā*. The third part focuses on the characteristics of the mentalities of the expected attendees of the *prajñāpāramitā* assembly. The fourth part explains what brings Suvikrāntavikrāmin to inquire into the series of issues related to the *prajñāpāramitā* practice. A more detailed discussion of these main points is offered below.

The Major Themes of the First Part

The first part is an outline of how the *prajñāpāramitā* teachings encompass the education of the *śrāvakayāna*, *pratyekabuddhayāna*, and *bodhisattvayāna* of cultivation and those who practice them. Since this section has not been well discussed, the entire passage is given here.

> We question the Tathāgata about this matter for the sake of all beings, for the welfare of all beings, out of pity for all beings. And why? The perfection of wisdom comprises all dharmas, i.e., the dharmas of disciples, of *pratyekabuddhas*, of bodhisattvas, and of fully enlightened buddhas. Therefore, O Lord, do expound the sphere of a tathāgata, the cognition of a tathāgata! When they have heard it, beings who are fixed on the disciple vehicle will

> quickly realize the stage that is without outflows. Those who are fixed on the vehicle of the *pratyekabuddhas* will go forth quickly by means of the *pratyekabuddha* vehicle. Those who have set out for utmost, right, and perfect enlightenment will quickly fully know utmost, right, and perfect enlightenment. But those who have not yet entered with any certainty on the path by which they will win salvation, who are not fixed on any of the three levels, will raise their heart to utmost, right, and perfect enlightenment. And much merit will be created for all beings by the Tathāgata's reply to this question about the perfection of wisdom.[14]

What Suvikrāntavikrāmin Bodhisattva explains reveals the basic capacity and vision. The discourse on multiple paths of cultivation can be summed up in the following five main points.

First, the all-encompassing nature of the *prajñāpāramitā* practice makes it possible not only for those of the *śrāvakayāna, pratyekabuddhayāna,* and *bodhisattvayāna* to take part in it, but also includes the path to all-encompassing and thorough enlightenment. This point warrants further discussion. If one recognizes the three paths as the result of a ramified sectarian movement or as three totally different claims, then there seems to be segregation among different paths. However, if one focuses on the *prajñāpāramitā* in terms of emptiness and nonduality, or even the proposition of the three paths as being derived from penetrating wisdom, then it is easier to comprehend that the *prajñāpāramitā* comprises all three paths.

Second, the *prajñāpāramitā* teachings remain open to those sentient beings who will remain fixed on the disciple path (*ye sattvā niyatāḥ śrāvaka-yāne bhaviṣyanti*). It is interesting to note that, to some extent, the *prajñāpāramitā* teachings will also help those who are already fixed on the disciple path to achieve their goals.[15]

Third, the *prajñāpāramitā* teachings remain open to those sentient beings who will remain fixed on the path of the *pratyekabuddhas* (*ye pratyekabuddha-yāne niyatāḥ bhaviṣyanti*). Again, to some extent, the *prajñāpāramitā* teachings will also help those who are already fixed on the *pratyekabuddha* path to achieve their goals.

Fourth, the *prajñāpāramitā* teachings are especially suitable, even indispensable, for those who have set out for utmost, right, and perfect enlightenment (*ye 'nuttarāṃ samyak-saṃbodhiṃ saṃprasthitāḥ*). Therefore, to some extent, the *prajñāpāramitā* teachings will help those who aim at utmost, right, and perfect enlightenment to achieve their goals.

Fifth, the *prajñāpāramitā* teachings remain open to those who are not fixed (*a-niyata*) on any of the three paths and are undecided about which learning path they will follow. Furthermore, it is hoped that after receiving the *prajñāpāramitā* teachings, these sentient beings will raise their hearts to utmost, right, and perfect enlightenment, and perhaps even opt for the *bodhi-mārga* as their first choice.

The Major Themes of the Second Part

The second part points out the mentalities that are not suitable for practicing *prajñāpāramitā*. Even though the *bodhi-mārga* champions the openness of the cultivation path and focuses on helping ordinary sentient beings, employing *prajñāpāramitā* as the main path of cultivation does not mean recruiting just anyone merely for the sake of gaining more members. Obviously, in terms of the context and requirements, there is a difference between the concept of the ordinary sentient beings it will help and the concept of a qualified practitioner of the path. Suvikrāntavikrāmin Bodhisattva clearly declares that the reason he asks the series of questions on the *prajñāpāramitā* teachings is not unlike forming a measuring ruler. He not only refuses to go with the flow and follow fashion blindly, but also will guard the gate strictly by identifying those whose temperament is incompatible with cultivation and excluding them.

> We do not question the Tathāgata for the sake of beings of inferior resolve, nor for those with weak hearts or poor minds, who are lazy or overcome by sloth . . . who exalt themselves and deprecate others, who attach weight to gain and honor, or are bent on food and robes . . . cheats, boasters, hinters, bullies, keen on making a profit. We do not question the Tathāgata for the sake of beings of that kind.[16]

Suvikrāntavikrāmin Bodhisattva then lists thirty characteristics that are not suitable for practicing *prajñāpāramitā,* starting from inferior resolve (*hīnādhimuktika*) and ending at being keen on making a profit (*lābhena lābha-cikīrṣuka*). Any qualities related to these are not appropriate for the cultivation of *prajñāpāramitā*. In other words, those to whom any of these characteristics pertain will not be suitable to practice *prajñāpāramitā,* at least for the time being. On reviewing the list, we see that none of these characteristics is personal—they are not about the religious preferences, religious identity, social status, ethnographic group, economic status, or political preferences of sentient beings. Furthermore, whether or not the practitioner is a layperson or a celebrity is totally irrelevant. All that matters is whether the would-be practitioners' attitudes, views, livelihoods, or habits are suitable for embarking on a path of cultivation.

The thirty characteristics listed by Suvikrāntavikrāmin Bodhisattva can be regarded as the insistence that Buddhism will not lower the bar merely to become popular, so as not to corrupt its purity and professionalism in cultivation. At the same time, it strives to provide those sentient beings that encounter choices of multiple paths of cultivation a mirror to inspect or reflect on their characteristics that are either revealed in their mentalities or steeped in habitual attributes. If there is serious damage or huge digressions, it is doubtful whether one can even continue as an ordinary person, let alone take on advanced and profound religious cultivation. As it turns out, the real opponents or obstacles to entering a path of cultivation are the ugly characteristics in the mentalities or habitual attributes of the would-be participants. As a result, the foundation of religious practice lies in the development of an upright character and the establishment of right views.

The Major Themes of the Third Part

The third part focuses on the characteristics of the mentalities of those who are the expected attendees of the *prajñāpāramitā* assembly. In addition to passively eliminating inappropriate characteristics, Suvikrāntavikrāmin also lists in two paragraphs the appropriate characteristics one should have toward sentient beings in general, and toward bodhisattvas.

> 1. But we question him for the sake of beings who strive after the cognition of the all-knowing, the nonattached cognition, the cognition of the self-existent, the unequaled cognition, the utmost cognition; . . .[17]
>
> 2. They do not apprehend even dharma, or feel inclined toward it, how much less that which is not related (adharma). They . . . attain to the highest perfection in all dharmas and have great skill in removing all kinds of uncertainty. For the sake of such beings, O Lord, of bodhisattvas, of great beings, do we question the Tathāgata.[18]

In the passage discussing sentient beings' practice, Suvikrāntavikrāmin Bodhisattva lists seven characteristics, beginning with striving for cognition of the all-knowing (*sarvajña-jñāna*), nonattached cognition (*asaṅga-jñāna*), cognition of the self-existent (*svayaṃ-bhū-jñāna*), unequaled cognition (*asama-jñāna*), and utmost cognition (*anuttara-jñāna*). On reviewing the list, it is not difficult to conclude that the family background and social status of the practitioners are irrelevant to *prajñāpāramitā* cultivation. The only important characteristics are those that are beneficial to the actual practice.

These seven characteristics proposed by Suvikrāntavikrāmin Bodhisattva as helpful in cultivating *prajñāpāramitā* cannot be easily or offhandedly dismissed. On the contrary, they are meaningful factors in retrospection, high standards, and correctional procedures. Some important characteristics are that one must really enjoy acquiring supreme wisdom through practicing *prajñāpāramitā;* one will not, in any case, be snobbish or despise the *prajñāpāramitā* practice and will continue in practice with a thoroughly constant modest mentality; one will eradicate all harmful or afflictive sentiments on life and death; and one will become accustomed to recognizing all things and events from the perspective of their important components, the perspective of equality based on emptiness.

In the context of the Prajñāpāramitā sūtras, especially in regard to the topic of how to cultivate *prajñāpāramitā,* it is clear that these seven qualities are not merely lumped together randomly, nor are they insignificant. Every characteristic is crucial, and one's ability to continue practicing depends on them.

Regarding the bodhisattvas' practice, Suvikrāntavikrāmin emphasizes that "they do not apprehend even dharma, or feel inclined toward it, how much less that which is not related" (*ye dharmam api nôpalabhante nābhiniviśante, kutaḥ punar adharmam*) that unfolds sixteen characteristics for bodhisattvas. While the path of cultivation of *prajñāpāramitā* is open to all sentient beings, most practitioners on this path are bodhisattvas. Examining them closely, we find that these sixteen characteristics do not include any quality that is irrelevant to practicing *prajñāpāramitā,* to the point that factors of family background or upbringing that most average people highly value are ignored. Yet the characteristics required for bodhisattvas are more extensive and advanced than those for ordinary sentient beings.

Since bodhisattvas form the majority of those who cultivate *prajñāpāramitā,* these sixteen characteristics can be regarded as a testimonial to the fact that *prajñāpāramitā* is an advanced practice. These sixteen characteristics can be grouped concisely and to lucid effect into four categories on how bodhisattvas should practice. First, bodhisattvas should maintain the mental purity required for decent practitioners of religious inquiry, and consistently overcome the various perplexities and obstacles with which they may be confronted. Second, bodhisattvas should continue working on the cultivation supported and motivated by a genuine undertaking and indomitable perseverance.[19] Third, bodhisattvas should be determined to accomplish *prajñāpāramitā.*[20] Fourth, bodhisattvas should act out their compassion and equality to guide sentient beings on the ways of life experience and paths of cultivation. Skillfully employing their merits, virtues, wisdom, and unsurpassed powers, bodhisattvas are dedicated to the world. In sum, bodhisattvas' strenuous practice in the *bodhi-patha* merges all of the four factors described above.

The Major Themes of the Fourth Part

The fourth part explains what has brought Suvikrāntavikrāmin Bodhisattva to inquire into the series of issues on the *prajñāpāramitā* practice. When the focus shifts from ordinary sentient beings to bodhisattvas, Suvikrāntavikrāmin, as one of the most brilliant bodhisattvas in the assembly, cannot, so to speak, hide behind the curtain. Even though there are only three factors, Suvikrāntavikrāmin directly expresses his reflections, which not only summarize the four parts from the beginning of the *Suvikrāntavikrāmi-paripṛcchā,* but also entail the following highly specialized discussion on cultivation of the *prajñāpāramitā.*

> We question the Tathāgata in the interest of the welfare of all beings, for their benefit, happiness, and pacification, bearing in mind the happiness of nirvana, the happiness of the buddhas, the unconditioned happiness. We therefore question the Tathāgata in order to remove the uncertainties of all beings. We ourselves, O Lord, want to be freed from uncertainty and then, freed from uncertainty, we wish to demonstrate the dharma to all beings, so that they also might lose their uncertainties. For all beings, O Lord, want happiness, but outside of wisdom we do not see, O Lord, any happiness for any being. Outside of the vehicle of the bodhisattvas, the great beings, there is nowhere any happiness for any being.
>
> Thereupon, considering this sequence of thought, we who wish to bear in mind the happiness of beings ask about the perfection of wisdom, and seeing this advantage to the bodhisattvas, we have asked the Tathāgata about this matter.[21]

All three factors elucidated by Suvikrāntavikrāmin Bodhisattva are useful in examining the intentions of Buddhist practitioners. At the very beginning, Suvikrāntavikrāmin, by implication, challenges the practitioners' intentions as to whether they have any hidden agenda, tend to create confrontation, or are inclined to denounce their opponents. The answer to this is a basic one: it is necessary to eliminate all negative scruples. In a positive sense, one can further scrutinize the following two issues based on these principles. First, what is the self-image promoted by these questions? Second, what is being questioned regarding the practitioners' intentions?

Regarding the first issue, the self-image promoted by these questions, if we recognize that the questions from the beginning of the *Suvikrānta-vikrāmi-paripṛcchā* are the self-description of most of the attendees of the assembly, then the portrayal, either truthful or idealized, can be discussed in two further aspects. On the one hand, what is the impression that is projected by cultivation of the *prajñāpāramitā* to the world? Simply put, in principle, the cultivation of *prajñāpāramitā* is always open to sentient beings who are ready to take spiritual practice seriously, and it encompasses all paths of Buddhist cultivation. In addition, it aims high at the unsurpassed states with the constant effort to make breakthroughs, leave all attachments behind, and reach the goal.

On the other hand, when ordinary sentient beings, practitioners in the *vimukti-mārga,* and bodhisattvas face the paths or the world unfolded from the cultivation of *prajñāpāramitā,* what positions do they take on? Which path or world can they expect? Once they embark on the cultivation of *prajñāpāramitā,* how much room for maneuver is there when choosing from multiple paths and approaches? What kind of result can be expected from the cultivation of *prajñāpāramitā*? And what kind of contribution can be expected from the professional cultivation of *prajñāpāramitā*?

In essence, ordinary sentient beings, practitioners in the *vimukti-mārga,* and bodhisattvas can expect the following as the result of the cultivation of *prajñāpāramitā:* to find and put into practice their own positions in life experiences and life practices; to be ready to start cultivating life practices and to actively expect themselves to do so, too; that there will be no limit at all in choosing from multiple paths and approaches, and even switching to another path is possible; to proceed until the goal is reached once the decision has been made, regardless of one's chosen path or approach; and to improve, solve, facilitate, and develop the thorough liberation of all sentient beings including oneself, so that all sentient beings can find their own tracks in their life paths, escape from their predicaments, and find their way out.

Regarding the intentions of the practitioners, this issue can be discussed further in terms of format and content. In terms of format, in addition to the *Suvikrāntavikrāmi-paripṛcchā,* many other scriptures are also structured as a set of questions and answers. There are many topics such as levels, clues, details, and mentalities to be discussed and comprehended further in regard to cultivation of the *prajñāpāramitā.* As a result, if the question about intention is framed properly, it will help bring out deeper levels of discussion and develop pertinent comprehension.

In terms of content, the discussion offers a perfect opportunity to clarify any concerns or confusion, and to correct any diversions from the intention to practice *prajñāpāramitā,* so as to come up with more appropriate approaches or performances. As a result, regardless of whether one has already started practicing Buddhist cultivation or not, he or she will certainly benefit from any engagement with the following: to realize the importance of intention in Buddhist practice, to comprehend the required intention in *prajñāpāramitā* practice, and to make a more appropriate decision in choosing one's path of cultivation. In other words, if it is necessary to assess the differences among different paths of cultivation in a broad view when choosing from multiple paths, then, by the same token, it is also necessary for one to honestly scrutinize one's intentions.

Summary of the Basic Points

In response to Śākyamuni Buddha's question, Suvikrāntavikrāmin Bodhisattva delineates in his opening remarks the outlines of the *prajñāpāramitā* practice, ordinary sentient beings, practitioners in the *vimuktimārga,* and bodhisattvas. Based on Buddhist scriptures and through this discourse, practitioners will have clear principles in mind when choosing from multiple paths of cultivation.

From the standpoint of learners, the basic principles on how to choose from multiple paths of cultivation delivered by Suvikrāntavikrāmin in the opening section can be grouped into the following four arguments.

1. The all-encompassing nature of *prajñāpāramitā* practice makes it possible that not only those of the *śrāvakayāna, pratyekabuddhayāna,* and *bodhisattvayāna* may take part in it, but the path to all-encompassing and thorough enlightenment is also included within it. On any chosen cultivation path, regardless of one's level of familiarity with the practice, one can certainly embark on the cultivation of *prajñāpāramitā.* In addition, the *prajñāpāramitā* practice can in fact help one to review their choice among multiple feasible paths of cultivation, and further help practitioners reach their chosen goal. In short, through the cultivation of *prajñāpāramitā,* there will be many options in the paths of cultivation providing practitioners their own choice of ways to reach ultimate enlightenment.

2. While the *prajñāpāramitā* practice is all encompassing, this does not mean that it is suitable for all sentient beings. In principle, none of the differences in one's religious preference, religious identity, social status, ethnographic group, economic status, or political preference is relevant in *prajñāpāramitā* practice. However, if too much agitation contaminates one's mentality, viewpoint, activities, or habits, such as inferior resolve or keenness on making a profit, then that particular sentient being is not suitable for such an advanced practice as *prajñāpāramitā.* Therefore, when choosing the path of cultivation, one should honestly evaluate

the compatibility of their own mentality with the practice of *prajñā-pāramitā,* as well as any obstructions they may have in unfolding a cultivation path in the future.

3. Again, while the cultivation of *prajñāpāramitā* is all encompassing, it is only suitable for certain particular sentient beings to practice. Those sentient beings or bodhisattvas who really enjoy acquiring supreme wisdom, and who are constantly in the state of cultivation, compassion, equality, perseverance, and responsibility, are great candidates for cultivating such an advanced practice as *prajñāpāramitā.* Therefore, when choosing a path of cultivation, one can also evaluate one's suitability for the *prajñāpāramitā* practice and explore the path to which *prajñāpāramitā* practice leads.

4. In every Buddhist cultivation path there are numerous exemplary professionals; Suvikrāntavikrāmin Bodhisattva is one such professional in both the *prajñāpāramitā* practice and the *bodhi-mārga.* As a result, a practitioner can employ Suvikrāntavikrāmin Bodhisattva as a mirror, a reference, or an exemplar to reflect on whether he or she is suitable for practicing *prajñāpāramitā* or the *bodhi-mārga.*

Conclusion

The cultivation of *prajñāpāramitā* offers at least three paths, that of the *śrāvakayāna,* the *pratyekabuddhayāna,* and the *bodhisattvayāna,* to accommodate, ripen, and offer more choices to sentient beings in choosing cultivation paths. How to choose an appropriate or better path from multiple alternatives depends on the particular sentient being's beliefs, attitudes, ambition, courage, comprehension, and rationale concerning his or her perspective on life, the world, values, and practice.

However, when facing multiple choices of cultivation paths, the decision is not so rigid that each sentient being can choose only one. For example, if one chooses to practice the *bodhisattvayāna,* then it is best to stay on that same path thereafter. Nevertheless, all-encompassing and thorough enlightenment cannot be achieved without the following measures: all the crucial dharmas in the *śrāvakayāna* and *pratyekabuddhayāna* are also required for practicing the *bodhisattvayāna;* all the abilities learned in the *śrāvakayāna* and the *pratyekabuddhayāna* are also to be learned for practicing the *bodhisattvayāna;* all the cognitions acquired in the *śrāvakayāna* and *pratyekabuddhayāna* must be excelled by the more thorough perspectives of emptiness and nonduality; and the levels of *śrāvaka*s and those on the way to becoming a *pratyekabuddha* will be transcended by the notion of nonappropriation. The *bodhisattvayāna* as such not only incorporates both the *śrāvakayāna* and the *pratyekabuddhayāna*, it also far surpasses dualistic opposition to the *śrāvakayāna* or *pratyekabuddhayāna*.[22]

The issue of choosing an appropriate cultivation path is not only important to the Prajñāpāramitā sūtras but is also prevalent in many other scriptures. When faced with the moment of choosing a cultivation path, it is possible to choose a particular path, to choose a path that incorporates others, or to choose all of the paths. For example, a passage in the *Vimalakīrtinirdeśa-sūtra* reads:

> Śāriputra: Goddess, do you belong to the disciple vehicle, to the solitary vehicle, or to the great vehicle?
>
> Goddess: I belong to the disciple vehicle when I teach it to those who need it. I belong to the solitary vehicle when I teach the twelve links of dependent origination to those who need them. And, since I never abandon the great compassion, I belong to the great vehicle, as all need that teaching to attain ultimate liberation.[23]

As this text is not within the scope of the major sources of this paper, I offer the quotation above simply as an important Buddhist reference without further textual analysis.

For some time within academia there has been a flood of papers on the *mahāyāna* or *bodhi-mārga* that focus mainly on such issues as disparities among sectarian groups, varied objects of worship, and whether or not the followers are laity. Furthermore, most papers tend to address only the oppositions, collisions, adaptation, or disputes between Mahāyāna and others. As a result, the important issue of the basic principles in choosing an appropriate path when faced with multiple paths of cultivation is overwhelmed by discourses emphasizing only the many oppositions and disputes.

This paper employs two texts, the *Aṣṭasāhasrikā* and the *Suvikrāntavikrāmi-paripṛcchā* from the Prajñāpāramitā sūtras, to focus on the basic principles for choosing the right path and moving in the right direction when faced with multiple paths of cultivation. From the above referencing, analysis, and discussion of these two texts, it is clear that the multiple paths of cultivation offered in Buddhist scriptures are not meant to foster hostile disagreement or confrontation. On the contrary, they are presented in order to help lead sentient beings to Buddhist paths of cultivation with wider capacity, more choices, and higher development. The Prajñāpāramitā sūtras are without doubt among the major Mahāyāna Buddhist scriptures. In light of the number of scholarly papers that are devoted to Mahāyāna Buddhism, it is important not to neglect the doctrinal themes of the Prajñāpāramitā sūtras.

In summary, this paper is concerned with one underlying theme: the cultivation of *prajñāpāramitā*. Through *prajñāpāramitā*, there are multiple choices in the paths of Buddhist cultivation entirely accessible all the way to their destinations. In addition, it is possible for practitioners to switch between paths even at the midway point on a certain path. Moreover, when choosing an appropriate path, the practitioner's mentality plays a major role. Therefore, the keywords for this underlying theme could be presented as wisdom, path, multiplicity, choice, mentality, switch, and thoroughgoing.

Notes

1 See Yao-ming Tsai, "Bodhisattva-niyāma in the Context of the Three Pathways as Depicted in the *Pañcaviṃśatisāhasrikā-prajñāpāramitā-sūtra*," *Newsletter of the Institute of Chinese Literature and Philosophy, Academia Sinica* 7/1 (March 1997): 109–142; "The Formation of Vehicles and the Proposition of the Three Vehicles in the Sūtras of the Perfection of Wisdom," *Special Edition of the 11th International Conference on Buddhist Education and Culture* (Taipei: Huafan University Press, 2000), pp. 130–164; "Teaching in Accordance with the Students' Aptitudes and the Distinction between Oneself and Others according to the *Analects of Confucius*, the *Āgamas*, and the *Sūtras of the Perfection of Wisdom*," *Journal of the Center for Buddhist Studies, National Taiwan University* 5 (July 2000): 37–78.

On multiple religious paths, see Stephen Kaplan, *Different Paths, Different Summits: A Model for Religious Pluralism* (Lanham: Rowman & Littlefield, 2002).

On Buddhist paths of cultivation, see Robert Buswell, Jr. and Robert Gimello, eds., *Paths to Liberation: The Mārga and its Transformations in Buddhist Thought* (Honolulu: University of Hawai'i Press, 1992); Geshe Lhundub Sopa, *Steps on the Path to Enlightenment*, 3 vols. (Boston: Wisdom Publications, 2004–2007); Joshua Cutler and Guy Newland, eds., *The Great Treatise on the Stages of the Path to Enlightenment*, 3 vols. Lamrim Chenmo Translation Committee, trans. (Ithaca, NY: Snow Lion Publications, 2000–2004).

2 Textual sources are mainly from P. L. Vaidya, ed., *Aṣṭasāhasrikā Prajñāpāramitā: With Haribhadra's Commentary Called Āloka* (Darbhanga: The Mithila Institute, 1960); "Chapter 1: Suvikrāntavikrāmiparipṛcchā Nāma Sārdhadvisāhasrikā Prajñāpāramitā," in *Mahāyāna-sūtra-saṁgraha* (Darbhanga: The Mithila Institute, 1961), pp. 1–74.

3 Lewis Lancaster, "The Dialogue Sūtras: A Study in Textual Structure," in Mano Ryūkai Hakushi Shōju Kinen Ronbunshū Kankōkai hen, ed., *Hannya Haramitta shisō ronshū: Mano Ryūkai Hakushi shōju kinen ronbunshū* (Tokyo: Sankibō Busshorin, 1992), pp. 3–7.

4 On different editions and translations in various languages of the *Aṣṭasāhasrikā*, see Edward Conze, *The Prajñāpāramitā Literature* (Tokyo: The Reiyukai, 1978, second ed.), pp. 46–55.

[5] T.220(4).7:764a; Vaidya, *Aṣṭasāhasrikā Prajñāpāramitā*, pp. 3–4; Unrai Wogihara, ed., *Abhisamayālaṃkār'ālokā Prajñāpāramitāvyākhyā: The Work of Haribhadra Together with the Text Commented On* (Tokyo: The Toyo Bunko, 1932), pp. 41–43; Edward Conze, trans., *The Perfection of Wisdom in Eight Thousand Lines & Its Verse Summary* (Bolinas, CA: Four Seasons Foundation, 1975), p. 84.

[6] T.220(4).7:769c; Vaidya, *Aṣṭasāhasrikā Prajñāpāramitā*, p. 17; Wogihara, *Abhisamayālaṃkār'ālokā Prajñāpāramitāvyākhyā*, pp. 131–133; Conze, *The Perfection of Wisdom in Eight Thousand Lines*, p. 96.

[7] T.220(4).7:763b; Vaidya, *Aṣṭasāhasrikā Prajñāpāramitā*, pp. 2–3; Wogihara, *Abhisamayālaṃkār'ālokā Prajñāpāramitāvyākhyā*, pp. 28–30; Conze, *The Perfection of Wisdom in Eight Thousand Lines*, p. 83.

[8] T.220(4).7:769a; Vaidya, *Aṣṭasāhasrikā Prajñāpāramitā*, p. 15; Wogihara, *Abhisamayālaṃkār'ālokā Prajñāpāramitāvyākhyā*, pp. 123–124; Conze, *The Perfection of Wisdom in Eight Thousand Lines*, p. 94.

[9] On *samyaktva-niyāma* see Tsai, "Bodhisattva-niyāma in the Context of the Three Pathways," pp. 109–142.

[10] T.220(4).7:767b (Conze, *The Perfection of Wisdom in Eight Thousand Lines*, p. 91):

> The Lord speaks of the "great vehicle." Surpassing the world with its gods, men, and *asuras* that vehicle will go forth. For it is the same as space, and exceedingly great. As in space, so in this the great vehicle of the bodhisattvas, the great beings. One cannot see its coming or its going, and its abiding does not exit. Thus one cannot get at beginning of this great vehicle, nor at its end, nor at its middle. But it is self-identical everywhere. Therefore one speaks of a "great vehicle."

T.220(4).7:778c (Conze, *The Perfection of Wisdom in Eight Thousand Lines*, p. 111):

> It is from the great ocean of the perfection of wisdom that the great jewel of the all-knowledge of the Tathāgatas has come forth.

T.220(4).7:847c–848a (Conze, *The Perfection of Wisdom in Eight Thousand Lines*, p. 252):

> When he trains in the perfection of wisdom, a Bodhisattva trains in that which is the highest possible degree of perfection for any being. For his merit is the greatest possible.

[11] On the transmission of different recensions and translations in different languages, see Conze, *The Prajñāpāramitā Literature*, pp. 56–58.

[12] T.220(16).7:1066a.

[13] T.220(16).7:1066a.

[14] T.220(16).7:1066a; Edward Conze, trans., "The Questions of Suvikrāntavikrāmin," in *Perfect Wisdom: The Short Prajñāpāramitā Texts* (Totnes, U.K.: Buddhist Publishing Group, 1993), p. 2; Ryusho Hikata (干潟龍祥), ed., *Suvikrāntavikrāmi-Paripṛcchā Prajñāpāramitā-Sūtra* 梵文善勇猛般若波羅蜜多經．序論文付 (Kyoto: Rinsen Book Co., 1983), pp. 4–5; Vaidya, "Chapter 1: Suvikrāntavikrāmiparipṛcchā Nāma Sârdha-dvi-sāhasrikā Prajñāpāramitā," p. 2.

[15] What is the benefit for those who stay on their original *śrāvakayāna* or *pratyekabuddhayāna* paths after receiving the *prajñāpāramitā* teachings? There are many major discussions and discourses in Buddhist assemblies. Among those, the

most worthy of notice is the systematic way of learning to liberate oneself through perspectives on issues such as emptiness, devoid of visual representation, nonduality, and absence of apprehension. Compare with the *Vajracchedikā-prajñāpāramitā*, T.220(9).7:981a–b.

16 T.220(16).7:1066b–1067a; Conze, "The Questions of Suvikrāntavikrāmin," pp. 2–3; Hikata, *Suvikrāntavikrāmi-Paripṛcchā Prajñāpāramitā-Sūtra*, p. 5; Vaidya, "Chapter 1: Suvikrāntavikrāmiparipṛcchā Nāma Sârdha-dvi-sāhasrikā Prajñāpāramitā," p. 2.

17 T.220(16).7:1067a; Conze, "The Questions of Suvikrāntavikrāmin," p. 3; Hikata, *Suvikrāntavikrāmi-Paripṛcchā Prajñāpāramitā-Sūtra*, p. 5; Vaidya, "Chapter 1: Suvikrāntavikrāmiparipṛcchā Nāma Sârdha-dvi-sāhasrikā Prajñāpāramitā," p. 2.

18 T.220(16).7:1067a–b; Conze, "The Questions of Suvikrāntavikrāmin," p. 3; Hikata, *Suvikrāntavikrāmi-Paripṛcchā Prajñāpāramitā-Sūtra*, pp. 5–6; Vaidya, "Chapter 1: Suvikrāntavikrāmiparipṛcchā Nāma Sârdha-dvi-sāhasrikā Prajñāpāramitā," pp. 2–3.

19 For example, the fifth factor out of the sixteen reads: "They carry the great burden, have mounted the great vehicle, live for the great task"; T.220(16).7:1067a.

20 For example, the twelfth factor out of the sixteen reads: "They . . . attain to the highest perfection in all dharmas"; T.220(16).7:1067b.

21 T.220(16).7:1067b–c; Conze, "The Questions of Suvikrāntavikrāmin," pp. 3–4; Hikata, *Suvikrāntavikrāmi-Paripṛcchā Prajñāpāramitā-Sūtra*, p. 6; Vaidya, "Chapter 1: Suvikrāntavikrāmiparipṛcchā Nāma Sârdha-dvi-sāhasrikā Prajñāpāramitā,"p. 3.

22 See Tsai, "The Formation of Vehicles and the Proposition of the Three," pp. 130–164; "Teaching in Accordance with the Students' Aptitudes," pp. 37–78.

23 Robert Thurman, trans., *The Holy Teaching of Vimalakīrti: A Mahāyāna Scripture* (University Park, PA: Pennsylvania State University Press, 1976), p. 60. Taishō Daigaku Sōgō Bukkyō Kenkyūjo Bongo Butten Kenkyūkai, ed., *Vimalakīrtinirdeśa: A Sanskrit Edition based upon the Manuscript Newly Found at the Potala Palace* (Tōkyō: Taishō Daigaku Shuppankai, 2006), p. 70: *āha: kiṃ tvaṃ devate śrāvaka-yānikā pratyekabuddha-yānikā mahā-yānikā vā / āha: śrāvaka-yānikāsmi śrāvaka-yāna-sūcanatayā, pratyekabuddha-yānikāsmi pratītya-dharmāvatāreṇa, mahā-yānikāsmi mahā-karuṇānutsṛjanatayā /.*

References

Buswell, Robert, Jr., and Robert Gimello, eds. *Paths to Liberation: The Mārga and its Transformations in Buddhist Thought.* Honolulu: University of Hawai'i Press, 1992.

Conze, Edward, trans. *The Perfection of Wisdom in Eight Thousand Lines & Its Verse Summary.* Bolinas, CA: Four Seasons Foundation, 1975.

—. *The Prajñāpāramitā Literature.* Tokyo: The Reiyukai, 1978, second ed.

—. trans. "The Questions of Suvikrāntavikrāmin," in *Perfect Wisdom: The Short Prajñāpāramitā Texts*, pp. 1–78. Totnes, U.K.: Buddhist Publishing Group, 1993.

Cutler, Joshua, and Guy Newland, eds. *The Great Treatise on the Stages of the Path to Enlightenment,* 3 vols. Lamrim Chenmo Translation Committee, trans. Ithaca, NY: Snow Lion Publications, 2000–2004.

Hikata, Ryusho 干潟龍祥, ed. *Suvikrāntavikrāmi-Paripṛcchā Prajñāpāramitā-Sūtra* 梵文善勇猛般若波羅蜜多經. 序論文付. Kyoto: Rinsen Book Co., 1983.

Kaplan, Stephen. *Different Paths, Different Summits: A Model for Religious Pluralism.* Lanham: Rowman & Littlefield, 2002.

Lancaster, Lewis. "The Dialogue Sūtras: A Study in Textual Structure," in Mano Ryūkai Hakushi Shōju Kinen Ronbunshū Kankōkai hen, ed., *Hannya Haramitta shisō ronshū: Mano Ryūkai Hakushi shōju kinen ronbunshū,* pp. 1–3. Tokyo: Sankibō Busshorin, 1992.

Sopa, Geshe Lhundub. *Steps on the Path to Enlightenment,* 3 vols. Boston: Wisdom Publications, 2004–2007.

Taishō Daigaku Sōgō Bukkyō Kenkyūjo Bongo Butten Kenkyūkai, ed. *Vimalakīrtinirdeśa: A Sanskrit Edition based upon the Manuscript Newly Found at the Potala Palace.* Tōkyō: Taishō Daigaku Shuppankai, 2006.

Thurman, Robert, trans. *The Holy Teaching of Vimalakīrti: A Mahāyāna Scripture* University Park, PA: Pennsylvania State University Press, 1976.

Tsai, Yao-ming. "Bodhisattva-niyāma in the Context of the Three Pathways as Depicted in the *Pañcaviṃśatisāhasrikā-prajñāpāramitā-sūtra,*" *Newsletter of the Institute of Chinese Literature and Philosophy, Academia Sinica* 7/1 (March 1997): 109–142.

—. "Teaching in Accordance with the Students' Aptitudes and the Distinction between Oneself and Others according to the *Analects of Confucius,* the *Āgamas,* and the *Sūtras of the Perfection of Wisdom,*" *Journal of the Center for Buddhist Studies, National Taiwan University* 5 (July 2000): 37–78.

—. "The Formation of Vehicles and the Proposition of the Three Vehicles in the Sūtras of the Perfection of Wisdom," *Special Edition of the 11th International Conference on Buddhist Education and Culture,* pp. 130–164. Taipei: Huafan University Press, 2000.

Vaidya, P. L., ed. *Aṣṭasāhasrikā Prajñāpāramitā: With Haribhadra's Commentary Called Āloka.* Darbhanga: The Mithila Institute, 1960.

—. "Chapter 1: Suvikrāntavikrāmiparipṛcchā Nāma Sārdhadvisāhasrikā Prajñāpāramitā," in *Mahāyāna-sūtra-saṁgraha,* pp. 1–74. Darbhanga: The Mithila Institute, 1961.

Wogihara, Unrai, ed. *Abhisamayālaṃkār'ālokā Prajñāpāramitāvyākhyā: The Work of Haribhadra Together with the Text Commented On.* Tokyo: The Toyo Bunko, 1932.

Contributors

Carl Bielefeldt (Stanford University, emeritus) specializes in East Asian Buddhism, with particular emphasis on the intellectual history of the Zen traditon. He is the author of *Dōgen's Manuals of Zen Meditation* and other works on early Japanese Zen, and serves as editor of the Soto Zen Text Project, an international effort to translate the scriptural corpus of the Japanese Sōtō Zen school.

Mark L. Blum (University of California, Berkeley), Professor and Shinjo Ito Distinguished Chair in Japanese Studies at the University of California, Berkeley, received his M.A. in Japanese Literature from the University of California, Los Angeles, and his Ph.D. in Buddhist Studies in 1990 from the University of California, Berkeley. He specializes in Pure Land Buddhism throughout East Asia, with a focus on the Japanese medieval period. He also works in the area of Japanese Buddhist reponses to modernism, Buddhist conceptions of death in China and Japan, and the impact of the *Nirvana Sutra* (*Mahāparinirvāṇa-sūtra*) in East Asian Buddhism. He is the author of *The Origins and Development of Pure Land Buddhism* (Oxford University Press, 2002), co-editor of *Rennyo and the Roots of Modern Japanese Buddhism* (Oxford University Press, 2005), and *Cultivating Spirituality* (State University of New York Press, 2011). His *The Nirvana Sutra, Volume I* (BDK America, Inc., 2013) is the first of a four-volume translation from Chinese of the Mahāyāna *Mahāparinirvāṇa-sūtra.* He is currently working on completing *Think Buddha, Say Buddha,* a history of nenbutsu thought, practice, and culture.

Robert E. Buswell, Jr. (University of California, Los Angeles) completed his B.A. in Chinese (1981), his M.A. in Sanskrit (1983), and his Ph.D. in Buddhist Studies (1985) from the University of California, Berkeley. He holds the Irving and Jean Stone Endowed Chair in Humanities at UCLA, where he is also Distinguished Professor of Buddhist Studies and founding director of the Center for Buddhist Studies and the Center for Korean Studies. He has published sixteen books and some forty articles on various aspects of the Korean, Chinese, and Indian traditions of Buddhism, as well as on Korean religions more broadly. His books include *The Korean Approach to Zen: The Collected Works of Chinul* (University of

Hawai'i Press, 1983), reprinted in a paperback abridgment as *Tracing Back the Radiance: Chinul's Korean Way of Zen* (University of Hawai'i Press, 1991); The *Formation of Ch'an Ideology in China and Korea: The Vajrasamādhi-Sūtra, A Buddhist Apocryphon* (Princeton University Press, 1989); *Cultivating Original Enlightenment: Wŏnhyo's Exposition of the Vajrasamādhi-Sūtra* (University of Hawaii Press, 2007); *Currents and Countercurrents: Korean Influences on the East Asian Buddhist Traditions* (University of Hawai'i Press, 2005); and *Religions of Korea in Practice* (Princeton University Press, 2007). He is also editor-in-chief of the *Encyclopedia of Buddhism* (Macmillan Reference, 2004), and coauthor with Donald S. Lopez, Jr. of the 1.2 million-word *The Princeton Dictionary of Buddhism* (Princeton University Press, 2014). Before returning to academia he spent seven years as a Buddhist monk in Thailand, Hong Kong, and Korea, which served as the basis of his book *The Zen Monastic Experience: Buddhist Practice in Contemporary Korea* (Princeton University Press, 1992). Buswell was elected president of the Association for Asian Studies (AAS) in 2008, the first specialist in either Korean or Buddhist studies to hold that position. In 2009, he was awarded the Manhae Grand Prize in Korea (as was Lew Lancaster before him) in recognition of his pioneering contributions to establishing Korean Buddhist Studies in the West.

Ronald M. Davidson (Fairfield University) earned his Ph.D. in Buddhist Studies in 1985, specializing in Indian Yogācāra philosophical problems. He is Professor and Chair of Religious Studies and the director of the Humanities Institute, College of Arts and Sciences. His primary area of research is in the domain of tantric Buddhism (Vajrāyāna, Mantrayāna, Mantranaya), especially in medieval India and early Tibet. His books include *Indian Esoteric Buddhism: A Social History of the Tantric Movement* (Columbia University Press, 2002) and *Tibetan Renaissance: Tantric Buddhism in the Rebirth of Tibetan Culture* (Columbia University Press, 2005). He is editor of *Wind Horse: Proceedings of the North American Tibetological Society* (Asian Humanities Press, 1981), and co-editor with Christian K. Wedemeyer of *Tibetan Buddhist Literature and Praxis: Studies in its Formative Period, 900-1400* (Brill Academic, 2005), and with Steven D. Goodman of *Tibetan Buddhism: Reason and Revelation* (State University of New York Press, 1992). His current research is on the transition between Mahāyāna *dhāraṇī* rituals and tantric Buddhism, to be published in *On the Threshold of Tantra: Mantra Rituals in Classical Mahāyāna Buddhism.* Following this, his further research is on the *uṣṇīṣa* system of earliest tantric Buddhism.

Robert Kritzer (Kyoto Notre Dame University) specializes in abhidharma and early Yogācāra, and is the author of three books: *Rebirth and Causation in the Yogācāra Abhidharma* (Universität Wien, 1999), *Vasubandhu and the Yogācārabhūmi: Yogācāra Elements in the Abhidharmakośabhāṣya* (The International Institute for Buddhist Studies, 2005), and *Garbhāvakrāntisūtra: The Sūtra on Entry into the Womb* (The International Institute for Buddhist Studies, 2014). He has written on the intermediate existence (*antarābhava*) and accounts of gestation and childbirth in Indian Buddhism, as well as on the meaning of the term Sautrāntika. Other interests include the relation between Buddhism and the Indian medical tradition. He was the Numata Visiting Professor at McGill University, Montreal, winter term 2006.

Richard K. Payne (Graduate Theological Union, Berkeley) is Dean and Yehan Numata Professor of Japanese Buddhist Studies at the Institute of Buddhist Studies, Berkeley. He serves as a member of the Core Doctoral Faculty of the Graduate Theological Union, where he initiated the Buddhist studies track in the doctoral program. His research focuses on the ritual tradition of esoteric Buddhism and continuing reflections on the contemporary interpretation of Buddhist thought. Recent publications include the co-edited volume *Esoteric Buddhism and the Tantras in East Asia* (Brill, 2011), and "Conversions of Tantric Buddhist Ritual: The Yoshida Shintō Jūhachi shintō Ritual," in István Keul, ed., *Transformations and Transfer of Tantra in Asia and Beyond* (De Gruyter, 2012). He is Editor in Chief of the Buddhism section of Oxford Bibliographies, and Co-Editor in Chief with Georgios Halkias of the *Oxford Encyclopedia of Buddhism* (forthcoming), and serves as Chair of the Editorial Board of the Pure Land Buddhist Studies Series, University of Hawai'i Press, and Chair of the Editorial Board of *Pacific World: Journal of the Institute of Buddhist Studies.*

Kennth K. Tanaka (Musashino University) taught at the Institute of Buddhist Studies of the Graduate Theological Union in Berkeley, California, before being appointed professor of Buddhist Studies at Musashino University, Tokyo, in 1998. He currently serves as President of the International Association of Shin Buddhist Studies and the Japan Association for the Study of Buddhism and Psychology, and serves on the board of The Society of Buddhist Christian Studies. His publications include: *The Dawn of Chinese Pure Land Buddhist Doctrine: Ching-ying Hui-yuan's Commentary to the Visualization Sutra* (State University of New York Press, 1990); *Ocean: An Introduction to Jodo-Shinshu Buddhism in*

America (Wisdom Ocean Publications, 1997); co-editor of *The Faces of Buddhism in America* (University of California Press, 1998); *Pure Land Buddhism: Historical Development, Contemporary Manifestation* (Dharmaram College, 2004); and *Amerika Bukkyō (American Buddhism)* (Musashino University Press, 2010) (in Japanese). He recently produced and appeared in a weekly year-long Buddhist television program, sponsored by Bukkyō Dendō Kyōkai. This program was broadcast in Los Angeles on Sundays in 2005; DVDs of the telecast are being distributed to religious and educational institutions throughout the world.

Yao-ming Tsai (National Taiwan University), received his Ph.D. in Buddhist Studies in 1997 from the University of California, Berkeley. He is Professor of Philosophy at National Taiwan University and editor-in-chief of the *Taiwan Journal of Buddhist Studies*. His teaching and research focus on Buddhist philosophy as well as philosophy of life. He is the author of four books: *The Teachings of Prajñāpāramitā and the Purification of the Buddha-field* (Right View Publications, 2001), *An Open Path for Constructing Buddhology* (Dharma Drum Publishing, 2006), *Research Methods and Academic Resources for Buddhist Studies* (Dharma Drum Publishing, 2006), and *Philosophy of Life and Worldview from the Perspective of Buddhist Teachings* (Wen Chen Publishing, 2012); as well as dozens of scholarly articles and book chapters on Buddhist studies. His current teaching and research are concerned with Buddhist perspectives on the challenging issues of bioethics, gender, and animals.